THE COMPLETE COMPOST GARDENING GUIDE

Banner Batches, Grow Heaps, Comforter Compost, and Other Amazing Techniques for Saving Time and Money, and Producing the Most Flavorful, Nutritious Vegetables Ever

BARBARA PLEASANT & DEBORAH L. MARTIN

Storey Publishing

The mission of Storey Publishing is to serve our customers by publishing practical information that encourages personal independence in harmony with the environment.

Edited by Gwen Steege and Delilah Smittle
Text design by Dan O. Williams
Cover design by Leslie Anne Charles/LAC Design
    and Dan O. Williams

Illustrations by Mavis Augustine Torke, except for those
    on pages 248, 255, and 264, by Kurt Musfeldt
Cover photography by © Donna Chiarelli, except for
    front cover, bottom center © hans slegers/iStockphoto
Interior photography credits appear on page 319

Indexed by Chris Lindemer, Boston Road Communications

Printed in the United States by Walsworth Publishing Company
10 9 8 7 6 5 4 3 2 1

Library of Congress Cataloging-in-Publication Data

Pleasant, Barbara.
  The complete compost gardening guide / Barbara Pleasant and
  Deborah L. Martin.
      p.   cm.
  Includes index.
  ISBN 978-1-58017-702-3 (pbk. : alk. paper)
  ISBN 978-1-58017-703-0 (hardcover : alk. paper)
  1. Compost. I. Martin, Deborah L. II. Title.
S661.P54 2008
631.8'75—dc22
                                        2007049729

DEDICATION

*To our families and friends
who have endured and (with time)
supported and encouraged
our composting experiments and adventures.*

Contents

How to Use This Book

A working compost garden is an interesting place, because you never know what kind of compost might be lurking beneath an innocent pile of leaves or perhaps a pen of withering weeds. The former might be a Nursery Reserve where pots of chrysanthemums have been tucked in for winter, and the latter might be the topmost layer of a Layered Crater or Honey Hole. If phrases such as these confuse you at first, please bookmark the glossary (pages 290–292). After you have read the definitions of important concepts a few times, and start experiencing your landscape as a compost-generating system, ideas like Comforter Compost or Hospital Heap will become as familiar to you as how to prepare a planting hole.

▶ **Materials.** When you have an abundance of anything from pulled weeds to cardboard boxes, review your options in the materials section that begins on page 50. Do the same if you are considering importing a load of manure or supercharging a weedy heap with a high-nitrogen plant meal to heat it up.

▶ **Techniques.** In part 2, beginning on page 130, we discuss dozens of methods you may want to try, starting with Banner Batches made in bins or pens, and then moving on to time-saving Comforter Composts and eye-appealing underground composting methods. There are also techniques to help you make your compost as good as it can be, which may mean deactivating weed seeds or sifting your black gold through a handmade screen.

▶ **Plants.** As compost's essential green portion, plants are at the heart of every Compost Garden. Part 3 covers plants that are especially responsive to compost gardening methods, including some to grow just so you can compost them. Throughout the book, plants that pair up perfectly with particular methods are featured in the Perfect Match boxes.

▶ **Learning from experience.** We don't want anyone to get hurt, so in situations where there might be a risk of injury, we've included safety tips worth knowing. Also look for snippets from Deb's Diary and Barbara's Journal, our firsthand reports intended to help you repeat our successes, avoid our failures, and join us in the creative fun of composting. As you learn from your own experiences, you can share your best ideas at **www.compostgardening.com**.

Part 1

Getting Started with Compost Gardening

1
Gardening in Garbage

YOU HAVE PICKED UP this book and opened it to the first page, so you probably expect it to show you new and better ways to compost. Great! The information, ideas, and projects here will certainly do that and a whole lot more, so find a comfortable chair and settle in for a while. This book will change the way you garden in such fundamental ways that a few seasons from now, you may look back at how you used to do things and wonder why it took so long for you to figure out that composting is, and always was, at the heart of your garden. Looking back, you may ask yourself: What was your heap doing hiding behind the bushes? Why were you carrying compost here and there instead of letting the process happen in places where the soil needs help? How many times did you worry that you were a composting failure because you never saw the faintest hint of steam rising from your heap? We used to ask ourselves the same questions, and this book is the result of that probing.

Seeing Is Believing

Like most gardeners who believe in the powers of compost, we followed directions we picked up from dozens of books and magazine articles, and from composting guides published by Cooperative Extension Service professionals and waste-management experts. We were repaid with pretty good results. Still, we sensed that there were some pieces of the puzzle missing, and we wondered if there were better ways to avail our gardens of the benefits of compost without facing endless work and frustration.

It's amazing what you can learn when you put aside ideas about the way things are supposed to work and pay attention to what actually happens in your garden. You may be surprised to discover that you can make better compost more easily by working with Mother Nature instead of working against her. Fortunately, she is a patient and persistent teacher, as shown in the following quick examples:

▶ **Compost in place.** For years we noticed how the soil beneath old compost piles turned dark and crumbly before it was touched with a turning fork. Instead of wasting this wonderful process in a remote corner, we moved it into the garden with techniques including layered Comforter Compost (see page 154) and Banner Batches of compost that "walked" toward where we needed them to go each time we turned them (see page 140).

▶ **Garden in compost.** After many seasons of watching volunteer pumpkin and winter squash vines tumble out of our old compost piles, we realized that these plants really like growing in compost. We began experimenting with the method we now call Grow Heaps — special compost piles that double as planting beds for compost-loving crops (see page 163).

▶ **Enlist earthworms.** Providing settings in which earthworms could help with composting made sense, but we asked ourselves: Is it really necessary to buy a special kind of worm and bin, and manage the worm bins in a particular way? In addition to saving time and money, working out the basics of a method we call Catch-and-Release Vermicomposting (see chapter 7) has made working with earthworms more fun and rewarding for us and for our gardens.

Perhaps you are already thinking "Of course! Why didn't I think of that?" If so, keep the part of your brain that's starting to get excited revved up and ready to rumble, because adapting *The Complete Compost Gardening Guide* methods to suit the unique needs of your garden is something only you can do. Don't worry. It's going to be far easier than struggling to make every composting project you undertake turn out a certain way; that is the fundamental flaw in how most gardeners think about home composting. In truth, what happens during the composting process is every bit as important as the result.

Are you ready to get started on compost gardening? We promise that the journey ahead will be painless, fascinating, and lead to endless satisfaction, season after season. It is good to be a gardener, but it's even better to be a compost gardener.

Use the easy Comforter Compost method to create fertile new beds. Earthworms, crickets, and other small animals help mix the materials in this layered type of compost.

SCAVENGING HAZARDS

Composting is all about recycling organic materials, so there will be times when you can't pass up a pile of perfectly good grass clippings someone left on the curb with their garbage, or maybe the salad scraps from a covered dish supper will ride home with you in the backseat of your car. Such acts of composting chivalry are fine most of the time, but do be aware that hidden hazards may lurk inside a seemingly innocent bag of leaves or grass clippings. Broken glass or pieces of wood studded with rusty nails may be present, and grass clippings may contain chemical residues or pet poo. Oddly enough, the most common foreign objects to turn up when commercial composters screen finished yard waste compost — the plastic mouth pieces from small cigars — are dangerous only to the people who discarded them.

6 Basic Rules of Compost Gardening

As a compost gardener, you will do much more than simply make compost. This book is a composting manual, but we take things further by presenting time-saving composting techniques that create new growing space, solve site problems, host beneficial insects, and invigorate soil during every season of the year. These techniques are covered in detail in part 2 (see page 130), and they have in common close adherence to the 6 Basic Rules of Compost Gardening listed here. While following these guidelines, you will no doubt invent even more ways to create compost in your yard and garden. As you do, keep in mind that the whole point of compost gardening is to put the natural decomposition processes first. From there on, everything else easily falls into place.

1 Choose labor-saving sites.

Keep your garden and compost as close to one another as possible. Compost in your garden whenever you can, or at least nearby. There is a catch, because while most garden plants grow best with plenty of sun, compost piles retain moisture best when situated in shade. Address this dilemma by using in-garden composting methods at every opportunity, and water as needed to keep the pile barely moist. Locate slow-rotting heaps in a shady spot near your garden, and site new garden beds close to your best area for making compost.

2 Work with what you have.

Compost what your yard produces first, and import materials only when they are convenient and of special value to your composting projects. Instead of yearning for materials you've heard make great compost, concentrate on doing the best job you can with compostable materials that you generate at home. Most landscapes produce plenty of fallen leaves, grass clippings, and withered plants; and kitchens spew out a steady supply of compostable riches (see page 56). When you do want to bring in outside materials, start looking for them along the curbs in your neighborhood, and stick with other sources close to home. In addition to being convenient and efficient, using local materials takes a bite out of local waste disposal costs and saves you unnecessary compost miles (see page 53).

3 Help decomposers do their jobs.

Compost happens thanks to the efforts of a vast population of organisms — from earthworms and pill bugs to microscopic fungi and bacteria — that live in, feed on, and otherwise process organic matter into nourishment for soil and plants. Creating optimal conditions for these essential composting critters is the key to your compost-making success. Keep them working by balancing compost ingredients between "greens" and "browns" (see page 54), adding high-nitrogen meals when needed (see page 122), and keeping compost materials moist. Additionally, you can aerate compost piles by turning them to stimulate microbial activity.

4 Reuse and recycle.

Reuse items from your recycling bin in your composting projects. Store finished compost in (well-rinsed) bulk containers, such as five-gallon plastic pickle buckets and detergent jugs. Turn cardboard boxes into bedding for your vermicompost bin. Place a thick layer of newspapers at the base of a curing compost pile to deter invasive tree roots. Look for novel opportunities to use compost-garden methods to shrink the waste stream generated by your household's day-to-day activities.

5 The magic is in the mix.

Decomposed leaves are called leaf mold, and rotted manure is . . . rotted manure. Both leaf mold and rotted manure have special uses, but they lack the diverse community of beneficial microorganisms found in true compost, which is made from a wide variety of materials. Each organic ingredient you put into a compost project — from carrot peelings to dead pepper plants — will host a slightly different group of microorganisms, and it is this diversity that makes compost greater than the sum of its parts.

6 Compost to suit your garden's needs.

Treat every plant you grow to some form of compost. Blanket beds as you renovate them between plantings, amend planting holes, or mix your best batches into homemade potting soil. Use rough-textured, partially decomposed compost as mulch, and sprinkle vermicompost into containers of flowers or houseplants. Match compost-garden methods to the situations you encounter most often in your gardens, and always put soil care first and plants second.

Who Owns Compost?

In the interest of clear communication, we have coined a number of phrases. For example: Comforter Compost and Banner Batches (see Glossary, page 290), and we use the word "composting" to refer to endless variations on "letting things rot." Such loose use of the word "compost" may bother those in the commercial-composting industry, because soil scientists have debated how compost should be defined and created for at least two decades. One camp maintains that the only true compost is produced through high-temperature processing, which requires close monitoring of materials, moisture, and oxygen.

Their point is that if we refer to everything that rots with help from human hands as compost, this loose interpretation of the word will corrupt the

In summer, a centrally located compost bin saves time by capturing compostable materials within a few steps of their source.

LOCAL COMPOST SOURCES

Depending on where you live, you may be able to buy bulk compost from municipal compost facilities, composted manure from nearby farms, or compost bagged from garden centers. Purchased compost can be of excellent quality, but some batches may include weed seeds, slugs, or other unwanted hitchhikers. See page 114 for a more detailed discussion of purchased compost, and remember that you always have the option of re-composting problem batches with materials from your own yard.

meaning of composting as a technical process. Their definition and method is one that industry or the government can use to solve pressing environmental problems presented by waste materials, such as sewage or swine manure. This is a good argument, but it is likely to earn little more than a questioning nod from millions of backyard composters.

Four out of five home-compost projects hardly heat up at all, so by this technical definition, they must be something else. But what? We composters know who we are, and in this book we claim the word "compost" as our own term and process. If commercial composters want to come up with a better word for what they do, bring it on. Meanwhile, the Purpose-Driven Composting chart should help clarify this bit of confusion.

PURPOSE-DRIVEN COMPOSTING

From start to finish, there are major differences between commercial composting and home composting. Home composting is much less technical, yet like its commercial counterpart, it should use methods that are aligned with its unique purposes.

COMMERCIAL GOALS	HOME GOALS
Waste management	On-site recycling
Pollution prevention	Improved soil quality
Financial savings	Self-sufficiency
Bioremediation of polluted sites	Healthy, productive plants

Why Compost?

Perhaps you are just getting into home composting, or maybe you've been composting for years and want to find ways to do it better. Or maybe you are one of the thousands of gardeners who tried to compost kitchen and yard waste and became so frustrated that they gave it up altogether. If so, are you ready to give it another chance? Composting to reduce the amount of garbage that leaves your house is an honorable primary mission, but compost brings so many benefits to your soil and garden that you may even consider buying compost to supplement your homemade supply.

In the following pages, we will discuss the following benefits of composting in detail:

▶ Compost increases the organic content of soil, which in turn improves its texture, drainage, fertility, and its ability to anchor plant roots.
▶ Compost invigorates the soil's food web by providing nutrients, moisture, and habitat for a huge range of beneficial life forms.
▶ Compost enhances plants' resistance to pests and diseases, and helps them respond quickly and effectively when faced with these and other unexpected health challenges, such as weather extremes.

Composting to Gain Organic Matter

Every gardener's goal is to make sure that the soil offers plant roots a pleasing balance of gritty mineral particles and spongy organic matter. The mineral particles may be large sand grains, extremely small specks of clay, or a mixture of sand and clay particles in various sizes. The size of mineral particles, which are basically ground-up rock, determines the soil's texture. An important job of the mineral portion of soil is to provide physical support for plant roots. Some plants prefer one type of soil texture over another, according to how their roots grow. Thick-rooted carrots, for example, grow best in

Carrots show fast, steady growth when grown in loose, well-drained soil enriched with compost. Vermicompost is especially beneficial to root crops.

Increasing the soil's organic matter content with compost improves its ability to hold moisture, which is much appreciated by plants with shallow, fibrous roots.

light-textured, sandy soil, while plants like lettuce, peppers, and others with more fibrous, shallow roots thrive in heavier soils that are less prone to drying out. However, when the mineral component of any soil is balanced with sufficient organic matter, soil texture becomes much less of a limiting factor in your choice of garden plants. Plenty of organic matter slows drainage and improves moisture retention in sandy soil, and it enhances drainage in heavy soil, while reducing its tendency to compact by creating tiny open spaces for air.

The Hows and Whys of Organic Matter

How much organic matter in soil is enough? Surprisingly little! Soil that contains only 5 percent organic matter is usually quite fertile, because at this ratio, mineral particles and bits of organic matter interact in ways that serve plants well. The mineral particles anchor plant roots in place and provide habitat for soil-dwelling life forms that set up communities within the root zone (the soil area below a plant occupied by its roots), while the organic matter feeds beneficial microorganisms and facilitates

Sooner or later, combined waste materials generated in your kitchen and garden (left) will become soil-enriching compost (right).

the movement of water and air between the mineral particles. You can easily increase the organic matter of your soil by using our compost-garden methods every chance you get.

Organic matter is being consumed constantly by beneficial organisms that live in soil and compost, so you must continually replenish it. Understanding this reality is fuel for the compost gardener's fire. You will rarely see a planting or growing situation that cannot be enhanced with the right use of compost. Depending on your purpose, it may be better to work with active organic matter, which is still actively decomposing; stable organic matter, which has rotted into humus; or a mixture of the two types.

Stable Organic Matter

This is compost that has pretty much finished decomposing. Ideally, about half of the organic matter in soil should be almost completely decomposed into humus. Soil scientists call this stable organic matter, and its value is mostly physical. Soil that contains plenty of stable humus is spongelike in its ability to hold and release air and water. However, many of its plant nutrients are long gone, having been taken up by plant roots or washed away by rain. Stable organic matter may include a few small sticks but is otherwise dark and crumbly, resembling rich, well-worked soil.

Active Organic Matter

This partially decomposed organic matter still has a way to go in its transition to compost, so it supports a diverse community of soil microorganisms, which release enzymes and acids that enhance plant growth, and sometimes form beneficial partnerships with plant roots that help the plants fix nitrogen or take up phosphorous, iron, and other important nutrients. "Active" is a relative term, because compost materials vary widely in how much microbial activity they can support. At one end of the continuum you could have a smoking hot heap (very high in active organic matter) or a slow-working, fall-to-spring Comforter Compost bed (see page 154). As long as you can identify chunks of leaf, strings of grass clippings, or bits of broccoli stalks in your compost, you are looking at active organic matter.

Finished compost that has rested, or cured, for a few weeks beneath a protective cover is an ideal source of both types of organic mater. Teeming with living organisms, the cured compost actively joins forces with plants, helping them take what they need from thousands of diverse nutrient molecules and root-friendly life forms. As they spread through the soil, the entire garden gets stronger.

Can You Have Too Much?

As a compost gardener, you may sometimes wonder if a certain garden spot has too much organic matter. This is a definite possibility, though whether the amount of humus is good or bad hinges in large part on which plants you are trying to grow. Some plants are happy to grow in pure compost (see Growing Pioneer Plants in Comforter Compost on page 158), but other plants, such as sweet corn or carrots, suffer when their roots are not in contact with plenty of good, gritty soil. In our experience, excessive organic matter is most likely to cause problems (evidenced by slow, thrifty growth) if there is a huge supply of stable organic matter, for example rotted sawdust, wood chips, or leaf mold. The light texture of such a growing medium makes it difficult for plants to anchor themselves firmly in place, and a shortage of mineral particles limits the soil's ability to retain nutrients. If a shallow-rooted plant like lettuce is asked to grow in such a soil, large amounts of supplemental water and plant food may be needed to promote strong, steady growth. Mulching the soil's surface to reduce evaporation can help, as can providing an extra helping of organic fertilizer, such as fish-based fertilizers or manure that has been composted, dried, and packaged.

Few gardeners, however, will ever complain about soil that contains a large amount of active organic matter. So-called muck soil, which is found at the bottom of bogs and shallow lakes or along the banks of slow-flowing rivers that flood periodically, can contain up to 30 percent organic matter mixed with extremely tiny soil particles, making muck soil a great home for many types of plants, provided that the soil is adequately drained. A raised garden bed filled with soil that has been thoroughly mixed with one part Banner Batch compost (see page 136) to two parts soil often compares favorably with extremely rich muck soil found in fertile bottomland sites, and the finished bed will drain like a dream.

Testing Organic Content

There are two ways to find out how much organic matter is present in your soil. You can have it tested by a soil lab (check with your county Cooperative Extension Service, or see the government pages of the phone book under Soil Testing or Agricultural Colleges), or you can observe how it behaves when you use it to grow plants. Soil-test labs use either chemical or electrical conductivity methods to

Raised beds filled with a soil mixture high in organic matter help improve drainage, which is naturally slow in compacted subsoil.

measure organic matter, neither of which can be replicated at home. But as you get to know how your soil looks and feels when you dig and turn it, and how it behaves when it's saturated with water, you can compare your observations to the characteristics of nearby soil that has not been improved by the addition of organic matter. In most soil, attaining an ideal level of 6 to 8 percent of stable and active organic matter usually takes three years if you mix in a 3" (7.6 cm) thick blanket of compost annually and use biodegradable mulches. So the three-year mark is a good time to have a soil test done to evaluate your progress. At this point, chances are good that soil-test results will show organic content of 6 to 8 percent, which is just about perfect for any type of plant you may want to grow — especially fast-growing vegetables and annual flowers. After three years, you can continue to enrich your soil with more organic matter to further improve its tilth, or you can ease off and use compost mostly for its "medicinal" value. As your soil steadily improves, you should need less bulky organic matter, but regular infusions of cured compost will still be essential to supporting an active, dynamic soil food web.

Secrets from the Rhizosphere

Compost's organic matter alone qualifies it as a top-notch soil conditioner, yet the greatest gift compost brings to soil is its huge array of beneficial life forms, which include fungi, bacteria, soil-dwelling insects, and numerous organisms that fall between these broad categories. Small populations of many of these are present in compost, but they do not take off until they enter the secret world known as the rhizosphere, which is the incredibly bio-active real estate where roots and soil come together. Some are fungi that assist plant roots as they take up nutrients, for example, the mutually beneficial relationship that exists between peas, beans, and other legumes, and certain strains of soil-dwelling bacteria (see Bold Bacteria on the facing page). In addition, numerous types of fungi have recently been found to help other plants take up phosphorous and other essential plant nutrients. In exchange for the microorganisms' services, plants exude sugary treats that nourish these and other soil-dwelling microorganisms.

Compost Condos for Beneficials

One of the best reasons to compost in or near your garden is that compost can serve as a habitat for crickets and ground beetles, which are two nocturnal insects that deserve more recognition as gardening allies. Crickets have a healthy appetite for protein-rich weed seeds, while ground beetles devour slugs and many other common garden pests, including squash bugs and spotted cucumber beetles.

SASSY SIDEROPHORES

Soil biologists have discovered that certain specialized large molecules, called siderophores, are the missing link between plants and iron. This essential nutrient is often in good supply in the soil but cannot be taken up easily by plants without the help of siderophores. Where do siderophores come from? They are produced by the same soil-borne microorganisms that create compost! Iron-challenged plants such as azaleas and blueberries often suffer from iron starvation, as evidenced by yellowing leaves and poor growth. Siderophores in compost help plants pick up, or chelate, the iron they need.

Both critters prefer places that are undisturbed, so a slow compost pile hidden behind your squash bed makes a great summer-long habitat. A Comforter Compost (see page 154) can also serve as a luxury hotel for crickets and ground beetles, because the material stays loose enough to allow them to move around freely. You can improve the shelter aspect of a compost pile by covering it with a blanket or cloth, or by topping it off with a loose layer of straw or other porous mulch. How about using a composting method we call a Pit-of-Plenty, which is topped by a plywood lid (see page 181)? This is a dream-come-true habitat for crickets, which seek out little seeds and other tasty tidbits and then leave behind manure (frass) that's rich in plant nutrients.

Above: cricket
Right: ground beetles

You need not worry that hosting crickets in your compost will lead to unwanted visitors in your house — as long as you keep outdoor lighting to a minimum during the summer months. Like many other insects, crickets are attracted to light, so leaving outdoor lights on at night can lead to strange and unpredictable disturbances in the overall balance of helpful and harmful insects in your home landscape.

Bold Bacteria

Peas, beans, and other legumes use the services of soil-borne bacteria to process airborne nitrogen and store it in nodules on their roots. In 1813, noted British writer and inventor Sir Humphrey Davy observed that "legumes seem to prepare the ground for wheat," but

WHO'S WHO OF NITROGEN-FIXING BACTERIA

In your garden, the most valuable nitrogen-fixing bacteria are the strains that assist peas and beans: *Rhizobium leguminosarum viceae* for peas and lentils, and *R. leguminosarum phaseoli* for beans. Both are included in products sold as "garden inoculants." Soybeans, crowder peas, and asparagus beans utilize different strains known as *Bradyrhizobia*, while alfalfa and most clovers team up with *R. meliloti*. Be sure to match the crop with the right bacterial strain when buying inoculant or when you are growing your own in compost-filled pots.

it was not until the 1880s that agricultural thinkers realized that nitrogen was involved. By then, most farmers had seen firsthand evidence that peas and beans grew better in soil where they had grown before, so by the early 1900s it was customary to take buckets of soil from places previously occupied by legumes, and scatter it into new planting furrows. These farmers were unknowingly inoculating their soil with beneficial bacteria, which remains a darn good idea (see Prime Your Soil for Legumes on page 22).

Since the 1950s, soil laboratories and garden catalogs have provided farmers and gardeners with inexpensive bacterial inoculants for legumes, but there is a new kid on the bacterial block. PGPB sounds like an acronym for a spooky chemical, but rather, PGPB stands for Plant Growth Promoting Bacteria, which encompass several types of bacteria that help plants grow better when added to the soil. PGPBs are available as ready-to-use products (for example, the over-the-counter brand Bio-Yield), but compost is a free, convenient, and renewable source of plant-growth-enhancing bacteria that also fall into the PGPB group.

How many types of bacteria are there in compost? Microbiologists usually manage to grow out about 300 different strains of bacteria from random samples of compost, including many of the strains that top current lists of most-wanted PGPBs.

Fantastic Fungi

Like legions of gardeners before us, we have seen plants that have been weakened or killed by powdery mildew, late blight, and other fungal diseases. So it is easy to understand why fungi have had such a hard time earning respect among horticulturists and gardeners, and why those claiming that fungi could actually help plants were dismissed as being too weird over the past 100 years. For example, exotic-plant collectors publicly wondered, in 1851, whether the demise of many hot-house orchids was due to a lack of fungi often present in the native soil beneath healthy plants. They were not taken seriously. It was not until German forest pathologist A. B. Frank conducted a landmark experiment in 1894 that the educated world began to entertain the possibility that some plants depend on fungi for their health and well-being. Frank sterilized a batch of soil, planted pine seedlings in it, and compared their pitiful growth to that of plants grown in soil that included native fungi. He subsequently coined the word "mycorrhiza," derived from the marriage of myco (fungi) and rhiza (root), to describe beneficial soil fungi.

Were Frank's pine trees a fluke? Hundreds of scientific studies since his time have shown that they were not, and the list of known ways in which soil-borne fungi benefit plants continues to grow. For example, fungi play crucial roles in helping plants metabolize nutrients and in helping some plants take up iron. Fungi also often galvanize plants' abilities to maximize phosphorous and may help keep plants' immune systems functioning at high alert. Recently, microbiologists have suggested using the word "mycorrhization" to describe the elegant relationships that exist between fungi that spend their lives in the soil and plants that wave their leaves in the sun. To a plant, a certain amount of liveliness among the bacteria and fungi living in the rhizosphere is exactly what's needed to make it feel at home.

Prime Your Soil for Legumes

When planting peas, beans, vetch, clovers, or other legumes in soil for the first time, gardeners are often advised to inoculate the seeds with nitrogen-fixing bacteria. Sold in a black-powder form, these legume inoculants are inexpensive and easy to use, or you can grow your own legume inoculant in containers of compost. Composting creates captive populations of nitrogen-fixing bacteria that can be used to inoculate new planting sites, as shown here. When using this method, keep in mind that different legumes utilize different strains of nitrogen-fixing bacteria (see Who's Who of Nitrogen-Fixing Bacteria on page 21 for more details). Be sure to match the legume you plant in compost-filled pots with those you plan to grow in your garden.

HANDLING INOCULANT

Legume inoculant looks like a dark powder, but it's teeming with resting bacteria. You are wise to wear a dust mask when handling large amounts of inoculant, but precautions are not necessary when coating small amounts of seed. Simply place the seeds in a jar, soak or dampen them well, and pour off excess water. Sprinkle with a teaspoon of inoculant, shake to coat the seeds, and they are ready to plant.

1 Go through your leftover seeds and find a legume you plan to grow again. Fill a 6″ (15 cm) pot with almost-done or fully ripe compost, plant five or so seeds, water, set the pot in a sunny window or in a protected spot outdoors, and let the seedlings grow. If you are growing more than one type of legume, label each pot so you will know which is which.

2 When the plants are 4 to 5 weeks old, or at any time before they start to flower, clip off the seedlings at the soil line and compost them. Enclose the pot in a plastic bag, or dump its contents into a bucket with a lid. Store the potted compost in the container, and place it in a cool, dark place. Keep it lightly moist until needed.

3 Empty the container onto the site where you plan to grow the legume, and mix it into the soil, or use it to line a planting furrow as you sow your seeds. Water well to distribute the bacteria in the soil.

4 Keep soil lightly moist to encourage germination as well as to support growth of nitrogen-fixing bacteria. Plants should begin fixing their own nitrogen by the time they have five true leaves.

Can Compost Make You Sick?

Because compost derives its life force from a teeming community of fungi and bacteria, common sense ought to tell you that you shouldn't eat it and that you should always wash vegetables grown in compost-enriched soil before you eat them. And, while working with compost does much more to improve your health than to hurt it, there are a few potential health threats of which compost gardeners should be aware:

Farmer's Lung

is a pneumonia-like illness caused by breathing in the types of bacteria and fungal spores present in rotted hay, sugar cane, mushroom compost, and other materials that decay at high temperatures. Acute cases are caused by intense exposure to spores, for example, spending a Saturday ripping through a round bale of rotted hay without wearing a dust mask. As a recurrent condition among farmers who often handle spoiled hay in late winter and early spring, farmer's lung has been recognized in medical literature for almost 300 years. The types of bacteria that produce the riskiest spores are actinomycetes, especially those that work at high temperatures. Hay or other materials that have been colonized by these bacteria usually include mats of dusty white or gray material containing billions of spores. To limit your chances of contracting this illness, always wear a dust mask when forking through moldy hay or any material that includes dusty white patches. When you are finished, change into clean clothes. Antibiotics are usually needed to treat acute farmer's lung infections.

Paronychia

is a painful infection located in the deep-skin crevices at the edges of a fingernail. Derived from Greek *para* (close) and *onyx* (nail), this common infection may as well be called nail-biter's nightmare, because it develops when bacteria enter openings in the skin. Prolonged moisture contributes to the problem, so you can unintentionally set the stage for a round of paronychia by working in compost bare-handed or by wearing wet, dirty gloves with holes in the fingertips. Soil that gets inside the glove holes can abrade the skin, much like sandpaper, thus providing access to moist crevices by *Staphylococcus* or *Streptococcus* bacteria, which are present almost everywhere. Minor cases of paronychia can clear in a few days with the help of warm-water soaks, but oral antibiotics may be needed to cure severe infections. To prevent this problem, replace gloves that have holes in them. If you

in susceptible people. However, the bacteria is not at all common, and it is killed by temperatures above 110°F (43°C). Lightly dampen very dry compost or potting soil before using it to reduce the possibility that you might inhale airborne spores.

Tetanus

is a disease of the central nervous system, caused by a toxin produced by *Clostridium tetani*, bacteria that are widely present in soil and manure. Tetanus is also called lockjaw because of the severe facial muscle spasms that are a symptom of the disease. Because the bacteria that cause tetanus are so widespread, even a minor cut creates the opportunity for exposure. Fortunately, vaccination provides excellent protection against tetanus. Every gardener should make sure his or her tetanus immunization is up to date — tetanus boosters are recommended every 10 years for adults. If you get a cut or scrape while gardening and don't know your tetanus vaccination record, call your doctor and get that shot. Public health departments sometimes offer tetanus shots as well.

have an injury in the fold next to a nail, keep it clean and covered and wear a medical exam glove under your gardening gloves until it heals. Once any glove gets wet and dirty, take it off, wash it, and switch to a dry one.

Histoplasmosis

is a respiratory infection caused by *Histoplasma capsulatum*, which is a yeastlike fungus that grows in bat or bird droppings. It is a common soil-borne fungus in the Midwest and Upper South, and many people come into casual contact with it all the time. Normal, functioning immune systems most often kill the fungus soon after it enters the lungs, but people can develop acute infections by breathing in large amounts of the dry fungus while gathering guano or bird droppings. Wearing a dust mask in such situations is an excellent way to prevent infection, but if you are exposed and experience breathing difficulties, seek medical care.

Legionnaire's Disease

is a respiratory infection caused by a rather uncommon bacteria, *Legionella pneumophila*, which is sometimes present in damp air conditioners or refrigerators. A closely related species, *L. longbeachae,* has been found in some potting soils in Japan, Australia, and the United States. Like its famous cousin, this bacteria can cause bacterial pneumonia

Derived from the Greek word *edaphos*, meaning "soil or ground," edaphon is the collective community of plant and animal life present in soil. In the 1980s, Vaclav Petrik, Sr., a Czechoslovakian-born soil scientist, published his attempt to quantify the edaphon of healthy soil with a high organic content of 7 percent. Of that 7 percent, Petrik estimated that 85 percent should be humus, or completely decomposed organic matter, 10 percent plant roots, and 5 percent should be made up of edaphon. Are you ready for more numbers? In Petrik's model, the best edaphon balance breaks down like this:

Fungi and algae	40 percent
Bacteria and microorganisms called actinomycetes	40 percent
Earthworms	12 percent
Other macrofauna	5 percent
Micro- and mesofauna	3 percent

Fortunately for us, replenishing the edaphon in soil is a simple matter of making and using compost! As for what the edaphon actually does for plants, keep reading.

Health Food for Soil

Compost is often too low in the major plant nutrients — nitrogen, phosphorous, and potassium — to qualify as a fertilizer. So what? While compost does contain some nutrients, more importantly, there are substances in compost that help dissolve iron, zinc, and other minor nutrients so that plants can take them up. Additionally, compost often supports starter populations of rhizomorphic bacteria and fungi, which in turn enhance plant nutrition. Compost can also suppress plant diseases, which can be every bit as important as soil fertility when you want to grow healthy, long-bearing, indeterminate tomatoes, discourage black spot on roses, or prevent root rot in a mass planting of ajuga.

How does this work? Germinating seeds and growing roots leak or actively exude sugars, which are, in turn, consumed by soil microorganisms. As long as there is plenty of diversity in the resident microbial community, beneficial life forms out-compete troublemakers that would otherwise invade root or stem tissues and damage the plant. And, because compost is basically the battleground left behind after wave upon wave of fungi and bacteria vie for dominance during decomposition, particles of cured compost often pack a good dose of natural antibiotics produced by the beneficial bacteria. The small mites, springtails, and other little insects that live in compost sometimes fulfill predator or parasite roles in the prevention of plant diseases, and then there is the mysterious matter of induced systemic resistance, or ISR. When grown in compost-enriched soil, many plants use substances present in the compost to prepare for future disease attacks. When a response is required, these "primed" plants produce more of the proteins needed to resist the disease.

Not all batches of compost can accomplish these wonders. For maximum effectiveness as a disease preventive, compost must be cured for at least several weeks, until the only recognizable materials are chips of wood or sticks. As the compost cures, microorganisms that were set back by high or low temperatures have time to recolonize the heap, dramatically increasing the compost's microbial diversity. Compost that has gone through hot, moderate, and cold conditions is most likely to contain exactly the microbial buffet needed to qualify it as health food for plants.

Synergistic Benefits

As a gardener, you want to grow vegetables, herbs, and fruits that are more flavorful and nutritious than those you can buy and flowers that produce a nonstop parade of colorful blossoms. Regardless of whether your special, pet plants are peppers or peperomias, if you were to assemble a top-notch panel of horticultural experts and ask them for the secrets of the gardener's art, they would give the same answer: Start with a quality plant variety or cultivar and then provide perfect growing conditions. We will give you some help choosing plant varieties in part 3 (see page 240), but here let's consider the role compost can play in providing those perfect growing conditions. Compost will condition the soil to make it more hospitable to plant roots, help plants to help themselves to soil-borne nutrients, and reduce the likelihood that you will be plagued by outbreaks of random, soil-borne diseases. These are big factors in perfect growing conditions. Compost cannot turn on the water faucet or work an organic fertilizer into a planting bed, but considering what you get for little or no cost, composting is a deal you can't refuse.

You will need to invest some thought and muscle, but by using the compost-garden methods discussed in part 2 (see page 130), your investments will yield greater returns than if you composted the traditional way, by piling compostable stuff up in a hidden corner of your yard. Now that you have a good idea of what's going on inside your compost bin or pile, it's easy to see why composting in or near the garden is such a sound practice. And, because many compost-garden methods benefit the garden while progressing, they will help you sidestep the most perplexing question asked by new composters: When will it be done?

Composting Fast, Composting Slow

In this age of microwave meals and speed-of-light Internet transmission, we all like for things to happen fast. Compost is not fast. Unless you really work it hard by achieving a perfect balance of materials and moisture and attentively turning and mixing it every few days to make a fast Banner Batch (see page 136), compost follows the rhythm of the seasons. Compost made in summer benefits from the work of micro-

LASTING DISEASE RELIEF

When you amend soil with compost, which contains natural antibiotics, to help prevent root-rot diseases or to strengthen plants' immune systems, how long will the effects last? The answer varies with climate, soil, and compost, but as long as you can see little tidbits of bygone sticks and leaves in compost-amended soil when you crumble some of it in your hand, the "good guys" are still working. Once the change from active to stable organic matter is complete, it's time to dig in more compost or blanket the surface with cured compost topped by a biodegradable mulch.

organisms that are active in warm temperatures, so it may be done in a matter of weeks. On the other hand, compost made from autumn's fallen leaves and frost-blackened plants usually does not become fully decomposed until the next summer rolls around. So, a certain amount of patience is required to be a happy compost gardener.

Sometimes you may want to put in extra time and effort to create a hot Banner Batch, which is a great way to neutralize pathogens in tissues of potentially disease-ridden plant debris and deactivate weed seeds, and also to make sure dangerous bacteria are cleared from animal manure. But most of the time, it is more enjoyable (and much less work) to allow compost to mature at its own rate. The materials you use have a mighty impact on a batch's speed (or lack thereof), and there is nothing wrong with tweaking a compost project to make sure you see enough ongoing change to keep you happy. At the same time, you will hear us saying time and time again that slow compost is good compost. Accepting and respecting the slowness of compost, the very essence of earth, can also bring balance to a high-pressure life that's burning too hot. Should you feel frustrated, remind yourself that this is earth you are dealing with, and pay attention to its lesson. If you need speed, find your car keys.

WEEDING IN SUPER SOIL

Need further persuasion to get into compost gardening? After a year or two of using compost-garden methods every chance you get, you will discover new pleasure in gardening. You'll notice that you can pull weeds more easily, and you may even look forward to weeding because it affords a justified opportunity to visit the vibrant underground world you have created. Pulling up a clump of crabgrass may produce a glimpse of the biggest, most iridescent night crawler you've ever seen, or maybe you'll begin gathering potatoes with your hands so that you can touch the crumbly texture of your wonderfully loamy soil. Having super soil brings its own satisfaction, which is really about leaving the world a better place than you found it.

Getting Intense

Soil that constantly gets what it needs from compost can be worked harder than soil that receives lesser care. Compost gardeners gradually fall into the habit of thinking of their soil's health status before they plant anything, because keeping the soil food web humming along is fundamental to growing robust plants. We learn to trust that if soil needs are addressed first, productivity logically follows. In an intensively managed garden, compost makes it possible to replace one crop with another without pausing to let the soil rest.

If you garden intensively, in raised beds or in a square-foot-type garden, your soil will often get little or no rest between crops. Whether your spring lettuce is followed by summer tomatoes, or perhaps you're planting a fall crop of kale where you just pulled out bush beans, a generous infusion of compost mixed into the soil between plantings is the best way to keep the soil from becoming exhausted. When you discover that a space will be empty for more than two or three weeks, pile on some compost and let it sit. Earthworms and leaching will pull humus and nutrients into the soil, getting the soil-enrichment process going while you attend to other things. When you're ready to plant, mix in the compost along with organic fertilizer sufficient to meet the needs of the crop, and you're good to go!

2
Tools for the Composter's Garden

I F YOU ALREADY OWN some basic gardening tools, you are adequately equipped to ease into compost gardening, but as you adopt and refine compost gardening methods for your garden, you will want to add a few specialized tools to your collection.

Don't get the idea that compost gardening requires a super-consumer mentality, because the opposite is true: Buying a lot of stuff to make compost runs contrary to the philosophy behind compost gardening, which is based on recycling on-site resources with minimal outside inputs. Certainly gardening catalogs and retailers offer a growing number of compost-related products — bins, tools, accessories, activators, and more — that promise to make the composting process better, faster, and easier. Some are worth their cost, and some are not. When you find yourself dazzled by shiny new tools and must-have potions, take a deep breath and remember that decomposition is a natural process that will happen whether or not you own a nifty tool.

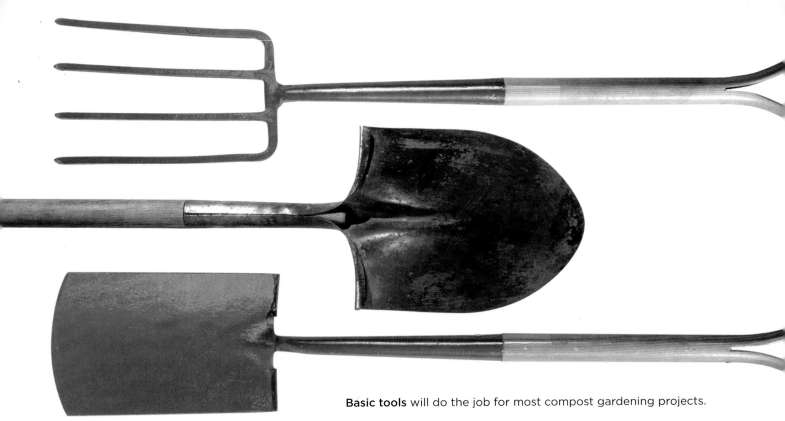

Basic tools will do the job for most compost gardening projects.

The Composter's Tool Shed

You should try compost gardening on for size before you start tooling up, because your tool needs will vary depending on your climate, available materials, and how much time you spend in your garden. Until you figure out which composting practices are the best fit for your site, soil, and personal gardening habits, it makes little sense to start acquiring special equipment.

Trusty Old Friends

The tools and equipment described in this chapter are things that we've found useful in creating and tending our own compost gardens and learning from the work of many other innovative, resourceful gardeners who know compost. When appropriate, we use recycled or "repurposed" items in the place of buying hard-to-get specialty items, and we encourage you to do the same. It's fun to buy new tools, but it can be more satisfying to build rich, healthy soil using tools you already own or can pick up for a fraction of their original price at yard sales, farm sales, thrift stores, or flea markets.

And then there are treasured tools, like the old knife with your grandfather's initials carved into the wooden handle, or the hoe you found in the garage while helping your parents move from your childhood home. Sometimes simply carrying the pocketknife your son bought you for a Father's Day gift is all it takes to turn a good gardening day into a great one.

Finding Great Tools

There will be times when you decide that the best thing to do is to pay retail price for a tool, but hardware stores, garden centers, and mail-order catalogs are not the only places to get good tools to facilitate composting. Balance your new tool purchases with efforts to get perfectly good used tools that are in need of new homes. Whether you're looking for the perfect tool to solve a perplexing problem or need to expand your tool inventory, here are some local tool sources that should not be overlooked.

▶ **Garage sales.** Folks who are moving often unload gardening tools before they go. Shop garage sales for excellent, lightly used tools.

▶ **Classified ads.** Watch the newspapers for estate sales that include gardening equipment, because well-made tools often outlast their owners — and may even outlast you!

▶ **Flea markets.** If your town has a nearby flea market, get to know vendors who specialize in old tools. They often get them from salvage dealers and sometimes run across unique finds.

▶ **Community gardens.** Does your city have a demonstration garden maintained by Master Gardeners? A friendly visit during a scheduled Saturday morning work session is a great way to see which tools local gardeners like well enough to carry in the trunks of their cars.

▶ **Freecycling.** "Freecycle" for what you want. Every community has an Internet group associated with the Freecycle Network and its Web site, www.freecycle.org, where you can list items and arrange to take or give away anything, as long as it's free, legal, and appropriate for all ages.

Whether you're shopping for used tools or new ones, keep in mind that cheap is seldom better, but expensive may not be that great, either. Long-handled tools like shovels and hoes can be costly, but these are heavy-use items that need to hold up well. You'll want to strike a balance between quality, durability, your budget, and your body — and be realistic about your tool-care practices, too. Do you always clean and store tools when you're through using them, or do you leave them out in the rain? Does your body "complain" when you do certain things, like lifting or bending? As the old saying goes, "the hammer can shape the hand, but it's better to get a hammer that does what the hand tells it to do." Here are some specifics to consider when choosing new tools:

▶ **Fit, comfort, and balance.** Buying tools firsthand, at a retail store or garage sale, has huge advantages over remote ordering. You can try the tools on for size, and obtaining the object of your desire does not require additional packaging made from

trees or fossil-fueled transportation (racking up extra compost miles). To test a tool, hold it as if you are working with it. Make sure the tool feels comfortable in your hands and that it is the right size and weight relative to your body.

▶ **Handles and attachments.** Is the handle sturdy and smooth? If the tool has a wooden handle, check for cracks or flaws where it could break during use. Look at how the tool head or grips are attached to the handle: Do they fit securely? Could you replace the handle if necessary? A heavy head is a virtue in mattocks and other tools meant for high-impact chopping, but no tool should be so heavy that you have trouble using it properly.

▶ **Cutting edges.** Shovels, spades, mattocks, hoes, and other tools meant for digging and cutting should have discernible cutting edges. For safety reasons, the edges on new tools are often left dull, and it's up to you to sharpen them. Still, you should see an obvious beveled (slanted) edge on new spades or hoes. On old tools, sharp edges usually can be restored by giving them a good working-over with a metal file (see pages 37 and 179).

▶ **Metal quality.** Beware of cheap metal tool heads that have been stamped out of a sheet of metal, or parts that are barely welded together. The flimsiness of such tools will be a continual source of frustration as they bend or break at the worst possible moments.

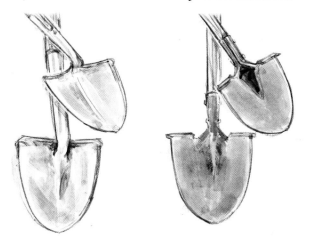

A sturdy, forged blade, such as that on the left, securely attached to a well-balanced handle makes digging tasks go more easily. Stamped blades, such as that on the right, are inferior.

Five Foundation Tools for Your Composter's Garden

The list of composting tools you will need on a day-in and day-out basis is surprisingly short — a spade, a garden fork, a hoe, a leaf rake, and a metal file for renewing sharp tool edges as often as needed. All come in a range of models, with sizes, shapes, and weights to meet your physical and composting needs.

Spades and Shovels

Whether you call a spade a spade, or call it a shovel, has little to do with which tool, technically speaking, it is. The two words vary in regional dialects (Barbara calls hers a shovel, but to Deb it's a spade), but what you call your digging thing does not matter if the tool does what you need it to do. Terminology in this matter is better left to folks who have time to argue the semantics and physical features of shovels and spades. Meanwhile, we have compost to tend! Spade or shovel blades may have a rounded shield shape with a distinct point, the cutting edge may be rounded, or it may be a flat blade with squared edges. The various shapes are suited to various tasks. To keep any spade or shovel in good working order, keep a file handy (see page 179) to use when restoring its edge to shiny sharpness.

▶ **Pointed-blade shovel.** For digging holes in hard-to-dig compacted clay soil, a pointed blade gives a bit of extra bite, along with a nice, clean slice.

▶ **Rounded-blade shovel.** If you have sandy soil and mostly need a spade for opening planting holes or mixing and moving composting materials, a smallish spade with a rounded edge is a good choice.

THE ADVANTAGES OF GARDENING LIKE A LADY

I was mildly offended, some years ago, when my husband presented me with a small-bladed shovel bearing the label "Lady Gardener" on its long wooden handle. It was nice of him to choose a gift in tune with my favorite activities, but I couldn't help wondering if he thought I was too delicate to manage full-sized tools. So I was pleasantly surprised when I eventually took up the shovel and found it well suited to any number of gardening jobs, including composting. One of my compost bins has a small door at its base for removing finished compost from the bottom of the pile. My full-sized

shovel's blade barely fits through that door, but my "lady" shovel enters with ease and her lovely long handle lets me scoop out as much compost as I need. She also saves me from myself when I'm moving compost or soil around, by allowing me to lift only dainty "bites" that don't overtax my back and shoulders. That small blade is just right for adding and subtracting plants from existing perennial beds, too, and it slips easily into the soil when I'm digging new holes for spot composting or planting. I guess Mom was right when she told me I should be more ladylike!

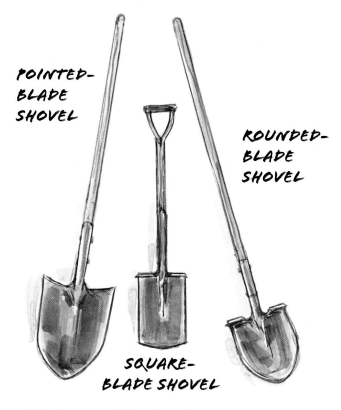

POINTED-BLADE SHOVEL

ROUNDED-BLADE SHOVEL

SQUARE-BLADE SHOVEL

Whether you call it a shovel or a spade, what matters most in a digging tool is a sharp blade and a comfortable grip.

▶ **Square-blade shovel.** For chopping piles of compost-bound materials on the ground, a square-point spade is hard to beat. Its long handle (straight or with a D-grip, depending on preference) lets you work in an upright position with gravity on your side, while the wide cutting edge makes the most of every chop through coarse stems.

Garden Forks

Choosing a fork for composting is not a question of etiquette, though your selection may depend upon which "course" your compost is currently serving. If it's a raw-materials appetizer, consider the humble pitchfork. A traditional pitchfork's thin, curving tines are meant to slide smoothly through hay and straw, and a pitchfork also works great for turning or moving matted layers of leaves. Its sharp tines make good pokers for breaking up compressed materials and for stirring layers together, but a pitchfork becomes less useful for lifting and turning compost as the pieces become smaller and slip easily through the spaces between the smooth, round tines.

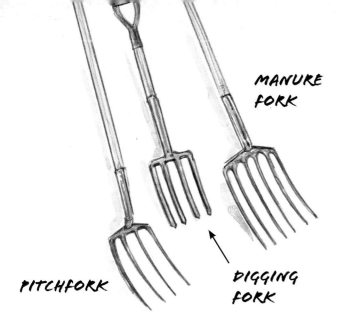

MANURE FORK

PITCHFORK

DIGGING FORK

Long, curving tines of pitch- and manure forks, are made to lift and scoop. Loosening soil is easier with a digging fork's short, straight, sturdy tines.

If you plan to regularly gather manure or stable bedding, you might want the pitchfork's first cousin, often called a manure, or compost, fork. These forks feature long, closely set tines that may be curved or straight. Manure/compost forks are meant for lifting mixed bedding and stable manure, or you can use one to turn moist compost-in-progress. Some models, called scoop forks, have 10 to 12 tines curved into a scoop configuration. Watch out, though, because a big scoop fork may allow you to lift larger loads than your back will bear.

Shorter, sturdier tines that are rectangular or diamond-shaped (in cross section) characterize digging and spading forks, also called turning forks. These

---

DON'T LOSE YOUR TOOLS

We all know that we should put our tools away each time we use them, but sometimes we don't and they end up lost. You will be less likely to lose track of your tools outside in the yard or inside your house if you wrap a stripe of brightly colored plastic tape (available at hardware, home, and discount stores) around their handles. Color-marking of tools is a standard loss-prevention practice among native-plant rescue groups, and it works in a home garden, too.

---

garden standbys can do the work of a pitchfork or manure fork pretty well, but their forte is loosening and lifting soil or compost. Stocky of handle and heavy of tine, digging forks are also useful for making planting holes or roughing the sides and bottom of a planting hole made with a spade or a shovel. In the compost garden, they're handy for turning compost or cultivating soil, for poking aeration holes in any site, and for leaning against when you're ready for a breather. If you choose only one type of garden fork, choose this one.

Hoes

For chopping matted leaves, breaking up clumps of grass clippings, or cutting bedraggled hay, straw, or weeds into smaller pieces for composting, a good hoe will do the job. Under the right soil and stem con-

GARDEN, OR NURSERY, HOE

WARREN HOE

STIRRUP HOE

You can stand up straight while chopping and mixing materials with the sharp, sturdy blade of a garden hoe.

ditions, you can even use a sharp hoe to take down compost crops ready to be harvested as greens. And then there is a hoe's primary purpose, which is to slice off weeds when they're young and tender. Teamed up with a digging fork or spade, a hoe makes short work of helping a Walking Heap (see page 140) move toward its final destination.

A hoe's design minimizes back bending, but you still need to hold your belly tight and let your arms

KEEP YOUR EDGES SHARP

Take care of your tools, and they'll take care of you. Maintaining the cutting edges on tools you use for digging, chopping, and cutting makes every job easier — and safer. Dull tools are dangerous: They slip and bounce over surfaces instead of cutting through them, and they cause you to use excessive force to make a cut. The harder you have to work, the more fatigued (and frustrated) you become and the more likely you are to hurt yourself (think strained back, cut finger, bruised foot), but there is no need to "go there."

Spend five dollars for a new steel file (commonly called a mill bastard file), or shop for a bargain used one, to use for sharpening the blades of shovels and hoes. A whetstone or diamond file for sharpening knives, axes, hatchets, and hand tools won't cost much more. Tool-tending is a fine task for bad-weather days, but don't wait too long between sharpening sessions. Instead, make a habit of sharpening your tools each time you launch into a new composting project. For how to sharpen a tool, see page 179.

and the hoe do the work. When done with proper form (knees bent, back straight), chopping anything with a hoe is darn good exercise.

The classic hoe has a rectangular metal head fixed at roughly 90 degrees to the handle; these types of hoes may be sold as planter, nursery, or grubbing hoes. Hoes with specialized blades — circular, stirrup (also called action), warren, goosefoot, and other shapes — are great for weeding but not as well suited for preparing compost ingredients. Their cutting edges tend to be in the wrong position for efficient chopping, and their blades may be too small or narrow to tolerate heavy use, so you may ding or bend them to ruination if you're not careful. Why risk it? Stick with a plain old hoe for compost work, and keep your sharpening file handy. When a hoe is used as a compost chopper, a sharp edge is essential. You'll see. Once you discover how well a sharp hoe chops, you'll touch up that edge every chance you get.

Leaf Rakes

If leaves are the most abundant high-carbon brown material generated in your yard, you need a good rake to make leaf gathering as easy and efficient as pos-

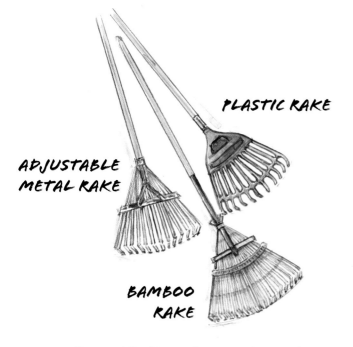

PLASTIC RAKE

ADJUSTABLE METAL RAKE

BAMBOO RAKE

You'll enjoy fall raking tasks more when you're equipped with a well-made leaf rake.

sible. You also can use a leaf rake to gather clumps of grass clippings or to remove old mulches and spread new ones. Look for a well-balanced tool that feels right when you stand in raking position. Consider it a failed fitting if you feel like the rake's head is pulling you forward (most of your energy will go into pulling the rake in the other direction).

A wide rake head will help you clear your lawn more quickly but also adds weight that can wear you out faster than a lighter model. An adjustable rake that lets you narrow the rake head to fit between shrubs and perennials is handy if there are leaves to be cleared from tight spaces. Choose metal tines for durability, plastic or bamboo tines for a slight weight advantage, or rubber-tipped tines if you'll be raking on paved surfaces and want to keep scraping sounds to a minimum. In fall, cheap rakes abound in home centers and mass-market retailers, but many are not the bargains they seem. If you're tempted by what appears to be a great deal, take a close look before you buy. Lightweight rigid-plastic tines break easily under even moderate use; a single bolt attaching the rake head to the handle is prone to loosen and be lost; a rough handle will quickly rub your hands the wrong way. You may not need a fancy-schmancy rake, but it's worth spending a few dollars more to make sure you get a tool you can use comfortably for several seasons.

Tools for Transporting Materials

Without realizing it, you may spend as much time moving garden-related "stuff" around as you do on actual gardening tasks. Depending on your day's gardening agenda, you'll need to get out the tools you'll use, and various composting materials, and pots and plants, and maybe even a "little one" strapped into an infant seat (our kids survived this nicely; babies love

to go outside and watch their parents do interesting things). Clearly, efficiency counts when it comes to moving materials, equipment, or whatever else you deem essential for a certain task. Even though compost gardening reduces much of the back-and-forth associated with traditional out-of-the-way composting, you'll still find plenty of things you need to move, so you'll need good ways to move them. For compost gardeners, this translates into a need for some sort of wheeled conveyance — typically a garden cart or wheelbarrow — accompanied by a collection of buckets, tarps, and bins.

Wheelbarrows and Garden Carts

Whether you choose to roll on one wheel (a wheelbarrow) or two (a garden cart) depends on factors ranging from the width of your garden paths to the weight of the things you most often move. A wheelbarrow's single wheel makes it easier to maneuver in tight spaces, while a cart's access is limited by the width of its wheelbase. Moving heavy loads tends to be easier with a cart, because its operator has less lifting to do to get a load balanced over the wheels. A cart is less prone to tipping than a wheelbarrow, but a wheelbarrow rolls more easily over rough terrain.

Perhaps you will need one of each — maybe a large cart and a small wheelbarrow, or a small cart and a large wheelbarrow. Carts and wheelbarrows are exceedingly useful for moving loads of loose, heavy materials, such as soil, manure, and compost. Container plants on their way to a bed or border, hand tools, full watering cans, stacks of newspapers for mulching, sunscreen, and a bottle of cold water are just a few of the many other items that will ride nicely to your job site in a cart or wheelbarrow.

The perfect choice for you will represent a good balance of durability versus weight. Models described as "heavy duty" may be too heavy for you to handle

IT'S A DRAG

Whether I'm settling in for a weeding session on a summer morning, or looking at an afternoon of leaf-raking in the fall, the one tool I'm sure to have on hand is my tarp. The current model is my third "official" gardening tarp, and compared to the sheets and shower curtains I've used in the past, it's deluxe — a sturdy 6′ x 6′ (1.83 x 1.83 m) sheet of tear-resistant, woven polyethylene with a strap handle at each corner. With the help of two metal carabiner-style clips that came with it, the handles can be fastened together to form a loose sack.

My tarp holds heaps of weeds, piles of prunings, and mountains (relatively speaking) of leaves. Sometimes it gets thrown over lawn furniture to keep it dry through a passing shower, and sometimes I use it as a drop cloth when I'm potting up plants in containers. Instead of sweeping up, I can drag the mess to the closest compost project. Given the choice between lifting and dragging, I'll drag every time.

It's hard to kill a good tarp, so my old tarps are still around. One protects a curing compost pile from exposure to the elements, while the other blocks weed growth in my garden path and provides shelter for a healthy population of crickets and earthworms.

when you take a pinecone for a ride; imagine pushing it up an incline loaded with 150 pounds of compost. If you think there may be times when you will want to lift the cart/wheelbarrow itself (into your vehicle or over a low fence, for example) is there a practical way to do it? Look for the combination of quality construction and utility that best suits you and your budget, and whenever possible, try out these big-ticket items before buying them. Often some assembly is required.

You may be totally satisfied with your wheelbarrow or cart but not with tires that go flat every time the wind blows. A bicycle pump can inflate an occasional low tire, but go to a tire store for help replacing tires that won't hold air. We know of one guy who got so frustrated that he filled his wheelbarrow tire with foam sealant from a can. The tire doesn't bounce anymore, but it never goes flat, either.

Buckets, Pails, and Tubs

It's hard to imagine compost gardening without buckets. For carrying small quantities of anything, buckets are downright indispensable. You can buy buckets in an almost endless array of sizes, colors, and materials — metal, plastic, recycled rubber, collapsible, with or without lids — to catch, contain, or carry whatever needs carrying. The world has free buckets aplenty, including sturdy plastic containers that once held cat box filler, drywall compound, donut icing, or other bulk materials.

Creative thinking can lead you to discover all sorts of bucketlike items that may be repurposed for a new life of service in your garden. Old laundry baskets, cracked kiddie pools, leaky trash barrels, and waxed corrugated cardboard boxes are just a few of the potential containers for transporting composting materials.

Wondering where to lay your hands on a few free buckets? Ask a building contractor to set aside some empty latex paint or spackle containers for you. Check with your favorite restaurant, bakery, or grocery store — items including pickles, olives, and cake frosting often arrive in 2½ or 5 gallon (9.5 or 18.9 L) plastic buckets. With a little bit of asking and ingenuity in seeking out sources, you can gather a good supply of these exceedingly useful tools. You'll quickly discover that you can't have too many, because in addition to using them for composting tasks, they can be brought into service as emergency cloches, rain barrels, and so much more. A sturdy bucket will even give you a nice seat for weeding, or to rest and admire your handiwork — just upend it and sit down.

Tarps and Slings

Also called drag sheets or ground cloths, the tarps sold for use in the garden are related to, but sturdier than, those meant solely for covering wood piles or leaks in your roof. A tarp makes a hard-to-miss target for collecting pulled weeds, or you can use one as a mobile dumping station for your lawn mower's bagger. In fall, a tarp becomes the ultimate leaf-gathering tool. Commercially available garden tarps often include useful features, such as reinforced handles and snap clips, but old sheets, blankets, bedspreads, draperies, or shower curtains can enjoy second lives as garden tarps.

If you fasten the opposite ends of a tarp or sturdy piece of cloth to long pieces of wood, you have a slightly different transporting device we call a Composter's Sling (see page 82). Sooner or later, you will want to make at least two of these versatile garden helpers for collecting piles of tossed weeds or shredded leaves, or for moving materials from one composting project to another. When you're not using them for moving materials, they make good shade covers for newly seeded beds, too.

Tools for Cutting and Chopping

The types of materials you use in your composting projects will determine which cutting and chopping tools you will find most useful. Power tools including a lawn mower, string trimmer, and leaf shredder will save time and work when gathering and processing

A basic pocketknife performs many garden tasks and lets you save your precision pruning tools for their intended purposes.

specific materials, and you can read more about them in chapter 3. Here we will talk about the most useful hand tools for cutting, slicing, dicing, hacking, or otherwise chopping compost materials.

Garden Knives

Years ago, a man was not considered fully attired unless he had a pocketknife on his person. When it comes to compost gardening, we think this belief still stands, and it certainly transcends gender. Habitually carrying a knife these days is more likely to get a person stopped at a security checkpoint than it is to earn him praise for being well prepared, but a garden is legitimate knife-wielding territory. You can use your knife to cut flowers or skewer vine borers, to take cuttings or to slice planting holes through a layer of cardboard mulch. As you work with compost, you might use your knife to break down cardboard boxes, remove the twine from a bale of straw, or cut ventilation holes in a plastic bin used for vermicomposting.

A cut above. Need-nosed pliers (left) can cut and bend slender wire, but you will need wire cutters (center) or metal snips (right) to cut through most types of metal fencing.

Even a very basic pocketknife may have a specialized blade or two, such as a screwdriver or a bottle opener. These can be quite helpful if you need to do on-the-spot equipment maintenance or if you get thirsty while working outside. For a few dollars more, there are now garden multi-tools that hold a folding hardware store. We don't trust ourselves to keep dirt or moisture out of the hinges of these super-knives — a definite complication if you're using your knife to slice through a dandelion root two inches below the surface or to scrape worm gunk from the bottom of a flowerpot.

Pocketknives are not alone as great compost-garden cutlery. A folding utility knife, or a knife with a sturdy canvas or leather sheath, can serve equally well. If you have trouble keeping up with small objects in general, buy an old set of steak knives at a thrift store and station them around your yard where you are sure to find them — one near each faucet, and another among your short-handled tools.

Metal Snips and Wire Cutters

For cutting metal hardware cloth or poultry netting (chicken wire), a pair of metal snips is the way to go. You can cut these materials with a wire cutter, too, but it's a much more painstaking process that way. You will want a wire cutter, though, if you're making a pen out of welded-wire fencing. A pair of pliers with a built-in wire cutter makes the perfect tool for cutting lightweight metal fencing and bending the cut ends to fasten it into a circular compost pen.

These are good occasional-use tools to shop for used, unless you've bought a big roll of steel fencing and need exactly the cutting tool for the job. In that case, do your preliminary shopping in a retail store and compare the gauge rating (thickness of your fencing) to the cutting ability of the various tools. It's better to buy a wire-cutting tool that's a little more powerful than it needs to be than to get one that can't bite through the wire you need to cut.

Scissors and Shears

Much like a pocketknife or utility knife, a small pair of scissors that fits into your back pocket is great for snipping strings, grooming plants, or cutting up paper or wet cardboard. A big pair of scissors or ready-for-retirement kitchen shears are useful for cutting compost materials into more manageable pieces, and they have no trouble cutting plastic fencing materials to size. For convenience, tie a piece of twine through the handle of your "trash" scissors or shears and hang them where you can find them easily when needed.

The same pruning shears you bought to shape up roses or other shrubs will prove handy for cutting woody or fibrous materials into compost-sized pieces. Resist the urge to use your good pruning shears for snipping twine or slicing the packing tape on a cardboard box, because you'll only dull the blades and make them less useful for the precision cutting they're meant to do. Come to think of it, cutting up random stuff is why you need a knife and a junky pair of scissors. Use your pruning shears only on compostable plant material, and only in a pinch.

Hand Scythe

If you grow lush, green Compost Crops to use in your projects (see Compost Fodder Crops on page 276), a hand scythe makes gathering them a snap. Its sharp, sickle-shaped blade also makes short work of other tasks, including cutting back tall weeds in spring or fading perennials in late fall. Whether long-handled or short, a scythe is a dangerous tool that should be kept where children can't reach it. Fortunately, a scythe hung high on a shed wall looks cool.

Mattocks and Pulaskis

The term "mattock" is applied to a variety of multipurpose tools that feature a metal head mounted on an ax handle. The tool head typically includes a broad hoe blade on one end; the other end of the blade may be a pick (known as a pick mattock), a cultivator, or an ax (sometimes called a cutter mattock). The combination of ax blade and broad hoe is also known as

THE LOST ART OF USING A SCYTHE

Over a thousand years ago, European farmers learned that a long-handled scythe worked better than a short-handled sickle for cutting down grain. Designed for working while standing nearly upright, a scythe is great for severing Compost Fodder Crops close to the ground, for harvesting spent pea or bean vines, or for beheading countless types of weeds, including young, green brambles, prickly thistles, and other plants best kept at arm's length. Slip the curved blade behind a cluster of tender plants, pull with a sudden tug, and they are on their way to becoming mulch. A scythe will also mow down overgrown grasses when swung like a golf club, but it can't handle plants with tough, woody stems. When properly handled, a scythe can do many jobs assigned to string trimmers, but without all the noise. Unlike a string trimmer, a scythe will never fail to start.

Swing a mattock as you would an ax.

a pulaski; these sturdy tools with intermediate-length handles are part of the equipment issued to U.S. Forest Service firefighters, and they are often used in the maintenance of hiking trails. Made to be swung like an ax, mattocks and pulaskis have plenty of uses in the composter's garden. The hoe blade makes holes in a hurry when you must dig into hard, compacted soil, and it's the best tool for chopping and mixing a big open heap of compost. The ax blade will cut tough stems into smaller pieces, and it's perfect for chopping through roots (assuming the tree can spare them). A pick or tiller mattock may be used to loosen and aerate a pile as it's turned, though the hoe blade usually does a better job.

Machete

As countless jungle movies have shown, there's nothing like a machete for hacking and chopping one's way through the thickest tangles of vines, brush, or small trees. If it works for all those pith-helmeted adventurers, it must be a worthy companion for our

Deb puts weeds, brush, and other compost-bound materials on the "chopping block" and cuts them up quickly with a sharp-bladed machete.

backyard adventures, too. Turns out that it is, and if you already have one of these big, sharp knives (or a similar tool with a hooked blade, called a brush ax) for clearing brush or other rugged landscaping activities, you'll find it's a great help for chopping up all kinds of materials for composting. The only downside of using your machete (or any short-handled cutting tool, such as a hatchet) as a compost chopper is that you need something to chop against, such as a great big stump or log. If you're stumpless, make a temporary compost-side chopping block from two bales of hay topped with an old sheet of plywood, or even a flattened, waxed cardboard box. Pile materials to be chopped on top of the "block," put on your goggles, and slash away.

Lawn Edger

Although it is made for slicing through the sod around beds and borders and at the edges of paved areas, you can also put an edging tool to use chopping up compostables. Most edging tools consist of a sharp metal blade shaped like a half-circle, which is attached to a long, straight handle. The blade may have turned treads on its top edge where you can push it down with your foot. The same features that make these tools work well for slicing through sod can make them equally successful at slicing through weeds, leaves, garden refuse, straw, and other compost materials. You probably don't need or want to buy an edger specifically for composting, but if you already have one in your tool shed, or come across a bargain at a yard sale, sharpen its blade and test it out next time you want to pulverize green materials for your pile.

Maintaining and Monitoring Tools

How much do you know about what's going on inside your compost? Do you care? Once a composting project is created, many experienced composters shrug off fussy details and trust the process to go on without constant fiddling. But maybe you want to mix and aerate a little more, or find out if you're getting any heat, or maybe you need to work out better ways to distribute water. For these and other compost-maintenance matters, there are special tools for each job.

Aerating Tools

Among the items gardening catalogs offer, you will often find one or two tools recommended for aerating compost. One is a pointed metal tool with a T-grip or a curved handle at the top and a pair of hinged wings just above the point; these wings fold in when the point is pushed into the compost, then open when the tool is pulled out. Like a giant fish hook, the aerator fluffs and stirs the compost with each pull. The other tool is a spiraled metal auger, much like the pointed, twisty stakes used for fastening down tents, mobile homes, and dog leads. You screw the auger into your compost pile, then pull straight out to mix up and aerate the contents. Both tools work well for their intended purpose, and if you are making compost in a plastic composter, one of these aerators is great for mixing and aerating materials without getting your hands dirty. Enclosed plastic composters make for difficult outright turning, generally requiring lifting the bin and reloading the mixed materials through the top. An aerating tool gets the job done without all the heavy lifting.

Auger-style (left) and winged (right) aerating tools help to mix and ventilate the contents of a compost bin.

WINGED COMPOST

After inadequately aerating my enclosed compost bin for years with the hollow aluminum leg from an old charcoal grill, I broke down and bought a winged compost aerating tool. It's so easy to use that I stir things up almost every time I visit the bin. In just a few minutes, it mixes and fluffs the composter's contents to about twice their original volume.

Hinged "wings" open at the tip of this aerating tool as it's pulled out of a compost pile.

The weight of a rebar stake makes it easy to drive it deep into a compost pile to open airways. Wiggle the rod to create larger channels.

Of course, you can go very low tech when it comes to designing your own aerators. Many compost aficionados swear by the "rebar method" of compost aeration, which entails poking a 3' to 4' (0.9 to 1.2 m) long concrete reinforcing rod into the pile, pulling it out, and repeating at other spots. The weight of the rebar rod helps you drive it into the pile, and you can wiggle it a bit to open larger airways in the compost. Another tried-and-true approach is to crisscross stout sticks or lengths of PVC pipe horizontally near the bottom of a heap, and give them a little jiggle when you think the compost needs air. In an open heap, you can do nothing at all in terms of aeration, because the heap has plenty of exposed surface area, and will make its own air pockets as the materials shrink and turn into compost.

Thermometers

A thermometer makes composting more interesting, whether you're measuring heat in the middle of a heap or checking to see if a container set in a Solar Cooker (see page 224) is hot enough to kill weed seeds. Special compost thermometers with metal-clad probes from 18" (45.7 cm) to 30" (76.2 cm) long can be costly, and you may be just as satisfied with a heat-resistant oven thermometer, which costs about five dollars and can be completely buried in the middle of the heap (mark it with a colorful piece of ribbon or yarn first; trust us on this one). If you want to hit the middle ground and like digital readouts, consider a soil thermometer, which is meant to be used for checking to see if soil temperatures are in the right range for seed germination. A cheap air thermometer enclosed in a waterproof freezer bag will work, too. Tie a colorful string or ribbon around the bagged thermometer to keep it from getting lost.

Don't forget that your skin can make a good substitute for a compost thermometer, if you know how to "read" it. For example, if you're standing at the edge of an open heap, chopping and turning as fast as you can, and you can feel the heat radiating onto your arms or legs, the pile is probably around 120°F (49°C). If you stick your hand into the hottest part of the pile and have to pull it out after less than five seconds, it's probably above 130°F (54°C). A rebar stake used as an aerator can do double-duty as a temperature indicator. If one end is in the middle of the pile, and the other end feels warm, the interior of the heap is likely around 120°F (49°C).

Watering Tools

Inadequate moisture is one of the most common reasons for compost to fail to make good progress. Compost microorganisms need moisture to live, so when a pile dries out, the "wee beasties" can't work. It is important to moisten ingredients as you add them to your pile, and to replenish moisture as you turn or aerate compost. A hose with a spray nozzle is the ideal way to do this, or you can use a water-

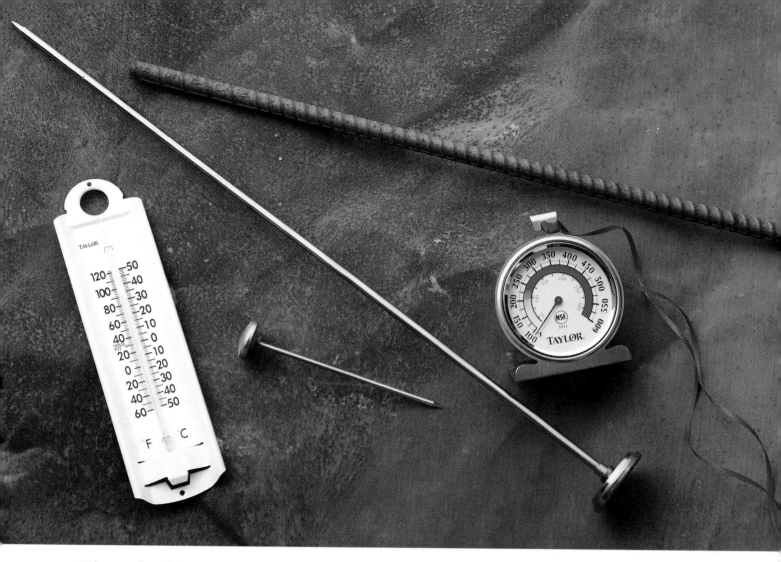

Take your heap's temperature with a thermometer (from left): air, soil, compost, or oven, or let your hand "read" the heat conducted by a metal rod stuck into the pile.

ing can if you're willing to make a couple of trips to deliver the drink. How much water your pile needs will depend on how dry things have become. If the contents are really dried out, you may need 3 to 5 gallons of water to rehydrate your heap, keeping in mind that you want things moist but not soggy. For a passive, no-turn pile, snake a soaker hose (or an old, leaky hose that you've punctured on purpose) through the pile as you build it. Then turn on the hose as needed to moisten the pile from within. If you go this route, monitor the moisture level within the heap to make sure things don't get too soggy.

Storage Containers

Finished, cured compost can be stored in any type of water-resistant container, including buckets with lids, plastic cat litter cartons, or rinsed-out detergent bottles. For short-term storage, you can reuse bags from purchased compost or potting soil, or other plastic bags. If you have a lot of compost to store, you can't do better than plastic storage bins, which have so many uses that it's a good idea to stock up when they are on sale, or if you see a size or color that you like while shopping for other things.

Plastic storage bins work seamlessly for Catch-and-Release Vermicomposting, and they're great for mixing up custom batches of potting soil. Large bins can prevent disaster if you must use your car to bring home treasure chests of manure, and you'll need one with a secure, clasp-on lid for dry storage of open bags of fertilizer, garden lime, gypsum, and other soil amendments.

Choose the right size bin for the task. Large bins can get too heavy to move when they are filled with damp soil, so we think the most versatile sizes are 15 quart (14.2 L) to 24 quart (22.8 L) bins. If you have four bins in service, you can stack them up in pairs and place a couple of boards over them to create an impromptu potting bench. When using plastic bins outdoors, keep them in a shady spot, because sun exposure will degrade the plastic, making it brittle in only two years. In winter, store your plastic bins in your garage to protect them from cracking during extreme cold. When a bin gets cracked or otherwise damaged, you can use it to hold bulbs being forced in a Nursery Reserve (see page 83) or to hide your supply of empty pots from view.

Evaluating Your Compost

As your compost nears completion, you can use "tools" you already have — your eyes, nose, and hands — to determine if it's ready. Visual inspection will reveal even color and consistency with a sprinkling of still-identifiable, undecomposed items, such as peach pits or chunks of corn cob. Your nose will detect an inoffensive, earthy smell with no sharp or sour odors. To the touch, your finished compost will feel cool (no apparent heating), moist, and crumbly.

Once your compost meets these standards, let a few lettuce or cress seeds pass final judgment. Combine compost with an equal amount of potting soil and plant seeds in the mixture. Sow the same kind of seeds in plain potting soil at the same time, and compare the progress of each planting. If the seeds grow equally well in both, your compost is ready to roll; slower growth in the compost mixture means your compost needs more time to mature before you use it in planting projects.

Knowing Your Needs

Just as you can catch a fish with a baited hook tied to a stick — or with a state-of-the-art rod and reel — you can compost plain or fancy. In addition to the tools discussed here, you will find suggestions for other handy items elsewhere in this book, including compost sifters (see pages 68 and 220) and attachment options for bins and pens (see page 143). Lawn mowers with baggers are discussed under grass clippings

WHY NO LIME?

When you make compost from very acidic materials, for example pine needles or sawdust, it seems logical to add a little lime to the mix to help nudge the pH into the neutral range. Not so fast! Especially in the early stages of decomposition, these and many other materials release a flush of organic acids — their way of inviting microorganisms that work best in acidic environments to the feast. Mixing in lime would sabotage this process and increase the amount of nitrogen lost as ammonia gas.

Besides, soil pH is determined much more by the mineral particles in soil than by its organic matter sources, so liming up a compost pile is putting your lime in the wrong place. When using lime to raise the pH of acidic soil, or sulfur to lower the pH of alkaline soil, it's best to work the minerals directly into the soil. Wait at least a month before using a simple pH test kit to evaluate the results of your efforts.

Soil Testing Is Serious Stuff

Wouldn't it be great if every country had a composter laureate? I would nominate Dr. William Brinton of the Woods End Research Laboratory in Mt. Vernon, Maine, because his work has been so crucial to the development of composting as a waste disposal technology. Establishing a set of indicators that reveal when compost is done is among Brinton's accomplishments, and if you like you can buy a Solvita compost test kit, just like the commercial composters use, and give it a whirl. I did, and it was an interesting adventure. The kit uses sensor paddles covered with chemical gels to measure ammonia and carbon dioxide gases given off by moist compost sealed inside a small jar. There is a 4-hour wait for a reading, so the Solvita is not nearly as exciting as doing

a 5-minute litmus paper soil pH test. You do get to match colors to a key, and if your compost is finished and/or cured it should rate a 7 or 8 on the index maturity scale.

Any gardener who's ever seen, smelled, or touched chocolate brown, cured compost can recognize on sight compost with a maturity index of 7 or 8 within 10 seconds. It's the good stuff. Within 5 seconds, you can inhale enough smelly gases from compost indexed at 1 or 2 to know that it has a long way yet to go.

One $20 test was enough for me, so I went back to the old ways of finding out if my compost is done. I look at it, crumble it in my hand, and give it a sniff. Then I share it with plants and see how they grow.

(see page 91) and you can look into leaf shredders (see page 80) as you figure out the best ways to handle your yard's abundance of leaves.

Quality tools that are kept in good working order make composting more fun, and trying new tools can lead you toward creative breakthroughs as you devise the best composting plans for your one-of-a-kind landscape. If you're having trouble with some aspect of composting, by all means become familiar with tools that can help. At the same time, we cannot over-emphasize that compost gardening revolves around reusing and recycling. It is not a consumer-based economy, so you can't buy your way in. Acquire tools you need and commit to actually using them. Time and nature will take care of the rest.

3

Materials for the Composter's Garden

I N MANY COMPOST-MINDED CITIES, trained volunteers staff telephone hotlines, or "rotlines," to answer caller questions about composting. The most frequently asked question is "Can I compost this?" The "this" can be anything from rabbit manure to the contents of a vacuum cleaner bag, both of which are among the thousands of materials that can be composted *under the right conditions.* Volunteers spend a lot of time exploring this topic with callers, because both parties really want to create more compost and less garbage. The core of any compost process is, after all, a happy marriage of materials and conditions. This chapter is about arranging many such happy marriages.

Getting to Know Compostable Materials

We must begin by setting forth a fundamental compost truth: When it comes to working with any compostable material, the work will teach you how to process the material. If you begin with rule number two of compost gardening, "work with what you have," it will take only a season or two for you to become familiar with good ways to handle the most abundant resources available in your own yard (for all six basic rules of compost gardening, see page 14). For most compost gardeners, these resources include fallen leaves, kitchen trimmings, plant parts gathered from the garden, and grass clippings, so we will spend many pages discussing each of these categories. Manure merits thoughtful attention, too, and we hope you will find out what you want to know about even more obscure materials in the Odd Compostables chart on page 128. Depending on where you live and who you get to know, marvelous composting materials like spoiled alfalfa hay or rabbit manure may be free for the taking from local sources. Almost anything that's local, free, or cheap and is inclined to rot can be an interesting addition to your composting projects.

By virtue of kitchen scraps alone, our compost piles can be quite omnivorous. Add to that the diversity of garden refuse, such as perennial prunings, spent annuals, weeds, and refuse from an array of vegetable crops, and a compost pile can become almost as unique as a fingerprint, its ingredients reflecting the particular likes and habits of the compost gardener who assembled them. Your composting projects may be completely different from those of your neighbor, or they may share certain characteristics based on plant residues and agricultural by-products that are common to your area. But it is unlikely that your compost ingredients will resemble the contents of a compost bin or pile in another region of the country, where different growing conditions require different crops and support different agricultural enterprises. This is as it should be.

Counting Compost Miles

One of the foundation concepts within the local food movement (see The Cost of Compost in Compost Miles on the facing page) is the importance of watching your "food miles." The farther your food travels from its source to you, the higher the costs to the environment become when measured in greenhouse gas emissions. Those harmful emissions vary with type of transportation used; they are higher for air and truck transportation than for ship or rail. Your car falls into the high-emission category, so you will rack up a few "compost miles" each time you venture outside your yard to obtain materials for composting. Compost miles count whether you are buying packaged additives, for example, alfalfa meal, or stopping by a horse stable to get a few garbage bagsful of manure.

YOU ARE WHAT YOU EAT

All compost is not alike, and many gardeners have two sets of standards for the compost they make and use in their yards. Compost destined for use growing vegetables, herbs, and fruits should be made from materials that are free of chemical contamination, but you may want to compromise if a supply of sludge (which often contains heavy metals) is easily available, and you are preparing planting space for nonedible trees or shrubs. Although it's often messy to handle, waste from most types of food processing is often of high quality. For example, you might pick up spent grains from a local brewery or cranberry-rice "cakes" created when cranberries are pureed and filtered for juice to make compost fit for the finest crop of tomatoes you've ever grown.

THE COST OF COMPOST IN COMPOST MILES

In 1995, Wendell Berry wrote of the importance of creating community-based food systems. Since then, talented thinkers like Gary Nabhan, founder of Native Seeds SEARCH in Arizona; award-winning writer Michael Pollan, *Mother Earth News* magazine; and many others have helped turn the quest for local food into an international phenomenon. When you eat locally produced food, you get the freshest possible food while supporting local farmers, and much less energy is needed for long-distance transportation. We think home composting calls for a similar approach and presents an irresistible opportunity for everyday people to reduce greenhouse gases. For example, a gardener in Indiana would log negligible miles composting his own yard's waste plus some used coffee grounds picked up in the neighborhood. Materials produced farther away rack up many more compost miles.

Material	Miles
kitchen waste	0
coffee grounds	0
hay or straw	20
alfalfa meal	300
peat moss	1500

As a conscientious compost gardener, you want to keep your compost miles as low as possible without getting overly rigid about it. This position makes for some interesting foraging! Once you step over your own property line, think about what types of compostable materials might be easy and convenient to find in your area. For example, used grounds from a coffee shop or the produce manager's trash box at your local supermarket may need little more than a procurement plan to get such compostables from their source to your compost. Also think about food or agricultural wastes generated in your area that need a better destiny than a landfill or ditch. Perhaps you will hit on a plan that helps your local environment, your neighbors, and your compost — without bingeing on compost miles.

Importing Solutions, Not Problems

Another reason to be careful when considering "imported" ingredients is that they can bring unwanted hitchhikers, be they weeds, chemicals from heavily treated lawns, drug residues in manure from livestock that have been dosed with antibiotics

HEAVY METAL THINKING

Sometimes the spooky phrase "heavy metals" is mentioned in association with compost, but most home composters have little to worry about. Yet there are exceptions. Rethink your plans if any of these factors affect your yard, because the composting process does not clear heavy metals, which can be taken up by some edible plants.

▶ **Lead.** The soil around old buildings in which lead paint was used decades ago can be contaminated. Have suspicious soil tested at a reputable lab. If the contaminated soil cannot be replaced, garden on top of it in large containers or planters.

▶ **Mercury.** This liquid metal travels in air, water, and in the bodies of animals. Aquatic animals that are high on the food chain — for example, fresh water bass or large saltwater game fish — often have high concentrations of mercury in their tissues, and sludge from sewage treatment facilities also can be high in mercury. Avoid using these materials in compost that will be used to grow edible plants.

▶ **Cadmium.** Unless you attempt to compost an old computer or other electronic devices, this contaminant should not be a problem. The special fees you may be asked to pay to dispose of TVs and computers help defray costs of specialized methods of disposal.

and growth hormones, or plant diseases, bugs, and slugs. Indeed, the probability of bringing in weeds, which may show an enthusiastic liking for various parts of your landscape, is so high that you should closely watch garden areas where you use the first compost batch made with a new material. Be optimistic yet careful, because the many benefits of many materials offset their liabilities.

Once you discover that a certain composting material is available to you without much bother, the next task is to come up with the best way to use it in your composting projects. When asked what kinds of materials they would like to have more of, most compost gardeners will immediately blurt out "high-nitrogen greens," but this may not necessarily be what you need. If your soil is tight clay, you might be better off looking into a good source for sawdust laced with manure, which is a combination that's hard to beat if you want compost that will fluff up your soil's structure. Or perhaps you're trying to shrink down an oversized lawn by converting it to garden beds, in which case you can take good advantage of the grass-smothering talents of cardboard covered with shredded leaves. If you're new to composting, take time to experiment with as many compostable materials as you have on hand, and limit imported materials to those that fill a specific need in your one-of-a-kind composter's garden.

Balancing Browns and Greens

A simple model for composting involves balancing materials that have a high carbon (C) content with others that contain abundant nitrogen (N). A numerical ratio of carbon to nitrogen, the C/N ratio can range between 30/1 for a lush wheelbarrow brimming with freshly pulled weeds to 500/1 for a truckload of dry sawdust. Combining two materials to achieve a new number, computed by adding the Cs and Ns together and dividing proportionately, makes it possible to control — to some degree — how much and how quickly a heap heats up (or if it heats up at all). Better yet, a C/N guesstimate gives you an idea of how long it will take for the compost to mature, as shown in these examples.

▶ **Fast.** The general trend is for mixtures with a low C/N ratio between 20/1 and 40/1 to heat up quickly and maintain their heat through two turnings. Techniques for turning out such fast, hot heaps are discussed further in chapter 4.

▶ **Medium.** If the ratio is closer to 100/1, the compost will still progress, but little heat will be generated beyond a brief initial surge, and the composting process may take three months in warm weather, or nine months in cold weather. Turning of this type of compost is optional once the materials are assembled or mixed and thoroughly moistened.

▶ **Slow.** A compost project with a C/N ratio in the 200/1 range, or higher, will morph along in keeping with changes in the weather, but it will probably need a second tour of duty in a second composting project before it's ready to cure and use. For example, you might combine shredded leaves with spent plants as you clean up your yard in autumn, allow the pile to sit through the winter, and then use the partially decayed materials in a new composting project the following summer.

RATIOS OF COMMON COMPOST INGREDIENTS

Compost progresses faster when you combine materials with low C/N ratios with others that have higher numbers.

Material	Carbon/Nitrogen Ratio
kitchen waste	15/1
horse manure	30/1
leaves	55/1
sawdust	440/1
cardboard	500/1

Composting Your Way to a Better Garden

Many existing composting manuals detail only the fast scenario, which is fun to do, but not always the most practical way to compost if your main objective is to grow a better garden. Slower, less labor-intensive methods often benefit soil more than the fast-and-hot approach, because composting that takes place over a prolonged period of time involves the activities of a broader range of life forms. Projects that involve composting *in the garden* benefit the soil below them, too. An in-garden compost project's soil-improvement properties start the day it is created, as earthworms gather at is base and nutrients leach from the pile into the surrounding soil. These benefits continue nonstop until the project is finished, or perhaps is renovated and transformed using a different composting technique.

As you explore the compost-garden methods in part 2, you will see that thoughtfully assembled, slow-composting cold heaps can be put to good use long before they are "done," such as for growing undemanding peas, beans, and various cucumber cousins in Comforter Compost. A heat-free approach is essential to sustainable home-based composting with worms, which we call Catch-and-Release Vermicomposting (see chapter 7). Should you take composting underground, compostable materials that are basically buried and forgotten often rot the smelly, anaerobic way, which would be offensive if exposed to open air but is of no consequence to our noses or to the plants that later benefit from the decomposed buried treasure.

Obviously, great compost is not built on C/N ratios alone. The condition of the compost materials is equally important. Large pieces of anything have less exposed surface area compared to smaller ones; dry materials support less microbial life than moist ones; and some materials won't start to rot until cell walls become fragile enough to break open, allowing their natural preservatives to leach away. In the pages that follow, you will learn about the stages materials must go through on their way down the composting road and discover ways that you can use that time to your advantage in your composter's garden.

In an enclosed composter or an open pile, alternating layers of high-carbon browns with high-nitrogen greens is a sound strategy.

Digging In

As you gain experience handling compostable materials, you will discover new and better ways to use them in your composting projects. In the following pages, we will discuss in detail the most common materials used in home compost, beginning with the big four: kitchen waste, garden waste, fallen leaves, and grass clippings. Then we will move on to materials that often are available from local sources, including manure, hay and straw, paper and cardboard, sawdust and wood chips, and compost itself. In addition, you can experiment with using high-protein grain meals as compost activators. These are discussed on page 122.

At this point, one thing should be clear: There is no single right way to compost. There are dozens of ways, and each composting project you undertake can be fine-tuned to accommodate available materials and bring you closer to your gardening goals.

Gathering the Goods: Start in the Kitchen

There is a joke going around that claims that the American diet is made up of three main food groups: sugar, fat, and meat. It's not really funny, but the main reason to remember this joke is that these are the three food groups that should *not* go into your compost. Anything else is fair game, including food items

that contain a little sugar (old applesauce) or a smidgeon of fat (stale muffins). As with all things, there are exceptions. See Compost: Those Special Cases on page 60 for how to compost unusual types of kitchen waste.

There are two great rewards for composting your kitchen scraps: Fewer yucky things end up in your garbage can, and your compost benefits from an incredibly diverse assortment of nutrient-rich ingredients. This diversity, in turn, supports an unimaginable variety of microorganisms, which is exactly what you want in a batch of finished compost. Kitchen scraps are considered "green" ingredients, which provide nitrogen, so adding only a little more "green" in the form of high-protein grain or seed meals can make a kitchen-scrap-based heap heat up fast. Or, you can take a casual approach by allowing your kitchen waste to decompose slowly on its own, without generating a noticeable amount of heat.

If you often cook and eat at home, your kitchen will produce a surprising bounty of compostable scraps. You may start off the day with used coffee grounds or tea bags and a banana peel and accumulate a bigger stash as you prepare a salad for dinner or give the day's garden harvest a good grooming. Your compost may overflow when you decide to clean out your cabinets (see page 58 for dozens of possible kitchen compostables), so you will need a system for collecting kitchen waste.

What's the best way? Not so long ago, every well-equipped kitchen had a bean crock and a cookie jar, but slow cookers and ready-made cookies have pushed both objects toward oblivion. This is good news for compost gardeners, because bean crocks and ceramic cookie jars make great countertop canisters for collecting kitchen trimmings, and you can find them at thrift stores for only a few dollars. The wide mouths help to minimize spillage, and the ceramic sides hide the contents from view while minimizing

An attractive ceramic container with a wide mouth is easy to fill and empty, and quickly rinses clean.

odors. You also can use flour canisters, large coffee cans, or a plastic bowl with a snap-top lid to collect your kitchen compostables. Do choose a container that is easy to clean inside and out, with a small footprint relative to its volume. Frequently you will move the container next to your cutting board so you can fill it as you chop. This close to working hands, you can't beat a container with a short, squat shape.

Filling a countertop kitchen-waste container is easy, but emptying one calls for advance planning. Grungy stuff stuck to the interior often refuses to leave without manual assistance, and the instinct that tells you not to stick your bare hand into a soup of rotting food is serving you well. Instead, keep an old spoon handy for scraping what a friend of ours calls "kitchen slurm" out of the container and onto your pile. Or, you can keep it from sticking in the first place by lining the inside of the container with a piece of newspaper or a used paper napkin, paper towel, or coffee filter each time you clean it out (they will rot just fine when dumped into your heap). Pouring a cup of warm water into your collection container a few minutes before you empty it can also help to loosen bits that have stuck to the bottom. After you've dumped the container's contents onto your compost pile, rinse the collection container thoroughly with hot water to remove potential odor-producing fungi and bacteria. Should things get too funky, clean your container with a bleach solution or other disinfectant, rinse thoroughly, and let it dry in the sun.

Keep It Simple

Beyond using a simple countertop collection container, compost gardeners around the world have experimented with other ways to capture kitchen refuse and deliver it to a waiting compost pile. There are devices you can add onto existing garbage disposals, but you still have to transfer the collected material to your compost pile by hand. In addition, using a disposal consumes electricity, generates noise, and rinses soluble nutrients down the drain. And for what? Food waste that is carefully chopped into small pieces is great for worm bins, but outdoor kitchen composting proceeds quite nicely when the heap includes everything from chunky pineapple tops and spoiled potatoes to tiny coffee grounds.

Many folks have tried under-the-sink collection cans, which work if you take care of them, but they tend to attract fruit flies if left uncovered, and they become stinky if left unattended too long. Lining an under-the-sink can with a biodegradable collection bag is another option, and these bags are invaluable

---

ANATOMY OF A KITCHEN COMPOST WORKSTATION

Most kitchen compost heaps are created by the dump-and-run technique, so they need to be ready for action at all times.

▶ Keep a bucket or watering can near your kitchen compost, and fill it with a few inches of water whenever you're using your hose. After you dump out your collection container, you'll always have rinse water ready and won't have to find the end of your hose.

▶ Station a turning fork or spade next to your kitchen compost so you won't have to search for the right tool when you add materials that need to be buried.

▶ Add a small, portable table in summer to provide a work surface for grooming and cleaning fresh-picked vegetables.

▶ Stockpile shredded leaves, dry grass clippings, or other "brown" material you can use to cover new infusions of kitchen waste.

As long as Barbara attends it daily, she can stash her collection pail for kitchen waste in a convenient kitchen cabinet.

in community composting programs in which participants leave their treasures on their doorsteps for collection. You can use them if neatness concerns are standing in the way of creative composting, but bags are just plain unnecessary when the longest distance your kitchen scraps ever travel is from your countertop to your backyard heap or compost bin.

Clean-Out-Your-Kitchen Compost Ingredients

Beyond the usual trimmings from fruits and vegetables, your kitchen may be a source of other compostable treasures that typically end up in the trash. Let's be clear: We're not advocating using still-edible "people food" to feed your compost. But even the thriftiest householder has the occasional expired food item that was accidentally pushed to the back of

the cupboard or lost in the refrigerator or freezer, and few of us make it through life without experiencing a pesky meal moth or grain weevil infestation in the pantry. When an exploration of the dark corners of your cabinets turns up an opened can of mixed nuts from last year's (or was it two years ago?) family gathering, or a bread mix that expired during a previous presidential administration, turn that potential trash into a treat for your compost pile or vermicompost bin. Even if it's no longer fit food for you to eat, the mighty microorganisms in compost will consume and transform it into food for plants.

TRAPPING FRUIT FLIES

The little gnat-like critters that swarm around a bowl of ripening pears, or the container where you keep your kitchen trimmings, are fruit flies (*Drosophila melanogaster*), which often become bothersome indoors in late summer and fall. You can gather them up with a vacuum cleaner, but it's easier to lure them to death by drowning in simple, homemade traps. In a day or two, a trap baited with apple cores or bruised fruit will net several hundred unsuspecting fruit flies.

There are many designs to try, from a plastic margarine or yogurt container with holes punched in the lid to a plastic drink bottle with entry holes cut into the sides. Bait the traps with apple, pear, or banana peelings and enough slightly soapy water to almost make the bait float. Fruit flies will enter the traps and drown as they try to feed or escape. Empty and re-bait the fruit-fly traps daily until your fruit-fly problem becomes history.

Wondering if various food items are still good? Nearly every packaged food has a "best if used by" or expiration date somewhere on the package. Absence of such a date may indicate food that's so old that it predates this widespread industry practice! Even if you're inclined to take the use-by dates as guidelines rather than deadlines, if today's date and the one on the box are more than a year apart, the item is past its prime. Recycle the packaging if you can, and put those bygone bread crumbs and stale coffee beans into your compost pile where they can do some good.

Managing Kitchen Compost

There are three important matters to consider as you devise the best plan for composting your kitchen waste: site selection, a workable design for your setup, and resistance to animals that may be attracted by the scent of decomposing food.

Select a Good Site

Convenience is key when selecting a kitchen-composting site, because you will be adding sloppy material to your kitchen compost at least every other day, and sometimes twice a day. It should be as close as possible to your kitchen door, yet you should also be able to reach it easily from your vegetable garden.

A water faucet should be nearby, because you will often trim and clean veggies heap-side before bringing them indoors. If you can't come up with a site just outside your kitchen door, keep a large plastic pail with a tight-fitting lid on your deck or patio, and use it for temporary storage of your kitchen waste. Every few days, add the bucket's contents to your kitchen compost pile, and then rinse the bucket. An indoor vermicompost bin also can accommodate some (but not all) of your kitchen waste. See chapter 7 for detailed information on composting with earthworms.

A back door waystation for compost-bound kitchen waste is a small investment and big convenience.

Compost: Those Special Cases

There's good news for adventurous composters: With careful handling, each of these special-case ingredients can make its way into your compost pile or bin.

Case #1: Dead Fish

You got lucky at the lake and brought home a stringer of fish. Can you compost the heads and entrails?

When it comes to smelly, high-nitrogen materials like fish heads and innards (or the shells and tails from a feast of peel-and-eat shrimp), ask yourself two critical questions: Do you have twice as much dry, high-carbon "brown" material on hand to mix with it and enough half-baked compost to cover the mixture at least 3″ (7.6 cm) deep? Or, can you secure it in a compost bin or pit so that animals can't reach it? If the answers are no, burying the stuff in a hole at least 12″ (30.4 cm) deep and letting nature take care of the composting is your best option. See Animal-Resistant Bins (page 63) and Pretty Pits-of-Plenty (page 181) for more juicy details on handling smelly food waste.

Case #2: Old Bones

You made a pot of soup from a turkey carcass, and it cooked long enough to soften the bones. Can you compost them?

The main challenge here is animal resistance, especially if you share composting space with a dog. Bones, particularly those of poultry, can splinter and get stuck in a dog's throat, so take as many precautions as needed to exclude dogs and other animals from a compost project that includes bones. On the plus side, well-cooked bones smell hardly at all when hidden away beneath 3″ (7.6 cm), or more of dense compost or other organic material, and they are a great source of slow-release phosphorous and calcium. Phosphorus aids in development of roots, flowers, and fruit. Calcium helps plants to build cell walls and grow, and is essential for preventing blossom end rot of tomatoes — a nutritional disorder that causes dark patches to form on the blossom ends of the fruits. In eastern states, acid rain leaches calcium from soil, so replenishing it with bones, bone meal, or crushed shells is a wise strategy.

Case #4: Nut Shells

You went out for dinner to a restaurant that provides endless bowls of peanuts all the way from the lobby to the table. Is it worth embarrassing your family to ask your server for a doggie bag (or two) of shells?

High-carbon peanut shells make a good compost mix-in for wet kitchen wastes, but they break down very slowly and may contain enough salt to poison microorganisms living in your compost. Thoroughly rinsing salted shells will remove some of the salt and get them nice and wet, which will aid decomposition. Don't worry if you are still seeing a spring infusion of peanut shells in compost that you harvest the following fall. Tightly interwoven cellulose tissues are slow to go, yet they persist as stable soil organic matter for a long time.

Case #5: Orange Rind Overload

Snack duty for your daughter's soccer game left you holding a bag of peels and pulp from a team's worth of orange slices. Should you toss the juicy mess into your cooler and take it home to your compost, or drop it into a trash can as you leave the field?

Citrus and other thick fruit rinds are good sources of nitrogen, so they are great for composting when combined with shredded leaves, sawdust, or other high-carbon materials. Citrus oil has antimicrobial properties, so citrus rinds tend to decompose very slowly in a casually managed compost pile. There is nothing wrong with slow decomposition, but if you like, you can speed things up by chopping the peels and pulp in an old blender or food processor before adding them to the pile.

Case #3: Mollusk Maneuvers

Your family-and-friends' clam bake at the beach yields a wealth of calcium-rich clam shells. Is there a way to turn this bounty into a benefit for your compost?

After the last clam has been dipped in butter and consumed, collect the shells in a large bucket and make sure it can't tip over or leak if it's being transported in your car. Clam shells (as well as oyster, scallop, and other mollusk shells) are mostly composed of calcium, an essential nutrient used by plants and soil organisms. Whole shells break down slowly, over a period of many years, but they perform passive aeration and provide shelter for earthworms and other compost residents along the way. To move things along, you can crush the shells by pounding them with a hammer on a hard concrete surface. Then sprinkle the calcium-rich dust and shell shards into your pile. Pulverizing clam shells with a hammer can be a source of great fun for young composters who are willing to wear protective goggles — a precaution that grown-up composters should also take when shattering shells.

Capturing Kitchen Compost

Once food waste leaves your kitchen, have a compost bin or pile ready to receive it. Here are five good options:

▶ **Bottomless plastic composters.** Enclosed composting containers that sit on the ground are a good choice for kitchen compost, especially if you have a small yard where every square inch of space is precious. Community-based composting programs often provide such plastic composters at a minimal price, and this is not an offer that should be refused. Small stationary composters make great year-round receptacles for fresh kitchen trimmings, or they can be a temporary stop for garden-bound kitchen waste.

▶ **Barrel-type composters** are great for kitchen waste, too, because you can quickly rotate the barrel to mix new materials with old, and barrel composters with locking lids offer superior resistance to animals. On the downside, barrel composters tend to be rather costly. Shop carefully for a model that suits your needs and your pocketbook, or get started by making a reasonable facsimile from a plastic garbage can equipped with a secure lid (see page 138).

▶ **Cylindrical plastic trash can.** As long as the garbage can is cylindrical rather than square or rectangular, you can roll the can over the ground to mix the materials inside. Or, if you happen to find just the right barrel with a reclosable door on the side, you can use a hammer and nail to perforate it with air

holes and roll it around to mix up the contents. If you like how this works, step up to a real barrel composter that rotates on a fixed stand.

▶ **Wire-enclosed compost pile.** Two-part, open, or semi-enclosed heaps work well, too, because you can flip-flop the two heaps, using material from the more advanced side to cover new additions made to the immature heap. In the interest of eye appeal and animal deterrence, it's always a good idea to enclose open kitchen compost-in-progress with welded wire, plastic fencing, shipping pallets, or something else that will keep the material from scattering about. If you don't like the looks of a wire pen, or one made from fencing, wrapping the wire sides with burlap or another type of porous cloth may solve the problem.

See Resourceful Compost Enclosures on page 142 for more ideas for building a simple bin.

▶ **Pit-type composters** are seldom used by gardeners, but they often make ideal dumping grounds for kitchen trimmings. Underground pits completely hide the compost contents from view, and let's face it — kitchen compost usually looks like a pile of garbage. The best way to make it pretty is to move the project underground (see Pretty Pits-of-Plenty, on page 181. Be sure to build a secure lid that is heavy enough to deter animals and hold the weight of a person who may mistakenly step on it.

Animal-Resistant Bins

Omnivorous animals including dogs, raccoons, opossums, mice, rats, and even an occasional bear, are drawn to kitchen compost. Whether you have problems with any of these animals depends on whether you are gardening and composting within their home range. With the exception of dogs, it is likely that animal aggravation is generally overrated, but you certainly don't want to create a neighborhood nuisance by attracting vermin with your unsecured kitchen compost.

These animals locate food sources using their sense of smell, which is often 50 (or more) times more acute than your own. When you cover a load of kitchen waste with a 2" (5 cm) thick layer of shredded leaves, grass clippings, or finished compost, chances are you will never pick up the slight whiff of decomposing broccoli or grapefruit rinds. Yet this level of burial is not enough to sidestep the sniffing talents of animals. Terriers can smell moles below 10" (25 cm) of soil, and raccoons and opossums often dig down 5" (13 cm) in search of earthworms and grubs. If you know a certain animal is likely to raid your

Take your pick. Lightweight plastic composters (**1**) can be moved easily between batches. Barrel-type composters (**2**) take care of the mixing for you. In open-air bins (**3**) wire fencing excludes unwanted animals. The boards on the sides of these bins (**4**) slide out when it's time to add materials or harvest compost.

GROUNDS FOR GREAT COMPOST

Running low on nitrogen-rich "greens" to kick-start your compost? Take a break from raking leaves and go out for a cup of coffee! Coffee grounds have a C/N (carbon to nitrogen) ratio of 20/1, making them a worthy substitute for fresh grass clippings in late-fall leaf piles. Take a clean, covered container, such as a five-gallon pickle bucket, with you to your favorite coffee spot and ask politely if they'll fill it with their spent coffee grounds (paper filters included). Most coffee shops will gladly share the highly compostable wealth with you, especially if you regularly give them your business.

To ensure that your coffee-ground collection goes smoothly, it's helpful to inquire in advance (before you arrive with bucket in hand) if they're willing to give you their spent grounds. Talk to the shop manager about the best days and times to stop in for grounds and plan your visits to avoid busy times when other customers are waiting for coffee service. Perhaps the best-known coffee purveyor, Starbucks, promotes coffee-ground recycling through their "Grounds for Your Garden" program, which encourages local stores to give spent grounds to gardening groups and individuals. Participation in this program is determined by individual Starbucks store managers, but most locations will pass along their spent grounds upon request. In response to requests from composters, many neighborhood coffee shops place bags of grounds outside on their doorstep as they close for the day.

If coffee shops are scarce in your area, you're not out of luck — we are a coffee-drinking society, and there are other places where quantities of spent coffee grounds may be gathered. Cafeterias in office buildings and on college campuses make a steady supply of coffee for employees and students, truck stops brew coffee around the clock, and then there are hospital waiting rooms (which may be staffed by helpful volunteers). Convention centers also generate a lot of coffee grounds, and church events can be a great source, too — sign up to help at the next fellowship breakfast or youth-group coffee house and go home with a warm feeling and a container of compostable grounds.

MODERATION IN ALL THINGS

A friend who knows about my composting habits called with a question one day: Should she worry about the amount of sodium she was adding to her compost when she tossed in the shells that resulted from her pistachio-snacking habit? Should she rinse the shells before adding them to the compost, both to moisten them for improved decomposition and to at least reduce their salt content?

I assured her that she was unlikely to create super-salty compost with pistachio shells unless she is eating the pricey snack by the 50-pound bag. Still, her question raises a useful point: Too much of anything, even a good thing, can create problems in your compost pile. Thick layers of dry ingredients that are slow to break down — or wet materials, which are prone to become slimy and smelly — can hinder the composting process, inhibit desirable microorganisms, and

make things so nasty that you lose interest in tending your compost pile. When you're assembling (or adding to) a compost project, keep three "Ms" in mind: Moderation, Mixing, and Microbes. Avoid large concentrations of any one ingredient — limit layers of wet, high-nitrogen materials like grass clippings or kitchen scraps to 1" to 2" (2.5 to 5.1 cm) deep and moisten dry ingredients like chopped leaves before adding them in layers no more than 4" to 6" (10.2 to 15.2 cm) deep. As a general rule, make shallow layers of finely chopped materials, wet or dry, and somewhat deeper layers of coarse materials like straw. Limiting the depth of the layers promotes better mixing of the ingredients, which in turn, encourages the development of a diverse microbe population that is better able to convert those ingredients into top-quality compost.

heap, tailor its design to make it a no-critter zone. For example, an excavated Pit-of-Plenty topped with a heavy, hinged lid (see page 181) makes it possible to compost kitchen waste in a backyard shared with a large dog. Where mice or rats are a problem, it is often easiest to work with an enclosed composter that is raised above ground, as are most barrel-type composters. If the composter's air holes are big enough for a mouse to squeeze through (their collapsible skeletal systems make it possible for them to make it through openings slightly larger than one-half inch), patch the holes with pieces of wire screening or fine mesh metal hardware cloth.

Life in a Kitchen Compost Pile

Imagine a huge crowd of hungry people of such different nationalities that they can barely converse about water, much less food. Then, all of a sudden, within various sectors of the crowd, tables laden with food appear — corn tortillas with beans in one place, curried stew in another, and rice scented with ginger and sesame right in the middle. It would be chaos of the highest order as people push and scramble to get what they recognize as food before it runs out.

Something similar happens each time you add material to your kitchen compost. A huge, diversified community of life forms occupy the compost, each with an appetite for a certain small link in the food chain that connects, say, a composting potato peeling first to mold (fungi) and slime (bacteria), later to earthworms, and eventually to a new plant root. The plant root enters the scene eager to take up nutrients left behind in the now shriveled, barely recognizable potato peeling, so it enlists the help of other compost-borne fungi that have been hanging around waiting for what *they* consider a great meal — steady helpings of nutritious root exudates that the plant pushes to the surface of its root tips. At the last minute, just as the potato peeling turns to humus (finished compost), a root-fungi relationship forms to give the plant roots and the fungi exactly what each needs.

This drama requires a huge cast, made possible by the incredible diversity of ingredients that are fed to kitchen compost. From fall to spring, the bulk of this activity is quietly carried on by fungi and bacteria,

but in warm weather, these microorganisms are often joined by insects attracted by the gases given off by fermenting fruit. Wasps and bees stop in for nips of compost "wine" if it's available, and at night crickets may use kitchen compost as a place to court and gorge at the same time. Take the time to look at these insects before dismissing them as pesky flies (some are flies, of course). If there are too many, start covering fresh material with a thick, 3" (7.5 cm) layer of compost or moist organic matter. Between deposits, cover the heap with a piece of cloth or a pillow of straw to help it escape the interest of insects.

As you turn or mix your kitchen compost, be on the lookout for tightly packed colonies of small, reddish, writhing earthworms. They may be red worms (*Lumbricus rubellus*), compost worms (*Eisenia fetida*), or another species that likes chowing down on kitchen waste. These worms are prime candidates for Catch-and-Release Vermicomposting, which is covered in detail in chapter 7.

Harvesting and Using Kitchen Compost

Advertisements for commercial composting devices often show happy gardeners holding a trowel loaded with beautifully finished compost, which they presumably pulled out of their composter just like that. Maybe they did, but before the picture was snapped, somebody picked out all the squash seeds, peanut hulls, and produce sticky labels that were still in the compost. Whether you let kitchen compost rot at its own pace or turn and mix it to speed things up, it is the nature of kitchen compost to morph into a mixture of recognizable tidbits surrounded by crumbly, dark-brown compost. It's easy enough to pick or sift out the stuff that needs more time to break down, and put it back into the pile with some active compost.

Finished kitchen compost hosts such a rich buffet of microorganisms — while holding enzymes and other compounds given off through millions of micro lives and deaths — that it should be regarded as the wonder tonic of soil amendments. If you think you have a soil problem, or want to keep from getting one,

AS FOR ANTS

Just like people, many of the critters with which we share our world are "into" sugar. It's the universal high-energy food, and a kitchen compost pile is likely to be the sweetest spot in your yard. Ants will rejoice as they discover the crust from a peanut-butter-and-jelly sandwich and quickly scout around for a nearby shelter where they can install their queen. A few ants here and there are not a problem, but the persistent presence of ants is a useful indicator that your compost pile is too dry. Adding water to it should send them looking for drier digs. Do not push your luck getting too close to fire ants and other bad biters. Instead, lure them away from your revamped damp pile with a drier one nearby, and then use an over-the-counter, spinosad-based ant control product to eliminate the colony. Spinosad is a biological pesticide, based on a naturally-occurring soil bacterium, that kills ants (and other insect pests including caterpillars, various flies, thrips, and some beetles) when they ingest it. Spinosad works better than chemical ant killers, and it is widely available at garden centers and farm supply stores.

WHAT'S WITH THOSE ICKY STICKIES?

There's nothing like sifting a first-rate batch of homemade compost through a screen and finding that its lovely brown, fine-textured surface is littered with perfectly intact label stickers that rode into the compost on apple peelings and onion skins. Known in the food industry as PLUs (price look-up stickers), those little buggers sail through the composting process and can often still be read after spending months in a vermicompost bin. Most PLUs are about as likely to break down as a synthetic hiking boot sole.

According to Alex Dietz, director of customer service for Sinclair Industries, the manufacturer of approximately half of the PLU stickers applied in the United States, Sinclair's stickers are made of a water-resistant "polyethylene material." They are mechanically applied with a food-grade adhesive to fresh produce as it is prepared for shipment. Retailers love PLUs, because the four- or five-digit code on each sticker tells your grocery store's computer how much each type of produce costs and helps the store track its produce inventory. Standardized PLU codes cut down on price checks, cashier mistakes, and other delays in the grocery checkout line. No question that's a good thing, but what's a compost gardener to do about the perpetual parade of pile-polluting PLUs?

Peel them off, suggests Dietz, noting that Sinclair Industries' PLUs are "tab-lift labels" that have a tiny, adhesive-free tab "so the consumer can peel it off easily." Still, you *will* miss a few, which you can watch for and pick out of compost that's being sifted and stored for use in potting soil or for topdressing containers. When you're digging PLU-laden compost into your soil, or simply letting them go, pause to take a walk down your culinary memory lane. For example, thoughts of the wonderful applesauce you made with 'Winesap' apples (4191) will make a brief return when your memory is jogged by those icky stickies.

small, therapeutic doses of kitchen compost are indicated. We like to sift some of our kitchen compost, allow it to dry (if necessary) until it's lightly moist, and then store it in airtight plastic containers for times when a plant or spot of soil seems to be in need of its medicinal powers. Unrotted chunks of broccoli stem or nut shells that are removed from kitchen compost make valuable additions to a new heap. Or, small pieces can simply be dug into biologically active soil.

Spreading the Wealth

It's also fine to spread the wealth by using partly done kitchen compost in other types of composting projects. For example, slipping a thin layer of kitchen compost into a Comforter Compost (see page 154) will inoculate it with fungi and bacteria that are found in rotting cantaloupe rinds or coffee grounds. Burying a bucket of kitchen waste at the bottom of a Treasure Trough (see page 187) moves the entire process to the root zones of garden plants, or you can use the Honey Hole approach (see page 191) to compost large seasonal infusions of food waste. From corncobs to shriveled jack o' lanterns, kitchen wastes bring the gift of diversity to any compost projects in which they are used.

KEEP YOUR COOL

Kitchen compost is usually rich in seeds, which you know by all the tomato seedlings that pop up in your garden! Tinkering with kitchen compost to get it hot enough to deactivate seeds isn't difficult (see page 137), but the heat treatment also will change the microbial makeup of your compost, eliminating many microbial species while favoring others. If you want to reduce the number of viable seeds in your kitchen compost while preserving remnant populations of beneficial microbes, avoid using heat during the latter stages of decomposition. Instead, stick with the low-temperature methods described in part 2 (see page 130).

Make a
Sling Screen Compost Sifter

The Sling Screen described here is enjoyable to use for screening compost, or you can use it to screen rocks, big acorns, or other objects from soil. In addition, you may find it handy when you need to cover a newly seeded bed to discourage visits from cats, dogs, or squirrels. When your Sling Screen is not in use, simply roll it up, secure the bundle with its attached piece of polyester clothesline, and stash it in a convenient place. See chapter 8 (page 218) for more plans and ideas for compost sifters.

Whether you use a Sling Screen or a compost screen of your own design, pick out earthworms and large sticks as you work, and toss them back onto your compost pile. You may find it easier to screen your compost after letting it dry a bit; dry compost is lighter in weight and often crumbles quite easily. However, the choice is yours.

MATERIALS AND SUPPLIES

- One 6'-long 1×2 (1.8 m-long 19×38 mm) pine or cedar, painted if desired
- Measuring tape
- Hand saw
- Pencil
- 2 small metal cleats
- 4 small wood screws
- Drill or nail
- Screwdriver
- 1 roll of 24"-wide ½" (61 cm-wide 1.25 cm) mesh polyester hardware cloth
- Scissors
- Staple gun
- Hammer
- One 48" (1.2 m) piece of polyester clothesline twine, or ¼" (0.6 cm) wide elastic

1 Cut two 26″ (66 cm) pieces from the 1x2 (19x38 mm). Set aside the scrap piece for another use. If desired, paint the cut pieces with exterior enamel paint.

2 On the narrow sides, measure and mark the center points of each of the cut pieces. Center the cleats over these marks, and mark the locations for the screws that will hold them in place. Make guide holes for the screws using a drill or a small nail. Firmly screw the cleats in place. ▼

3 Measure the width of the cart or wheelbarrow you will use to collect your screened compost, and add 8″ (20 cm) to this measurement. Use the scissors to cut a piece of hardware cloth to this length.

4 On a flat surface, lay the 1x2s (19x38 mm) on their broad sides, with the cleats on the outer edges. Position the edge of the cut piece of hardware cloth atop one of the 1x2s (19x38 mm), ¼″ (0.6 cm) in from the edge, and staple it in place. Repeat with the other side. Go back and add more staples if needed to make them no more than 2″ (5 cm) apart. Pound the staples in tightly with the hammer.

5 Loop and knot one end of the clothesline twine over one of the cleats. Lay the sling across the top of your cart or wheelbarrow, pass the free end of the twine underneath, and attach it to the other cleat. The sling need not fit tightly and will work better if it sags slightly.

6 Place a gallon-sized pile of compost on the sling, and use gloved hands or a hand trowel to fluff and rake it over the Sling Screen. ▼

Turning Garden Refuse into Garden Rewards

Along with the by-products of your kitchen, the plants growing in your yard and garden are the next most likely source of materials for your composting projects. What could be more natural than recycling some of the nutrients that those plants took from the soil into compost, which will replenish that same piece of ground? Nothing; because this is how it is done in nature, time and time again. Compost moves the process up a notch by not only putting back some of the nutrients your plants borrowed during the growing season, but by doing so in a bigger and better package, which is laced with beneficial microbes, growth-promoting nutrients, and organic matter, all of which help the soil function even better than it did before.

Waste Not, Want Not

For many people, fall garden cleanup is an annual *rite* that is not always done *right*. At the end of the growing season, they remove plant "waste" and burn or bag it for disposal. Or, in a more progressive turn of events, they compost it in another part of their landscape. They may then turn and pulverize the denuded garden soil, further disrupting the microbiology that is going on below ground. Then they leave the soil bare and exposed to the elements, which leach nutrients away over the winter months. Spring fertilizer applications serve up the nitrogen, phosphorus, and potassium (N-P-K) essential for plant growth, but do little or nothing to replenish the soil-support system that sustains long-term plant health. The real "waste" in this approach is not the spent plant parts that are dutifully dragged away. What gets wasted are the little, but important, things — micronutrients and

Every leaf and stem that withers in your garden can come to rest in compost.

microorganisms — that play big roles in garden success, along with precious human time and energy.

Compost gardeners do things differently. We don't miss a chance to tighten the connections between plants and soil, and by doing so, we minimize the need for applications of fertilizers, pesticides, and other outside inputs that are meant to keep plants healthy. And we do it with less work! For example, instead of clearing away spent pea vines, carrying them to a distant compost pile, and then cultivating and fertilizing the soil before replanting (there went half the afternoon), you can chop the vines with a sharp hoe or shovel blade and layer on some weathered leaves and finished compost to make a Comforter Compost bed. Now you're ready to plant pole beans, cucumbers, or another crop that knows what to do with a vacant pea trellis. From start to finish, the renovation should take less than half an hour.

A Compost Gardener's View of the Garden

When you look at your garden through a composter's eyes, you'll see a wealth of potential compost goodies, like frostbitten pepper plants, fading annuals, dried flower stalks, and your garden's favorite weeds, to name just a few. In fact, you may begin to appreciate some plants as much for their compost potential as you do for their fruits or flowers. Here is where you may cross the line, entering into biodynamic gardening, a discipline in which living and once-living plants become essential pieces in the healthy garden puzzle. There are dozens of plants that can be grown for the primary purpose of making more and better compost, and every compost gardener should make friends with a few of these terrific plants (see Biomass-ters of the Compost Garden on page 73, as well as the Compost Fodder Crop profiles that begin on page 276).

The amount and type of garden refuse you have on hand for stoking your compost will vary over the course of the growing season. In spring, it may take the form of winter mulches that have served their protective purpose; by early summer you may have spent pea vines and bolting spinach plants to add to the mix. All summer there will be succulent young weeds, wilted plants, and pruned plant parts. In fall, things get more interesting, as you gather up leaves, stalks, stems, and roots of dead annuals from alyssum to zinnias, along with a small mountain of vegetable-garden has-beens.

Your flower beds, shrubs (evergreen and deciduous), and mixed borders can provide fodder for the compost pile, too. Pinching and pruning produces tender tidbits that will feed your heap in summer, followed by withered stems and leaves in fall. Whether you tidy them up in the fall or leave them standing for architectural interest (and wildlife habitat) through the winter, dried flower stalks, such as those of daylilies, hostas, and sunflowers, make great additions to the compost pile. You can chop them into manageable segments for speedy decomposition, or leave them long and layer them higgledy-piggledy in your heap to help create channels for air to get into such a slow-cooking pile.

Make Room in Your Garden for "Compost Central"

Whenever possible, compost your garden refuse where it happens, rather than carting it from your garden to a distant compost pile. That way, you'll move closer to returning nutrients to the soil they came from, and you will promote long-term relationships that naturally form between plants and soil microorganisms. On-site composting, the hallmark of compost gardening, also saves you literally tons of labor — a cubic yard of compost (27 cubic feet, or 8.25 cubic meters) weighs roughly 1,000 lbs (454.5 kg), so you only have to turn such a heap twice to start measuring your efforts by the ton.

Here are four simple ways to incorporate composting into an existing garden. All of these techniques, and many more, are discussed more fully in part 2 (see page 130).

▶ **Put up a pen.** Use chicken wire or plastic or welded-wire fencing to form a simple cylinder and set it up in the center of a bed or in a convenient corner of your garden. If necessary, fasten the pen to a stake or fence post for stability. As you pull weeds or clean up crop remains, toss them into the pen. Add other compost ingredients as they become available over the growing season, and moisten the contents of the pen each time you have the hose handy for watering your garden. Sometimes, it's possible to use the outside of a pen to support pea vines, pole beans, morning glories or other annual climbers. If the pen gets full before summer ends, set up another one in a different part of the garden. Whenever you're ready, remove the pen and kick-start this cool, slow pile with an infusion of grass clippings or alfalfa meal. Cook it for a month or so, and you have garden-grown compost ready to use in your garden or to put to work in a new composting project.

▶ **Start a Walking Heap.** Similar to the pen described above, a Walking Heap differs by starting on one end of a garden bed and gradually moving to the other, dribbling organic matter into the soil along the way (for step-by-step instructions, see page 140). Begin by simply piling weeds and garden refuse in a designated area of your garden. Moisten the pile as you build it, and add other materials as they become available. When the pile gets to be 2' (0.6 m) deep, and the garden area next to the pile is free of productive plants, turn the pile by moving it to the adjacent space in the garden. If you like, plant something in the pile's initial footprint. Meanwhile, continue adding weeds and spent plants to the pile. Repeat this process until the pile reaches the far end of the bed. If it's not finished at that point, change directions and keep going.

▶ **Set up Comforter Compost.** At the end of the growing season, gather up all garden plants that have reached the end of their road. Spread the spent plant materials into a flat-topped pile and cover with other materials, such as chopped leaves, spoiled hay, grass clippings, composted manure, or sawdust, balancing high-carbon browns with nitrogen-rich greens as you go. Pile things on thickly, moisten everything well, and you'll have a super-fertile planting spot by spring. (For more on Comforter Composting, see chapter 5.)

▶ **Hit up some trenches.** The Treasure Trough method (see page 187) takes a bit of work upfront, but doesn't require any structure and is ultra easy to manage once the trench is dug. Make an 8" to 12" (20 to 30.5 cm) deep trench along one side of your garden, and toss weeds and garden refuse into it. Top the trench with soil as you fill it in. When you finish filling one trench, dig a new one in another part of your garden and repeat the process. Grow plants alongside the compost-filled trench the first season; plant right on top of it the following year.

Composting Ailing Plants and Weeds

Whatever else it produces for your use and enjoyment, your garden will certainly yield ample amounts of compostable materials. The good news for compost gardeners is that almost everything that comes *out* of your garden is fair game to go back *into* your garden via compost, including diseased plants and weeds that bear seeds. We are not kidding. You really can compost sickies and weedies as long as you quarantine them in their own intensively managed heap or composter. We realize that this sounds like composting heresy, but consider these two points:

▶ **Most fungi and bacteria** that cause plant diseases are seriously set back by the competition for nutrients in the microbial compost-sphere. Those that don't starve may be poisoned or consumed by their ever-changing neighbors. Survival becomes a long shot during microbial shift changes caused by changes in temperature, with high temperature microbes (thermophiles) the most lethal of all. If you subject mildewed squash plants or blighted tomatoes to a fall-to-spring compost cycle, you can finish

Compost Fodder Crops:
Biomass-ters
of the Compost
Garden

There are safer ways to improve compost than risking the ambiance of your automobile interior by fetching funky manure in it. You can think (and work) vegan by growing nutrient-rich compost fodder crops right in your garden. These are long-respected members of the cover crop and green manure plant clubs, which can be grown for the primary purpose of making great compost. True, Compost Fodder Crops often improve the soil while they are growing, *and* they smother weeds, but it's the copious amount of plant matter, or "biomass," that makes these plants so valuable in a composter's garden. Your choice of Compost Fodder Crops will vary with your climate, available space, and what you want to see happen in your garden. Do you need to break in new gardening space, or give a well-seasoned garden bed a restorative vacation? After looking through the brief descriptions below, turn to the plant profiles that begin on page 276 to learn more about using these talented plants in your garden.

Alfalfa (*Medicago sativa*) is a perennial legume that grows into a knee-high mass of nitrogen-rich foliage. In most climates, it can be cut back and composted twice a year.

Austrian winter pea (*Pisum sativum* ssp. *arvense*) is another legume that is good to grow in colder conditions than most vegetables can take, so it's a good fodder crops to grow from fall to spring in cold-winter areas.

Borage (*Borago officinalis*) is an herb that produces more beautiful blue flowers the more often you cut back the big, bristly plants.

Buckwheat (*Fagopyrum esculentum*) will turn any bare spot into a sea of green in a matter of days and will please the palates of numerous beneficial insects if you allow it grow until the flowers open before cutting it back.

Crimson clover (*Trifolium incarnatum*) makes a great winter annual in the South, or it can be grown as a summer compost crop in the North.

Crowder peas (*Vigna unguiculata*) are first cousins to black-eyed peas, but they are more efficient nitrogen-fixers and ideal for midsummer fodder in hot climates.

Hairy vetch (*Vicia villosa*) usually grows as a hardy annual, and it's the finest of all fodder crops for building soil nitrogen in late fall and early spring.

Mustard (*Brassica rapa*) produces huge leaves quickly, which shade out weeds. They are a fast fodder crop to grow from late summer to fall.

Cereal rye (*Secale cereale*) is fast and hardy, and can be sown in fall and mowed down first thing in the spring.

Wheat (*Triticum aestivum*) and other grains do double duty as food and fodder crops, and some varieties can also be grown for their decorative seedheads.

off any survivors by using one of the heap-heating methods discussed on pages 123 and 140 and call it your Hospital Heap. Then let the compost cure for a month or so, and it's safe to use in your garden.

▶ **Weeds** that show up in your garden are fair game for compost, even if they are holding seeds. Green plant material is green plant material, and weeds take nutrients and moisture out of the soil just like any other plant in your garden. Weeds that have not yet begun to bloom and lack viable root buds that help them grow into new weeds can be added to any compost project, but it is important to keep weed seeds to a minimum every chance you get. This gets easier once you get to know your garden's resident weeds and how they behave (keep reading), but you will still miss a few seed-bearing bad boys. The solution is to compost weedy or invasive plants in their own heap, which can be the same one you use for diseased garden refuse. Slip in a little heat treatment for your Hospital Heap, let the batch cure, and you're good to go!

Managing Incoming Weeds

Into every garden some weed seeds must fall, and most of us know, all too well, several species of weeds that find our yards precisely to their liking. Some of them get away from us and set seeds, and we stack the seed-bearing plants into our compost piles, thinking that we will worry about them another time. We

envision a heap smoking with 130-degree heat, which will cook the weed seeds into oblivion, but what if that doesn't happen? What should we do then?

There are several ways to deactivate the weed seeds lurking in your compost, and these are valuable skills to have. Even if you never toss a seed-bearing weed into your compost, it may still be rich in unwanted seeds carried in by animal manure or kitchen scraps. Tomato seeds are such valiant survivors that they often become downright weedy, but finding random fruit and vegetable seedlings in your compost is fun and can sometimes lead to wonderful crops. Several de-weeding methods to use on almost-finished compost (because it's less bulky, and thus easier to process) are covered in detail beginning on page 222. But you can make the biggest impact on potential weed problems at the front end, by setting aside one heap or compost bin to handle only weedy materials. That way, you won't have to worry about weeds sprouting in your primo composting projects.

Where Do Weeds Come From?

Before you can sentence weedy materials to their own heap, you must know where they originated. Many garden weeds are secretive with their seeds, and numerous species can continue to produce new blossoms after they have fattened up a nice crop of seeds (chickweed is a prime example). Manure from animals that feed in open pastures is often rich with strange weed-species seeds, and mulch materials that seem well behaved, such as hay, can be a source of weed seeds as well. Hitting only one or two clumps of seed-bearing crabgrass with your mower can liberate thousands of seeds into a load of grass clippings, and then there are all the weeds you pull by hand from your vegetable and flower beds. They would make dream greens for compost if not for those seeds. On the other hand, fallen leaves and pine needles are reasonably free of weed seeds, and the same is true of rotted sawdust, wood chips, and shredded paper; all are fine carbon sources (browns) for a weed-free heap.

In every climate there are plant criminals known as noxious weeds, with noxious being the highest level of invasiveness a plant can attain on many state government lists of problem weeds. Bindweed, Canada thistle, and quackgrass fall into this category along with dozens of other plants. Most of these superweeds reproduce by shedding seeds and by developing hundreds of root buds. Unless you are confident and committed to processing the compost made from noxious weeds with a high-heat procedure, collect them in a black plastic garbage bag and subject them to various forms of torture before dumping them in an inhospitable place. Cook bags of them in the sun, add water and let them soak into slime, and keep track of what works and what doesn't. If your superweeds survive your torture methods and you don't have a spot in your landscape suited to use as a little landfill, discard them as garbage.

What About Buggy Plants?

As you make and use more and more compost in your garden, you will find that serious insect-pest problems become few and far between. Many studies have shown that stressed plants actually give off chemical signals that attract pests to them, as do plants that are producing fast, "soft" growth in response to excessive nitrogen fertilization. Besides preventing these types of stress, the biologically active soil of a compost garden supports many beneficial insects and arthropods that help to control would-be pests. And, compost itself can "prime" plants to better defend themselves when random leaf-nibblers do appear.

Still, every garden will play host to occasional insect infestations. In some years, your beans will get chewed by Mexican bean beetles, and in others your pumpkin plants will get girdled by squash vine borers. Many garden pests do overwinter in garden debris, so as you clean up, you will probably move many to your compost. Out of their element and deprived of food in the pile, insect pests become weak or die from starvation. High temperatures or the physical disturbance of turning the pile spells doom for most stragglers, and the last survivors become food to millions of invisible comrades in your compost. It's a grisly story, but at least it has a happy ending.

Horseradish from Hell

Over the years, I've dealt with noxious nasties from Johnson grass to ground ivy, but the most dangerous plant I know is horseradish (*Armoracia rusticana*). My first lesson came years ago, when I naively ran a tiller over a clump of dormant roots. Horseradish sprang up everywhere I tilled, and it took all day to dig up the plants. Luckily, I was able to throw them over the fence to my neighbor's donkey, who took one taste before expressing his negative opinion by pulverizing the pile with his little donkey hooves.

Fast-forward twenty years, during which I decided that I really like eating horseradish. I bought a root at the grocery store and planted a wiener-sized piece in soil so compacted and acidic that nothing should grow there. The plant grew 3′ (1 m) tall in its first season, and in the fall, I dug up enough horseradish roots to open every clogged sinus cavity in the state.

I thought I got them all. Fat chance! Spring brought a rollicking gang of little horseys, and by the time I dug them up in early summer, they showed me their 1′ (0.3 m) long roots as thick as my finger. I was getting scared now, so I set some aside to dry in the sun and managed to stuff others into a clear-plastic bag. Final report: Horseradish roots that are dried until they as hard as leather can come back to life, but those that swim in slime for a couple of months in a plastic bag can't.

Five quiet composts come of age.

Leaves and Pine Straw

A certain measure of sorrow marks the end of the growing season, but that grief can be lightened by the realization that a new composting season is beginning. In most temperate landscapes, the largest infusion of organic matter of the year comes with the new crop of autumn leaves. Depending on your climate, the harvest of leaves or pine needles shed by trees can stretch on for four to six weeks, allowing plenty of time to gather the season's compost bounty.

If you have deciduous trees on your property (or your neighbor does), leaf management can consume a lot of time each fall. Fortunately, raking is good exercise, and it keeps you warm while you enjoy being outdoors on those crisp fall days. Gathering up leaves is good for your lawn, too, because matted leaves can suffocate your grass. A light layer of leaves can simply be mowed over, thus returning the tidbits to the yard's soil as organic matter; it is free fertility for grass and trees. Many composters treasure the mixture of grass clippings and leaves collected in early fall, with the help of a bagger, because it's a ready-made mix of high-carbon leaves and high-nitrogen grass clippings. Later, as the grass stops growing, the harvest will gradually become nothing but ready-to-rake leaves. Each year as leaf season begins, review the 12 Rules of Raking (page 81) to make sure you're making the best use of your time, energy, and leaves.

LEAF MOLD

CHOPPED LEAVES

WHOLE LEAVES

Leaves in stages of decomposition.

Composting with Leaves

Leaves vary in how long they take to decompose, because they are not all alike. Thin leaves that are high in calcium and low in lignin — for example, those shed by dogwoods and birches — will rot in the course of a winter, while thicker oak or magnolia leaves may take two years or more to make the transition from fallen leaf to morsels of humus. Some gardeners think that mixing leaf species together in a compost pile helps to even out the time difference, and this is partially true.

Lignin molecules break down when they are ready, which is usually after leaves have been thoroughly leached and then worked by various types of fungi. Composting has little or no effect on the initial leaching stage, but after the leaching is done, the increased microbial diversity that is achieved when different leaf species are mixed together in compost may help the slower decomposers move along a bit faster. Leaves are low in nitrogen and high in carbon, with an average C/N ratio in the 50/1 to 60/1 range. Don't hold their low nutrient composition against them, because some of the nutrients present in green leaves shift to the dormant buds as the trees and shrubs prepare to let them go. These concentrated sugars are utilized as chemical antifreeze in the buds — an elegant self-preservation strategy that proves the wisdom of long-lived woody plants.

Composting provides endless opportunities to compensate for the low nutritional value of leaves by combining them with materials that are higher in nitrogen. Or, you can not worry about nitrogen at all and simply appreciate the substantial contribution rotted leaves can make to your soil's bank of organic matter. Either way, it is unrealistic to expect to see

Coarsely chopped leaves (left) make a fine mulch for partially shaded flower beds. Pine straw (right) is easy to handle and has a neat, tailored appearance.

much decomposition from leaves during their first winter. Shredded leaves used as mulch or layered into Comforter Compost usually show rapid decomposition as the weather warms in spring. Whole leaves may not be ready to do much with until well into the summer — a good time to combine them with kitchen waste, grass clippings, or other sources of nitrogen. Meanwhile, you can use your new crop of shredded or whole leaves to create Nursery Reserves. Covered in detail beginning on page 83, Nursery Reserves use a leaf pile's natural insulating properties to protect marginally hardy plants through winter, or you can use a Nursery Reserve as a chilling chamber for spring-flowering bulbs planted in pots.

Pining for Pine Straw?

With a C/N ratio of 500/1, pine needles are about as far as you can get from a material likely to fire up a compost heap. Yet pine straw is great for mulching beneath shrubs and trees, or between perennials. Pine straw stays put and rots slowly while retaining soil moisture and suppressing weeds. After a year, pine straw's burnt sienna color weathers to gray, at which point it can be raked up and composted, or you can simply cover it with a fresh supply. Successive layers of decomposing pine needles will push the soil's pH into the acidic range, which is fine for plants that prefer acidic soil, such as azaleas, blueberries, strawberries and rhododendrons. When using pine straw as a long-term mulch for other plants, simply dust on a little garden lime each fall to keep the pH from dipping too low. Don't worry about pine straw's effect on soil pH if you are simply using it as an attractive cover for a fall-built compost heap or Comforter Compost, because pine needles do not begin to decompose until they have been thoroughly leached by a winter's worth of rain and snow, and a single season under pine straw will have minimal effects on the soil's pH.

Pines vary in the length of their needles and when they shed them, but all tend to let go all at once, over a period of a few days. If you rake up all needles just as they begin to fall, you can be assured of a clean catch of fine-textured pine straw. If you don't need collected pine straw for mulch right away, simply stuff it into garbage bags and keep it in a dry place.

Do not attempt to compost synthetic pine straw, most of which is made from recycled plastic. Even when fluffed every other year, synthetic pine straw loses its color after four to five years, at which point it should be raked or swept up and discarded. You can ask about recycling it at your local recycling center, but don't get your hopes too high. Degraded plastic strings mixed with soil are more likely to pollute the recycling stream than be given another life as a welcome mat or food container.

Chopping and Shredding Leaves

Chopped or shredded leaves make nicer looking mulch and work much better than whole leaves for most composting projects. If left to rot into leaf mold (see page 85), shredded leaves will make the transition in only a year or so, compared to two to three years for whole leaves. Best of all, chopping leaves reduces their volume by about two-thirds, or sometimes more, so they take up much less composting space than whole leaves.

You can use a lawn mower, string trimmer, or leaf shredder to chop up your leaves. Here are some technical points to consider when you are using power equipment to shred leaves.

LEAF LOVE ON THREE LEGS

I prefer garden tools that serve more than one purpose, such as a combination blower/vacuum rather than just a leaf blower, or a mattock with one end that slices through roots and makes planting holes and another that pries out rocks. So I wasn't immediately smitten with the electric leaf shredder I received as a gift several years ago because it does only one thing: It chops up leaves, using what is essentially a double-bladed string-trimmer mounted at the bottom of a 3-legged hopper.

With experience, however, I've come to love this single-use machine because it does what it does so well. Large piles of whole leaves are quickly reduced to small piles of shredded leaf bits that are just right to use for composting and mulching. Since it weighs no more than 20 pounds, I can set up the shredder anyplace that I can reach with a heavy-duty exterior extension cord and chop leaves where I want the shredded results. By setting the machine's spindly tripod legs on a tarp, I can catch the chopped leaves and move them to my compost pile or nursery bed. With its legs removed, the shredder will sit on top of a barrel, so I can shred leaves directly into a container to stockpile for future projects. In the fall, I often set it up right in a garden bed and shred leaves from the surrounding lawn. The blanket of shredded leaves protects the soil over the winter; in spring I cover the weathered shredded leaves with top-quality finished compost, and the bed is ready for planting.

Current leaf-shredder models are priced at around $150, a cost that may take a few seasons to recover in terms of less purchased mulch and less gas used to power your mower while chopping leaves. Because it runs on electricity rather than gas, and because it's easily turned on and off as needed, a leaf shredder creates less air pollution during a leaf-shredding session than a gas-powered mower used to shred a similar quantity of leaves.

▶ **Mower.** A lawn mower can be a mighty ally during leaf season. To gather chopped leaves with a bagger, begin by raking the leaves onto a paved surface. Run over them two or three times with your mower. When using a walk-behind mower, you may need to raise the mower's cutting height as high as it will go, or raise up the front wheels by pushing downward on the handle to keep the leaves from choking the blades. Wear heavy shoes or boots, long pants, and eye protection as precautions against flying debris. When using a bagger to collect the shredded leaves, you will get a cleaner catch if you reset the wheel height to the lowest level (see safety information on page 91).

To shred leaves without a bagger, run your mower over a leaf-covered area so the chopped leaves fall into a long spine. On your return, position the mower's chute so it spews more leaves onto the first pile. When the leaves are coarsely chopped, you can rake or sweep them onto a tarp or Composter's Sling (see page 82). Another option is to start at the outer edge of your lawn and mow in a square or circle, always with the mower's chute facing the center of the yard. With each pass around the yard, the mower will move the leaves inward, so you can collect them from a small space.

▶ **String trimmer.** If the best leaf chopper you have is a string trimmer, you can put whole leaves into a barrel, stick the string trimmer in, and chop. Shredding leaves with a string trimmer is messy and dusty, and you will need to watch your string trimmer for signs of overheating. Be sure to wear protective goggles when you're leaning over a barrel of leaves and chopping them up with a string trimmer.

▶ **Leaf shredder.** Electric leaf shredders cost $200 or less, and even though they are less noisy than gas-powered models, they still emit sound levels in the 85 decibel range, which is the maximum safe volume for unprotected ears. These little wonders are basically a string trimmer mounted on a stand, into which leaves are fed through a hopper (see Leaf Love on Three Legs, on page 79. It takes a little practice to learn exactly how to feed leaves into a shredder, and small shredders cannot handle sticks, acorns, or other large objects. Larger gas-powered shredders can chop up small sticks, but they are expensive and noisy. Renting a big shredder/chopper for a weekend is usually smarter than buying one.

However you tackle this task, chopping up leaves is dusty, dirty work. Lightly moistening the leaves, or working while they are slightly damp with dew, will reduce dust and give the leaves enough extra weight to keep them from blowing away while you're working. Use your hose to apply a very fine mist over a leaf pile before shredding it. Keep it light, because too much

Shredding leaves greatly reduces their volume, and enhances their value as mulch or as additions to compost.

moisture will make the leaves stick together and clog your equipment. Even if you moisten your leaves, wear a dust mask while shredding to avoid inhaling leaf dust and fungal spores — especially if you have allergies or asthma. If a manufacturer recommends ear protection, it is usually because the machine emits more noise than human ears are built to handle. Follow their advice, or risk permanent damage to your ears.

What About Leaf Vacs?

Some leaf blowers convert quickly to leaf vacuums, which are especially handy if you have a large deck or driveway that stays covered with leaves every fall. But blower/vacs can be more trouble than they're worth out in the yard, because the small collection bags must be detached, emptied, and reattached often, and then you have to restart the thing. Restarting is not an issue with electric models, but their small size limits their usefulness except in tight spaces like your deck or patio. Small blower/vacs don't shred leaves, either, and larger models that do cost well over $1,000, drink gasoline, and make a lot of noise. If we may suggest an alternative, consider paying for help if you're so overwhelmed with your leaf harvest that you are having nightmares in which you are being chased by a howling leaf blower. In many communities, members of high school service clubs raise funds in the fall by working as yard clean-up teams.

SAFEGUARD YOUR EARS

You've been mowing and shredding leaves for an hour when you realize that your son is waving at you from the back door because dinner is ready. If you didn't hear him when he called loudly, the machinery you're using probably emits more than 80 decibels. Short sessions at this noise level are probably safe, but the longer you are exposed to noise levels above 80 decibels, the greater your risk of hearing loss. You can slash this risk by wearing foam earplugs or noise-blocking earmuffs when using mowers, shredders, and other loud yard care equipment.

---

12 Rules of Raking

1 Always rake with the wind, and rake downhill whenever possible. Leaves are light, but they have enough weight to respond to the pull of gravity.

2 Share the wealth with your lawn. Leaves contain some of the nutrients that trees and shrubs have taken out of the soil, and it's in keeping with Nature's plan that you should give back some of those purloined nutrients by mowing over part of your annual leaf-fall, thus returning organic matter to the soil from whence it came. This works best in early fall when the first leaves are coming down and grass still benefits from mowing. In addition to helping the lawn, it's easier to rake turf areas that have been smoothed over by a good mowing.

3 Keep whole leaves from blowing away by stomping through the pile. If you are using a bin or other enclosure, leave it open on one side until you're through collecting leaves. That way, you can rake or dump right into the pile without lifting your loads over the sides of the bin, and your leaf pile will be accessible for walk-in stomping.

4 Minimize how far you move your leaves. Rake them directly onto nearby beds that won't be worked until spring. Use shredded leaves as mulch beneath foundation shrubs. Maintain leaf piles in different parts of your yard so you won't have to drag or carry tarps full of leaves any farther than necessary.

5 Match your rake to the type of leaves you have in your yard and to your body. At stores, try rakes on for size before you buy. Rakes with metal tines last longer than plastic ones, but plastic tines may be lighter.

6 Use your mower to shred what you can (see page 79). Put shredded leaves to work in active compost projects such as Comforter Compost or Nursery Reserves. Set aside whole leaves in a separate pile, and deal with them later when you have more time.

7 Mix leaf species whenever possible. Leaf-eating microorganisms that get started on thin maple or dogwood leaves will move on to thicker oak leaves as the pile decomposes.

8 Wear gloves to prevent blisters. Cloth gloves are comfy, but any glove that protects your skin from rubbing on the rake handle will suffice.

9 Wear a dust mask when shredding leaves with your mower, especially if you have allergies or are easily irritated by dust.

10 Don't pick up leaves unless you must. Instead, use an old sheet as a tarp, pick up the corners, and carry or drag the bundle to your piles. Few carts or wheelbarrows have the capacity and portability necessary to make them worthwhile during leaf season. Use a sheet, tarp, or Composter's Sling (see page 82) to collect and move shredded leaves.

11 Watch the noise. When you're not in the mood to mess with your mower, or the sound of a leaf blower or shredder would ruin your neighbor's quiet afternoon in their yard, fall back to manual raking and collecting methods and work with whole leaves.

12 Work a little at a time, and stop when you've had enough. Keep in mind that leaf season will last for several weeks, so you have plenty of time to let yourself enjoy the weather and the work.

Make a Composter's Sling

In less than 10 minutes, and for less than $10, you can make this versatile composter's sling. Use it to collect and move shredded leaves, grass clippings, and even the weeds you pull from your garden. When excavating a garden bed, place the sling beside the hole and stock-pile the soil on the sling rather than on the ground. When you're ready to refill the hole, lift the far side of the sling and dump it in one fell swoop. You also can use your sling as a repot-ting mat (to catch spilled potting soil), and it makes a great shade cover for newly planted beds. Roll up the sling and stash it in a dry place when you're not using it. When the fabric becomes fragile due to dampness or old age, pry up the staples with a screwdriver, remove the old fabric, and replace it with a new piece.

You can use any type of fabric, from burlap to old curtains. If you want to improve your sling's eye appeal, before you assemble the sling, paint the 1x2 (19x38 mm) lumber a color to match the fabric.

MATERIALS AND SUPPLIES

- Steam iron
- Two 6' (1.8 m) long pieces of untreated 1×2 (19×38 mm) pine
- 2 yd (1.8 m) lightweight fabric at least 45" (1.1 m) wide
- Staple gun with staples

1 Press under a 1" (2.5 cm) hem on both of the long sides of the fabric.

2 Place the 1 x 2 (19 x 38 mm) boards on a level surface, broad side down, so they are parallel and about 3' (0.9 meters) apart.

3 Position one of the hemmed edges over one of the 1 x 2 (19 x 38 mm) boards and staple it in place, allowing 4" (10 cm) or so between staples. ▼

4 Repeat Step 3 with the other long, hemmed edge of the fabric and remaining 1 x 2 (19 x 38 mm) board.

Make a Rake-in Leaf Pen

Capturing leaves inside a bin or pen is the only way to keep them from blowing back into your yard, and in fact you can even use a blower to help fill a Rake-in Leaf Pen. And because leaves are so light, they can be easily contained by a pen made from plastic garden fencing or plastic hardware cloth secured to a few upright stakes. See the discussion of pens and bins on page 142 to consider the many options you have when erecting a structure for containing leaves.

The distinctive feature of a Rake-in Leaf Pen like the one shown below is that it is left open on its broadest side until leaf collection season is over. That way, leaves can be raked or blown right into the pen, with no lifting required. You can make a Rake-in Leaf Pen in any shape provided it is open on one side. After you've finished loading the bin, you can easily reach the pile to chop through it with a hoe, mattock, or other manual macerator whenever you're in a chopping mood. As long as they are dry, leaves from the bin can be fed into a leaf shredder.

A storage bin buried in a leaf pile makes a good place to chill spring-flowering bulbs potted up in the fall.

Using Your Leaf Pile as a Nursery Reserve

Whether the leaves are whole or coarsely shredded, a leaf pile will compact during the winter, but mostly it will just sit there as rain and melting snow help leach out tannins and other substances that inhibit decomposition. Why not give it a job? Your damp leaf pile can be used to shelter dormant container-grown plants from the ravages of winter, or you can use it as a staging point for forcing spring-flowering bulbs. When employed in these and other ways that enhance the growth of plants, your leaf pile becomes what we call a Nursery Reserve. In spring, leaves from a Nursery Reserve can go on to comprise parts of other composting projects.

Ideally, a Nursery Reserve is made of coarsely shredded leaves, which pack down better than whole leaves, making it possible to create a heap that will keep its size and shape through the winter. If you base your heap's shape on its purpose and remember accessibility issues, you will probably come up with many unique ways to use this simple technique in your garden.

Heeling In

To create a place to overwinter, or heel in, container-grown dormant perennials, take a head count of your plants in need of winter protection and line them up in a single or double row. Now that you know how much sheltered space your collection requires, find a

At the height of leaf season, set up a pen left open on its most accessible broad side. Rake or blow leaves into the pen through the opening.

Forced Hyacinths

In addition to being the most fragrant of spring-flowering bulbs, hyacinths are also the easiest ones to force into bloom in pots. Buy bulbs in September, as soon as they appear on store shelves, put them into a paper bag, write the date on the bag, and close and set the bag in your refrigerator. Ten weeks later, plant the bulbs, one to a pot, in 4" (10.2 cm) diameter pots, positioning the bulbs high so that their tops (pointed ends) show at the soil line. Water well, and place inside a bin or other container that's buried in your leaf pile. Begin to check the pots after a month; bring them indoors when fat leaf buds emerge. After a month in a cool, brightly lit room, each bulb will produce a beautiful bloom spike studded with enough fragrant florets to perfume a large room. If you apply a half-strength soluble fertilizer with each watering and grow them on a sunny windowsill, you can transplant the hyacinths to the garden in spring. Mound up cured compost around the plants to help them settle in and start storing up food reserves for the next year's flowers. Most fancy hyacinths will persist in the garden for years with little help. The blooms of naturalized hyacinths are seldom as large as those seen the first year after planting, but they are still wonderfully fragrant.

spot for your Nursery Reserve that's five times bigger than the collective footprint of your plants. Pile shredded leaves in two parallel elongated loaf-shaped heaps, and place your plants in the open slot between the two heaps. Be sure to dampen the leaves as you go, or thread a soaker hose through the layers. Add more shredded leaves until the plants are surrounded on all sides by 12" to 14" (30.5 to 35.6 cm) walls of leaves. You will need to add additional leaves after two to three weeks, because the pile will become compacted as the material settles into place.

You can use a similar approach to shape a Nursery Reserve leaf pile into more than one compartment. For example, once you get your container plants nicely tucked in, perhaps you want similar space to force spring-flowering bulbs. On the roomiest side of the first heap, begin shaping up a second one around a large plastic storage bin with its lid snapped shut. Later on, it will serve as your chilling chamber for bulbs planted in pots. Position the bin so that you can easily reach it from one side, and pile fewer leaves on the access side.

Get the idea? You can use this basic plan to create a protective enclosure for other situations, such as when you need a holding place for a shrub you've dug up and plan to replant when its new space is ready. You also can use a Nursery Reserve as a place to heel in bare-root trees and shrubs, or as storage space for mesh bags filled with seed potatoes or Jerusalem artichokes you plan to set out in spring. If a plant or root needs cold, moist storage through winter, a Nursery Reserve often makes an opportune spot.

Waiting Out Winter

Many of us start out the leaf season with plenty of ambition and energy, but after a few weeks of raking, shredding, and piling, we start slowing down. Fine! Simply pile your remaining whole leaves together in different parts of your yard, stomp on the piles to compact them, enclose the piles with a corral of wire or plastic fencing to keep the leaves from blowing away, and forget about them until spring. If you want to get fancy, you will find that a whole leaf heap will hold its shape and moisture level better if you alternate layers of leaves with well-dampened hay, straw, or perhaps some weathered grass clippings. Spent plants pulled from the garden can be used to strengthen a leaf pile's structure, too. Ropy tomato stems, for example, work somewhat like tie rods when layered into a leaf pile. There is no need to include high nitrogen materials, because the leaves will not be ready to interact with them in meaningful ways until spring (at the earliest) and any heat generated by high-nitrogen materials in fall will be wasted.

It is nearly impossible to keep the contents of a new leaf pile uniformly moist. Some leaves repel water, and all leaves are prone to packing together into dry clumps. These conditions improve after a winter of rain and snow. The following spring or summer, begin chopping through your leaf pile with a sharp hoe from time to time, or slice and dice it with a machete or mattock. Give it a good soaking each time you chop, and soon you will notice that the leaves are becoming much more fragile, and that the heap is actually holding water! Now you have the perfect carbon base for a Banner Batch juiced up with grass clippings, kitchen waste, or a high-protein meal (see page 136).

A final option is to do nothing, and let your leaves rot into leaf mold at their own pace. This is a very worthwhile undertaking because it requires so little work yet yields a wonderful substance for digging into beds or blending with other ingredients into homemade potting soil mixes.

The Mysteries of Leaf Mold

If nature graces you with more fallen leaves or pine needles than you can use in compost, let them morph into leaf mold, or "mould" as it's known in Great Britain. Don't be deterred by possible ickiness from something called mold, because leaf mold is one of the nicest forms of organic matter a gardener can have — dark, crumbly, and smelling of the earth. Typically very low in weed seeds, leaf mold is what happens after leaves leach and weather until they rot. Should you unexpectedly need some high-carbon organic

---

MIRACLE LEAF MOLD

All organic matter increases the soil's ability to absorb water, but leaf mold does it best. Like a dry kitchen sponge, dry leaf mold can absorb five times its weight in water, making it an ideal soil amendment for dry shade. Worked into the soil and used as mulch, leaf mold's water-holding talents help compensate for moisture taken up by tree roots, transforming dry shade into moist shade suitable for growing woodland beauties, such as foamflowers, heucheras, and trilliums.

Leaf mold can be substituted for peat moss in most potting soil recipes, or you can use it to make a special mix for plants grown in pots or planters stationed in the shade. Or, use it to implement this easy solution for the problem of chronic dryness in spots dominated by tree roots. Fill plastic nursery liners with this simple potting mix, add some impatiens (summer annual), Lenten roses (winter-blooming perennials), or hardy ferns, and "plant" the pots up to their rims. The buried pots will turn away thirsty tree roots, and you can hide the rims from view with leaf-mold mulch.

In a roomy bucket or bin, mix together:

1 part lightly moistened leaf mold
1 part sand (such as play sand)
2 parts loamy soil (or purchased topsoil if your soil is heavy clay)

Store any leftover mixture in a moisture-proof container, or mix it into another recipe, such as those on page 234.

---

matter for another composting project at any point during this process, you can get all you need from leaf-mold-in-the-making. Once it's finished, leaf mold can be substituted for peat moss in homemade potting soils or other garden projects.

One of the great things about leaf mold is that it so closely follows nature's plan: Take some leaves, add moisture, allow enough time, and you get leaf mold. To see this plan in action, poke around under the trees the next time you take a walk in the woods. Most of the stuff covering the ground is leaf mold in

Breakdown in a Bag

For three straight weeks every fall, my deck gets a fresh blanket of white oak leaves every day. The deck railing makes it hard to sweep them over the edge, so a few years ago I started collecting them in heavy-duty black plastic bags with drawstring tops. Each time I stuffed in more leaves I walked over the bag to crunch up the contents. By the end of leaf season I had three big, puffy bags of compacted leaves.

I could have added water and some finished compost to start making leaf mold right in the bags, but why not use them just as they are? Invention's good mother, necessity, soon provided answers to my question. One bag, thrown over a new planting of tulips and hyacinths, kept squirrels from digging up the bulbs. Another became a one-piece winter mulch for a bed of marginally hardy four-o-clocks. I ran out of bags before I ran out of uses, and after being carried around all winter,

taking on a little rain now and then, and freezing and thawing more times than I could count, the leaves inside were perfectly primed for composting the following spring. They ended up stacked beside the Pit-of-Plenty that receives leavings from the kitchen, where they are a ready source of high-carbon browns to mix with all those greens. Still, I was bothered about the plastic. Garbage bags are not at all attractive lounging on the deck, and even when handled gently, they suffer plenty of punctures and tears when filled with leaves and sticks. Sewing up three drawstring leaf bags, the same dimensions as the commercial ones, from indestructible polyester fabric remnants turned out to be two hours (and about $10) very well spent. The cloth repels much of the rain that falls on the bags, but enough moisture seeps through to enhance early leaching of the leaves. With luck, the bags should last at least three years.

some stage of decomposition. You'll probably be able to see distinct layers that represent the leaf fall over a few years. Next to the soil, the layer will be dark and fine-textured, like compost. Above that, you'll see bits of leaves that are chocolate brown and crumbly but still recognizable as leaves. Topping it all off will be the leaves that fell in the previous season or two, with

some of them stuck together with white, threadlike mycelium (the vegetative form of mushrooms). Leaf mold is not particularly nutritious to plants, but it makes an excellent substrate for fruiting fungi (mushrooms) as well as fungi that form mutually rewarding relationships with woodland wildflowers including wild orchids, galax, and many other species.

Making Leaf Mold

Making leaf mold, like making compost, can be managed as much or as little as you want. At a bare minimum, simply pile up fallen leaves in an out-of-the-way spot, stomp them down, and try to keep them wet. With no other effort on your part, you'll have leaf mold at the bottom of such a pile in about two years. With a little more tweaking, you can move things along more quickly and have good-quality leaf mold in only one year. Here are four ways to speed the transition of leaves to leaf mold.

▶ **Shredding.** Reducing the size of dry leaves by chopping or shredding allows moisture to leach their tannins out faster and exposes more surface areas to the actions of decomposing organisms once the pieces are moist. See page 78 for a variety of leaf-shredding methods.

▶ **Watering.** Piled leaves tend to shed water and may be quite dry in the center even after heavy rains. If you're piling up leaves for a "let-it-happen" heap, thread a soaker hose through the middle of the heap as you make it. Or, make a habit of setting leaky jugs on the pile. Water-filled milk jugs or detergent bottles with small holes punched near their bottoms will slowly drip their contents into the leaf pile below.

▶ **Turning.** As a leaf pile settles, the leaves become packed down so that air and water cannot move through the pile. A laid-back attack with a turning fork will do little to relieve this situation compared to an all-out assault with a mattock or a sharp hoe. Instead of thinking in terms of turning, make it more of a chop-through when the materials at hand are compacted leaves.

▶ **Inoculation with decomposers.** If you have some finished compost made mostly from leaves, by all means sprinkle some into your evolving leaf mold. It also can help to stir in a nitrogen source, such as alfalfa meal, grass clippings, or coffee grounds — even a little bit will help compost microorganisms gain a foothold in your leaf pile. This option can speed up decomposition, especially when the leaf mold is almost done.

Azaleas and Rhododendrons

Rich compost is great for most plants, but woodland shrubs like azaleas and rhododendrons prefer leaf mold. It's more acidic than compost and hosts fewer microorganisms, which is just fine with these beautiful shrubs.

Tackling Tree Debris

If you share your yard with trees, they will provide you with twigs, sticks, and seed structures (like acorns and cones) in addition to leaves. Piled together in an out-of-the-way place, sticks and other tree debris create shelter and habitat for birds, chipmunks, and other friendly forms of wildlife. After a stick pile has been out in the weather for a year or so, it's usually easy to chop through it with a hoe or mattock, after which you can add the weathered wood chips to many different types of composting projects. Many people who have outdoor fireplaces or chimineas burn their sticks as kindling, and then enrich their garden beds with light sprinklings of wood ash.

Tree debris gets stuck frequently in drainage gutters, where damp conditions help it to begin composting into "gutter goo." Left where it is, chunks of gutter goo will eventually become clogs, which is why gutters should be cleaned periodically, even if they are outfitted with screens. Goo from metal roofs is usually cleaner than the version that accumulates from shingles, which often includes sand particles from the roofing material. Go ahead and use it in your composting projects anyway! When you (or someone else) cleans your gutters, spread a water-repellent tarp on the ground to catch the mushy mess. There's nothing quite like the simple satisfaction of knowing you have clean gutters and interesting new things going on in your compost.

Composting Grass Clippings

We don't want to go so far as to say that every landscape should have a lawn, because keeping a good lawn is usually a high maintenance proposition. Most lawns require supplemental water and fertilizer, and there are valid questions about the environmental integrity of lawns in climates where swaths of grass are way out of sync with nature's plan. For example, using water to keep a lawn green is a waste of a precious resource in areas where water is in short supply, and even if you use organic fertilizers, keeping a lawn well fed will cost you in terms of time and money.

On the plus side, an established lawn can do a good job of perpetuating itself when given thoughtful care (see Compost Your Lawn with Clippings on the facing page), it can greatly enhance the curb appeal of your house, and there's nothing like a nice patch of turf for outdoor play. Lawn areas play important roles in landscape design by creating a feeling of openness and allowing the eye to rest between visually busy garden beds. A lawn also can help cool your yard on hot days, when turf is often 14°F (8°C) cooler than bare soil, and 30°F (17°C) cooler than asphalt.

Most importantly, your lawn can help energize your garden when the juicy green grass clippings are used in various composting projects. Grass clippings also make great mulch provided they are spread over the soil's surface in very thin layers (layers more than 1" deep pack down and repel water). You can use thicker layers when applying grass-clipping mulch over sheets of newspaper or cardboard.

It is not too far off target to think of grass clippings as the "manure" produced by urban and suburban landscapes. High in bioactive nutrients, fresh grass clippings are a dependable energy source for compost, which needs a dose of nitrogen to make it cook. But unlike animal manures, grass clippings do not need to be composted before they are used as mulch, and you can even mix light sprinklings right into your garden provided the soil is biologically active.

Grass clippings are a valuable composting commodity, and should be regarded as an important natural resource that happens to grow right under your feet. Grass clippings are rich in nutrients (usually with an N-P-K around 4-1-2), they're over 80 percent water, and they have a low carbon/nitrogen ratio of 17/1, or so. If you want to induce a cold heap to generate heat levels high enough to kill pathogens and weed seeds, mixing in fresh grass clippings will often do the trick. For best results, thoroughly mix in enough fresh green clippings to equal one-third of the mass of the pile, and turn the heap every two days for a week. It should be finished and ready to cure about two weeks later.

Whenever you make use of grass clippings' high nitrogen content by teaming them up with materials high in carbon, it's important that the "browns" be in appropriate condition for active decomposition. Otherwise, there will be little interaction between your hot clippings and cold compostables. Freshly fallen leaves or fresh sawdust are "no-goes," because both of these materials must leach out their tannins for several months before they are ready to be colonized by fungi and bacteria. Weathered leaves, cardboard, and most forms of paper, on the other hand, usually rot readily when thoroughly dampened and mixed with an equal amount of grass clippings.

Should you find yourself with more grass clippings than you can use, spread them in the sun for a day or two to dry, mound the dry clippings together, and cover the pile with a waterproof tarp or other rain-resistant cover. You also can store dried clippings in a cardboard box or plastic garbage bag kept in a dry place. Dried clippings don't pack down and turn slimy the way fresh ones do, and they retain their nutrients in concentrated form. Be sure to add enough water to rehydrate the dried clippings when using them in your composting projects.

Gathering Grass Clippings

During their seasons of active growth, most lawn grasses need to be mowed about once a week. Allowing the clippings to rot where they fall recycles their nutrients back into the turf, so at least half of your mowing sessions should end with a light layer of uncollected small clippings heading back to the soil from which they came. However, there are times when harvesting grass clippings benefits the lawn, the garden, and your compost, too. Here are six common situations in which collecting clippings makes great sense:

▶ **Overgrown lawns.** Heavy rains or a vacation lead to an overgrown lawn in which the clippings are likely to be more than 2" long. Long clippings often form persistent clumps that block light and decompose very slowly, so they are better collected than left on the lawn.

▶ **Entertaining.** You plan to use your lawn for entertaining, and don't want people tracking clippings into the house. This is also a good reason to collect lawn-grass clippings from areas near entryways as often as you like.

Fresh grass clippings will energize any compost.

▶ **Weeds.** Persistent lawn weeds are holding mature seeds, and you want no part of replanting them in your lawn. Gathering seedy clippings and hot-composting them is a strategic move toward reducing the number of weed seeds that lurk or sprout in your turf.

> ### NEED MORE CLIPPINGS?
>
> You can easily procure all the lawn clippings you could ever want by linking up with someone in the landscape-maintenance business. Many lawn-care customers prefer to have their clippings collected, so landscape maintenance crews often end each day with a truckload of fresh, green grass clippings. Talk with crews that work in your neighborhood, and ask for clippings from lawns that have not been treated with herbicides or pesticides. Some lawn chemicals can survive the composting process and can cause abnormal growth when taken up by plants.

▶ **Mulch.** Your vegetable garden needs a tidy, soil-improving (and free) mulch.

▶ **Compost.** You need some grass clippings for a special composting project, the lawn needs mowing, and it's a great day to work outside!

▶ **Fall compost.** A late fall mowing will yield mixed grass clippings and chopped leaves for composting over the winter.

When Not to Mow

The best lawn grasses have been bred with regular mowing in mind. Regardless of species, lawn grasses that are well suited to their site, soil, and climate usually need to be mowed once a week during their active season of growth. Ideally, grass should be mowed when doing so will lop off one-third of the length of the blade. Keeping the cutting height on the high side helps the turf do a better job of shading out weeds. Yet there are times when mowing is not good for your lawn, and possibly not good for you, either.

▶ **New grass areas.** Let newly seeded, sodded, or repaired areas grow for up to three weeks before mowing them.

▶ **During dry spells.** If the weather is dry, stop mowing before conditions develop into a true drought. Do not mow when drought-related water restrictions are in force.

▶ **Never mow wet grass.** The mower blade will chew at the grass rather than slicing the tips off cleanly, and wet grass clippings form slippery clumps that make mowing downright dangerous.

▶ **Do not mow at night.** This seems like common sense, but some people seem to love mowing too much to quit when the sun goes down. This is not smart, or perhaps you like going to the emergency room? If being popular in your neighborhood is important to you, we also suggest no mowing before nine o'clock on Saturday mornings and doing your part to keep Sunday mornings comfortably quiet, too.

Working with a Bagger

Raking up grass clippings is painfully slow, but it's fast and easy to collect clippings if your mower has a bagger attachment. Mowers of all sizes including several

---

MOWER KNOW-HOW

Mowers with baggers often have extra safety features to help keep the mower operator from making careless mistakes, such as trying to remove the bag when the blades are spinning. Never disable any mower's safety features, and add a little safety equipment of your own in the form of sturdy mowing shoes or boots. Mower-related injuries put more than 80,000 Americans in the hospital each year, and a third of those involve amputated toes. Other common injuries, such as skin lacerations or eye injuries caused by flying bits of debris, are less likely to occur if you're using a bagger, but they are still a good reason to wear long pants and goggles and make kids and pets stay a safe distance from a working mower.

---

electric models often include this feature as standard or optional equipment. Baggers *cannot* be attached to mowers that are not designed to accommodate them.

Baggers are usually sized to work well with the mower for which they are made, and you will learn, with a little practice, how full the bag should be before you stop to empty it. When a bagger attached to a walk-behind mower gets too full, you will feel its drag and may hear the blades strain against a logjam of clippings in the chute. Overloaded baggers are heavy, too, and once clippings become compacted inside, you may need to reach in and pull out clumps of clippings by hand. In general, it's best to empty a mower's bag when it's about three-quarters full of dry clippings, or half full if the clippings are on the moist side. This makes for a lot of stopping and starting and may double your mowing time. This is no big deal if you're harvesting clippings to use in a composting project, such as layering them with compost, sifted soil, and weathered leaves in a Comforter Compost bed. On a blue-sky summer day, there is a satisfying rhythm to mowing up a bag of clippings, sandwiching them with other compostables or fluffing them into a heap being turned, and then heading back to the lawn for another batch.

GETTING RID OF GRASS STAINS

A session spent gathering grass clippings will leave you thoroughly striped and splashed with green grass stains. They will wash right off your skin, but clothes are a different matter. Before you toss grass-stained clothes into the washer (which can set the stains and make them permanent), douse the stains with a half-and-half mixture of rubbing alcohol and water, and work it in well. Then hand-rinse the problem spots in cool water. If the stain persists, try a half-and-half mixture of either vinegar or lemon juice and water. To be on the safe side, test these natural stain removers on a part of the garment that is not seen, because they may bleach the color. Better yet, keep a grungy outfit just for mowing and gathering clippings, and wear those stains as badges of honor.

Composting Manure

Historically, farmers and gardeners made compost mostly to stretch their supply of manure. The fertilizer produced by the family milk cow or flock of laying hens simply went further when it was mixed with moldy hay or cornstalks before being set aside to rot. Compost made with manure is rich, plush stuff that will tickle the fancy of any plant fortunate enough to encounter it, and composting manure is fun for compost gardeners, too. Even if you handle manure only occasionally, it is enlightening indeed to watch the miracle unfold that has fascinated gardeners for thousands of years.

Okay, so you're not interested in using manure. If your religious beliefs support only compassionate treatment of animals, and you follow a vegan diet, you may feel more comfortable excluding manure from your composting projects. This is infinitely doable by using high-protein plant meals when a potent nitrogen source is needed. See page 122 for more information on composting with alfalfa, soybean, canola, and other plant meals.

Perhaps your reservations about using manure have to do with cleanliness. Good, because you should know what you are getting into before you agree to clean out the stall where a friend boards her horse. All animal manures contain a buffet of bacteria that can make you very sick if you put them in your mouth.

Manure must therefore be handled with respect, and scooping and piling manure is not generally enjoyable work. Manure never smells good, and some types smell downright awful, plus it's often gloppy and sticks to your shoes. As for those bacteria, they fight a losing battle that begins the moment the manure becomes involved in active composting, and they are pretty much gone by the time the compost is ready to use. Still, remnant populations of some bacteria may linger, which is why you should always wash your garden-grown goodies before you eat them. Manure produced by meat-eating animals can host pathogens that make the ones in a ball of horse hockey seem rinky-dink, so you should never include dog, cat, human, or wild animal scat in your composting projects. And, we must note here that urine is much cleaner than manure, microbially speaking, so we will not deny those so inclined the occasional deposit of personal liquid nitrogen in their compost piles.

Sourcing Manure: Six Smart Questions

Most home landscapes produce no manure, and adventuresome compost gardeners can't help but want some to work with from time to time. As you consider possible manures and their sources, you are wise to do so with a careful look at the animals themselves. You should also work with the animals' owner so that the doo-getting operation ends up as a winning proposition for everyone involved.

▶ **What are your time and fuel costs for importing this manure?**
Remember the Compost Miles concept back on page 53? Whenever you must drive to secure manure, you incur fuel costs (monetary and environmental), plus the inconvenience of outfitting your vehicle with boxes, bins, and tarps to prevent spillage. High-quality manure is worth a reasonable drive, especially if other errands can be incorporated into the trip. Can you buy farmstead goat cheese and pick up some stock-piled manure at the same time? Does the stable where your child takes riding lessons make manure or stable bedding available for patron pickup? Can you bunny-sit for a vacationing friend and collect your payment in compost-enriching rabbit manure?

▶ **Do you share any level of personal responsibility for the generation of this or other manure?**
If you regularly eat meat, eggs, or cheese and other dairy products, plenty of animals are producing tons of manure on your behalf. You are already in the game, so making a place in your garden for manures that might

otherwise pose pollution problems is an honorable goal. Maybe you can't do anything about the area three states away that's unlivable because of the stench from a commercial hog operation, but you can help out local dairies, and poultry and egg operations, by stepping up to the bat and facing down a fair share of manure.

▶ What do the animals eat? Is this a healthful and appropriate diet for this animal?

Goats and cows that are fed a heavy grain diet look nice and plump, but some of that grain goes undigested. By comparison, grazing animals that eat grass and hay primarily, with seasonal grain supplements, often produce healthier, high-fiber manure as a result of more complete digestion. Alpacas, llamas, cows, goats, and sheep have multi-chambered digestive systems designed to extract the nutrients available from grass. If you see them grazing in pretty green pastures or pens that open into hay-strewn paddocks, it is a good sign. Poultry manure can be quite rank under the best of conditions, but if you can locate an organic chicken or turkey farm, it won't take long to learn the art of handling it in compost (see Comparing Manures on page 94). Animals raised for organic meat, and fed organic food, eventually produce organic manure, which is a dream come true for compost gardeners in search of the perfect manure.

▶ Are horrible weeds present in the area where the animals browse or graze?

Many weed seeds pass through the digestive tracts of grazing animals intact, so you should bypass manure from animals that have been eating weeds like crabgrass and henbit whenever possible. If there are well-known noxious weeds in your area, be especially careful to look at the animals' access to seeds of invasive weeds like Johnson grass (in the South) or quackgrass (in the North). All pasture-fed animals will have weed seeds in their manure, but many seeds can be killed by using our various high-temperature composting methods. Still, you are wise to limit how many manure-borne weed seeds enter your compost — and your garden.

Direct from the source. Pasture-fed sheep and goats produce fiber-rich manure that's great for composting, and not unpleasant to handle.

▶ Is space available to begin the composting process at the site?

The animals' owner may appreciate your help in moving the manure out of the animals' living quarters so much that she is willing to set aside a place for the manure to begin rotting. Like other compostables, manure shrinks as it decomposes, so you will have less volume to transport if you can partially compost the manure before you bring it home.

▶ How distasteful do you find the manure-gathering experience?

Try manure-gathering on for size before you commit to collecting large quantities. Some manures are much nastier to work with than others, and it's possible that you can find a better source if you look long enough. If the best word to describe your feelings about gathering manure is "gross," you may be better off using composted manure, which can be purchased in bags or in bulk at garden centers and big box stores, or at landscape supply companies.

Comparing Manures

Animal manures are typically rich in nitrogen, but the amount varies with the animal and what they eat. You can use many different methods to compost manure, but all animal manures should be given time to decompose before sharing with actively growing plants.

Alpaca • Llama • Horse • Donkey

The C/N ratios for these high-fiber manures range between 15/1 and 25/1, but don't hold those modest numbers against them. Slow, cold heaps such as Walking Heaps (see page 140) benefit from the buffet of microcritters and chemical compounds found in these not-so-hot manures. They are also good choices for inclusion in the lower layers of a Comforter Compost bed you plan to put into service right away.

ALPACA, LLAMA

Characteristics: Neat, oblong manure "beans" have little odor and are easy to collect. These animals eat mostly grass and hay, with minimal grain supplements.

Carbon Partners: None generally needed, because this manure is grass-based and low in nitrogen. Can be combined with many other types of material, including weathered leaves.

Handling Tips: These animals often leave their manure in concentrated patches. Rake the material into piles before picking it up with a flat-bladed shovel.

HORSE, DONKEY

Characteristics: Rounded manure nuggets have a fibrous texture and little odor. Often contains viable weed seeds as well as intact corn, wheat or grain seeds.

Carbon Partners: Versatile manure to use in numerous types of composting projects. Often is already mixed with straw or sawdust bedding.

Handling Tips: Use a spade to gather material into piles, and then scoop it up. Rehydrate dry nuggets before composting them.

Chicken • Turkey • Rabbit

With C/N ratios ranging from 4/1 (without bedding) to 10/1 (mixed with trampled, shredded straw), these manures contain so much nitrogen that they give great results when combined with high carbon materials such as cardboard, paper, or sawdust in Comforter Compost, or you can use them to create a Hospital Heap for garden waste that harbors diseases or weed seeds.

POULTRY

Characteristics: Concentrated manure includes both solid and liquid wastes, very high in nitrogen. Initial strong ammonia odor decreases within a few days, or when mixed with other compost materials.

Carbon Partners: Mix with high carbon materials such as sawdust, paper, cardboard, or weathered leaves. Less volume needed compared to other manures. Leaching reduces nitrogen.

Handling Tips: Gather with a spade and transport carefully, because poultry manure is smelly stuff. Can be dried in the sun and stored in airtight containers until needed for compost.

RABBIT

Characteristics: Tidy, rounded pellets have little odor. Rabbits kept in hutches eat alfalfa-based feeds, so their manure is high in nitrogen and other important plant nutrients and contains few weed seeds.

Carbon Partners: Versatile manure to use in composting projects, or can be mixed with grass clippings or another weed-free material to make potting soil–quality compost.

Handling Tips: Manure accumulates beneath hutches, where it can be scooped up with a spade. Easy to transport in plastic bags or bins.

Cow • Goat • Pig • Sheep

The C/N ratios for these manures vary from 10/1 to 15/1, depending on the animals' diets and bedding present in the mix. Composted with little or no additional high-carbon brown material and protected from leaching by rain, these manures rot into rich compost worthy of use as a garden fertilizer. These versatile manures work well in underground composting projects (see chapter 6) and make lovely layers for Grow Heaps created in autumn for planting the following spring.

COW

Characteristics: Circular "pies" with soft centers are often wet and messy. Manure from grain-fed animals frequently has a strong odor. Watch for weed seeds.

Carbon Partners: Combines beautifully with weathered hay or straw. Even without turning, this mixture produces superb compost.

Handling Tips: Cow manure gathered in dry weather is lighter and less messy to handle. Use a digging fork or spade to lift manure "pies" from beneath when collecting them.

GOAT

Characteristics: Mostly nuggets, though texture varies with animals' diets. Goats raised for milk production enjoy clean housing and balanced grass/grain diets.

Carbon Partners: Mix with garden waste to create wonderful compost. Goats eat large amounts of grass or hay, which is passed on to their manure.

Handling Tips: Can be quite smelly when fresh. Pre-compost on-site when possible. Gather in dry weather to reduce weight and aroma.

PIG

Characteristics: Mixture of nuggets and pasty glop, which is promptly trampled. Often very smelly until it is mixed with other materials. Manure from homestead or hobby farm pigs preferred to that of commercial operations.

Carbon Partners: Pigs often are pastured on mud, so the resulting pure manure should be mixed with straw, weathered leaves, corn cobs or stalks, or other high carbon material before composting.

Handling Tips: Gather in dry weather; dry pig manure is easier to handle and less aromatic. Fork into a pile, and pick up with a spade. Transport in an open truck or trailer.

SHEEP

Characteristics: Nuggets that fall apart easily when trampled. Primarily grass or hay residue, but may contain abundant weed seeds, depending on pasture conditions.

Carbon Partners: Can be mixed with straw if no bedding is already present. Sheep manure–straw compost can be used in the garden as soon as it is done, or mixed into other compost projects.

Handling Tips: Sheep barns are cleaned often in winter. Pre-compost on site when possible. Less manure is available in summer, when sheep are put out to pasture.

LESSONS LEARNED FROM MANURE

Good manure has enough advantages to make it worth a certain level of inconvenience. Still, it's the fortunate gardener who has a manure-appropriate truck. Those of us who move the stuff in an enclosed vehicle face manure's dark side long before we enjoy its benefits. Take the smell, for example. Manure's pungent punch is bearable in open air, but it quickly becomes overpowering inside a closed car on a warm day. Leaving the windows open is not enough, as I learned the day I gathered goat manure at a friend's house and then lingered too long, chatting away. When I opened the car door, I was greeted by dozens of flies and other assorted creatures, which buzzed around my head, landed on the manure, then on me, over and over, until cruising speed, open windows, and a few stifled screams blew them away. More flies appeared as I unloaded the manure, and hung around for a few days, reminding me of my misadventure.

Securing Manure

Finding a good source of manure may be easier than you think. Remember to look under every rock, as the saying goes, for local resources before considering distant locations. Here are six easy ways to find local manure stockpiles in need of a good home.

▶ **Yellow pages.** Look in the Yellow Pages under farms, stables, or dairies, and make a few calls. Drive slowly as you pass local stables; many post signs at the gate if they have manure available.

▶ **Advertise.** Place an ad in a local newspaper or community-based marketing publication.

▶ **Freecycling.** Post a message in your town's freecycle group (freecycle.org), an Internet-based exchange hub for all sorts of free things.

▶ **Farmers' markets.** Check around at the farmers' market to find local producers of eggs, cheese, and other products that involve animals.

▶ **Cooperative Extension.** Call your local Cooperative Extension Service office to find out if there is a 4-H livestock club in your area.

▶ **County fairs.** Go to the county fair in the fall, and meet area hobby farmers who raise heritage poultry, rabbits, or fiber-producing animals.

Rare Riches from Rabbits

Traditional rabbit hutches offer would-be manure gatherers the chance to skip scooping in favor of much easier manure-collection methods. Most bunny homes are raised off the ground and have poop-through wire-mesh floors. If there is room, recycle an old child's wagon (a true garage sale treasure) and park it under the hutch. Fill the wagon bed with sawdust, chopped straw or shredded paper to absorb excess moisture, and let the rabbits do the rest. Depending upon how many rabbits reside in the hutch, it may take two weeks or more than a month for the wagon to fill. When you're ready, roll out the wagon, empty it, and get set up for the next batch.

Where sub-hutch clearance is too tight for a wagon, try a plastic tarp, an old shower curtain, a custom-sized Composter's Sling (see page 82), or even

Rabbits are ideal backyard livestock for composters in need of manure. The area beneath the hutch is a constant source of high-nitrogen pellets.

a double layer of corrugated cardboard. Place your tarp or other liner under the hutch, top it with a light layer of absorbent carbon material, and wait. When a 1" (2.5 cm) thick layer of manure has accumulated on the liner, slide it out from beneath the hutch and start over. Be gentle when removing a cardboard–bunny manure "pizza," because cardboard decomposes quickly when combined with nitrogen-rich rabbit manure.

Manure by the Bag

Every large garden center sells some form of composted manure, which can be used in compost projects almost like the fresh version. Bagged manure is sold by volume rather than by weight, and it is best to buy easier-to-carry bags that are somewhat dry and stored in a place protected from rain. Keep in mind that bags of manure often spring leaks as they are moved, so be sure to line your car trunk with a waterproof tarp before loading up with bags of manure. You also may encounter fertilizers made from poultry or other manures that have been composted, formed into pellets, and dried. When working with such products, you will need to add sufficient water to soften the pellets as they are mixed into compost. Store unused pelleted manure in a cool, dry place.

Composting with Manure

Because manure carries such a heavy bacterial load, many composters subject it to a two-phase composting process. First it is combined with an appropriate carbon source and turned often to ensure a good mix

Good Neighbors to Have

For the past five years, I've had a Black Angus bull and his harem of heifers as next-door neighbors. Their job is to eat, sleep, and reproduce. In summer they eat everything in their pasture, and in winter they get a daily ration of feed along with hay. Several times a year, I collect cartloads of manure, combine it with rotting hay, and end up with a batch of dream compost.

Looks (like dreams) can be deceiving, and using this manure has led me to make plenty of experiments with de-weeding methods (see page 223). But the biggest lesson I've learned is this: Always wait at least two weeks after the cows are turned into fresh pasture to gather manure. When allowed to gorge on lush grass, their output is best described as green slime. On a grossness scale of 1 (not gross) to 10 (gag gross), brown slime pies are a 4, but the green

versions get an 8. It is no fun at all to clean level-8 green gunk from your cart, spade, gloves, and shoes.

Why do I bother? It goes against my nature to let a great compost ingredient go to waste, and runoff from the sloping pasture has polluted a human neighbor's fish pond and made the fish inedible. But mostly it's about the cows. These animals would never choose to live inside a barbed-wire enclosure, so I do my part to make things better for them by cleaning up the places where they like to hunker down in bad weather. I'm cow-accountable here: Some of my favorite shoes are leather, I love cheese, and then there's the pleasure of bedtime snacks of Graham crackers and milk. I may not know the individual cows who feed me, but I know these. The only remaining question to be asked has to do with who is serving whom.

and achieve a high level of heat. As soon as it begins to cool down it is recomposted with materials that decompose slowly, such as leaves and garden waste. Precomposting manure in this way quickly causes huge shifts in the microbial makeup of the material, with the majority of problem-causing bacteria being banished in favor of more beneficial life forms.

When using manure to make a Banner Batch, cover the pile to avoid losing nutrients to heavy rains. Nitrogen also can be lost to the air, so turn manure piles quickly and then cover them with a tarp, cloth, or blanket of straw or hay. As with other types of compost, how much turning you do after the materials are thoroughly mixed and moistened is entirely up to you. If you are not concerned about creating enough heat to deactivate weed seeds, it is perfectly

fine to let manure-based compost perk along at its own speed. Only a little change may be apparent for the first few weeks, and then you may be surprised to find your manure compost completely rotted into beautiful black gold.

You also can include manure (preferably partly pre-composted) in many types of composting projects. Horse manure makes wonderful stuff to layer into Comforter Compost beds, and any manure that is weedy or smelly can be buried at the bottom of a Treasure Trough. A few vegetables develop problems when too much composted manure is mixed into the soil in which they are grown. Carrots, for example, often develop forked roots when grown in heavily manured soil, and potatoes may show symptoms of scab — a disease that causes rough patches on the

ANIMAL BY-PRODUCTS FOR COMPOST

Meat, milk, and manure are only the beginning of the many things made from animals. If you need a nitrogen pick-me-up for compost or soil, a bag of feather, fish, or blood meal may do the trick. Also consider plant meals, which are described on page 122. Most garden centers carry some form of powdered animal by-products, but these are the big four.

Feather meal is made from poultry feathers that are cooked, dried, and pulverized. With an analysis of 13-0-0, it compares to blood meal in nitrogen content but degrades more slowly, usually over a period of two to three months. Feather meal makes an excellent addition to finished compost to be used as a pre-plant fertilizer, but it is less powerful than grain meals for heating up compost.

Bone meal contains abundant phosphorous and calcium, but little nitrogen, so it won't do much to heat up compost. It won't give you mad cow disease, either, but its best use is as a fertilizer for bulbs and other plants with large storage roots.

Fish meal brings a bit of balance to the picture with an analysis of 10-6-2. It will release its nutrients in a sudden flush, provided temperatures are above 60°F (16°C) or so, so it's a good addition to warm-weather compost that needs a nutrient boost.

Blood meal carries an N-P-K analysis of 13-0-0, and all that nitrogen can burn plant roots when blood meal is used as fertilizer in warm weather. This is not a problem when you use it in compost, though you may be deterred by hemophobia (fear of blood), or concerns about mad cow disease (there is no evidence that this rare form of encephalitis is actually carried in blood meal, and if it were, scientists say it could not be taken up by plants). The scent of blood meal seems mild to human noses, but it is easily picked up by curious scavenging animals and could serve as a welcome mat for uninvited varmints.

FEATHER MEAL

BONE MEAL

FISH MEAL

BLOOD MEAL

spuds and shortens their storage life. Heavy feeders such as corn and cabbage family crops can usually handle all the composted manure you care to give them.

Harvesting and Storing Composted Manure

Most types of compost are best regarded as soil amendments with a medicinal edge, but well-made composted manure often qualifies as true fertilizer because it is so rich in the big three of plant nutrients, which are nitrogen, phosphorus, and potassium (N-P-K). It also contains numerous trace nutrients along with humic acids and other beneficial by-products of the composting process. Capture these nutrients for future use in your garden by uncovering the pile during a period of dry weather. Then spread the compost on a tarp or cloth until it is only slightly moist. Collect your treasure and store it in moisture-proof containers in a cool place until you need it to mix into potting soil, dig into beds, or use as a topdressing over the roots of your favorite plants. We caution you to not use composted manure to make compost tea, which can revive almost-gone populations of problem-causing bacteria. When applied to food crops, it can create a serious health hazard. If you really like the idea of compost tea (see page 227), use it only on your plants' root zones, or on nonedible ornamental plants.

Hay and Straw

Gardeners who grow grains can harvest homegrown hay or straw, and both materials are easy to obtain should you want to add them to your composting projects. Most feed stores sell at least two types of hay by the bale, and most garden centers stock bales of straw. In spite of appearances, they are very different materials! Hay, which is meant to be eaten by animals, is basically grasses and/or legumes that are cut while lush and green, allowed to dry in the sun, and then tied into rectangular bales ("square" bales in feed store lingo) or rolled into big, round bales (which are usually left in the field because they shed rain). Straw, on the other hand, is the hollow stems and dried leaves that are left standing after wheat, oats, or other grains have been harvested and are a second crop for the grain grower. Hay and straw share a common texture and presentation, but they bring different gifts to a composter's garden.

Hay varies tremendously in its nutrient density and weediness depending on its source, and these factors are reflected in its price. Super-nutritious hay made from dried legume foliage, such as alfalfa or timothy hay, has enough nitrogen to earn C/N ratios between 15/1 and 25/1. Naturally, they are the most costly types of hay to buy, and they typically carry a very light load of weed seeds. Grass hay is much less expensive, and usually has a C/N range between 35/1 and 50/1, but it's often laced with a robust crop of pasture grass and weed seeds. Forage grasses are tough, persistent plants that recover quickly when grazed by animals, so they are not welcome visitors in the garden.

Straw often contains a few grain seeds, but it is seldom extremely weedy. It is also not nearly as nutritious as hay when fed to cows, horses, goats, or other animals, because the grain plants are on the brink of death when the straw is harvested. Some animal

---

WHEN SPOILED IS A GOOD THING

Hay and straw that become moldy cannot be fed to animals, but it makes great mulch. Farmers who produce hay as a cash crop (as well as dairy farms, horse stables, and other places that stockpile hay) often have spoiled hay in addition to the good stuff, and spoiled hay can be quite a bargain. For the cost of the farmer's fuel and time, you may be able to get a quantity of spoiled hay for next to nothing. If you arrange to pick it up yourself, take along a batch of homemade cookies or a similar non-monetary expression of appreciation. Your money may be refused, but everyone likes cookies.

Hay (left) and straw (right) differ in texture and weediness.

owners do use straw for bedding, but most of the straw sold at garden centers is used to set up decorative fall scenes in your neighbors' front yards, or to lightly mulch over soil that has been seeded with grass. Wheat straw (C/N 140/1 to 150/1) is the most widely available type, but you may run into a source of oat, rye, or triticale straw, which are usually richer in nitrogen (C/N 70/1 to 90/1). Oat straw has the further distinction of containing chemicals that inhibit the growth of other plants as they leach into the soil, which is a talent best used by applying oat straw as a weed-deterrent mulch around established plants or in walkways before feeding it to your compost. In any species, straw described as "bright" straw was harvested in perfect weather and baled before it could be moistened by dew or rain.

Handling Hay and Straw

Transporting bales of hay or straw is easy if you have a truck or utility trailer, but be sure to take precautions before hauling a bale in your car. Bits that break off lodge in automotive carpeting, and the only way to get every last one is to pick them out by hand. Avoid this complication by wrapping each bale in a full-size flat bed sheet before lifting it into your car. Be forewarned that with no strings to hold on to, hefting a bale is much easier for two people than for one.

Once you get a bale home, keep it dry until you are ready to start using it. In addition to using the hay or straw itself, you can put the bound bales to work temporarily as enclosures for open compost piles, cold

FUNGI AMONG US

When moldy hay or straw must be gathered with a pitchfork or digging fork, treat it with great respect for the sake of your health. Numerous types of fungi form teeming colonies in damp hay or straw, so work in damp weather if possible to reduce airborne dust and wear a dust mask to avoid breathing fungal spores. For more information, see Can Compost Make You Sick? on page 24.

frames, or erosion barriers on disturbed slopes. Wet hay or straw is much heavier than the dry version, so be sure to move bales where you want them before they get soaked by rain. Whether dry or wet, if you find a bale too heavy to handle, simply break it apart into "leaves" or "books." Baled hay naturally comes apart into flattened layers, which can be pulled off in any thickness you desire.

Moldy or rotted hay is worthless as animal feed (and often free for the taking, as a result), but such bales quickly become fragile after they get wet. It is usually easier to push or roll a weathered bale onto a tarp and then drag it than to attempt to pick it up. You can also use a sturdy piece of cardboard as a "sled" for moving a bale without lifting it.

Fresh hay or straw is bound together with polyester or fiber string or twine, which should be snipped and collected as you take a bale apart. Small pieces of untreated hemp or jute baling twine will decompose in compost, but other baling materials will end up getting a stranglehold on your lawnmower's blade or your tiller's tines if they are allowed to get loose in your yard. When working in spoiled hay, spending a few minutes pulling and clipping the baling twine also makes forking faster because you aren't stopping every few seconds to pull string out of your digging fork.

Seeking Straw and Hunting for Hay

In rural areas, sources of hay and straw may be numerous and nearby, but tracking down a few bales can be like looking for the proverbial needle in the, um, haystack for gardeners in urban and suburban locations. The laws of supply and demand apply here, as well: A bale of straw that sells for $3 at the local feed-and-grain supply store may cost five times as much when sold as festive fall décor at a garden center or craft store! To avoid logging an excess of compost miles in your quest for a few bales, consider all your options for getting the bales that your compost pile needs.

▶ **Farmers' ads.** If a feed store is a distant proposition or a distant memory, depending on where you live, you may find individual farmers selling hay or straw through the classified ads. Look in the most local paper you can find, especially free weekly papers. In the fall, scout your neighborhood for homes with bales used as decoration. Introduce yourself to the occupants and see if they have post-Halloween plans for their straw. If you can save them the task of dragging a wet bale to the curb, they may be happy to have you take it away.

▶ **Hayrides.** If there are Halloween hayrides in your area, ask the operator what happens to the straw once the wagons are parked for the winter. They may be willing to give you a bale or two or sell them to you at a reduced rate, especially if the bales have been exposed to rain.

▶ **Ornamental grasses.** Don't overlook potential straw sources in your own yard. Like their grain-bearing cousins, ornamental grasses produce plenty of straw. It won't be nicely baled, but the dried stems from fountain grass and other ornamental-grass species are great for composting.

Controlling Weeds in Compost

Just as seed-bearing weeds from the garden should be composted separately from weed-free materials, so it is with hay. Nature's penchant for diversity often shows clearly in grass hay, which may be rich with grass seeds, weed seeds, and seeds of pretty meadow wildflowers. Legume hay sometimes bears watching for weed seeds, too, especially if the legumes are clovers, which can be invasive when let loose in a garden. The more you know about where the hay came from, the better you can plan for its best use in your garden.

One way to reduce the weed seed load brought in with hay is to let it spend a season as mulch placed over a sheet-type bottom mulch, such as cardboard or newspapers. All summer, weed seeds will fall prey to crickets and other seed-eating insects, or they may sprout and then shrivel in the sun. By fall, the hay will be no more weedy than grass clippings and can be raked up and layered with shredded leaves and garden waste in a heap, or you can use it when building a Comforter Compost. As long as weathered hay is thoroughly moistened, its stringy texture adds structure to a heap made mostly with leaves, making it easier to turn and improving the heap's ability to retain moisture.

Loose pillows of hay make a good covering for any compost pile, though again it's important to keep weedy ingredients together, which may mean opting for straw rather than hay if your purpose is to improve the eye appeal of a compost pile. Straw is actually quite good at this job, because the shafts and stems "knit" themselves together to form an almost cloth-like cover over a rounded compost pile. If you want to remove the straw covering to turn the heap, try rolling it up like a rug, and then rolling it back on when you're finished.

Make-Your-Own Mushroom Compost

Of course, you always have the option of going straight to compost with an imported bale of hay or straw, and this is where manure often enters the picture. When roughly equal parts of horse manure and straw are mixed together, moistened, and turned every three days, after three weeks you have the

Hollow wheat straw stems help compost hold air. When used as mulch, the straw knits together into a weed-smothering carpet.

THE ARACHNID ADVANTAGE

The old folk song "Turkey in the Straw" notwithstanding, a more apt ditty might tell of spiders in the straw. Unless you suffer from severe arachnophobia, a healthy spider population is among the advantages of incorporating hay or straw into your compost gardening plans. These eight-legged good guys of the garden are particularly fond of straw mulch, which creates plenty of spaces for spider habitat. In exchange for the accommodations, the spiders will provide round-the-clock, chemical-free insect-pest control for your garden. If you're the slightest bit uncomfortable about welcoming spiders into your territory, focus on the kinds of spiders that set up housekeeping in your garden, such as hairy wolf spiders, hairless crab spiders, or the brown garden spiders that scurry about pushing their egg sacs. These and most other garden-spider relatives like daddy longlegs are not poisonous, nor are they interested in moving indoors when the weather cools in the fall.

Other critters to watch for include mice (who love to nest in dry hay or straw) and the snakes that eat them. Be careful when attacking a stockpile of straw in warm weather, when snakes are active.

CREATIVE WAYS WITH STRAW AND HAY

If you're buying baled hay or straw for your compost gardening projects, it makes sense to get your money's worth by using those bales in and around your garden before adding them to your compost. In addition to performing useful roles in your garden, these simple bale-based projects give the straw time to weather a bit before it goes into the compost pile, making it more inclined to decompose once it gets there. Bear in mind that this weathering will gradually reduce the bales' structural integrity, making them harder to lift and move without breaking apart. Set up bale structures as close as possible to where you eventually want to compost straw or hay.

▶ Make a bin out of stacked bales in your garden or right next to it and fill with garden refuse throughout the growing season.

▶ Stretch your gardening space by placing bales on the ground, cut side up, and then plant space-gobbling vine crops in planting pockets in the bales. Dampen the bales, and then use a pick or hand-sized digging fork to make an 8" (20 cm) square hole in the top of each bale. Fill the hole with a 1:1 mixture of soil and compost. Plant pumpkins or winter squash in the pocket and watch them

take off. Keep an eye on moisture throughout the growing season, because these bale-bound planting pockets can dry out quickly. By the time you're picking pumpkins, the bales will be ready to knock down and compost along with the spent vines.

▶ Frame a Nursery Reserve (see page 83) leaf pile with bales to create the perfect winter shelter for hardy container-grown plants.

▶ Insulate compost bins or pens with bales to keep them cooking over the winter, then compost the insulating material in the spring.

perfect substrate for growing button or Portobello mushrooms. Growing these mushrooms is easier said than done (growing fruiting fungi is far different from growing plants), but many gardeners buy bags labeled as mushroom compost.

Commercial mushroom growers create mushroom compost from a manure/straw compost (sometimes combined with organic fertilizers), which has been further "processed" by cultivated, edible fungi for up to two months. The partially composted result

tends to be quite aromatic, at least for a few days. This pungent fragrance, however, does not happen when you allow manure/straw or manure/hay compost to mature naturally. With or without turning, the marriage of manure and either hay or straw produces a beautiful, black compost ideal for mixing into potting soils or planting beds for heavy feeders like spinach or broccoli. Should de-activation of weed seeds be desirable, you can use one of the Banner Batch hot-compost methods described on pages 123 or 136.

Manure-Free Hay or Straw Compost

You can compost hay or straw without manure by combining it with garden debris, kitchen waste, or whatever compost ingredients you have on hand. This is one situation where it is often beneficial to add a portion of soil (say, a tenth of the total mix) because hay and straw can hold too much air for rapid, steady decomposition. Soil works like magic to help pack down compost that's overly fluffy due to a heaping helping of hay or straw.

Paper and Cardboard to Compost

Money may not grow on trees, but paper and cardboard do! A tiny percentage of paper is made from short-lived plants like cotton and kenaf, but most paper and cardboard starts out as wood pulp. With few exceptions, paper and cardboard can be composted just like other tree by-products, such as leaves, sticks, sawdust or wood chips. All are high-carbon (brown) materials, and various paper-based materials often have C/N ratios ranging from 200/1 to over 500/1. When torn or shredded into small pieces, paper and cardboard combine easily with kitchen waste, manure, and other materials that are rich in nitrogen.

Some forms of paper should routinely go into your home compost. Coffee filters, used paper napkins, thin uncoated paper plates, paper towels used in food preparation, and newspapers used to catch spilled potting soil during planting sessions are good examples. These types of soiled paper cannot be recycled, so they would end up in the garbage, and eventually a landfill, if you did not compost them. There is no doubt that composting is an appropriate way to recycle many types of paper, and it can be enlightening and even

Uncoated paper plates are infinitely compostable.

enjoyable to park a chair in the sun, straddle a water-filled bucket, and fill it with torn pieces of junk mail. Do relieve envelopes of their translucent windows, which are basically plastic rather than paper.

Paper to Recycle

With some types of paper, including newspapers, magazines, clean cardboard, or the output from your office shredder, it may be better to recycle them instead of feeding them to your compost. Why? The economics of recycling strongly support a "like begets like" theme; few resources are needed to turn old newsprint into new newsprint, so newspaper recycling is efficient. The opposite is true of glued-together food boxes with moisture-resistant coatings, which are tricky to recycle or to transform into compost.

Composting with paper involves a long cascade of personal decisions, beginning with those that affect how much waste paper you generate on a day-to-day basis. You can take a huge chunk out of your personal waste-paper trail by choosing products with minimal, biodegradable, or easily recycled packaging, for example, a large plastic bottle of soda versus a fridge pack of cans. In both cases, the containers themselves are recyclable, but not the coated cardboard packaging for the cans. Consider your local recycling resources, too. Most recycling centers want as many newspapers as they can get because they are easy to recycle (see What Happens to Recycled Paper, at right), but they often reject coated boxes used to package frozen pizzas and other frozen foods. Such materials will eventually decompose when torn up and mixed into compost, though they may leave behind a trail of residual chemicals. When it comes to paper, the best way to reduce your overall personal environmental liability is to think green every chance you get, which means consuming less paper in all of its incarnations.

Inks, Dyes, and Coatings

The age of lead-based ink is over, and today much printing is done with soy-based inks. Synthetic dyes and plastic coatings often *are* of chemical origin. Laser printers (and photocopiers) use toner rather than ink, and toner contains plastics or waxes that bind to the paper as the page is printed. The residual effects of toner in soil are unknown, and the same is true of the array of chemicals that fall into the category known in the paper industry as "wet strength additives," which are plastics and waxes that keep paper from softening when exposed to moisture. We do know that soil that is active with plenty of fungi and bacteria often does an amazing job of breaking down some man-made chemicals. Still, if you want to grow the purest possible food crops, it is best to avoid putting things into the soil that are laced with chemicals. Bleached paper and wax or plastic-enhanced toners fall into the unnatural category, so you may opt to use compost made with plasti-paper in soil used to grow ornamental plants rather than those you intend to eat.

Glossy magazine pages often get their sheen from clay-based materials, which are biodegradable and usually safe to use in compost. But like toner-printed paper, glossy papers are far from organic or natural, so most people recycle magazines rather than composting them.

Dealing with a Sticky Situation

Most glues and other paper adhesives are water soluble, but remember that dissolving is not the same as disappearing. Like heavily inked or coated paper, paper products that carry a heavy load of glue are best fed to compost in small doses, if at all. When preparing glue-bearing paper to use in compost or as bedding in a vermicompost bin, it can help to soak the paper in a bucket of water for a few minutes first. Then pour off the water in an area not used to grow plants, such as a paved driveway.

What Happens to Recycled Paper?

There is no doubt that you've done the right thing by sending most of your excess paper to the recycling center, but what happens to it then? With newspapers, the recycling process is pretty simple: The paper gets chopped and mixed with water, rinsed, and bleached, and then pressed into new paper. The contents of the mixed-paper bin require more elaborate processing including more chopping, more bleaching, and spinning or filtering to remove unusable chemicals and fibers. So, if you want to do your bit to reduce energy consumption, water pollution, and conserve air quality, you can start by finding ways to compost paper that would otherwise end up in the mixed-paper bin. Old envelopes and even phone books disappear quickly when torn into pieces and combined with kitchen waste, or you can use paper as the base layer in Comforter Compost projects.

Talking the Talk, Walking the Walk

Like most green thinkers, I have a pet environmental issue: forest conservation. A few years ago, I realized I was talking the talk more than I was walking the walk, so I set myself on a straighter course toward tree conservation. For starters, I began putting catalogs, elaborate solicitation packages, and unwanted magazines that arrived in my mailbox into a special "pre-recycling" box.

When the stack got heavy, I paid my underemployed teenage daughter $5 an hour to call the toll-free numbers and ask to be removed from each company's mailing list. The volume of incoming unwanted paper mail shrank like magic. My kid, in turn, got to practice phone-courtesy skills, learning that when you ask nicely, you usually get what you want. I have since found that the drill needs to be repeated every few months, as my name and address get picked up by new vendors selling everything from shoes to mutual funds. Next came reducing random packaging, which meant buying fewer things by mail order, checking packaged goods, from cereal boxes to bathroom tissue, for recycled content, and remembering to take cloth bags with me when I went shopping. Beyond getting out of the "paper or plastic" loop, the cloth shopping bags hold so much stuff that they make toting groceries from car to kitchen fast and easy, and most stores will give you a dime or two as "bag credits" if you remember to ask.

The few tradeoffs I've made have been pretty painless. My office paper with a high recycled content isn't quite as bright white as what I used to buy, cloth napkins and handkerchiefs add a little bulk to my laundry loads, and shifting to paperless billing means you can't ignore messages that appear in your computer's inbox. And the rewards? They meet me face to face each time I walk through leafy woods, surrounded by chattering birds and oak trees that began bearing acorns long before I was born.

Cover Your Paper Trail

In some areas, paper is a hot composting commodity because other carbon sources are in short supply. Cold, arid climates, for example, support few leaf-producing trees, and paper makes a fine stand-in for leaves when mixed with nitrogen-rich kitchen wastes. Paper and cardboard also make excellent bedding for vermicompost bins, provided they are thoroughly dampened first (see Composting Cardboard on page 108).

If you use a barrel or other enclosed composter, it's a good idea to keep a stash of dry paper on hand for times when conditions get a little too soupy in your composter. Paper absorbs water well, so mixing dry paper into overly wet compost is a fast and easy way to put the skids on composting conditions that are slipping into slime. In addition, the flaky flatness of paper can be used to good advantage when starting a Comforter Compost in a grassy area, or when you want to deter tree roots intent on colonizing a

Damp newspapers and veggie trimmings refresh living conditions in a small vermicompost bin.

CARDBOARD COMPOST SANDWICH

When turning a weedy spot into gardening space, start small and use labor-saving compost garden methods to plan ahead for future expansion. Before you start digging, place several pieces of cardboard alongside the site and pile the weeds on it as you dig them out. When the cardboard is covered, add a second layer of cardboard followed by more weeds. After a few days of warm weather, when the weeds are nicely shriveled, dampen your cardboard compost sandwich, and cover it with grass clippings, shredded leaves, or another attractive mulch. This version of Comforter Compost (see page 154) will host beetles, crickets, night crawlers and other beneficial critters as it rots. When you're ready to expand your bed, simply chop and mix the cardboard compost sandwich into the soil.

finished batch of compost set in a shady spot to cure. The paper works as a barrier between the ground and the compost, smothering existing vegetation or slowing down the invasion of tree roots.

When using torn or shredded paper in an open or semi-enclosed heap, keep in mind that bits of paper look pretty trashy, so this type of mix is best hidden from view. Paper likes to take flight, too, so it's important to cover a paper-amended heap with materials that are both heavy and damp. You can prevent eyesore and windblown litter issues by using paper primarily in enclosed heaps or by covering open paper-enriched heaps with a tarp or piece of cloth weighed down with rocks or buried along its edges.

Composting Cardboard

Composting is the best thing to do with cardboard that has become wet or dirty, for example, the remnants of a cardboard box you filled with compost and used to grow plants, or cardboard you used as a light-blocking mulch (covered with straw, grass clippings, or another organic material) to control weeds in your garden pathways. If you keep a worm bin, you also may want to use a corrugated cardboard box as bedding. Despite cardboard's acidic pH and high carbon content (its C/N ratio is 560/1), earthworms use bits of corrugated cardboard as both food and shelter. They often squirm into the little channels in corrugated cardboard for a bit of privacy, while other worms gather beneath torn pieces to socialize.

To prepare a cardboard box for your worm bin or compost pile, pull out any metal staples with a screwdriver and pliers. If you skip this step, sooner or later you will find the staples, sharp and rusty, when you're digging in your garden or worse yet, strolling around barefoot. Strip off tape that comes off easily, because most packing tapes are plastic and will persist almost forever in your soil if they don't first get caught up in your tools. Next, either tear the box into large pieces or set it out in the rain while still whole. Place dry pieces in a wheelbarrow or other large basin filled with a few inches of water, and let the cardboard soak for ten minutes or so. Most of the remaining tape or stickers will float off easily, and wet cardboard is easy to tear into hand-sized pieces. The cardboard is now ready to be added to any type of compost, including vermicompost bins. Pour the soaking water into the ground away from sensitive or edible plants, because it probably contains a buffet of chemicals from dissolved glue. Although not particularly toxic, dissolved cardboard glue is not at all organic, and may contain enough boron (a plant trace-mineral nutrient) to burn the roots of some types of plants. When glue residue is transformed via compost, it is broken down by fungi and other microorganisms.

What About Waxed Boxes?

The cardboard boxes covered with a waxy coating that often are used to ship perishable produce are not good candidates for composting, and they are not accepted by most recycling centers. On the plus side, they make great storage containers for cured compost, or you can cut them to appropriate sizes to fit into the trunk of your car, and use (and reuse) them as transport containers for materials you can't resist bringing home to your heap. For example, your car won't start smelling like a barn if you gather stable manure in garbage bags and set the filled bags inside waxed boxes.

Using Paper-Based Compost

Like compost made from other tree by-products, paper-based compost may have an acidic pH, depending on the materials with which it is mixed. This is not a problem in itself, and several university-based studies have found that compost made from paper pulp makes a good alternative to peat moss (which is also acidic) when used in potting mixes. Paper-based compost has the potential to be weed free as well, though you must scrupulously avoid introducing seed-bearing materials to get seed-free results. Vermicompost made primarily from paper and kitchen scraps is often rich in growth-enhancing humic acids, which make it especially valuable as a topdressing or soil amendment for container-grown plants.

WHAT CAN YOU GROW IN A BOX?

The large, extra-sturdy boxes used to package televisions and other appliances can do a short tour of duty as enclosures for Comforter Compost (see page 154), or you can use them as Grow Heaps for potatoes or other garden crops. Simply place the box where you want to smother weeds or improve the soil, fold in the top flaps and fold out the flaps on the box's bottom, and then fill it with mixed or layered compostable materials. As you fill it, you can tuck in green potatoes gathered from your garden or container-grown plants that need protection from the ravages of winter. If you like, it's easy to improve the appearance of the box by covering it with a piece of burlap or other cloth. When the box softens and begins to collapse, tear it up and add the pieces to any working compost heap, or feed them to an enclosed composter.

Wood Chips and Sawdust

For decades, many gardeners have avoided using wood chips and sawdust in their gardens because of the belief that they deplete the soil's supply of nitrogen. This is partially true. When undecomposed wood particles are mixed into soil, they tie up nitrogen that would otherwise be available to plants. But when wood chips or sawdust are used as mulch or combined with high-nitrogen materials, such as grass clippings, in compost, they pose no threat to nitrogen-hungry plants. Indeed, as long as you wait until wood chips or sawdust have decomposed to the point where they are dark brown or black in color before mixing them into soil, they are among the best materials you can use to improve your soil's texture. In addition, the cellulose fibers in composted wood chips or sawdust often persist in the soil for several seasons as late-stage active organic matter, prolonging the tenancy of microorganisms that help prevent outbreaks of soil-borne diseases.

There is no argument that the transition from fresh tree tidbit to stable organic matter takes time. The

Know your source. Cabinet shops use untreated woods, so they are a good source of compost-worthy sawdust and wood shavings.

C/N ratio range for wood chips or sawdust is often as high as 500/1, and the situation is further aggravated by the presence of natural compounds that help wood resist rotting, which is a basic survival strategy trees use to live long, healthy lives. Some of these natural chemicals are leached away when woody materials are exposed to soaking rains, but the next stage of decomposition, which is presided over by talented types of fungi, is best measured in months or even years. You can put time on your side by planning a series of jobs for wood chips or sawdust. In their first season, you might use them either as mulch beneath trees or shrubs, or for paving garden pathways. After a year of weathering, wood chips or sawdust should be ready to use in any type of composting project, particularly those that stretch on for several months. By the time the composted wood nuggets become intermingled with soil, they have lost their power as nitrogen magnets, and instead become garden-friendly reservoirs of water, air, and microbial life.

Free for the Taking

Depending on where you live, both of these materials may be in good supply. Tree trimming crews generate

---

DON'T COMPOST THIS WOOD

For years, gardeners have been told to avoid using chips or sawdust from cedar, redwood, or walnut trees, because substances that leach from these types of wood were thought to be toxic to plants. As it turns out, walnut is the only natural wood known to inhibit the growth of other plants, including most vegetables except for beans, grains, and onions. Walnut's secret weapon, juglone, degrades after a year of composting, but it's best to compost walnut sawdust or chips separately, at least 20 feet from your garden. Never compost any type of treated wood, which carries a heavy load of chemical contaminants.

---

load after load of wood chips in urban and suburban areas, while sawmills and woodworking shops are usually good sources of sawdust. Do be choosy when it comes to sawdust, and bypass any supply that may contain dust or shavings from treated wood, for example, sawdust from new home construction. The chemicals used to make wood resistant to moisture and termites have changed in recent years, but they are still not worthy of good garden soil.

Handling Wood Chips

Obtaining a pile of wood chips is easy, especially following storms, when fallen trees and limbs must be cleaned up in a hurry. Listen for the sound of chain saws, and you will soon find a tree-trimming crew who will much prefer dumping a load of wood chips nearby to hauling it to a disposal site. Some tree-service companies are even set up to take phone and email requests for free loads of wood chips, dumped wherever you want them.

In summer, such a load may include enough green leaves to earn it a C/N ratio in the 200/1 range, but in winter it will be mostly wood and bark (C/N 500/1). Expect the pieces to be far from uniform in size, which means they will decompose at different rates. The type of wood will affect how quickly the chips rot, too, because soft wood such as pine and poplar rots faster than oak, hickory, and other hardwoods. Chips of dense hardwood that are more than ½" (1.3 cm) thick and 2" (5.1 cm) across are not likely to rot for four or five years, compared to only a year or two for smaller chunks the size of a marble, or matchbook-size pieces of pine. If you like, you can pick through the pile by hand to remove oversized pieces, dry them in the sun, and store them for future use as firewood. Even if you don't burn wood yourself, anyone who has a woodstove or outdoor fireplace will be happy to have a bag of dry wood chips.

Sometimes tree maintenance crews leave piles of chips along roadsides, in vacant lots, or in other places where you may feel comfortable helping yourself. Check with nearby property owners before making plans to claim the chips as your own. Some towns maintain wood-chip piles, or they may mix wood chips with leaves and other yard waste. Be wary of piles of chips that have been sitting on the ground for more than a few weeks, as they may have been discovered by foraging termites. Rotting piles of wood chips also attract ants in search of dry nesting sites,

No-Work Sweet Corn

Twenty-odd years ago, I heard an organic farmer from Tennessee talking about no-work corn. In the fall, he tilled his plot, covered it with a 5" (12.7 cm) thick layer of "broiler litter," which translates as chicken doo mixed with sawdust, and let it weather over the winter. In spring, he poked sweet-corn seeds into the weathered sawdust crust, and they sprouted and grew like crazy in the fertile, weed-free bed.

My gardening partner, Brice, had a funky old farm truck and he knew a chicken farmer, so we decided to try it. Getting the litter was easy enough, thanks to the farmer's front-end loader, and we lucked into a cool, breezy autumn day for spreading our riches over the next year's corn patch. Then a warm front came through, complete with soaking rain. Overnight, the stench of the manure settled over the yard like an evil cloud, and it stayed. Brice and his wife, Melanie, learned to take deep breaths before dashing from their cars into the house. The relative values of sweet corn and breathable air became topics of lively debate in their household, but the damage was done and there was nothing to do but wait.

Two weeks passed before the odor became bearable, and we had almost forgotten about it by spring, when we found that the sawdust litter had, indeed, mellowed into a chocolate brown seedbed perfect for corn. Yes, the project was a success, but not one I plan to repeat in this lifetime. Noses can only take so much abuse. I later learned that "stable litter," which is sawdust mixed with horse manure, is much less aromatic, and it's become one of my favorite additions to my composting projects.

and it's easy to get the two insects confused. Termites have a straight abdomen, with no waist at all, while ants always have a thin waist. Many ants will bite you when alarmed, but termites only bite into wood.

Good planning is needed for an effective wood-chip rescue. Wood chips are hard to pick up with a digging fork or spade, so they can be wily things to handle. The easiest way to collect them is to place a tarp at the edge of the pile, and then use a hoe to chop and scrape the chips onto the tarp. You can then carry them in a bundle, or transfer them to boxes or bins for the ride home. Keep in mind that dry wood chips are lighter and less aromatic than wet ones, and that the chips' sharp edges will turn even heavy-duty garbage bags into confetti.

Wood chips darken as they decompose, and make a long-lasting mulch for perennial beds.

Best Uses for Chips

Leaving a pile of wood chips to weather for a while is a simple, passive way to smother unwanted weeds or grasses, or you can site a pile where it will channel rainwater toward or away from various parts of your landscape. Should you decide to use the chips as mulch, remember that they may float around a bit when lifted by flooding rains, so you may need some kind of edging surrounding the mulch. Also be watchful when using wood chips from weathered piles as mulch, because they may contain slugs, earwigs, and other plant-eating critters. If you discover this problem after you've spread the mulch, encircling the trunks of trees and shrubs with band-type sticky traps will ensnare pests that attempt to cross the traps.

Wood chips used as paving for garden paths usually stay put because they are pressed into the ground by repeated footfalls. Many vegetable gardeners use wood chips to cover sheet mulches of paper or cardboard, which provides a clean surface for walking, or for rambling pumpkins and other vining crops.

Working with Sawdust

Compared to wood chips, sawdust has much more exposed surface area, so it readily absorbs water and

Coarse sawdust makes a foot-friendly paving material for permanent garden pathways.

is easily infiltrated by numerous types of fungi. These factors add up to faster decomposition compared to wood chips. Sawdust is also easy to move with a shovel, light in weight (as long as it is dry), and looks lovely when used as mulch over paper, cardboard, or bare ground. Fresh sawdust contains no weed seeds. After only one season of surface weathering, sawdust can be mixed into the soil or gathered up and used to add bulk and carbon to compost projects. Sawmills, cabinetmaking shops, and hobby woodworkers are all good sources of sawdust.

Ready-Made Compost Blend

Because sawdust is absorbent, inexpensive, and easy to handle, it is a popular bedding material for horses, poultry, cattle, and other types of livestock. When a stable or poultry house offers manure, it is often already mixed with sawdust, which has absorbed the animals' urine along with the trampled solid waste. So, for a short time anyway, the sawdust is quite saturated with nitrogen, which quickly causes it to darken in color. When piled up soon after it is infused with animal waste, sawdust will heat up quickly, usually in a matter of days, and cool down just as fast. At this

---

GLOBAL WARMING: A CATTLE COMPOST CONNECTION

When it comes to creating the big three of greenhouse gases — carbon dioxide, methane, and nitrous oxide — cattle are major producers. Some of those gases are given off as cows digest what they eat, and more are released as manure decomposes. Manure that is mixed with other materials and composted produces fewer of these gases, and less nitrogen is lost when the manure is composted with wood chips compared to straw. A research study from Agriculture and Agri-Food Canada showed that cow manure–wood chip compost retained 80 percent more nitrogen than cow manure composted with straw.

point you could go ahead and mix the partially rotted sawdust into your soil, but what's your hurry? The cellulose fibers in the sawdust will persist for a couple of years no matter what you do, so you have plenty of time to put them to good use keeping Comforter Compost nicely aerated, attending to drainage problems in an otherwise great gardening site by installing a Treasure Trough, or finding other ways to make use of sawdust's ability to hold on to both water and air. Until the last crumbs of sawdust retire to become humus, they support aerobic microbial communities, and the more of those you have in your compost, the better. Combining sawdust with high-protein meals (see page 122) can help it rot faster and produce a finished compost that's black, fluffy, and somewhat rich in plant nutrients.

Using Composted Wood Chips and Sawdust

Even when fully composted, wood chips retain their rough character. This is not necessarily a bad thing, and it may be a very good thing if you garden in clay soil. Introducing chunky composted wood chips can improve the drainage of clay soil, and this benefit can play out over several seasons. To be on the safe side, be sure to provide plants with ample nitrogen by using a good organic fertilizer (remember that a high first number in a fertilizer's analysis, such as 6-4-4, means it has abundant nitrogen) in appropriate amounts for the crop, and add composted wood chips in small helpings rather than all at once.

When combined with manure or another high-nitrogen material, such as high-protein meals (see page 122), sawdust matures into black gold with a rich, velvety texture. It makes beautiful mulch for high-visibility flower beds and is equally suited to function as a splash-guard between soil and leafy greens. As long as it contains few (if any) weed seeds, composted sawdust can be used in place of vermiculite in potting soil mixtures, or you can use it as mulch for container-grown plants.

Purchasing Compost

Because composting depends on microorganisms to transform raw materials into finished compost, it can be compared to making sourdough bread. The depth of flavor in sourdough bread comes from using a "starter" culture of yeast that is kept growing in a nutritious substrate of powdered grain (flour). The yeast community takes off like a rocket when given a more abundant food supply (the fresh batch of dough). A similar chain of events takes place when you add finished compost to a fledgling compost project. Presented with a suitable food supply, the microorganisms in the compost colonize the new batch. By adding finished compost to young composting projects, you can rest assured that waves of hardworking fungi and bacteria are present and ready to do their jobs.

If you have been composting for a while, you can simply use compost starter taken from your finished batches to inoculate new projects with helpful microorganisms. New composters who have no "mother" heaps from which to borrow starter cultures can simply buy a bag or two of compost and use the

---

BAG-HANDLING TIPS

Less mess. Prevent a mess in your car by spreading an old shower curtain or other water-resistant liner in your trunk or hatch before buying bags of compost or other soil amendments.

Take it easy. If you will be loading the bags, choose smaller bags to avoid injuring your back. Take along a pair of work gloves to keep your hands clean.

Neat and tidy. Open the bags by cutting across the top. Fold down the tops of partially used bags and secure them with a clothespin to keep out rain.

Reuse. Save empty bags, and use them to store future batches of finished compost or potting soil that you make.

of farm-animal manures, and sometimes from growing mushrooms.

Shopping for Compost

In terms of compost miles, buying compost is often less costly than you may think. Because compost is heavy, and therefore expensive to ship, both the bags and small mountains of compost found at garden centers are often produced close to home, usually within 50 miles (80.5 km) from where they are sold. Check the labels on bags, and you will probably find out where the product was made. Choose local compost whenever you can.

Compost Industry Standards

You will likely find a number of products that fall into the broad category of soil amendments, which include compost, humus, composted manure, and various soil conditioners and planting mixes (see "What's in the Bag?" on page 116). Laws define only general guidelines for labeling over-the-counter soil amendments (unless they contain enough nutrients

purchased compost to inoculate new heaps with ready-to-work microbial decomposers. In addition, situations often arise in which your need for compost far exceeds your supply, such as when you are radically expanding your growing space or are planting a hedge of shrubs. There is no shame in not having enough homemade compost to be generous as you prepare soil to support an ever-expanding collection of vegetable and flower beds. Instead, head to the garden center and buy the compost you need in bags or in bulk. Compost is also often available from municipal leaf piles, or you may find local farmers who make more compost than they can use from various types

When shopping for bagged compost, check labels to find good products manufactured in your area.

TRY BEFORE YOU BUY

The county where I live allows residents to buy compost at its municipal compost facility for a nominal fee per five-gallon bucketful. This gave me a chance to try out a few containers of its product before I invested in the price of 3 cubic yards (2.29 cubic meters) of compost (the delivery was the expensive part of the transaction). I was happy with the quality of the compost I purchased by the bucket. I could see that it was thoroughly finished (few identifiable uncomposted components), the texture and particle size were consistent, and it had no noticeable odor beyond a mild, earthy smell. Like almost every municipal compost I've ever seen, it did contain visible contaminants — mostly plastic — that had been reduced to thumbnail size by the grinding and screening processes.

As for the big pile I had delivered to my front yard and moved to the backyard one wheelbarrow at a time, I have some nagging questions. Until I used it, my yard was totally free of jimsonweed, but not anymore! It cannot be pure coincidence that jimsonweed now grows only in the places in my lawn and flower gardens where I used that compost. Lesson learned: I now keep closer tabs on the ingredients that go into the compost I make for my vegetables and fruits and take fewer chances with the county's compost.

to qualify as fertilizers), and producers tend to focus more on attractive packaging than promoting what's inside the bag. As industries go, the soil-amendment business is still young, but it's beginning to find its feet. Challenged by the same diversity that's found in nature (leaf mold and rotted turkey manure have little in common), producers struggle to clarify products and standards, and they're making progress. A national association of producers and equipment manufacturers, the Mulch & Soil Council (www. mulchandsoilcouncil.org) offers definitions for terms like "compost" and "planting mix," while the U. S. Composting Council, an international, nonprofit alliance of scientists, compost producers, and equipment manufacturers (www.compostingcouncil.org) created a voluntary quality-control program.

Still, you are pretty much on your own when it comes to trying various products. To find a favorite, buy an assortment of sample bags, bring them home, and put them to work. You may find that a bag labeled "humus" works better for you than one touted as compost. Packaged composted manure typically costs a little more than other types, but for your money, you'll get nitrogen in addition to a healthy band of composting microorganisms.

Mushroom compost tends to be quite aromatic if it is very fresh or has been allowed to get wet, but you can often buy it weathered and odorless. Planting mixes often include plenty of gritty, black soil along with some compost. Check out what's cheap and local, and proceed from there.

What's in the Bag?

The soil amendment definitions used by the Mulch and Soil Council include many of the words and phrases listed below. Compost or composted manure is often the best source of compost-energizing microorganisms, but in some cases you may want the additional weight and grittiness that's typical of soil conditioners and planting mixes.

▶ **Compost** is decomposed organic matter that has been mixed and piled to promote natural decay, while minimizing pathogens, weed seeds, and odors.

▶ **Composted manure** is processed or composted animal manure combined with organic bedding or other materials needed to maintain sanitary conditions and conserve plant-food elements.

▶ **Planting mix** is a blended material suitable for growing indoor or outdoor plants, and is made primarily from natural soils, humus, compost, and/or manure. It may include fertilizers, pesticides, and/or additives intended as soil conditioners, such as peat moss or charcoal.

▶ **Potting soil** is a material suitable for growing potted plants. It is made primarily from natural materials, such as bark, peat, humus, compost, and/or manure, and may also include fertilizers, pesticides, and/or additives such as perlite, vermiculite, or charcoal.

▶ **Soil conditioner** is derived primarily from the decomposition of animal or vegetable matter. It should resemble finished compost, or humus.

▶ **Topsoil** is rich soil that is high in organic matter. It is made chiefly from natural materials, such as soils, peat, humus, compost, and/or manure.

Using Public Compost

Many towns and cities maintain compost facilities where leaves, chipped Christmas trees, and other yard wastes are piled, turned as time and weather permit, and then offered free or cheaply to local residents. When government agencies make compost, their primary goal is to keep organic matter out of the waste stream, but producing a superior soil amendment may or may not be on their list of priorities. The quality of municipal compost therefore varies widely between mighty and mediocre. It's possible to luck into some fine stuff, but you may also get a few things you don't want, like noxious weeds, legions of slugs, or the odd plastic bag or other non-biodegradable item.

Proceed with caution, however. We've seen the sad remains of a new gardener's ambitious flower planting project, in which five flats of bedding plants were consumed in three days by "zillions" of slugs that hatched from the muni-compost she spent hours digging into the beds. Choose and use municipal

compost carefully, and consider setting it aside to cure while you experiment with it in a small spot. If you detect a problem, re-composting the compost will usually get it under control. Take the time to test each new batch, because the contents of muni-compost can vary considerably from one load to the next.

The Best There Is

Finding an organic dairy, poultry, or egg farm that makes compost on the side is not as easy as picking up a few bags of compost at a discount store, but discovering one is worth the search. Certification guidelines specify that animals used to produce organic milk, eggs, or meat must be fed organic food, so they may eat even better than you or I do! Just like conventional farms, organic farms that house numerous animals often produce more manure than they need, so they combine their excess with other materials, such as locally produced yard waste to make compost, and sell it for a small profit.

A few such farms produce labeled, bagged compost, but most small operations simply maintain large piles of cured compost, which should be kept covered with a tarp or sheet of plastic. Shop carefully and maintain your own quality control standards by checking batches for weed seeds or unwanted critters, and rejoice if you find a source that is close by, values excellence, and is staffed by dedicated, likeable people. When it comes to purchased compost, local organic-farm-based compost is often the best there is.

Compost Activators

As a compost gardener, you want every project you create to steadily degrade in the best possible way. There are many factors to consider. The speed of decomposition will be determined primarily by the materials themselves. Moisture and air temperatures also will play important roles, as will the presence, or absence, of fungi, bacteria, and larger organisms whose sole life missions are to create compost. The use of compost activators is based on the assumption that something is missing, and that the lack of this essential ingredient is holding up the composting process. Getting your time and money's worth from activators is a matter of identifying the problem and choosing the right activator for the job.

Activators should always address a specific problem, assuming that there is a problem. If your compost is stalled at a point in its cycle when it should be showing clear signs of decomposition, take a careful look at where the process may have gone astray, keeping in mind that patience and moisture monitoring will cure most general composting problems. It's easy to be patient if you do your best to combine materials in ways that make the most of their characteristics and parallel your gardening goals. Then you can simply support the composting process with thoughtful infusions of water and air.

When Activators Are Called For

This said, you may encounter special situations in which the use of a compost activator is worthwhile. Compost activators can supply microorganisms, or nitrogen, or they can include substances that enhance a heap's ability to retain water. In the interest of clear thinking, we have divided activators into four general categories, which are described in detail below. Of these four categories — microbial, mineral, biodynamic, and nutritional — we think that nutritional activators based on high-protein plant meals, such as alfalfa, corn, and soybean meal, are the most useful. Why? They are a reliable and effective way to transform a cold heap into a hot one. Step-by-step instructions for making this little miracle happen are outlined on page 123.

Types of Activators

Whether you buy activators or make them yourself, play it smart by tailoring your choices to what your compost project needs. Then use the same "close to home" approach with activators that you use in other aspects of compost gardening by looking first at locally available resources.

▶ **Microbial activators.** A sterile heap, completely bereft of fungi and bacteria, would never rot. However, a sterile heap is an impossible phenomenon given the load of microorganisms present in only 1 cubic inch (2.5 cubic cm) of outdoor air, plus there are all those little hitchhikers that ride in on leaves, plants, and other materials. Even the slowest of heaps includes colonies of adapted microbes, but why not have more? This is the idea behind microbial compost activators, which are typically dry powders that contain compost-ready fungi and bacteria.

It can be argued that using microbial activators is like selling ice to the good people of Iceland. Why would they need more ice? And if they did need ice, why not use some of their own? You probably already possess the best microbial activator you can use, which is homemade compost. Your own compost (especially almost-finished compost) contains an overflowing buffet of microorganisms that have proliferated in the unique setting of your own yard. They have a proven ability to work your one-of-a-kind compostable waste stream. They haven't been imprisoned in a package, so they are ready for action. Need we say more? If you're starting your first composting project and don't want to wait for a resident population of decomposers to evolve on its own, buy a bag or two of compost (see page 114) to invigorate your homemade compost's microbial life. All future batches can be laced with a few shovelsful borrowed or saved from your more advanced composting projects.

▶ **Mineral activators.** Plants need minerals as do people. Unfortunately, most soil-borne minerals are rock particles that dissolve very, very slowly, and compost, being mostly organic matter, is pretty lean when it comes to minerals. Using mineral-based compost activators that contain rock powders or ground seashells will infuse compost with calcium and other minerals, which can lead to a slight increase in the long-term nutritional value of your compost.

SULFUR

CRUSHED OYSTER SHELL

GARDEN LIME

ROCK PHOSPHATE

GYPSUM

Mineral activators contribute nutrients and much-needed minerals to small amounts of compost.

On the other hand, mineral activators will not trigger a heating response in a cold compost pile, and compost activators that contain lime (intended to offset the natural acidity of decomposing leaves) may alter the pH in ways that handicap the ability of leaf-decomposing fungi and bacteria to do their jobs. Adding minerals to uncomposted material to prevent an "off" pH or other mineral issue in finished compost is putting the cart before the horse.

Mineral fertilizers certainly have their place in a compost garden, but not in the compost itself. Their best place is in the soil, where they can leach slowly, over a period of years, and meanwhile bind closely with their brethren, the mineral (rock) particles that make up 90 percent or more of any soil sample you might scoop up in your hand. If you have naturally acidic soil, you will need to learn to use lime appropriately and effectively, and gardeners with alkaline soil will require similar skills with sulfur. Other naturally occurring powdered minerals including gypsum, granite dust, or rock phosphate can enhance soil

fertility, too, and there is no finer time to apply them than when you are working a fresh infusion of compost into your soil. We think that mineral compost activators can make excellent soil amendments, but their value as compost activators just leaves us scratching our heads.

▶ **Biodynamic activators.** In 1924, an Austrian scientist named Rudolf Steiner founded a school of thought known as biodynamic farming. In addition to making full use of sound, organic soil-building methods, biodynamic practices incorporate techniques intended to tap in to esoteric energies, or the spiritual realm. Understanding biodynamics, therefore, requires thinking outside the box, particularly when it comes to composting, which is at the foundation of biodynamic gardening. In much the same manner as homeopathic medicines are used to enhance human health, biodynamic practitioners use special preparations that are believed to bring vitality and balance to compost. These preparations, made from six key plant-based ingredients

RABBIT FEED

DOG FOOD

CHICKEN CRUMBLES

Nutritional activators heat up compost rapidly.

— yarrow, chamomile blossoms, stinging nettle plants, oak bark, dandelion flowers, and valerian flowers — are added to working compost at exacting times and in precise locations in the heap.

We don't claim to be biodynamic experts. In all honesty, we have not tried the formulas ourselves, mostly because it's an all-or-nothing proposition to do it right. So, we would be on shaky ground if we said they were not of value. Admittedly, the additives are weird, and when it comes to making compost, weirdness is optional.

Much less weird, yet equally fascinating, are the biointensive methods developed by the modern American food gardening researcher and author John Jeavons and his colleagues, which blend the best of biodynamic with intensive gardening practices (see the reading list on page 293). Bottom line? Unless

you are making and selling compost labeled as biodynamic, think carefully before spending your money on a biodynamic activator.

▶ **Nutritional activators.** The most common reason for compost to stay cold is that it does not contain enough bioactive nitrogen. Adding nitrogen lowers the C/N ratio, which should make the heap heat up, right? Not necessarily. Adding pure nitrogen in the form of ammonium nitrate (a cheap, widely available nitrogen fertilizer) will burn or pickle many life forms that live in the heap, but it will barely lift the mercury in a thermometer buried in the heap. The story is different if you add organic nitrogen sources that degrade in a burst of transformative energy when mixed with moist compost. High-nitrogen, plant-based meals or pellets made from alfalfa, canola, corn, cottonseed, and soybean waste make dependable acti-vators when you want a heap to cook.

The availability of these materials at feed stores varies from region to region; naturally, they are most abundant in the areas in which they are produced. For example, alfalfa meal or pellets are easy to find in the Northeast, the Upper Midwest is canola meal coun-try, and every farm supply store in the South is well stocked with cottonseed meal. The urban/suburban alternative is to use cheap dry dog food (mostly corn meal) or other animal feeds (see Feed Store Specials, on page 122).

We think that being able to fire up a cold heap is a skill worth practicing, because compost made with diseased or weed-seed-bearing plants is unacceptable for most uses until it is subjected to high tempera-tures, which can happen during the composting cycle with the help of high-protein meals. Various ways to do this are detailed in the following pages.

Reasons to Get Hot

Creating a hot compost heap requires extra work. You will likely need materials not found in your yard, and you will need to pay close attention to details, so it's not a project to take on unless you have a good reason to do it. Two good reasons are to neutralize resting weed seeds and/or to eliminate the last remnants of powdery mildew, fusarium wilt, or other fungal-plant

Adding high-nitrogen meals to a working compost heap will heat it up quickly. Fre-quent turning provides needed oxygen.

diseases that can survive in dead plant tissues. When used to address these problems, you're not just run-ning a hot heap, but keeping what we call a Hospital Heap. It's also just plain fun to push your turning fork into a hot heap and watch the steam billow into the air. The first time you do it, you'll feel the way you would if a magic trick you had practiced a hundred times in front of a mirror finally worked out right.

The heat-killing threshold you're after is 130°F (54°C) to 150°F (66°C). The lower temperature will effectively kill weeds and pathogens if it can be sus-tained for several days, while the higher temperature

---

ACTIVATORS IN A BOX

It sounds like a dream come true: To make a great batch of compost, all you must do is open a box of powdered compost activator, sprinkle it through your heap like fairy dust, and stand back. This can work, because most products sold as compost ac-tivators are high-protein meals that provide a fast shot of nitrogen. Read the labels, and you will find they are made of alfalfa meal, fish powder, blood meal, or cottonseed meal. In a situation where you think you need an activator, it is often cheaper and easier to work with straight plant meals or animal feeds made from them.

can neutralize these problems in a matter of hours. If you think you may be pushing temperatures even higher, use a long-shanked compost thermometer (see page 46) to make sure the hottest parts of the heap stay below 170°F (77°C). Temperatures rising above that level lead to excessive casualties among beneficial microorganisms, as well as undesirable changes in the compost's basic chemistry. Frequent turning prevents overheating and increases the likelihood that all of the material will get a turn in the middle, where temperatures are highest. Hot heaps lose water as steam, but it can be a mistake to flood a hot heap each time you turn it. As long as the heap is heating well, try to keep the moisture level as constant as possible, and certainly not overly moist, but about as moist as a wrung-out sponge.

It's also best to do hot composting in warm weather, because the maximum temperature inside the heap will be higher if the temperatures outside the heap are warm, too. Warm air temperatures limit the exterior cooling of the heap and encourage the proliferation of microorganisms that work best at high temperatures.

The frequent turning required to run a hot heap is a lot of work, so it's best to wait until a weedy or disease-laden heap has shrunk down to a manageable size to put it through a hot process. If you pile together problem-prone materials in their own heap in the fall, they will be ready for hot processing by May or June. The advent of warm weather plus the addition of high-protein meals and grass clippings will work together to help you turn your would-be criminal heap into well-behaved compost. In addition to the Hospital Heap project at right, see page 124 for more proven recipes for making steaming-hot compost.

Working with High-Protein Meals

Let's say you have a batch of compost that you want to heat up, and you have selected a high-protein meal that is inexpensive and easy to obtain. If it is a concentrated powder, for example cottonseed meal, the meal will get hot right away, resulting in spotty temperature spikes in the heap, but the activity will peak almost as soon as it started unless there is additional organic material present that the microorganisms can easily colonize. Fresh grass clippings or coarsely chopped immature weeds will do, or you can add an infusion of foliage from a Compost Fodder Crop (see page 276). Having a second form of bioactive material present is essential if you expect to prolong the heat-producing capacity of highly "combustible" seed meals. It is like starting a fire with newspaper. Once the paper starts burning, you had better have some kindling at the ready if you expect to be able to warm your hands.

Things may go differently if you use alfalfa pellets or the nuggets of corn meal known as dry dog food. These materials have a bit more food to sustain thermophilic bacteria, so they have a slightly longer burn time. Still, it is prudent to supplement the activator with an infusion of nitrogen-rich greens or manure to make sure you get the results you want.

Run a Hot Hospital Heap

Here are the five basic steps for firing up a hot compost heap using high-nitrogen meals as activators.

1 Choose a location at least 8' (2.4 m) square, with easy access for flip-flopping a heap back and forth. Chop and moisten a pile of weathered material at least 12 cubic feet (3.6 cubic meters) in size. (A hip-high bin of weathered leaves or other compostable materials 40"/1 m across is good.) Use a hoe to break up big pieces, and keep a hose or watering can handy to douse dry pockets.

2 Mix in fresh green materials equal to about 20 percent of the heap's mass, along with your chosen activator. Sprinkle the powders or pellets onto the heap in layers, with 3" (7.6 cm) of compost between each heavy dusting of meal. Lightly spray the meal layers with water as you build the heap.

3 After three days, mix and turn the heap, and add water if needed to moisten any dry pockets. Heat may come from parts of the heap, but not uniformly.

4 Mix and turn the heap every two to three days for two weeks, moving material from the outside to the center. In about a week, the heat inside the heap should be quite high, evidenced by abundant steam and a white, ash-like coating on some of the material. A thermometer should read above 130°F (54°C) from day 6 to day 12, and sometimes beyond. Don't skip any turnings during this crucial interval.

5 After two to three weeks, the heap will cool down except for isolated warm pockets. Continue to turn it every few days, adding water if needed to keep it moist. When heating ceases, cover the heap with a cloth, tarp, or fabric weed barrier, and let it cure for at least a month. If tree roots are likely to invade it from below, pile it atop a piece of weed barrier, burlap, or scrap carpeting the last time you turn it.

HOW MUCH ACTIVATOR DO YOU NEED?

The answer depends on the size of the heap, the condition of the materials, and the C/N balance already present in the heap, as well as the potency of the activator. As a general rule, we have found that the following rates result in a rapid warming of 12 cubic feet (3.6 cubic meters) of half-done compost when supplemented with grass clippings or other fresh greens equal to 20 percent of the volume of the heap (one part grass clippings to four parts compost). Twelve cubic feet (3.6 cubic meters) is less than the 1-cubic-yard (0.76 cubic meters) measurement often used in composting manuals, but it comes closer to the size of most home compost heaps. Measured in forksful (easy enough to do while turning), 12 cubic feet (3.6 cubic meters) is about 60 lifts with a loaded digging fork.

ACTIVATOR	HOW MUCH TO USE
Cottonseed meal	8 lbs (3.6 kg)
Dry dog food (corn and soybean meals)	20 lbs (9.1 kg)
Rabbit feed (alfalfa pellets)	20 lbs (9.1 kg)
Poultry feed (soybean meal)	20 lbs (9.1 kg)
Soybean meal	10 lbs (4.6 kg)
Canola meal	10 lbs (4.6 kg)
Organic fertilizer (a blend of meals)	8 lbs (3.6 kg)

Haste Avoids Waste

When using a high-nitrogen additive to heat up compost, it's crucial to work the heap intensively by turning it at least every two days, because the heat created by the decomposing plant meal won't last long. In most situations, the core temperature within the pile will warm noticeably within 24 hours. If you introduce the additive in layers, it's a good idea to turn the heap one or two days later to achieve a good mix. Then, continue to turn and mix the heap every two days to make sure material from the outside of the heap is moved to the inside. Maximum heating will usually occur from days five to nine, with heat decreasing slowly after that. So, you really have a short window of time to work with if your goal is to kill

pathogens and weed seeds by the time the fire goes out. If you need to add small amounts of water, using water that has warmed up in a watering can or in a dark-colored garden hose set in the sun will further conserve the biological heat generated by the pile through the turning and moistening process.

Odds and Ends for the Composter's Garden

A popular parlor game among compost-minded folks could be called "What's the Weirdest Thing You Ever Composted?" Because every living thing is bound to decompose sooner or later, the list of things you *could* put into a compost pile is necessarily broad. That doesn't mean you *have* to compost every conceivable bit of organic material you encounter — there are certainly things you should avoid (see What Not to Use on the facing page) and others that you'll want to avoid because they create more problems to process than they're worth.

The vast majority of compostable odds and ends that wind up in a home compost heap arrive in such small amounts as to have little effect on the composting process. Bits of cotton string too short for any other use, for example, or the wreckage of a toothpick-and-glue school project may be tossed into the bin to decompose along with other more abundant materials. If your pile is working properly, the decomposers in it will be able to take the occasional oddball item or experimental ingredient and break it down along with more standard fare. Diverse ingredients in your compost pile encourage diversity in the organisms that work to decompose them and result in a wider range of nutrients and other beneficial compounds in your finished compost. "Feeding" your

My Personal Best

Spring has sprung, and the once gigantic heap I started last fall from shredded leaves, late-season grass clippings, and lots of random plant parts (including my nemesis, smartweed) is nicely shrunken and ready to be "cooked." Should I go with what I know, and fluff in lots of fresh, green grass clippings, or "cheat," and heat it up fast with the addition of a little dry dog food? Another protein-rich meal like alfalfa meal would be better, but it's 20 miles (32.19 km) from my house to the nearest farm supply store, and I can pick up the dog food when I hit the supermarket next time.

Why not use both? While I'm doing the deed, my neighbor stops by, takes it all in, and suggests that I move the heap out into the sun, where it will get even hotter. Too late for that! I'm into compost-craziness mode, even starting to get sloppy about rounding up rolling nuggets of dog food. "Last night a raccoon got into the barn and ate the milk supplement for the cows,"

my neighbor Marion tells me. "Bet he'll like that dog food."

Three days later, when I turn the heap to get a good mix, the dog food is really "on a roll." Six inches (15.2 cm) inside, the heap registers a solid 120°F (49°C). Two days later we're at 130°F (54°C), which is not the best time for the thermometer to go missing inside the heap, but it's gone. It doesn't appear in the next turning, but the next one, done overnight by the "bionic" raccoon, produces the errant thermometer, which I found lying at the edge of the scattered pile. Answered prayer or sweet coincidence? After a few small repairs, the heap's temperature slips to 120°F (49°C), then 100°F (38°C), and the contents still look chunky, with wisps of grass clippings hanging on as I cover it to cure. A month later, the "raccoon compost" made the grade for use in potting soil, but to call it my personal best would be wrong. That batch was just plain blessed.

compost a variety of ingredients is like eating a balanced and varied diet and enjoying the health benefits of an array of vitamins and minerals.

As with so many things in life, moderation and balance are the keys to success. If you happen into a large quantity of organic material that seems compost-worthy, go for it! But give some thought to the nature of that material and what you'll need to mix with it to create the conditions needed for lively composting.

Gathering odd ingredients is just like gathering any other materials for your compost pile: Watch your compost miles and the time and labor costs involved and make sure the effort you invest is repaid with suc-

cess in your compost garden. And above all, keep your eyes on the goal of making good compost, which you will use to build healthy soil.

What Not to Use

Some materials simply do not belong in compost. These are things that pose dangers to human health and/or the environment. Many of them have been mentioned above, but it's worth a quick review to make sure that your compost garden is both successful and safe. Use these guidelines to evaluate untested ingredients before you put them in your pile.

▶ Will it decompose?

There's little point in putting petroleum products, plastics, metals, or glass into your compost, because these materials will break down at a glacially slow pace, if at all. Plastics, for example, will degrade, which means breaking into increasingly smaller pieces, but they will never decompose into compounds that are useful to soil organisms or plants. Most building materials fit into this category, too, especially things like scraps of treated wood and insulation. Gypsum board (often called sheetrock or plasterboard) is an exception; it is basically gypsum sandwiched between layers of paper.

▶ Is it a potential source of pathogens that could make people sick?

The answer to this one takes the manures of omnivores and carnivores off your list of compost ingredients (see Composting Manure on page 92), as well as the carcasses of poultry, wild birds, and wild animals. Besides being unpleasant, handling these materials is not worth the associated risks. Raw eggs can host salmonella, so rinse eggshells thoroughly before adding them to your heap.

▶ Will it help or hinder the composting process?

Cleaning products and other household chemicals, paints and thinners, pesticides, motor oil, and coal ashes all are materials that can wipe out enough of the decomposing organisms in your pile to bring the whole thing to a screeching halt. The whole point of compost gardening is to create healthy organic soil, so there's no sense in risking that by putting toxic chemicals into your compost bin. The small amounts of fat and oil found in kitchen wastes pose few problems in a well-managed compost pile, but emptying the deep-fryer into your bin would be nearly as damaging as pouring on the used motor oil from your car.

▶ Will it create compost-management problems?

Most composters leave meat and dairy products out of their piles, not because the materials won't break down, but because they attract animal pests and flies and may produce unpleasant odors as they decompose. Many problem ingredients can be managed successfully by mixing them with other materials, keeping them in enclosed bins, or using an underground composting method, and limiting them to a small percentage of a pile's ingredients. If your "cheater's compost" is within sight or smell of your neighbors, however, it's important to consider their noses as well as your own.

Adventures in Composting

Making compost is an extremely creative and personal endeavor. As we've already noted, your compost pile will be as unique as your fingerprints, even if you use the same basic ingredients as your neighbor. Once you're comfortable with the fundamentals of composting, it's fun to explore the boundaries of the process to find out just what those busy decomposers in your bin really can do.

Even if you start composting as much for waste disposal as for soil improvement, use common sense and a "let's see" approach to choosing ingredients. As long as you carefully avoid things that can harm you (disease pathogens) and things that can shut down the composting process completely (petroleum products, pesticides, harsh chemicals), a "try it" pile can help you learn the best ways to compost all kinds of materials, be they novel new ones or familiar favorites. For certain success, dedicate a separate pile to trial materials, or work in an enclosed bin or pit if you anticipate problems with animals or odors. If you're worried about having too many projects going at once, use your quarantined pile of seedy, weedy stuff as your experimental compost. It can be a fascinating adventure!

The transformation from raw materials to compost proceeds quickly in a barrel composter.

Odd Compostables

Material	Pros	Cons	Notes
Agricultural by-products, such as buckwheat and rice hulls, cocoa bean shells, coconut fiber, corn cobs and silage, sugar cane waste	Processing leaves these materials in ready-to-compost condition. Often free or cheap. Few if any weeds.	Becoming less available as farmers find ways to minimize wastes. Need a large supply of matching green compost materials. Many nutrients removed during processing.	Mostly high-carbon browns. May be sold as mulch or peat substitutes. Be wary of the compost miles associated with exotic ingredients like cocoa bean shells and coconut fiber (coir).
Animal carcasses	Nitrogen source. Composting offers alternative to disposal in household garbage.	Gross, smelly, potential sources of dangerous pathogens. May attract other animals to your compost.	Very-high-nitrogen greens. Underground composting in an out-of-the-way place is your best option.
Carpeting, rugs	Good for weed-blocking base layer under more attractive mulch in pathways.	Synthetic fibers will never decompose. Even natural-fiber carpets may be treated with chemicals to prevent decomposition.	High-carbon browns, but impossible to mix with other materials. Reuse is the next best thing to recycling in compost.
Cigarette butts	None.	Cellulose acetate filters are not biodegradable. Residual nicotine has pesticidal effects that may harm beneficial organisms in compost.	High-carbon browns. Decomposition time ranges from 10 to 80 years.
Dryer lint	Fine, fluffy texture offers lots of openings for decomposers.	May contain inorganic fibers that will degrade very slowly but will never decompose or provide any benefit to compost or soil.	A compost-neutral brown material with very little to offer your pile.
Fabrics and fibers, such as cotton, hemp, linen, ramie, silk, wool	Add diversity to compost ingredients. Animal-based fabrics (silk, wool) provide nitrogen.	Require thorough wetting to allow decomposition. Finishes and coatings may be slow to break down.	Best regarded as high-carbon browns. Small scraps will quickly disappear in working compost. Avoid synthetic fibers, which will not decompose.

Material	Pros	Cons	Notes
Fruit wastes, such as apple pomace from cider making, citrus wastes, grape wastes from wine making, spent hops from beer making	Grinding/pressing makes material well prepared for composting. Materials used in food production are unlikely to contain toxic compounds. Free or cheap for the asking.	May be wet, messy, smelly, hard to handle. Finely pulverized materials may mat down in compost pile and impede decomposition.	Regard as high-nitrogen greens. Hobbyists and small-scale producers are the best local sources. Add to compost in shallow layers; after a few days mix in the materials well.
Hair (human and animal)	Nitrogen source. Free and abundant.	Repels water and decomposes very slowly.	High-nitrogen (yet low volume) greens. Get a bagful from the barber (men use less "product" on their hair) or the dog groomer; mix thoroughly into pile to avoid water-repelling mats.
Leather, leather dust	Nitrogen source.	Repels water and decomposes slowly. May be contaminated by heavy metals used in tanning.	Works as a green when thoroughly dampened. Dust and small pieces will break down fairly quickly.
Pet bedding, such as mixed shavings or paper and droppings/spilled food from enclosures for mice, hamsters, gerbils, birds, etc.	Mix of spilled food, animal wastes, and bedding creates good balance of nutrients for composting.	Small risk of exposure to disease pathogens; practice proper sanitation when handling. Dry bedding may repel water and resist decomposition.	Typically available in small amounts. Moisten thoroughly when adding to pile.
Spoiled bird seed	Source of nitrogen, other nutrients.	May contain viable seeds that become weeds in finished compost.	Regard as a green unless numerous hulls are present. Composting is best use of spoiled, rancid, or infested seed that birds won't touch.
Vacuum cleaner contents	Diverse nutrient source.	May contain inorganic fibers and materials that will not decompose. Messy to handle.	Compost-neutral at best, in spite of potential range of ingredients.
Wicker	Good "fiber" for compost allows air movement.	Paints and finishes may impede composting.	Dry, high-carbon brown, slow to decompose. Unfinished wicker will break down gradually while creating air channels in your pile.
Wood ashes	Excellent potassium source.	High alkalinity can disrupt decomposers if used in large quantities.	Regard as a mineral amendment, neither green nor brown. Sprinkle over layers as you make a new compost pile and mix well.

Part 2

Compost Gardening Techniques

4
Banner Batches

A SURPRISING NUMBER of otherwise successful gardeners will admit to being, in their own opinions, composting failures. Their heaps didn't heat up; their stalks didn't break down; the pile turned smelly and slimy; the pile just sat there. For any number of reasons, their compost didn't happen the way they expected it to. To all these gardeners, we have one thing to say: Don't give up. Armed with the information in this chapter, your future composting projects not only will be successful but also will be easier to create and tend. First we will cover the basics of the composting process as it is done in heaps, bins, or enclosed composters. With a working knowledge of the process to guide you, you can make better decisions about composting enclosures (see page 143) and eventually move on to curing and storing the best compost you have ever made.

Making Compost in Piles, Heaps, Bins, and Pens

When a compost project fails to perform as expected, the problem is not with the compost but with the expectation. You can't *make* organic matter become compost any more than you can *make* a seed grow into a flowering plant. What you can do is create the conditions that allow and encourage these natural processes to take place. In compost gardening terms, this means working with the materials you have available and using methods that are appropriate for the materials and for the level of work and commitment you wish to invest. Frequently you may opt for a non-heap method, such as Comforter Compost or underground Treasure Troughs, which we explore in the other chapters in this section. Still, you will invariably tinker with a heap or two, or perhaps make compost in an enclosed composting appliance.

Most composting manuals describe one composting model, which is a heap that heats up as the materials decompose. This model is far too limiting, because a successful compost pile does not have to

be a hot pile, nor does it have to be turned, fluffed, enriched, or monitored on a daily basis. These are all things you may choose to do, depending on your goals for a specific compost project, but they are not essential to the production of good-quality compost. Mother Nature does not chop, stir, blend, or turn the wealth of organic matter that falls on the earth every single day, and yet our forests and grasslands are not buried beneath mountains of undecomposed material. Why not? Because natural systems process those materials into food for composting microorganisms, animals, and plants.

Gardening and composting are not natural systems (unless you count well-developed permaculture landscapes), and the more time and trouble you put into your compost projects, the less natural they become. Whether you're tending an intensely managed barrel composter or a neglected, let-it-happen open heap, it's important to remember that compost happens *when the conditions are right for the materials that are present to break down*. If you keep this in mind and manage your compost projects accordingly, they will never fail.

Becoming a Compost Connoisseur

It may take a few tries to figure out which methods and conditions are best for your most abundant materials. Then you will be well on your way to making Banner Batches of top-quality compost. As you refine your composting projects to fit in with the way you garden, you may find yourself dabbling ever more deeply in the composting arts: chopping and mixing and moistening materials, balancing nutrients by adding high-protein plant meals or manure, monitoring temperatures, and turning and mixing the materials as much for your personal pleasure as for the benefit of the heap. It will take only one or two successful projects to get you hooked on these and other aspects of composting. Every composter's garden is run by a compost connoisseur.

As a compost gardener, you will probably have several compost projects going on in different parts of your landscape (we average four to five at any given time in our average-sized yards). Some may be

How you contain your compost — if you do so at all — may depend upon how it looks and who's looking at it.

The Tortoise and the Hare:

A Race to the Rotten End

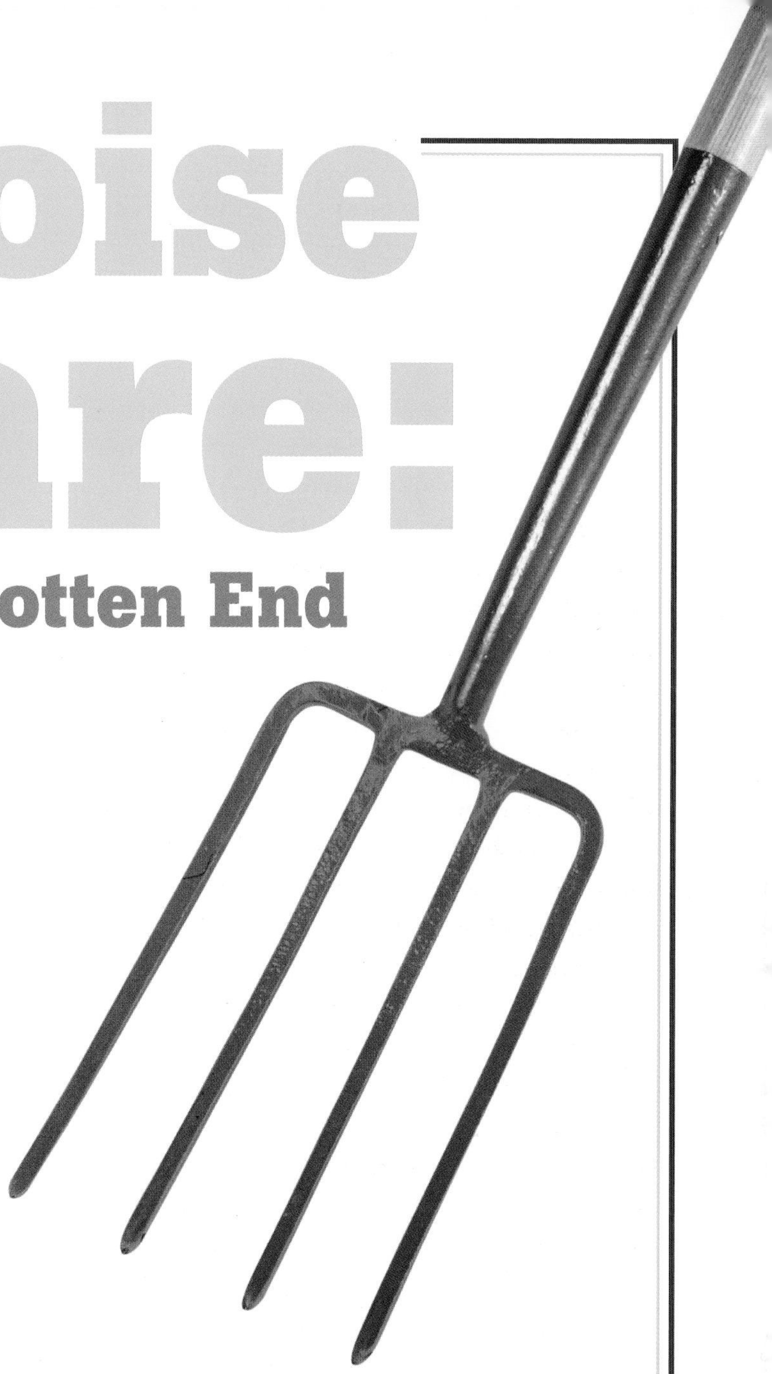

Banner Batches may be hot and fast (as the hare) or cold and slow (as the tortoise). In this race, slow and steady doesn't always win, and haste doesn't always make waste. Both approaches to composting have their place in composters' gardens. Many projects start out as slow heaps and are briefly converted to hot ones as they advance toward maturity.

Method	Pros	Cons
Hot	Fast; you may have finished compost in as little as two weeks. Sustained high temperatures can kill weed seeds and disease organisms.	Labor intensive; requires regular monitoring and turning on a rigid schedule. High temperatures may kill some beneficial organisms and deplete nutrients.
Cold	Lower temperatures allow greater diversity of microorganisms and plant nutrients. It requires little or no labor once established.	Slow; may take as long as a year to yield finished compost. Low temperatures may permit weed seeds and disease organisms to survive.

closely managed hot Hospital Heaps meant to neutralize weed seeds and diseases. Other projects meant to produce high-quality compost for potting soil may focus on balancing materials and allowing time for the broadest possible range of microorganisms to work their wonders. We recommend using labor-intensive methods only when you have a supply of superior ingredients (rabbit manure comes to mind), the time to tend them (turning every three days), and a specific goal (producing weed-free compost for your pet plants). Composting more while working less is one of the themes in a composter's garden. Especially when working in heaps or enclosed batches, artful composting is done as much with your head as with your hands.

The key to making Banner Batches — which we define as compost made in heaps or enclosures — is to plan compost composition for successful decomposition. You can use Banner Batch techniques with any compostable materials as long as you mix them in proportions that create a desirable carbon-to-nitrogen ratio, and then manage air and moisture to provide optimal conditions for decomposition.

Making Fast Banner Batches

In compost gardening terms, fast Banner Batches represent what you may recognize as traditional, labor-intensive compost making. Making a fast Banner Batch requires your active participation in the process; the most obvious payoff for the extra labor is finished compost within two or three weeks' time, not counting setting the finished compost aside to cure for several weeks before using it (see page 150). A fast Banner Batch can function as a Hospital Heap for weedy or diseased materials, or you may make one just because you want to do it. Cured compost from a fast Banner Batch is the best kind of compost for making potting mixes or using as velvety black mulch

---

TREES IN YOUR COMPOST?

If you count apricots, peaches, plums, and almonds among your favorite foods, sooner or later you'll probably discover a *Prunus* species tree sprouting from the discarded pits in your compost. If you catch the seedling early, while the "nut" is still attached to the roots, you can probably identify the species, but be forewarned that the foliage of these *Prunus* cousins is so similar that it can be impossible to tell them apart. Like many nut-bearing trees, seeds from various *Prunus* species germinate best after they have been subjected to a cold, damp period, which is easily provided in a slow-working compost heap.

Are volunteer almonds or peaches worth keeping as garden plants? It can be interesting to watch them grow, but in general, seedlings are rarely as vigorous or productive as grafted plants purchased from a good, regional nursery. Take almonds, for example. In the United States, most almond trees are grafted onto peach rootstocks, and the rootstocks vary from region to region. And, because almond trees are not self-fertile, a second pollinator variety must be present before a tree can set fruit. But even if you never pick a nice fruit or nut from a compost-borne *Prunus* tree, you may want to keep your volunteer to enjoy its pretty spring flowers if you have the space for it. When a plant shows such a determined will to live, it's just plain hard to say no.

---

in containers or exhibition flower beds, but you should only undertake this project when appropriate materials are available and you have the time to monitor and turn the compost every few days. Here are the essential issues involved in building and tending a fast Banner Batch from start to speedy finish:

▶ **Get the right stuff.** Balance browns (carbon materials) and greens (nitrogen materials) to achieve a ratio of roughly 30/1 (see page 54). For your first fast batch, it can help to follow a fixed recipe, knowing you will get a predictable result. See Recipes for Fast, Hot Compost on the facing page for several tried-and-true combinations.

▶ **Prepare the materials.** Since you'll be turning this compost every couple of days, there's no need to worry about leaving some large pieces of this or that to create air spaces in the pile. Do shred leaves and chop up dry stalks and stems, and cut chunky kitchen wastes, such as melon rinds, into 1" (2.5 cm) cubes. These smaller pieces of compostable material have more surface area, so they are more accessible to fungi and bacteria.

▶ **Manage moisture.** Moisten dry ingredients as you add them to the pile, and check for dry pockets every time you turn. Use a hose with a spray nozzle or a watering can to dampen a pile that's too dry; use a fork to fluff and turn a soggy pile or mix in additional dry ingredients, such as sawdust or chopped straw. You shouldn't be able to squeeze liquid out of a handful of mixed materials, and nothing in your heap should be dry enough to light with a match.

▶ **Turn, turn, turn.** Three days after you assemble a hot Banner Batch, turn and mix the materials and add water to dry spots. After the second turning, with the materials evenly mixed and moistened, you should start feeling some heat. Now is the time to use a thermometer (see page 46) to see if the inside of the mix is warming to 120°F (49°C) or more between turnings. A pile that's not heating up may be too dry, or it may need a nitrogen booster, such as fresh grass clippings or a high-protein meal (see page 122). Turn the pile every two or three days for the next two weeks, and don't stop when temperatures begin to drop. The microorganisms that take over after the high-temperature phase peaks are every bit as important as those that work at higher temperatures.

▶ **Finish and cure.** When the pile is no warmer than a few degrees above the air temperature, the compost is finished. You can go ahead and use it in other composting projects, but making the best possible Banner Batch requires a month or more of curing under a tarp or similar cover to protect it from losing nutrients through rain leaching (see more on curing later in this chapter). Now you have the kind of compost you have always dreamed of, and you will probably want to do it again and again.

RECIPES FOR FAST, HOT COMPOST

Some compost gardeners like it hot, and we know how it feels to crave the excitement that comes with working a fast, hot heap. If you want guaranteed high-heat thrills, these recipes can get you started. All of these recipes will benefit from the addition of a few shovelfuls of active compost, and most require materials that are not generated by the average home landscape. Once you get the feel of how hot compost works, you can begin using more of the materials available in your yard, and less of those that must be imported. Meantime, use these recipes to heat-treat diseased or weedy materials, Hospital Heap–style. Use a large bucket or pail when measuring materials.

▶ Equal parts horse manure, rotted hay, and damp straw or ground corncobs

▶ 4 parts fresh grass clippings, 1 part sawdust, 1 part active compost

▶ 3 parts fresh grass clippings, 1 part kitchen scraps, 1 part damp straw

▶ 3 parts shredded leaves (weathered through winter), 1 part packaged dehydrated cow manure, 1 part green or partially rotted garden waste

▶ 3 parts fresh grass clippings, 1 part kitchen scraps, 1 part moist, shredded paper

▶ 2 parts rabbit or poultry manure, 1 part shredded leaves (weathered through winter), 1 part sawdust, 1 part green or partially rotted garden waste

▶ 20 pounds cheap, dry dog food, 3 bushels (60 forksful) of mixed, moistened yard waste or partially rotted garden waste

▶ 20 pounds rabbit food (alfalfa pellets), one wheelbarrow load each of shredded dry leaves, fresh grass clippings, and green garden waste

Try Garbage Can Compost

Making a Banner Batch in the confines of a barrel or tumbler is almost like test tube compost — you can maintain precise control over materials, moisture, and mixing, with no interference from curious critters or compromising weather. Purchased composting barrels or tumblers can be pricey, and a garbage can experiment is a good way to give tumbler-style composting a try before you invest in a commercial model. If you're satisfied with the results you get with a modified garbage can, you may want to shop for a barrel or tumbler that's specifically designed for this task. After rolling a garbage can around your yard, you'll have a greater appreciation for barrel composters that are designed for easy turning!

MATERIALS AND SUPPLIES

- Cylindrical metal or plastic garbage can with secure lid

- Drill with 5/16" bit or hammer and large nail (4 or 6 penny size)

- Elastic tie-down (bungee cord) twice as long as the can's diameter

- Duct tape (optional)

1 Use the drill or hammer and nail to punch 15 to 20 evenly spaced holes in the sides and bottom of the garbage can. ▼

2 Set the can upright in an area where there's room for it to roll around. Add prepared (chopped/shredded) ingredients to the can in alternating layers; moisten dry ingredients as you add them to the mix. Fill the can two-thirds to three-fourths full. ▼

3 Put the lid on the garbage can and fasten it with the elastic tie-down run over the lid and hooked on each side to the lip at the base of the handle. If the lid does not seem secure, lash it on with a few strips of duct tape. Tip the can onto its side and roll it around to thoroughly mix the contents. ▼

4 Roll the can daily, making at least three full revolutions, for at least two weeks. To check for heating, feel the outside of the can with your hand. Every three days or so, you may want to open the lid and check the moisture level of the contents, watering enough to keep the contents as moist as a wrung-out sponge, and to break up large clumps with a turning fork or other long-handled tool.

5 When heating subsides, you'll know your compost is nearing completion. Continue to roll the can every two to three days for another week. By this time the temperature in the can should be the same as the air temperature outside. The compost is now ready to set aside to cure for two weeks, which can be done in the can or in an open pile, covered with a tarp.

Working with Slow Banner Batches

Slow Banner Batches make it easier to use materials that are abundantly available in most yards and communities, especially those, such as autumn leaves and wood chips, which must be leached by water and processed by fungi before they can become food for composting bacteria. Slow composts, also called cool or cold composts, lack the high-spirited appeal of their hot, steamy counterparts, but they are so simple to create that compost gardeners make slow compost much more often than they undertake hot heaps. Compost projects you may have thought were failures were more likely slow heaps that did not act like hot heaps — an all too common mistake in judgment. Slow compost is good compost, and it may contain more disease-suppressing microorganisms than compost made using higher temperatures. Research has shown that trees, shrubs, and perennials grow better in soil amended with slow, cool compost.

To make Banner Batches using a slow and steady approach in place of hot composting's fast and furious techniques, use these basic steps to assemble and maintain simple heaps. In addition, try the slow, labor-saving, in-garden methods we describe in the next three chapters to enrich your garden.

▶ **Build in some balance.** Balancing the ratio of carbon to nitrogen in cool compost is less critical than in hot methods, but it's still important to have a good mixture of browns and greens. Alternate layers of brown and green materials, moistening dry materials as you work. Add fine-textured ingredients, such as sawdust or grass clippings, in thin layers to prevent them from forming impenetrable mats. Remember that you can always add more of anything at any time.

▶ **Plan for passive aeration.** Part of the appeal of a slow, cool compost pile is that it works with less

Work a Walking Compost Heap

Many people flip-flop heaps from side to side as they turn them, but a Walking Heap moves closer to its final destination each time you turn it. Each turning creates a fertile footprint, so this is an ideal method if you have wide rows. Simply walk the heap from one end of a row to the other. If you're working on a slope, start up high and "roll" the heap down the hill using a hoe rather than a turning fork. In any site, shape the heap to fit the space below it where the soil is in need of compost's rejuvenating effects.

MATERIALS AND SUPPLIES

- 4 wheelbarrow loads of compostable materials
- Hose or watering can
- Turning fork
- Garden hoe
- Pen type enclosure (see page 143), optional

1. About 15′ (4.5 meters) from where you want to use your compost, set up a large heap with enough of it to fill a pen 3′ (0.9 m) across and 2′ (0.6 m) tall — about 4 wheelbarrow loads of stuff. Chop and moisten as needed to get a good mix.

2. After a month or two, chop, mix, and turn the material in the direction of its final resting place. It should travel about 6′ (1.8 m).

3. The mass will shrink considerably over the next few weeks. Turn and mix it again to move it 4′ (1.2 m) closer to the finish line. At this point you might want to amend the mix with a high-protein meal if you want to subject its materials to high enough temperatures to deactivate weed seeds and microorganisms that might cause plant (or people) diseases.

4. Two more turnings should get the heap where you want it, ready to mix into soil or use as excellent quality mulch. If you're not quite ready for it, simply cover the pile with a tarp and let it cure.

turning than a hot, fast heap. However, you still need to arrange ways for air and moisture to get in and out of the pile. One way to do this is to leave dry stems and stalks in larger pieces, or to toss in several handfuls of twigs. If it is a large heap, you may lay lengths of PVC pipe peppered with holes across layers of your pile as you build it, allowing the ends of the pipes to stick out of the compost. Or create "chimneys" using cardboard tubes or bundles of coarse stalks and sticks placed vertically in your compost with the ingredients layered around them. Building your pile on a base layer of coarse brush, or in a bin with a raised and perforated bottom, also promotes a healthy air flow through the layers.

▶ **Build a healthy heap.** Include layers of soil and/or active compost in your new pile. It's okay to build a slow, cool pile over time, adding materials as they become available, but do try to keep the heap's long-term balance in mind. When the pile reaches 3' to 4' (0.9 to 1.2 m) high and wide, consider it complete and start a new one. Before moving on, cover the pile with an outer layer of water-shedding straw or whole dry leaves, or cover it loosely with a tarp. In dry climates or seasons, make a depression in the top of the pile to hold water supplied from a hose or watering can.

▶ **Be patient but not absent.** Once it is assembled, your slow Banner Batch will do its thing with little involvement from you. Do keep an eye on moisture and don't hesitate to give your heap a drink when you're watering plants in your garden — or you can outfit it with a soaker hose (see page 46). If the materials seem soggy, you may need to inject a bit of air into the pile using a compost aerating tool or a length of rebar (see Aerating Tools on page 45).

▶ **Turn when the mood strikes.** After a couple of months, turn the pile to move and mix the materials, moisten dry pockets, and chop big pieces into smaller ones. A month or two later, turn it again. At this point you're pretty much done, and the compost should be ready to cure. Cover it up, wait, and you will soon have beautiful compost.

PERFECT MATCH

Johnny Jump-Ups and Touch-Me-Nots

Would you like to stock your yard with colorful flowers that plant themselves? Let a Walking Heap do your seed cleaning and sowing for you by welcoming Johnny jump-ups (*Viola tricolor*) or touch-me-nots (*Impatiens balsamina*) into your yard — and your compost. Both flowers will reseed without your help, but you can "plant" them in the footprints of a Walking Heap by placing plenty of spent plants in the heap. As the compost rots and rolls toward its final destination, it will leave a trail of seeds and active organic matter to help nurture the seedlings. Should seedlings of either flower become too numerous, they are easy to pull up and use as composting greens. Cold-hardy Johnny Js are likely to pop up just about anywhere — including your lawn, walkway crevices, or beneath the shade of summer veggies. Warm-natured touch-me-nots need at least a half day of shade, so they make colorful companions for the same moist, shady places where you are likely to make Walking Heaps.

Roses

Unlike many human beauty queens, roses aren't afraid to help themselves to a well-stocked buffet of nutritious foods. These beauties must indulge their appetites to maintain their classic good looks. If roses play a starring role in your beds and borders, or if you would like for them to do so, you can keep them happy and healthy by loading up the soil with your best Banner Batches of cured compost, made from only the finest ingredients. In the book *Growing Roses Organically*, author Barbara Wilde recommends compost for every phase of a rose's life, starting with preparing the planting site well ahead of time with a cover crop (see Compost Fodder Crops, page 276) or by digging in 4″ to 6″ (10 to 15.2 cm) of compost or leaf mold, preferably in the fall prior to spring planting. When it's time to plant, remove the enriched topsoil and set it aside, then divide the subsoil taken from the hole and mix half of it with more compost before backfilling the hole, topsoil first, then the subsoil-compost mix. Once roses are in the ground, Wilde advises further pampering them with a 1″ (2.5 cm) thick layer of compost mulch to conserve soil moisture, encourage beneficial microorganisms, and prevent diseases. "Compost," Wilde says, ". . . is an absolute must for growing roses organically."

Resourceful Compost Enclosures

To contain or not contain — that is the question that stops many would-be compost-makers short. The answer is "it depends." Whether you make your compost in a sturdy wooden bin or in a loose heap, whether you make compost above ground or below — these decisions and others will depend on several factors, including these:

▶ **Your climate.** In dry climates, composting in an enclosure or pit helps keep materials from drying out; in rainy regions, composting above ground with plenty of circulating fresh air helps keep things from getting too soggy.

▶ **Your neighborhood.** Urban and suburban composting often requires careful containment to exclude animal pests, prevent odors, and satisfy aesthetics. Being a good compost citizen may mean working with enclosed composts or keeping open compost projects in eye-appealing bins.

▶ **Your materials.** As we've noted previously, a visible pile that includes kitchen scraps can look like a pile of garbage, especially to a neighbor who's less enamored with making compost than are you. Leaf piles must be contained to keep them from blowing away, and animal exclusion can be an issue with kitchen scraps or manure.

The Benefits of Bins

The words bin and pen are used every bit as loosely and variously as the structures they describe. In composting circles, a compost bin is usually a structure made of wood, concrete blocks, sheet metal, plastic, or other durable materials. A pen is a more transient affair that can be made of wire mesh, plastic fencing, or even sturdy fabric supported by fence posts, metal rods, or similar supports. A bin may be completely enclosed on all sides; or it may have a solid top and sides but be open on the bottom where it rests on the soil a pen is typically a permeable frame with neither top nor bottom. Bins may be either open or closed composting systems, while pens are almost always open systems.

For our purposes, we'll refer to the whole range of solid-sided compost containers, including barrels and tumblers, as bins. These are structures that are meant for making compost, but not necessarily for moving from place to place. Pens, as you'll see below, can be put up almost anywhere. Pens may be used to enclose working compost piles or to stockpile materials. Bins may be homemade or commercially manufactured; whether you build or buy is up to you.

Choosing a Pen Style

Compost gardeners who use enclosed bins or composting containers for making Banner Batches still need places to stockpile their materials. Pens are the answer, and you can be endlessly creative when finding ways to corral leaves, grass clippings, manure, or other materials until they are needed for compost projects. Bales of hay — which afterward can be used in compost — make great walls for low pens, but they

A three-bin composter provides a space for stockpiling materials, one for an active pile, and one for curing finished compost.

require a lot of space. Pens made from fencing, which is usually attached to posts, need less room and can be relocated in only a few minutes.

In the charts that follow, we compare the various materials you can use for the three parts of any pen — posts, enclosures, and fasteners that hold the pen together. Decide what the pen will contain before choosing its location and component parts. Also consider how the pen will look when it is finished and filled with compost, leaves, or waste from your kitchen or garden. Pens are only as unattractive as you make them.

Comparing Open vs. Closed Composting Systems

System	Pros	Cons	Examples
Open	Easy to build; easy to add ingredients over time. Contact with soil gives access to desirable decomposing organisms. Takes advantage of moisture from rain/snow. Passive aeration is easier to achieve. Easily accessible for turning, removing compost.	Ingredients may dry out quickly or become too wet during heavy rains. Attractive/accessible to animal pests, flies. May be unattractive. Ingredients on the outside of the pile may break down very slowly.	Piles, pens, three-sided bins, open-slat bins.
Closed	Compost is secure from animal pests. Kitchen wastes and other unappealing materials hidden from view. Conserves moisture, heat, and nutrients. Materials decompose more evenly.	Can easily become soggy and smelly without regular turning or aeration. Limited capacity may require stockpiling of ingredients. May exclude beneficial organisms, such as earthworms. Can be difficult to add ingredients/remove finished compost.	Barrels, tumblers, enclosed plastic bins, tightly built wooden bins.

My Parents' Roses

My father grew up in rural Mississippi, so naturally he gardened all of his life. Gradually my Chicago-born mother became a gardener, too, and together they went through a decade-long period as rosarians, skilled and dedicated cutivators of roses. On warm afternoons our backyard was enveloped by a cloud of rose perfume, and I was taught how to cut stems, polish leaves, and arrange buds and blossoms to be taken to church or to the homes of friends and relatives.

But there was trouble in paradise. My detail-oriented mother wanted to follow all the prevailing guidelines she had learned from fellow rose growers, while my father wanted to put more trust in compost. He had invested in a big, beautiful compost tumbler, had seen what it could do, and was ready to break some rules.

Instead of quibbling, my parents divided the roses into "his" and "hers" beds. They could do what they wanted in their half and take pride in their own results.

A year later, the two beds looked different. Dad had moved his composter right up to the back edge of his bed and covered the ground between plants with a 3″ (7.6 cm) thick layer of compost. Mom's bed made a prettier picture with its pine-needle mulch. Both groups of roses prospered, and the question of who had the best blossoms became a family joke that even came up at their 50th wedding anniversary party. The lesson here is simple: One of the secrets of a long and happy marriage is to never, ever, let compost come between the two of you. Another is to always make time to smell your roses.

Comparing Features of Bins

Bin Construction	Comments
Wood	Most common and economical. Will eventually decay from contact with compost and soil; use nontoxic product to paint or seal to extend bin life. You can buy a wooden bin or make one from boards or shipping pallets, using basic carpentry skills and tools. Heavy once completed, wooden bins become a semi-permanent installation in your landscape.
Plastic	Common material for bins offered through municipal yard-waste reduction programs. Exposure to sunlight and weathering causes degradation of plastic. Generally unobtrusive in landscape, plastic bins offer good protection against animal pests while hiding the contents from view. Turning the contents can be challenging, and the impermeable plastic may promote anaerobic conditions unless adequately ventilated.
Concrete block	Sturdy and long-lasting. May be stacked into desired shape and size; you can set blocks over rebar or metal posts driven into the ground for additional stability; blocks can be disassembled and moved as needed. Not very attractive, and may require a wire screen or wooden lid to exclude animal pests.

Parts of a Pen: Posts

Material	Pros and Cons	Cost and Availability	Ease of Handling	Tools Needed
Metal fence posts	Sturdy enough to support a tall bin. Easiest installation if soil is free of obstructions. Long-lasting when repainted periodically to prevent rust.	4' to 6' (1.2 to 1.8 m) posts cost about $2 to $4. Compare prices at home supply, farm supply, and fencing contractors.	Heavy; can be difficult to remove when securely installed in clay soil.	Hammer or mallet, small piece of scrap lumber. A manual tool called a post setter makes installation easier, but requires skill and upper body strength.
Rebar rod (concrete reinforcing bar)	Relatively easy to pound into hard soil. Must be painted to retard rust. Lasts practically forever.	Standard sizes available at building supply stores are sold by 1/8" (0.3 cm) diameter increments and by length	Solid steel rods are heavy. (A 6' long, 1/2" diameter rebar rod weighs 4 lbs.) Perfectly plumb installation is a challenge. Short rods make good mounting pegs for PVC pipe uprights, which slip over the pegs.	Heavy mallet or hammer; small piece of scrap lumber. Use a hack saw to cut, or have a welding shop use their special equipment to cut rebar to custom lengths.
Wooden stakes	Inexpensive and easy to make from 1x2 (19x38 mm) or 2x2 (38x38 mm) lumber. Accept staples and can be painted or stained. Last five or more years.	5' (1.52 m) long tomato stakes are widely sold individually or in bundles. If you cut your own from 2x2s (38x38 mm), each 4' (1.2 m) stake will cost about $1.	Fast to install or pull up, and can be attached to enclosure material with staples. Wear gloves: Splinters are a constant hazard.	Heavy mallet or hammer; small piece of scrap lumber. Can be cut to length using ordinary hand or circular saw.
PVC pipe	Inexpensive and easy to make from 1" or 1 1/2" (2.5 or 3.4 cm) diameter pipe. Can be painted. Lasts seven or more years when used outdoors.	Sold in 6' to 12' (1.8 to 3.7 m) lengths at home supply stores. Prices range from $.25 per foot for 1" (2.5 cm) PVC to $.47 per foot for 1 1/2" (3.4 cm) pipe.	Lightweight and easy to install and move. Remove soil that clogs pipes by soaking them in water.	Heavy mallet or hammer; small piece of scrap lumber. Can be cut to length using an ordinary hand saw or circular saw.
Sticks	Inexpensive or free when gleaned from tree prunings. Bamboo is attractive and fun to work with. Sticks become brittle and weak after one to two years.	Easier to make than to buy. Look for land where construction is planned, and get the owner's permission to gather usable sticks.	Lightweight and natural, but prone to rot when pushed into damp soil. Use short PVC-pipe sleeves, pounded into the ground, to secure the base of stick-type posts.	Lopper or pruning saw for gathering sticks and cutting them to length. You will need pruning shears for trimming away small side branches.

Parts of a Pen: Enclosure Material

Material	Pros and Cons	Cost and Availability	Ease of Handling	Tools Needed
Wire fencing (galvanized steel or vinyl-coated)	Strong support with some resistance to animals. Lasts many years. Posts often are not needed for circular or oblong shapes.	50' (15.2 m) rolls of 3' to 4' (0.9 to 1.2 m) wide fencing cost $25–$55. Widely available at hardware and home improvement stores.	Two people working together make cutting much easier. Can be rolled for storage.	Bolt cutters and heavy gloves required to cut fencing to length. Use heavy pliers to bend protruding wires inward.
Garden fencing (plastic)	Lightweight, portable, and easy to clean. Commonly available in green, black, and orange. Lasts several years.	100' (30.5 m) rolls, 48" (1.2 m) wide, cost about $35. Available in other widths and lengths at home improvement stores.	Easily cut and handled by one person. Can be stapled, tied, or pinned in place. Scraps useful for other garden jobs.	Can be cut with heavy-duty scissors or a utility knife.
Poultry netting (Chicken wire, wire coated with plastic, or all plastic)	Inexpensive, but prone to crumple as compost shrinks. Plain wire lasts several years; plastic or coated versions last slightly longer.	Available as galvanized wire, wire coated with plastic, or all plastic, in widths ranging from 18" to 48" (0.4 to 1.2 m). Coated or plastic versions most attractive.	Can be cut and handled by one person. Coated version easier to handle than plain wire. Scraps useful for other garden jobs.	Wire snips and heavy gloves needed to cut material to length. Cut ends can be stapled to 1x2 (19x38 mm) lumber to keep them straight.
Hardware cloth (wire mesh)	Inexpensive and sturdy. Lasts many years. Range of mesh sizes useful for other tasks, such as screening compost.	Sold at home improvement and building supply stores, typically in 24" (0.6 m) wide by 10' (3 m) long rolls. Other widths and lengths may be available.	Can be cut and handled by one person, but easier with two.	Cut with wire snips; wear gloves to protect hands from sharp wires. Ends can be pinned, clipped, tied or stapled.
Cloth	Inexpensive and easy to handle. Burlap is a good choice, or you can use other fabrics. All hide contents of pen from view. May require periodic retightening.	Check stores for usable remnants (short pieces of fabric sold at a discount). Standard fabric widths are 36", 45", and 60" (91.4 cm, 114.3 cm, and 152.4 cm).	Easy to cut or fold to desired size. Sew pieces together to create custom shapes. Coordinate colors with other features in your yard.	Cut with scissors, bind ends with duct tape, if desired, to prevent ragged edges. Ends can be pinned or stapled to posts. Can be installed over fenced enclosures.

Material	Pros and Cons	Cost and Availability	Ease of Handling	Tools Needed
Wood pallet	Usually free for the asking from businesses. Sturdy; will last for five years or more. Heavy, unwieldy to lift and transport.	Any business that receives products on pallets is a likely source of free pallets.	Pallets are self-supporting or can be set over fence posts or rebar rods. Too big to fit easily into a car.	None. Set three pallets on their sides in a U-shaped arrangement to form an open bin; tie together at corners with wire or cord (or set over posts). Add two more pallets to make a second bin.
Wood and wire panel	Requires simple assembly with basic tools; can be made to desired size. Paint wood to protect against moisture.	Make a wood frame using 3′ to 4′ (9 to 1.2 m) lengths of 1x2 (19x38 mm) lumber; cut sections of wire or plastic fencing to fit and staple to frame.	Finished panels are easy to move. Fasten four together with wire or cord to form a bin. Can stack and store flat.	Hammer and nails or drill, screwdriver, and screws to assemble. Staple gun and staples to attach fencing to frames. Wire or cord to connect panels at corners or use hook-and-eye connectors on one side to allow opening and closing.

TRY PVC SLEEVES

Need to throw up a compost-ingredient holding pen in a hurry? Keep handy several sets of "post sleeves" made from 1′ long (0.3 m) pieces of 1½″ (3.8 cm) diameter PVC pipe. When you want to set posts for a pen, pound the sleeves into the ground, and then insert posts made of wood, bamboo, or 1″ (2.5 cm) diameter PVC pipe into the sleeve. Pull the sleeves up and rinse them off between uses. If you don't like seeing the sleeves, paint them dark green or brown to help them blend in with their surroundings.

Parts of a Pen: Fasteners

Material	Pros and Cons	Cost and Availability	Ease of Handling	Tools Needed
Detachable clips (metal)	Strong enough to resist tampering from animals. Aluminum is lighter and more weather resistant than other metals.	Cost varies with size and materials. Inexpensive aluminum clips often are sold in assorted colors. Sold at camping and home supply stores.	Very easy to handle, provided movable parts are kept clean and lubricated. Between uses, scrub well, dry thoroughly, and work a drop of lubricant into hinge or slide.	None. If a hinge locks up due to corrosion, apply spray lubricant or light machine oil, and then tap lightly with a hammer to break adhesions.
Biodegradable string (cotton, hemp, jute, sisal, cotton ribbon or seam binding)	Fast way to attach and detach open fencing to posts. Textures and colors can bring a decorative touch to pens. Ribbon can be reused.	Try fibers available locally, and pick a favorite. Cotton and sisal are weaker and degrade faster than hemp, jute, or ribbon.	Easy and interesting to handle. Can be tied, used as lashings, or woven through fencing to add strength and visual texture to a pen.	Scissors or sharp knife. Wait a few days after assembling a pen to trim off long ends; knots may need retying. Snip knots to disassemble pen. Compost used pieces.
Cable locks (plastic)	Long-lasting, resist animals, and come in different colors and weights. Not reusable. Can fasten several together to create longer ties.	Inexpensive in quantity bags sold at home centers and hardware stores.	Easy to use. Eventually will break or locking mechanism will fail. May leave bits of plastic in compost or grass.	None. Most are permanent once locked; cut with heavy-duty shears to take apart pen.
Clothespins (spring type)	Minimally animal resistant, but infinitely handy for assembling shallow or temporary pens. Plastic pins last longer than wooden ones.	Standard-sized clothespins are widely available, but look for extra-large versions, which are typically made of plastic.	Easy to use, and easily lost in grass and mulch. Set up a place to keep them in your composting areas.	None. Lightly rubbing dry, wooden clothespins with a cloth moistened with vegetable oil will help weatherize them.
Twist ties	Animals can sometimes pull these apart, but they are fast and easy to use. Especially handy for preliminary assembly of a new pen.	Ties sold in garden centers are longer and more versatile than those found in the produce section of the supermarket. Most are unobtrusive green.	Easy to use, provided you can reach inside to guide ends to the outside of a pen. Work especially well with plastic garden fencing.	None. Use scissors if necessary to shorten long ties or snip through weathered ones that will not untwist.

Curing Finished Compost

The word "finished" is never truly accurate when used to describe compost, because compost continues to change for up to two years after the most active phases of decomposition are history. It's still a convenient word to use, but what most gardeners call finished compost is really *stable* compost, which generates no biological heat and has an earthy smell.

You can test for heating by placing some compost in a bucket with a thermometer and seeing if the temperature changes over a period of three to four days.

To assess smell, place some moist compost and air in a sealed plastic bag and open it after a day or two and take a sniff. Compost that's not quite stable will give off faint whiffs of ammonia or other yucky aromas, whereas stable compost will smell pleasantly earthy.

Stable compost is fine to use as mulch beneath flowers or to add to other composting projects, but a final important transformation is yet to come if you want your compost to be in proper condition for mixing into potting soils or spreading over the surface of your salad patch. When given additional curing time, stable compost undergoes the following four crucial changes that dramatically improve its safety and quality:

▶ Volatile organic acids decrease, reducing the possibility that the compost could damage plant roots.
▶ Particles become smaller and more uniform in size, giving the compost a rich, fluffy texture.
▶ Nitrogen content of stable compost increases as microorganisms recover nitrogen "borrowed" by earlier generations of fungi and bacteria.
▶ The pH stabilizes, often approaching the neutral range (6.0 to 7.5 on a pH scale, depending on the pH of the primary materials in the batch).

All in all, cured, or stable, compost is compost as plants prefer it to be, and working with cured compost is among the finest delights of compost gardening.

Timing the Transition

How long compost should be cured depends on what it was made of, how it was made, and how far it has already progressed toward maturity. The four changes described om page 149 vary with materials, particle size, and the moisture and air supply the compost received during its heyday on the road to rot. For practical purposes, the appearance of earthworms in a heap or bin is often a sign that the compost is moving itself from the stable phase into final curing. In comparison, you will see few earthworms in a hot Banner Batch made outdoors that stopped regenerating heat after you turned it last week. It is a newcomer to the stable phase, so the curing process has just begun.

On the materials variable, if your hot heap was activated with high-nitrogen plant materials (including high-nitrogen meals), a 6-week minimum curing time will probably be sufficient. But if you used animal manure as a primary nitrogen source, 12 weeks is a better estimate of how long the compost will need to reach full maturity. Part of the long wait has to do with food safety (see Patience Pays below).

Taking the Cure

If left alone, any type of compost can be counted upon to cure itself. The finished product, however, will be of much better quality if a thoughtful compost gardener oversees the process by protecting the curing compost from leaching, monitoring its moisture supply, and perhaps aerating the material a time or two to

PATIENCE PAYS

Studies have shown that some manure-borne pathogens can persist in stable compost produced using high temperature methods, but that they disappear as the compost cures. A long curing time (12 weeks or longer) also benefits cold compost made from leaves or other acidic, high-carbon materials, because it takes them longer to complete the physical (reduced particle size) and chemical (nutrient and pH normalization) changes associated with curing.

PERFECT MATCH

Garden Cress

The spicy little salad green known as garden cress (*Lepidum sativum*) is so sensitive to compromised soil chemistry that it will refuse to grow in soil containing even small amounts of natural or synthetic herbicides, or in immature compost. If you're not quite sure if a batch is finished with its active phase, see what happens when you put some in a pot and plant a dozen or so cress seeds in it. If the plants are ready to pluck and put on a sandwich after three weeks, you can be assured that the compost is advanced enough for most garden uses. Cress varieties vary in leaf texture and flavor. Frilly 'Wrinkled Crinkled Crumpled' makes a beautiful addition to salads and stir-fries, while flatter, broad-leafed varieties are better for sandwiches. All varieties of cress have a peppery bite, so most people mix the leaves with milder greens when using them in salads.

keep the process moving along. You can meet all three goals easily by placing compost over a breathable cloth barrier when it's ready to be cured (the barrier will deter tree roots from invading the pile and reduce nutrient leaching from the bottom of the pile) and then covering the compost with a rain-resistant tarp or other cover. Keep a hose or watering can handy for adding water as needed to keep the mixture barely moist, but not as moist as active compost (no water should squish through your fingers when you squeeze a handful tightly). A few light chops with a turning fork will add air, but aerating a curing heap is usually done more out of curiosity than necessity.

You also can cure compost in an enclosed container, for example a garbage can, storage bin, or a large plastic pail. In this situation you will need to open the lid to refresh the compost's air supply every few days at first, and then every few weeks as the compost nears maturity.

Storing Cured Compost

After working with a fine batch of compost for several weeks or months, and then allowing it to cure for a few more, it is pure pleasure to store up a nice supply for future use. We like to sift our black gold through a screen before storing it (see chapter 8 for our favorite screening techniques), but sifting is not necessary if the compost contains only a few small sticks or intact acorns. Whether or not you sift it, you probably do need to dry your cured compost a bit before packing it away in buckets, bins, or bags. Cured compost typically has a moisture content of

35 to 40 percent, which should be reduced to 15 to 20 percent for long-term storage (6 months or more). Reducing the moisture content keeps the compost from souring due to recolonization by aerobic bacteria, but there should be enough water present to sustain anaerobic life forms. How can you tell when compost is dry enough to store? If you don't trust yourself to guess, simply use your bathroom scale to measure moisture loss. Fill a large, clean bucket with cured compost and weigh it. Add or subtract compost as needed until the bucket weighs at least 10 pounds. Place the open bucket in a dry, sunny spot and stir it with a hand cultivator every day or two to encourage evaporation while mixing the moist and dry portions together. Weigh the bucket when you notice a significant weight loss. Allowing a pound for the weight of the bucket, the compost should be at the right moisture level for long-term storage when the weight drops to 6 pounds.

You won't have to use your scale more than a few times to learn what your compost looks, smells, and feels like when it is perfectly dried for storage. The cured, dried compost can be kept in a plastic pail topped with a lid, or you can use plastic storage bins, garbage cans, or the large containers used to package cat litter, birdseed, or laundry detergent. If you leave a little headroom before closing the containers, you can aerate the stored compost by giving the containers a good shake, roll, or jiggle from time to time. Keep the closed containers in a cool place, protected from sun and moisture; your compost will be ready to use at a moment's notice.

5

Comforter Compost and Grow Heaps

BEGINNING ON YOUR FIRST DAY as a gardener, you will need more good ground in which to grow plants. There is no easier way to turn a piece of lawn or patch of weeds into a garden bed than to make Comforter Compost, which is so named because it blankets the soil with cushy layers. Simply select the spot where you want to create a new bed, layer on compostable materials, and let them rot. You don't have to dig out grass or weeds to get started, and with a little planning, you can actually grow plants in your Comforter Compost.

Some plants grow so well in customized compost that the seeds can grow from the same heap in which the parent plants rot — an almost effortless way to help your garden perpetuate pumpkins, squash, or tomatoes. We call these tweaked heaps Grow Heaps, and once you discover the fun of watching Grow Heap crops explode from seeds buried in made-to-order compost piles, you may never be without them again.

Working with Comforter Compost

The advantages of Comforter Composting, which is basically an intensified version of an older method called sheet composting, are not limited to creating new beds or improving the soil in established parts of your garden. You can also use Comforter Compost techniques to stabilize sites that turn into rutted washouts after heavy rains, or to create planting pockets atop soil that's too rocky or root-ridden to dig. Depending on your purpose and the materials you use, Comforter Compost can benefit you and your garden in six important ways:

▶ **Labor-saving site.** Comforter Composting is a perfect example of the first rule of compost gardening (see page 14), which is to choose labor-saving sites, because Comforter Compost always occurs in the garden. Once it's done, the only place Comforter Compost goes is into the soil beneath it. Do think strategically by choosing a centrally located bed or row for Comforter Composting projects. Then alternate 3" (7.6 cm) deep layers of green garden debris and grass clippings with partially decomposed leaf compost, soil, and whatever other organic materials you have on hand until the comforter is 1' (0.3 m) deep. With a little advance planning, you may be able to locate new Comforter Composts within easy "pitching" distance from any point in your garden.

▶ **No-work method.** Comforter Composting borders on being a no-work method, because there is no turning or mixing of materials until both the compost and the gardening year are done. Your only job is to keep piling things on and add water as needed to keep the materials moist. The composting process takes care of the rest.

▶ **Self-weeding.** You don't have to dig out existing grass or weeds before getting started, because Comforter Compost will smother existing vegetation by depriving it of light. Some particularly invasive plants, such as Canada thistle or Bermuda grass, will survive, so it is best to dig these types of troublemakers out before setting up a Comforter Compost.

▶ **Year-round.** A true all-season method, Comforter Composting can be done at any time of year. A project set up in spring often can be used as growing space right away, or you can use summer Comforter

Create new beds or invigorate old ones with Comforter Compost made from alternating layers of compostable materials.

Compost as a "fallow" or resting rotation in an intensively managed garden. As a way of "tucking in" garden soil for the winter, Comforter Composting is beyond compare.

▶ **Soil builder.** The soil-building potential of Comforter Compost runs deep, thanks to work done by night crawlers and other earthworms that make permanent tunnels beneath the heap. Earthworms know a great habitat when they find one, and few setups are more earthworm-friendly than the base layers of a Comforter Compost. You will see the results of this passive soil improvement when you fork finished Comforter Compost into the soil.

▶ **Natural beauty.** Comforter Compost can be just plain cute. It is fine to let a Comforter Compost go au naturel from a visual point of view, but you can get as creative as you want in order to make the project look pretty. For example, you can bring in color by using cloth or colored fencing as a low enclosure, and it's fast and easy to top off Comforter Compost with cloth or an attractive mulch material, such as pine needles or straw. Comforter Compost will disappear from view entirely when covered with a thin layer of soil or finished compost.

Once you become familiar with how you can best use your most abundantly available materials in Comforter Compost, it may emerge as one of your favorite ways to garden. Do keep in mind that thoughtful layering of materials is important (keep reading), and realize that although Comforter Composting is a fine method, it's not a miracle. If your goal is to create perfect new space fast, Comforter Composting will not give you loose, rich, well-drained soil that reaches 14" (35.6 cm) or more below the surface in a single season; sooner or later you will have to get behind a digging fork or spade to work it into the soil. However, Comforter Composting will jump-start the process by smothering existing vegetation, attracting earthworms and other creatures that help build better soil, and introducing an on-site source of active organic matter.

PERFECT MATCH
Raspberries

Raspberries are packed with healthful antioxidants, and they taste great, too. Most summer-bearing red raspberries (*Rubus idaeus*) propagate themselves by seed, by tip rooting of long branches, and by sprouting from root buds every chance they get. New plants often pop up several feet (meters) from the parent, where the soil may be in desperate need of an upgrade. Comforter Composting is an excellent way to improve soil conditions for these plants, and it smothers competing weeds and grasses. Simply rough up surrounding soil with a sharp hoe, and then layer on chopped or weathered leaves, partially rotted compost, and grass clippings. In addition to nurturing the new plants, this method can trigger the emergence of more nearby raspberry root sprouts, which often appear after the soil's surface is disturbed.

Fall-bearing raspberries don't sucker as freely as those that bear in summer, but 'Heritage' and other fall-bearing varieties are still great subjects for Comforter Composting. In fall, spread layers of compostable materials around the plants, but wait until late winter to cut back the old canes. To help the soil to warm promptly in spring, rake the weathered compost to the sides of the row when new cane tips appear.

Comforter Compost Basics

Any non-smelly materials that can be composted can be included in Comforter Compost, provided that they are layered in ways that enhance decomposition. Topping high-nitrogen greens with high-carbon browns is the general rhythm. If you want to grow plants in Comforter Compost, it helps to include thin layers of soil, which add density that helps plant roots to stay securely anchored.

The texture of the layered materials is important, because unlike other types of compost, which are worked primarily by microorganisms, the maturation of Comforter Compost results in large part from the work of soil-dwelling animals. Earthworms, ground beetles, and numerous species of millipedes, centipedes, and other crawly things will make themselves at home in Comforter Compost, tunneling and chewing their way through the layers with each passing day. Most of these critters like a little grit in their gullets, as well as shelter from predators. Alternating coarse materials with finer substances, such as a layer of bush bean corpses topped with half-decomposed shredded leaves, enhances the habitat value of a Comforter Compost for these and other squirmy, jumpy, and crawly decomposers.

Free-Form or Framed?

Enclosing a Comforter Compost bed with boards, plastic fencing, a cloth corral stapled to stakes, or

STRATEGIC LAYERS FOR COMFORTER COMPOST

If you begin with the end in mind, your Comforter Composting projects will produce huge dividends from the modest investment of labor you put into them. Consider these guidelines when deciding how to stack a new project together.

PURPOSE OF PROJECT	LAYERING STRATEGY
Smother grass and weeds in preparation for creation of a new bed.	Start with a base layer of several sheets of biodegradable newspapers or a single layer of cardboard. Top with alternate layers of grass clippings, leaves, garden waste, and soil.
Create growing space for legumes or other pioneer plants.	Make layers with whatever you have, including some soil. Make a trench filled with soil for planting seeds.
Rest and reinvigorate an established bed or row.	Place your richest material at the base, and add layers of any weed-free materials. Top with attractive mulch.
Prevent erosion and create planting space on sloping sites.	Use plenty of long-fiber materials, such as hay or straw. Pound short stakes or sticks into the ground to improve stability.

other material helps to create a neat edge and can add color and texture to your garden scene, but a frame is not necessary equipment for Comforter Composting. Allowing some of the material to trickle out around the bed's edges will do no harm, especially if it spills into garden pathways. In our gardens, we constantly transition selected patches of oversized lawn into garden by setting up oval or circular enclosures made from 14" (35.6 cm) wide pieces of plastic garden fencing. These little enclosures can be attached to wood, PVC pipe, or bamboo stakes with twist-ties or string if you want a square or rectangular bed, but you can let the fencing stand alone if a rounded shape will do. If you already have raised beds framed with a certain material like cedar boards or composite decking, you can simply erect a new bed and fill the frame with compostable goodies arranged in interactive layers as outlined above.

To turn lawn into garden, work from the top down with Comforter Compost. After the layers decompose, dig them into the passively improved subsoil.

Another great option is to incorporate Comforter Compost into a larger planting plan, so that nutrients leached from the compost trickle to roots of nearby plants *and* the compost serves as habitat for beneficial insects. For example, you may start with four upright-growing, long-lived plants, such as staked tomatoes or peppers, or a quartet of roses. Plant them in a circle or at each corner of a square or rectangular bed, making sure you can easily access the open space in the middle of the bed. Use that space to create a Comforter Compost consisting mostly of garden waste generated in nearby beds or rows. Provide a low enclosure if necessary to prevent unwanted avalanches of compost from smothering the bases of surrounding plants. The plants will shade the compost, making it easier to keep moist. As the season progresses, the plants will send foraging roots into the nutrient-rich compost. When you renovate the site in the fall, you can spread out the compost and dig it into the soil, or cover the bed with a new multi-layered Comforter Compost.

Managing Moisture

Water is the last thing you want in the comforter that keeps you warm at night, but undercover composting organisms require even moisture to do their work. Comforter Compost tends to dry out unless supplemental water is added. When a Comforter Compost is new, this is especially evident: It may absorb astounding amounts of water as each tidbit sponges up all the moisture it can hold. Standing around with a hose in your hand gets old fast, so plan in advance to keep your Comforter Compost from going thirsty. Here are four easy ways to hydrate a comforter heap:

▶ **Slow soak.** Arrange a short length of soaker or drip hose over the bed or row just before you add the topmost layer of material. If you like, you can make a

PERFECT MATCH

Asparagus

Most gardeners hold visions of succulent spears pushing up through late spring snow, even as they plant wiry rooted asparagus crowns. Within a few seasons, they will learn two more things about asparagus: The ferny foliage looks great in cut-flower arrangements, and established plants are nearly impossible to kill. Here's another secret: Asparagus can *move*. If the plant senses that it could grow better if it held its buds deeper down or closer to the surface, it can it expand or contract its roots to alter their depth.

This uncanny talent makes asparagus a perfect subject for a care regimen that centers on Comforter Compost. In late fall, after thoroughly weeding the patch, set up a three-layer Comforter Compost using a 2" (5 cm) deep layer of rich, cured compost (or a 1/2" [1.3 cm] deep layer of vermicompost), a 3" (7.6 cm) deep layer of chopped leaves or garden refuse, and an eye-appealing 3" (7.6 cm) deep top layer of straw or pine needles. Once plants are established (in about two years), gather all the spears that emerge in spring before your last frost date, and for two more weeks after that. When you stop picking, feed the plants with a balanced organic fertilizer to support strong foliar growth. Repeat the cycle each fall.

drip hose from a scrap piece of garden hose peppered with nail holes and capped off at the end.

▶ **Drip it in.** Collect several large milk jugs or plastic pails, and punch small holes an inch (about 2 cm) or so above the bases of the containers. Fill with water and let it slowly drip into the compost. The weight of the water that remains below the holes will help to keep the jugs from blowing away. Empty the jugs at least every five days to discourage mosquitoes.

▶ **Throw in the towel.** Cover the top of a Comforter Compost with old cotton towels, which can then be hidden from view with a thin layer of grass clippings or other mulch. When the towels feel dry, you know it's time to add water. Pieces of scrap carpeting make good moisture barriers, too.

▶ **Wrap it up.** Reduce moisture lost to surface evaporation by using scraps of sheet plastic to wrap the sides and top of a Comforter Compost after it has soaked up its fill of water. If desired, you can cover the plastic with mulch to hide it from view.

Growing Pioneer Plants in Comforter Compost

We usually think of pioneers as people who strike out into an unknown land, surviving on pluck and persistence, but some plants are also pioneers. Many weeds have a pioneer bent, and the same goes for garden plants, including beans, peas, and other legumes, as well as several members of the squash family. How do they do it? Back in 1813, leading British scientist Humphrey Davy went out on a limb by asserting that legumes "seem to" prepare the ground for wheat, but it was not until the 1880s that horticulturalists began to truly understand how peas pack away nitrogen they take from the air in storage nodules on their roots, which is an amazing survival strategy that helps them set a good crop of seeds when grown in poor soil. More recently, soil scientists have learned that zucchini and other members of the squash family can enlist the help of soil-dwelling fungi to help them take up phosphorus — a plant nutrient that is crucial for healthy root growth.

Natural Partnerships

It is therefore no small surprise that members of these two plant families are prime candidates for growing in Comforter Compost or Grow Heaps (for more information, see page 163). Both methods provide settings that are nicely outfitted with an available workforce of fungi and bacteria capable of teaming up with plants that come into the world ready to form cooperative relationships within the soil food web. Plants grown in Comforter Compost often benefit from light fertilization when they are young, but once they recruit the help of root-friendly compost microbes, they often show unstoppable vigor. See part 3, Plants for the Composter's Garden, for tips on making the most of these natural partnerships in your garden.

Using Comforter Compost in the Landscape

Beyond using Comforter Compost to prepare new planting spaces, it is also a useful method for improving the growing conditions of established plants. Here are five situations where strategic placement of Comforter Compost can be of tremendous benefit to garden plants by suppressing weeds, retaining soil moisture, and improving the soil from the top down:

▶ **Ring around a tree.** You can lay down a ring of Comforter Compost under an established tree or shrub, provided that you don't smother the base of the tree with more than 3" (7.6 cm) of material, which can deprive surface roots of oxygen and invite problems with diseases and gnawing rodents. This technique increases soil fertility, insulates surface roots from drought, and forms a basin that helps to retain water. If the tree (or large shrub) is deciduous (sheds its leaves in winter), the Comforter Compost can become a planting site for spring-flowering bulbs or an evergreen groundcover, such as pachysandra, or Japanese spurge (*Pachysandra terminalis*), periwinkle (*Vinca minor*), or a variegated English ivy (*Hedera helix*). Each of these knows how to put winter and early spring sun to good use, and then they are content to rest in the shade in the summer.

PERFECT MATCH

Reblooming Daylilies

Rustic strains of daylilies (*Hemerocallis* hybrids) have gone wild in ditches around the world, which we take as evidence that daylilies, in general, thrive when regularly doused with fresh infusions of decomposing organic matter. To their credit, the buds of most old-fashioned daylilies are a gourmet treat when lightly sautéed in olive oil (don't try this with the newer thick-petaled tetraploid flowers). This is a just balance for daylilies' flaws: The blossoms last only a day (sometimes two), and most varieties bloom but once a year.

Vigorous new varieties of reblooming daylilies are capable of blooming again and again, in flushes or nearly continuously from early summer through fall. Yes, there's a trick. For top performance, rebloomers need a steady supply of nutrients and moisture, because they produce new bud-bearing scapes from new fans of foliage. The mulch zone of a daylily bed is therefore a great spot for Comforter Composting during summer's second half, when rebloomers work the hardest. As you pile on the compostables, allow some open space around the base of each clump to avoid shading the leaves and limiting photosynthesis.

Spot Compost for Landscape Plants

Let's say that you want to plant some bulbs or woodland wildflowers in the fall, or tuck in some quickie annuals in spring. The problem is that the site you want to plant has drainage issues and soil that is even too poor to support weeds. Spot compost to the rescue! It's fast, it's easy, and it really works.

TOOLS AND MATERIALS

- Weed trimmer
- Hatchet
- Hoe
- Digging fork
- Used newspapers
- Garden hose and nozzle
- Shovel
- Garden rake
- Compost ingredients, green and brown
- Finished compost or organic mulch

1 Cut all vegetation back to the ground (unless it's woody or seedy, you don't need to gather it up). Be mean to invasive plants, and use a hatchet if necessary to chop into their crowns. ▼

2 Use a sharp hoe to rough up the surface of the soil. Then use a digging fork to perforate it with holes. ▼

3 Cover the area with layers of newspaper, 10 to 12 sheets thick. They will stay put better if you wet them first in a wheelbarrow of water, or you can dampen them as you put them on the ground. Be sure to overlap the edges to block light that might wake up lurking weed seeds. Corrugated cardboard works well for this layer, too, and it's an effective weed-blocker. ▼

4 Top the layer of newspaper or cardboard with a 3" (7.6 cm) deep layer of mixed compost ingredients, such as shredded leaves, grass clippings, and decomposed garden waste, or perhaps wet straw or hay mixed with manure or a nitrogen-rich meal. Water thoroughly. ▼

5 Cover the active compost with a 2" (5 cm) thick layer of attractive mulch, such as aged sawdust, pine straw, or even finished compost. Plant through the compost layers. ▼

6 As the compost shrinks, add a 1" (2.5 cm) thick layer of soil, and repeat steps 4 and 5. Your former pocket of wasteland is now a hot spot for gardening!

▶ **Marginally hardy perennials.** Deep mulching is often recommended to enhance the cold hardiness of flowering perennials, and Comforter Compost can pass for deep mulch any day of the week. In climates where the soil does not freeze in winter, set up 6" (15.2 cm) deep mounds of Comforter Compost over elephant ears (*Alocasia odora* or *Colocasia esculenta*) or over the bases of fig trees (*Ficus carica*) in late fall. In colder climates, wait until the soil freezes to create Comforters for hardy hibiscus (*Hibiscus syriacus*) and other marginally hardy perennials.

▶ **Walking shrubs.** A few long-limbed shrubs including forsythia and climbing or rambling roses often self propagate by burying the tips of arching branches in nearby soil, where they take root and grow. The locations they choose often surprise gardeners, making it impossible to prepare fertile places for the new plants to grow. You can do these "walking" plants a favor by covering the spots where the stem tips touch the ground with Comforter Compost, which will suppress weeds and grasses, expand the rooting media for shallow roots, and improve soil fertility all at the same time. This is a refinement of the propagation technique known as tip layering (below). You can use Comforter Compost in a similar way when doing simple layering of clematis and other ornamental vines.

Tip layering beneath cones of Comforter Compost is a sure, easy way to propagate bramble fruits and most perennial vines.

TURNING A DITCH INTO A LAWN

My entire yard is on a slope, and what sloping yard is complete without an eroded ditch? The one on my property was pretty big — roughly 10' wide x 15' long (3.05 m wide x 4.75 m long) — shady, and really hard to reach with a hose. Why not fill it in with compost and plant a little grass? I have two boys, and they could do with more room to play, plus smoothing out the terrain would make mowing much easier.

I started the renovation by raking leaves into the ditch, tramping them down, and raking in more. It seemed that adding a little structure would help, so I put down a layer of cardboard and covered it with a topping of chopped leaves. The materials stayed put through the winter, and in the spring I added countless cartloads of municipal compost and finally seeded the filled rut with grass seed.

Did it work? Sort of. As the bottom layers of leaves decomposed, the filling sank down more than I had hoped, meaning that I should have piled the compost a few inches higher than the surrounding lawn. Now I have an area that's less depressed and nicely green, but it would make a better miniature golf hole than an actual lawn. The boys like that idea, so it may turn out to be a success after all.

▶ **Expanding edges.** The best way to manage the weed-prone battleground area where a flower bed merges with lawn is to install a brick or stone mowing strip, which separates grass from mulch and provides a smooth surface for lawn-mower wheels. As a temporary margin, you can use a broad ribbon of Comforter Compost, which will deter weeds, keep mulch from the flower bed from washing out into the lawn, and provide visual contrast and definition for the edges of the bed. And, if you decide to expand the flower bed, the Comforter Compost will have begun the soil-improvement process in a passive, labor-saving way.

Of course, a masonry mowing strip is not your only long-term option for providing an attractive, yet functional, frame for a bed filled with flowers, herbs, veggies, or a mixture of all three. Depending on your climate, you might be able to make use of perennial edging plants, such as liriope, candytuft, or creeping thyme, or you can replant the edge each summer with edge-worthy annuals, such as ageratum, sweet alyssum, annual gypsophila, dwarf zinnias, or compact curly parsley. Edging a bed with Comforter Compost in fall is an excellent way to prepare soil for plants such as these, in subsequent seasons. Simply turn under the compost, mix in a balanced organic fertilizer, and bring on the plants.

▶ **Mound-layering shrubs.** If you want to propagate shrubs that multiply by growing new stems from root buds (often called suckering), you can use Comforter Compost as part of the mound-layering process. When you place Comforter Compost directly over the base of a red-twig dogwood (*Cornus sericea*), spirea (*Spiraea* species), or cotoneaster (*Cotoneaster* species), for example, the moist compost will encourage stems buried in it to form above the soil line. The following spring, as soon as the buds begin to swell, you can pull back the compost and use a sharp knife and small spade to dig out these well-rooted suckers, with roots attached, and transplant them to a new site. Rake the remaining Comforter Compost into the hole left behind and the parent plant should recover quickly.

Getting Started with Grow Heaps

We wish we could take credit for coming up with the idea of intentionally stocking compost piles with seeds of desirable plants, which sprout and grow into welcome volunteers, but that would be like claiming fame for a natural process that has been going on for more than 10,000 years. As early humans shifted from being hunter-gatherers to living in settlements, they realized that they needed to do something better with their waste than scatter it willy-nilly. Why not throw everything together in one place, thereby achieving some control over stench, flies, and vermin? In this way, the first garbage dumps evolved, which were long known as middens (derived from an archaic Danish word for dung). As primitive societies became true communities, in some places middens even developed into primitive kitchens — doughnut-shaped trash piles with a fire pit in the center that were used to prepare foods that needed to be harvested and cooked before they were stored.

The Earliest Grow Heaps

Archaeologically speaking, some of the best-preserved middens are found near bodies of water, where people threw the shells of clams and other shellfish year after year, along with other stuff they regarded as garbage. Seeds and plant parts recovered from shell middens provide information about what people ate and how they lived, but we must use our imaginations to contemplate the diets of early people who generated trash that decomposed faster and more completely than shells. Seed- and root-bearing plants were always part of the mélange of materials in a midden, so the midden (being basically a compost heap) provided plants with a nutrient-rich environment in which to grow. Enter species that became "camp followers" by enthusiastically springing up in or around middens, offering humans their first look at what plants can do when grown in compost. These plants, known as ruderals (from the Latin word for rubbish), were probably among the first of all garden crops. It is likely that beans, melons, and many other food crops caught the attention of earth's earliest gardeners by growing as robust volunteer plants in the midst of middens.

The Genetics of Grow Heaps

Since bygone eras, plants have not lost their liking for life in the compost pile, and most compost gardeners see a steady stream of seedlings popping up where they have spread their compost, or in the heap itself. These plants are often a source of curious delight to gardeners, and there are many reports of compost-borne tomatoes that show remarkable disease resistance, and watermelons that exhibit supernatural exuberance when allowed to stake out territory on the outskirts of a compost pile. We have spent our share of growing seasons enthralled by the sheer vigor of winter squashes that spewed forth from our heaps, but not all stories of compost volunteer plants have a happy ending. The truth be told, it is always a gamble when you accept and nurture random plants that sprout in your compost. Yes, you may get a great pumpkin vine that becomes the plant your kid remembers for the rest of her life, or you may harvest tomatoes that are hard and flavorless.

The explanation for this variability has nothing to do with the quality of your compost. Rather, the growth habit, appearance, and flavor of compost-borne seedlings are genetically determined, and unless you take steps to manage the plants' genetic heritage, you will encounter chaos. The reason has to do with hybrids. If the seeds that sprout in your compost were produced by hybrid parents (most supermarket tomatoes, peppers, and cucumber family crops are hybrids), the seedlings carry an unstable assemblage of genes. Hybrid varieties are created to be one-generation wonders that exhibit characteristics from two carefully selected parents. Those characteristics can be crucial to the success of your garden (for example, in the case of tomatoes that are hybridized to provide resistance to a prevalent disease), but in the generations that follow the hybridized ones (the pop-up seedlings in your compost), you may get throwbacks to rather feral grandparents, or you may get something really great. So, while growing a hybrid variety is often the best way to prevent a serious disease, when it comes to practicing planned parenthood of compost-borne seedlings, you are wise to look at high quality, regionally adapted, open-pollinated parent varieties.

Backyard Breeding of Open-Pollinated Varieties

Superior open-pollinated varieties are created by allowing a certain strain of a plant to perpetuate itself with thoughtful human help. Open-pollinated varieties are the result of "selective" breeding, which has been happening since the first gardeners began making choices, or selections, as they decided which plants would become the bearers of seeds. As a human seed saver working with an open-pollinated variety, you have four important tasks:

▶ **Isolation.** Prevent the "crossing" of the original strain with a different one, as can happen when bees or other insects carry pollen from flower to flower. Backyard plant breeders (and every seed saver is a breeder) use one of three approaches to "isolate" a plant from unwanted cross-pollination. These include using staggered planting times to make sure that plantings bloom far enough apart so that pollen will not be shared between different varieties, by separating plants by a distance of at least 100' (30.5 m), or by covering plants with floating row covers to exclude pollinating insects. When pollinators are excluded, the breeder must hand-pollinate flowers of crops that are not self-fertile.

▶ **"Roguing out."** Eliminate the weak and encourage the strong by pulling out plants that show unwanted traits, such as slow growth or substandard flavor. This step is called roguing out, and it is essential to making sure that the next generation is at least as good, if not better, than the one that came before it. This is also the most important step toward selecting seed-producing plants that show superior performance in the unique growing conditions in a given garden.

▶ **Passage of time.** Allow ample time for the plants to develop fully ripened seeds. Plants often look shabby as they devote all of their energy to nurturing seeds, but only totally ripe seeds can be counted upon to germinate when given good sprouting conditions.

▶ **Harvest and store.** Harvest, clean, and store the seeds in an air-tight container under cool conditions until it is time to replant them. Many other life forms share an interest in seeds, so keeping seeds safe from fungi, bacteria, and hungry animals is mandatory. The exceptions are cases in which you use a compost pile as a seed storage facility, which is what using Grow Heaps is all about.

Working with Grow-Heap Crops

A handful of popular vegetables have a long track record of success as compost volunteers, and these are the best candidates for Grow Heaps. If you have been composting for several seasons, you have no doubt seen some of these plants elbowing their way into your garden. Unless they are restrained, tomatoes, winter squash, and other Grow-Heap crops can become downright weedy.

Good Grow-Heap crops produce an abundance of sound seeds that survive cold composting with ease, and then germinate at appropriate times. So, using Grow Heaps can save you many hours of time and trouble. Simply make a compost heap or enclosed pen where you want the next season's crop to grow, bury a few ripe "mother fruits" in it, and the compost will clean the seeds, hold them through winter, and provide them with a fertile spot to sprout and grow when the weather warms in spring. Be prepared to see too much of a good thing. As reluctant as you may be to pull up perfectly good seedlings, thinning is a crucial step in managing Grow-Heap crops.

A detailed discussion of creating and using Grow Heaps follows, but we cannot overemphasize the importance of treating Grow Heaps as specialized compost projects in which *no seeds are allowed except for those you want to grow*. Only non-seed-bearing kitchen waste can be permitted in a Grow Heap. If you are careless with this detail, you will have no way to tell

A large Grow Heap set up in fall can produce a bumper crop of pumpkins the following summer.

the difference between plants that grow from seeds you put into the Grow Heap and chance volunteers.

Grow-Heap Essentials

Grow Heaps can be made from a huge range of materials, but from a practical standpoint, it is best to set them up in the fall as a specialized type of Comforter Compost. A good Grow Heap differs from other types of compost in that it contains several layers of soil along with compostable materials. The soil provides sturdy anchorage for plant roots, helps to satisfy plants' constant hunger for dissolved minerals, and improves the heap's ability to retain moisture. When we tried using soilless Grow Heaps (close to 100 percent organic matter), the plants often showed symptoms of nutrient deficiency and drought stress, even when the compost was never allowed to dry out. The nutrient shortage can be fixed by pouring on plenty of water-

soluble organic fertilizer (we like liquid fertilizers made from fish emulsion and seaweed), but drought stress is a more perplexing problem that is easily prevented by including soil in the heap.

The Importance of Transpirational Pull

Perhaps this seems illogical. Organic matter typically increases the moisture-holding ability of soil, so why should plants growing in pure compost have so much trouble taking up water that they severely wilt in midday, develop brown leaf tips, and show symptoms of inadequate pollination? The explanation lies in the extremely porous, spongy structure of compost, which contains larger and more numerous air pockets compared to a mixture of compost and soil. In an all-compost environment, the excessive air in the root zone causes a slowdown of the pumplike movement of water from root to leaf, which is called transpirational pull. Here's how this elegant system works: Within all plants, the cells that carry water from the roots to the leaves, flowers, and fruits are lined up end to end, forming an uninterrupted chain of moisture. At the bottom of this ingenious system, water (along with dissolved nutrients) is gently pulled into roots in much the same way you might suck water through a straw. When no moisture is available to the roots, the plant does what it can to wait out the problem by closing its leaf stomatas (pores on the undersurfaces of leaves) and allowing its cells to evenly sacrifice their water supply. Symptoms we see in drought-stressed plants include flaccid lettuce leaves and squash foliage that looks like half-folded umbrellas.

Now imagine that instead of sipping water through a straw, you are trying to enjoy a frozen drink, but every few pulls on the straw you come up with nothing, because the moisture you have removed as been displaced by air. You must wait until the air pocket is filled with liquid to get another sip, but the number of dry slurps declines as the drink melts into denser slush. Including soil in a Grow Heap has a similar effect, in that it helps eliminate interruptions in a plant's transpirational pull.

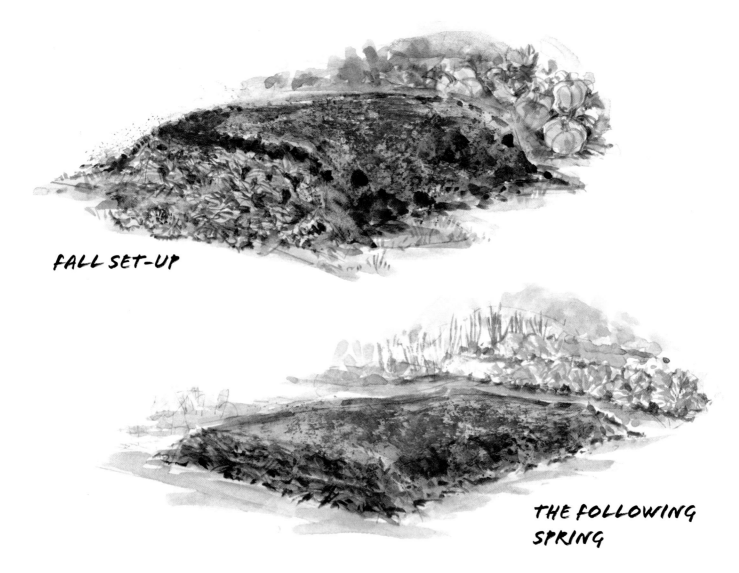

FALL SET-UP

THE FOLLOWING SPRING

A Grow Heap set up in the fall will shrink to half of its original depth by spring.

The amount of soil needed in a Grow Heap varies with the crop, but about 20 percent of the total mass of the heap is a good rule of thumb. If you make a Grow Heap in the fall using one part soil to four parts leaves, grass clippings, or weedless yard waste, the organic matter will show substantial shrinkage by spring, resulting in a shallow heap that is closer to equal parts soil and active organic matter.

Planting Seeds in a Grow Heap

The first time you plant a certain crop in a Grow Heap, you will probably begin with a seed packet of a good open-pollinated variety (see variety suggestions in the Plant Profiles that begin on page 245). At the correct season for planting, simply bury the seeds in your prepared heap and keep them moist until they sprout. Sow seeds a little closer together than you would when planting them in a bed or row. To encourage strong germination, it can help to dig out small planting pockets or trenches in the heap and fill them with soil, because most seeds sprout best when they are in close contact with moist soil. After the seedlings appear, thin them as needed to prevent crowded conditions.

As summer progresses, select a few perfect fruits as the seed-bearers of next year's crop. If it's too early to place your seedy specimens in a new Grow Heap, fill a bucket or cardboard box with moist, mature compost, cut the fruits into golf ball–size chunks, and bury them at least 3" (7.6 cm) deep. In the fall, after you have created a new Grow Heap, plant the contents of the containers — or seed-bearing veggies cut into halves or quarters — by burying them 6" to 12" (15.2 to 30.5 cm) deep in their new home. The fruits will rot over the winter, but most of the seeds will be in perfect condition to sprout at just the right time in spring. If you like, you can turn and mix the heap to move some of the seeds closer to the surface, but this is an optional step with Grow Heaps. Once a Grow Heap is set up in fall or in spring, all you need to do is add water often enough to satisfy the needs of the plants and the microorganisms in the Grow Heap.

PERFECT MATCH

Forget-Me-Nots

Few ornamental plants are as adaptable as dainty, blue-flowered forget-me-nots (*Myosotis sylvatica, M. alpestris*). Sometimes they grow as perennials that are hardy to Zone 3, but more often new plants grow from seeds shed in late summer and behave as hardy annuals. Want more forget-me-nots? Wait until the plants have finished nurturing a new crop of seeds, and then gather up the seed-bearing branches and mix them into a Grow Heap located in a moist, shady spot near where you want to see clouds of blue the next year. Cover the heap through summer to keep the materials lightly moist. In late summer, give the heap a thorough chopping and then spread the compost 2" (5 cm) deep where you want the forget-me-nots to grow. Some seedlings will appear as the soil cools in the fall, followed by more in spring. This technique is also a good way to preserve and distribute the seeds of reseeding annuals, such as sweet alyssum, portulaca, and cleome.

THE GROW-HEAP FAMILY PLAN

There is a happy symmetry in the fact that the best Grow Heap crops belong to two plant families — the tomato family (*Solanaceae*) and the cucumber family (*Cucurbitaceae*), which are discussed in more detail in part 3. In some climates, beans work in Grow Heaps, too, but more often birds and other critters consume them before they can sprout and grow.

Fortunately, there are only a few diseases and pests that infest both the tomato and the cucumber family, so it is usually safe and practical to flip-flop Grow Heap crops, as well as Grow Heap sites, by growing tomato-family crops in compost made from cucumber-family waste, and vice versa. You can include plants from other botanical families in Grow Heaps, but do avoid stocking a Grow Heap in which you plan to grow tomatoes with dead tomato-family plants, and don't expect to grow super-healthy squash in the residue of last year's zucchini. The leaves and stems of spent plants may be infected with a range of fungal diseases, from early blight of tomato to powdery mildew of squash, and they also may harbor pupae or adults of troublesome insects that overwinter in plant debris. Grow Heaps heat up very little, if at all, so some troublemakers are likely to survive within the heap.

To ensure that your Grow Heap crops get a fair start at lifelong health, compost the residue from different plant families in separate Grow Heaps, and then use the heap made with tomato family plants to grow cucumber cousins, and vice-versa.

Grand Finales for Comforter Compost and Grow Heaps

The hardest part of working with Comforter Compost or Grow Heaps is taking them apart at the end of the season, which is actually not hard at all. If a large volume of finished or almost-finished compost remains, you may need to move some of it to another nearby spot, but usually you can dig it into the soil right where it sits. Always use a digging fork rather than a spade for this job, because the soil under these types of compost projects is often teeming with earthworms. There will be casualties regardless of how gently you dig, but fewer earthworms will get sliced to smithereens if you work with a fork.

In some climates it may be practical to skip the digging and move right into a new Comforter Compost or Grow Heap, but doing so may set the stage for problem populations of plant-eating slugs and snails. Indeed, should you notice that a heap of any kind is morphing into a mollusk mansion, mobilize to get these slimers under control by studding the heap with slug traps made from shallow dishes of beer. Keep in mind that a slug-infested compost project is not necessarily a bad thing, because it encourages your enemies to mass together in one place. It may take several nights of trapping to reduce snails and slugs to a manageable number once they colonize a heap, but this is much easier than trying to hunt them down in every corner of your garden. If you live in an area where slugs or snails are chronic problems, you may even begin using Comforter Compost as an intentional habitat that attracts slugs and snails that would otherwise be chewing holes in your favorite plants. To make a heap even more attractive to slugs, lay down a line of cornmeal in a moist area along the edge of an infested compost pile, and cover it with a board or a piece of damp cardboard just before the sun goes down. First thing in the morning, you should find several sticky specimens on the bottom of the board, which can be scraped into a watery grave — a pail of soapy water.

6
Composting Underground in Craters, Trenches, and Holes

INFINITELY USEFUL yet woefully underutilized, composting in excavated holes or trenches is a method every compost gardener should know. It is the best way to take soil improvement to new depths when creating planting space in sites with rocky or compacted subsoil that must be cracked into to make them suitable growing places for deeply rooted plants. Underground composting also works well in porous, sandy soils, because deeply buried organic matter is insulated from leaching by rainwater as it moves through the soil. In any soil situation, as well as in gardening sites that are not particularly problematic, underground composting puts organic matter exactly where it is needed, right within easy reach of foraging roots of your garden plants.

The Compost Problem Solver

Underground composting methods also work well in hot, dry climates, because buried composting materials are insulated from surface heat and evaporation. But the most attractive aspect of taking compost underground is that it cannot be seen or smelled. With the help of a buried compost project called a Pit-of-Plenty, designed to receive kitchen wastes, you will never again scurry to hide your compost from view should you decide to host a social event in your yard. Even the fertile leavings from a fish-cleaning session won't come back to haunt you once they are securely buried underground.

On the practical side, some underground composting methods provide safe ways to put weedy manures or other problem materials to good use. When buried more than 1' (30.5 cm) deep, most weed seeds will eventually perish. Some long-lived weed seeds will survive for several years, but they will never sprout if you take care not to bring them within 4" (10.2 cm) of the surface.

Some may consider it a disadvantage that finished underground compost can be awkward to scoop out compared to an aboveground heap, but this is not an issue if the compost is never scooped. If you make compost in the dark depths where topsoil and subsoil come together, and later grow plants on top of your masterpiece, the compost is exactly where it needs to be, with no need to dig or move it at all. With the exception of a permanent Pit-of-Plenty (see page 181) created to receive fresh trimmings from the kitchen, underground composting methods are basically on-site in their nature, so they should be used in spots where you want more and better soil for garden plants.

In the following pages, we will explore four simple ways to put underground compost to work:

▶ **Layered Craters.** These ready-to-plant beds combine the benefits of double digging with Comforter Compost–type layers, so they are an ideal way to wake up a new garden space.

▶ **Pit-of-Plenty.** Hide your kitchen wastes from view with a permanent composting pit topped with a critter-proof lid.

▶ **Treasure Troughs.** Do you need to extend a bed or add a row to the outside edge of your garden? Dig a trough, fill the bottom with compostable waste, and start planting.

▶ **Honey Holes.** Use underground compost as the heart of a working garden bed.

The Legacy of Latrines

Pardon our coining of catchy phrases, but underground composting needs an image makeover because of its historical association with outhouses and latrines. Humans have been disposing of their own biological wastes in holes dug into the earth for tens of thousands of years, and in some places they do it still! Beyond its association with human sewage, pit composting also has been extensively used as a means for controlling odors from animal manures. George Washington's home in Mount Vernon, Virginia, included a stone-lined "dung pit" to shield the house from the sights and smells of rotting stable manure. In the Bible, dung pits are repeatedly mentioned as the worst possible environments for people. With or without actual dung, holes dug in the ground are great places to make compost from bad-smelling materials.

Granted, compost that matures in the ground is different than other types of compost because it decomposes with a limited supply of air. Most aboveground composting methods are powered by aerobic bacteria, which need oxygen to do their work, while buried compost is more likely to be worked by anaerobic life forms, at least during the early phases of the decomposition process. This is the well-known, stinky-slimy phase often associated with overly wet compost, which is not bothersome when it occurs below the ground. If you like, you can use ventilation pipes to run air into underground compost (see the Composter's Conduit project on page 180), which will help to bring about a balance between anaerobic and aerobic bacteria. Regardless of who does the work — anaerobic or aerobic bacteria — sites improved by using underground composting methods can have soil equal in quality to that of spots that have been dug and amended with compost made above the ground, but the renovated soil has the benefit of stretching deeper into the earth.

We have little hard science available to enlighten us on specific characteristics of compost made underground in a home-gardening situation. Digging holes for the purpose of burying waste has few practical applications in agriculture, so it has simply not been studied. But because beauty and pleasing smells are high priorities in a home landscape, underground composting can be very practical, indeed. Give various underground methods a try, and you will see proof of the benefits of composting underground right before your eyes.

Historically, stable latrines were used to collect and compost ever-present horse manure.

Underground vs. Aboveground Composting

Input/Effect	Underground Compost	Aboveground Compost
Initial Labor	Digging required to create composting space.	Materials can be placed on top of unworked soil.
Materials	Can handle smelly or weedy materials, as well as very moist materials.	Malodorous materials hard to handle. Weedy materials must be quarantined.
Moisture	Retains moisture by reducing evaporation. Dry pockets occasionally require attention in new projects.	Water easily lost to surface evaporation. Moisture requires ongoing monitoring.
Leaching	Nutrients released as gases or water-soluble compounds retained in soil.	Nutrients released as malodorous gases (such as nitrogen) often lost to open air.
Mixing/Turning	Little or none required after project is created.	Must be mixed or turned to achieve superior results.
Harvesting	None required.	Can be collected and stored for future use.

Secrets of the Subsoil

Gardeners who like to dig holes and have a natural curiosity about the rocks, roots, and worms that form the soil's infrastructure will enjoy using underground composting methods, because all of them require digging into the compacted zone known as the subsoil. A hard layer of subsoil covered by a few scant inches (centimeters) of softer topsoil is natural in many ecosystems, but it also can be man-made. For example, gravity and natural compaction (from atmospheric pressure, rain, and the movement of animals) helped to form hard subsoils in more than 30 million acres (12.1 million hectares) in North America alone. Mountain sites often have a thin layer of topsoil over rock, and in arid regions, a layer of concretelike caliche forms as minerals being pulled upward by evaporation meet and meld with those washed downward by occasional rains.

In many neighborhoods, farms, and gardens, humans bear responsibility for the presence of hardpan (hard, impermeable subsoil). When bulldozer operators create an earthen building pad for a house, they often import clay soil because it is so dense; it does a good job supporting the structure's foundation. Or, as new housing developments are created, subsoil from one lot may be scraped off and pushed or dumped onto another, resulting in a patchwork of topsoil and subsoil situations. Topsoil is brought in later on, when a new house is almost finished, but an 8" (20.3 cm) layer of topsoil in foundation beds and 4" (10.2 cm) of topsoil for lawn areas (customary builders' specifications in many areas) does not make up for the glaciers of clay or rock hidden just below the surface.

Finally, a layer of hardpan often forms beneath soil that is cultivated repeatedly to a certain depth. It's a physical thing. Small soil particles break free as the soil is cultivated. They drift downward, dry, or they mix with rain and move down as thin mud, eventually creating a layer of subterranean stuccolike material. Modern low-till farming methods have helped to reduce this problem in farm fields that are maintained with tractors, but it remains an issue in gardens managed with garden tillers.

Subterranean composting conserves moisture in arid regions and helps loosen compacted clay soil.

TREES NEED SUBSOIL

Garden plants grow much better in soil in which drainage and fertility have been improved by opening and renovating the subsoil, but not trees. Long-lived trees and shrubs often grow best when their roots are securely anchored in compacted subsoil. In fact, some experts recommend making separate piles of topsoil and subsoil as you dig planting holes for trees and large shrubs. Put the subsoil back on the bottom of the hole as you refill it, and shovel the topsoil on top. This procedure sets the plant up from the get-go to make itself at home in the site just as it is. We have to wonder if deep roots actually need the comparatively sterile conditions of subsoil as opposed to the rowdy biological circus present in the organically enriched topsoil.

Because of this, underground composting methods are not suitable for preparing planting holes for trees and shrubs, particularly native or near-native species. Yet the surface area over these plants' root zones is a great place to use casual Comforter Composting methods (see page 154) or to simply use compost as mulch. Either technique will intensify nature's pattern of enriching the soil from the top down, without distracting plants from their important work of establishing reliable roots.

Exceptions may erupt from time to time. Do you yearn to grow a luscious, self-fertile cherry tree or a head-high reblooming rose? These and many other popular woody plants have a proven track record of responding dramatically to soil that is amended with up to 30 percent cured compost, which is blended with the excavated soil as the planting hole is backfilled.

Opening the Drain

Any time you crack into compacted subsoil, you improve the site's drainage by creating fissures through which excess water can move. Only bog plants grow well in soil that is very poorly drained, and we think that naturally occurring slow-draining sites that collect rain should be left with their subsoil intact and used as rain gardens comprised of plants that tolerate wet roots, help purify water, and look pretty, too. Garden sites that aren't natural mud puddles, yet refuse to be penetrated beyond the first few inches (centimeters) when probed with a digging fork or spade, must have their subsoil opened before they are asked to support cultivated plants. The composting methods in this chapter go a step further by infusing the subsoil and the topsoil with biologically active organic matter.

Whether you are setting up a new underground composting project or doing some double digging, gaining access to compacted subsoil is hard work that calls for patience, perseverance, and special tools. Following the sequence of steps below will make excavating easier and help you make wise allotments of available time and energy.

1 Identify the area you want to bring into cultivation. If possible, perforate the surface with numerous vertical holes by pushing down with a digging fork. If this gets you nowhere, use a hammer and a large nail, tent stake, or thin steel rod (rebar) to make the holes. This is a great job for kids who like to bang on things.

2 Flood the site with water to soften the soil. Wait a day or two, and conduct a probing mission if you suspect the presence of a buried boulder. Use a hammer and a piece of metal pipe or a rebar stake to poke around in order to rule out this possibility. When you hit solid rock, it has a distinctive sound and feel. ▼

3 Assuming the site passes the buried boulder test, attempt to remove the topsoil with a sharp spade or digging fork. You may need to use a pick to break up the chunks. Set the excavated soil aside in a wheelbarrow or cart, or pile it up on a Composter's Sling (see page 82) or a piece of scrap plywood placed at one side of the hole. ▼

4. Keep a bucket handy, and fill it with rocks or other obstructions as you find them. Use a pry bar to loosen and lift rocks that are larger than your head. Resist the temptation to use your long-handled shovel or spade to pry out large rocks, unless you are prepared to risk bending the blade and breaking the handle. Should you encounter a stout tree root, stop and reconsider what you are doing. Trees may suffer a slow death when primary roots are cut or seriously injured.

5. Wearing protective goggles, use a splitting maul or ax (both wood-splitting tools) to shatter rocks that show a willingness to crumble. If you have never before handled one of these tools, take the time to practice a sound, safe swing: Keep your knees loose, hold your back and belly tight, and let the tool land the blows. You also can break out rock with a rock chisel or hatchet, but be sure to protect your eyes from flying shards. Set aside low-quality, rocky subsoil in a shady place. Later, you can sift out the rocks and use the soil in other projects.

6. Stop digging when you have gone 24″ (61 cm) or as deep as you can go. Excavating to only 12″ to 14″ (30.5 to 35.6 cm) is not a failed project! Repeat step 1 to perforate the floor of your excavated site with drainage nooks and crannies, and you're ready to fill it with a Layered Crater or another type of underground compost.

7. To bring the site into cultivation right away, add additional aboveground root space by using raised beds, Comforter Compost, or Grow Heaps for a couple of seasons. Then try deep digging again, because the microbial activity of the soil — and physical penetration of fissures in the subsoil by plant roots — will have made the bottom of the hole much more friable.

Working with Layered Craters

If you take the basic idea behind Comforter Compost and layer the materials into an excavated hole or trench rather than piling them up on the ground, you have a Layered Crater. This is an ideal method for making huge, lasting improvements in sites that have compacted subsoil or thin to nonexistent topsoil.

Like other underground methods, Layered Craters require a substantial amount of work up front, with little or no follow-up labor. If your soil is especially compacted or rocky, you could spend a weekend transforming enough space to support three tomato plants in a Layered Crater. The good news is that after only one season, a Layered Crater will show you how good your previously awful soil can become if you juice it up with plenty of biologically active organic matter.

Historically, the Layered Crater method shares its background with a well-known innovation made by market gardeners living near Paris, France, in the 1830s. They discovered that by digging the soil very deeply — to 24" (61 cm) or more and improving its tilth with organic matter, they could get large yields from plants spaced closely. This practice of "double digging" became the foundation of the French Intensive method of gardening, and there are many parallels between double digging and making Layered Craters. In both situations, the topsoil is dug up and set aside, and then the subsoil is removed. When double digging, the two piles are enriched with organic matter as the site is refilled, with the enriched topsoil placed at the bottom. When making a Layered Crater, the excavated soil is returned to the dug site sandwiched between layers of compostable organic matter. It matters little whether the topsoil and subsoil are kept separate.

Most gardeners who make Layered Craters do so because their soil needs a lot of work. Rocks may need to be broken up, lifted out, and sifted from the excavated soil using a Compost Sifter or similar device (see page 220). Sifting out rocks and roots reduces the volume of the excavated soil, about half of which should be piled next to the hole for layering back into it along with other materials. Still, you will need a place to set aside extra excavated soil. Having such a stash of soil is great if you're using Comforter Compost (see page 154) or Grow Heaps (see page 163) to grow plants, because plants grow best when

Once the digging's done, fill your Layered Crater with goodies that will benefit your plants and the surrounding soil for seasons to come.

their roots have access to at least a little actual soil. Set-aside soil also can be incorporated into home-made potting soil (see page 230).

Creating a Plantable Layered Crater

There are no special instructions for excavating a crater beyond those outlined on the facing page, with the exception of stockpiling half of the soil you dig out alongside the hole or trench. The hole can be of any shape but should not be so large that you cannot reach the middle when you kneel at the edge. Once created, the Layered Crater will become a footfall-free zone where physical compaction is kept to a minimum, so your plan for the site should include pathways that allow easy access.

After digging as deeply as you can, begin filling the crater by covering the bottom with a 3" (7.6 cm) thick layer of coarse compost materials, such as stemmy dead plants, hay, or small sticks broken into small pieces. Using a coarse, slow-rotting base layer will keep a little air trapped at the bottom of the crater, and help to provide drainage in the event of prolonged wet weather. Next, add a 2" (5.1 cm) thick layer of shredded leaves or other high-carbon brown material, topped by a 1" (2.5 cm) layer of soil. Sprinkle a light dusting of a dry organic fertilizer over the soil and water well. As an insurance policy against having the bottom layers dry out, this is the best time to install a Composter's Conduit (see page 180).

Now the crater is ready for a 2" (5.1 cm) thick blanket of high-nitrogen green material, such as grass clippings, manure, or chopped foliage from a Compost Fodder Crop (see page 276). Top the green matter with a 2" (5.1 cm) thick layer of browns, 1" (2.5 cm) of soil, and a light sprinkling of organic fertilizer. Drench with water. Continue adding layers (greens, browns, soil, and fertilizer) until the top of the Layered Crater is 4" (10.2 cm) higher than the surrounding soil.

The filled crater will begin to compact and sink immediately, which is not a problem if you want to plant it with seed potatoes or sturdy tomato seedlings. If you plan to direct-seed the Layered Crater with beans, peas, or a cucumber family crop, make 4" (10.2 cm) square holes and fill them with good soil taken from another part of your yard. Plant the seeds in the soil-filled holes, because seeds germinate best when they are in close contact with soil.

Compaction will continue as your plants grow, so plan to add more compostable material or mulch as needed to keep it from becoming a sinkhole. At the end of the season, use a digging fork to lift and mix the material in the crater, which should be nicely decomposed by this point. If the texture of the mix seems too light and fluffy, mix in more soil. You may find a ready supply in the previously rock-hard sides and bottom of the Crater, which will have softened after several months of close contact with moist organic matter. Or, use soil sifted from your standby mountain of dug dirt. After this bit of fine-tuning, your Layered Crater can be worked like any fertile, deeply dug bed. After the mixing is done, do check the bed's pH if soil conditions in your area tend to be acidic or alkaline. Follow package directions when adding lime to raise the pH of acidic soil, or powdered sulfur to lower the pH of alkaline soil.

Make a Composter's Conduit

The lower portions of a Layered Crater have no access to fresh air beyond the spaces between the coarse materials at the bottom. Should the materials dry out, it can be difficult to restore moisture to all of the layers simply by watering from the top. Installing a Composter's Conduit helps get air and water down into the crater, and the conduit provides an easy way to deliver water to plants you are growing in the site.

The dimensions we give here are for a Composter's Conduit suitable for a 6' (1.8 m) long row that is 18" (45.7 cm) wide, but you can make a conduit of any size — and there is no rule against using a Composter's Conduit in other types of composting projects. Once installed, you can leave it in place for a year or more. Before reusing your conduit in a new project, soak the pieces in a wheelbarrow filled with warm, soapy water, and then use a strong stream of water to clear any blocked holes.

MATERIALS AND SUPPLIES

- Hack saw
- Drill with ⅜" (1 cm) bit
- One 8' (2.4 m) long piece of 1½" (3.8 cm) diameter PVC pipe
- Two 1½" (3.8 cm) diameter PVC elbow connectors

1 Saw the PVC pipe into three pieces — one 5' (1.25 m) long and two 18" (45.7 cm) long.

2 Place the long piece on a flat surface and drill numerous holes, spacing them 2" to 3" (5.1 to 7.1 cm) apart, in one half the length of the pipe. Also make several holes in one half the length of each of the two short pieces. ▼

3 Use the corner connectors to assemble the conduit by attaching the two short legs to the long horizontal piece. They should fit together tightly enough to hold together without glue if you handle the conduit gently. Rotate the pipes so that the perforations of each piece face away from the center. The holes in the long piece should face downward, and the holes in the side pieces should face outward. ▼

4 Place the conduit in your Layered Crater atop 3″ to 4″ (7.6 to 10.2 cm) of compostable material. The open ends of the conduit should extend about 5″ (12.7 cm) above ground level. ▼

5 Keep the two side pieces of the conduit vertical as you complete your Layered Crater. After it is installed, air will flow continuously through the conduit. When deep moisture is needed, simply fill the conduit several times with water from a hose. ▼

Pretty Pits-of-Plenty

The best way to use a Pit-of-Plenty, the underground counterpart to an aboveground enclosed compost bin, is to install one as a convenient place to dump kitchen waste and organic refuse generated by nearby garden beds. But unlike a bin, heap, barrel, or composter, a Pit-of-Plenty doesn't stick up above the ground, so it's easily hidden from view. This is an important consideration if you need a place to compost kitchen waste only a few steps outside your back door — and every compost gardener does! If you have to carry your countertop collection crock more than fifteen paces, you're walking too far.

Finding the right spot for a Pit-of-Plenty may take some study, because the areas closest to entryways are already high-value gardening real estate:

▶ They are the best places to grow kitchen herbs so sprigs can be gathered quickly in all types of weather.

▶ They are entryways, where welcoming flowers are mandatory.

▶ They may be dominated by outdoor living areas that include a deck or patio.

The truth be told, most types of compost simply do not fit in well visually in this high-activity landscape sector. However, an unobtrusive trap door that rises only a few inches above the ground is easy to camouflage, and much more attractive than any type of aboveground bin. Once a Pit-of-Plenty is installed, the lid or top will be the only visual evidence that you have yucky-looking compost in progress within easy dumping distance of your back door.

Designing a Practical Pit

The best versions of the Pit-of-Plenty concept are nothing more than roomy holes topped with a lid to keep out animals and excess rain. Any spot where you

Ethiopian Potatoes

Barbara's Journal

My newest bed was a 6' (1.8 m) long, double-wide swath of lawn converted to Comforter Compost. In its first year, it supported spring peas and summer pole beans, but the soil under the compost zone was still a mess of compacted clay and rock. It was time to dig in. Dig is not exactly the right word, because my newly sharpened spade hit the bricklike subsoil only 2" (5.1 cm) below the surface. I ended up sitting on the side of the hole cracking into the subsoil with a hatchet.

After five hours, I had hauled off at least 100 lbs (45.6 kg) of rocks, one bucket at a time, and carved out a hole 15" (38.1 cm) deep and 20" (51 cm) wide. The next day, it took another hour to refill the crater with 15 alternating 1" (2.5 cm) layers of sifted soil and decomposed leaves, fresh grass clippings, and half-rotted horse manure. The hours spent rock-crushing gave me time to think about what I was doing and to wonder whether other folks had tried the same thing. My research turned up a project in Ethiopia where agricultural aid workers taught local farmers to plant potatoes in compost-filled trenches. Of course! Yellow-fleshed fingerling potatoes would be a perfect test crop for my new bed.

I started with seven little green potatoes, and after two months I pulled my crop. Each plant produced 20 to 30 usable tubers! That's an impressive return, but here's the biggest thing I learned about potatoes grown in a Layered Crater. They ask for nothing. They are happy. And being in the presence of such satisfied, productive plants makes me happy, too.

can dig a hole at least 14" (35.6 cm) deep (without encountering buried utilities) that also meets your access needs, will work for a Pit-of-Plenty. The size and shape of the hole are up to you, but we think a rectangular hole, 20" (50.8 cm) wide by 36" (91.4 cm) long is big enough to do the job. Smaller is better for aesthetic reasons, and a trench this size is easily and securely covered by a quarter sheet of ¾" (1.9 cm) thick exterior plywood — a precut size that's widely available at home supply stores.

You can be as creative as you like in making a lid, which should blend in with the adjacent areas of the landscape. You could use an old door and hinge it to a frame made from stock lumber or landscape timbers. Or, keep it simple with plywood stained or painted a neutral color (for details, see Top Off a Plentiful Pit on page 184), attached to a simple box frame with hinges. Do make sure the lid can stand the weight of a child or other unsuspecting person who mistakes it for a spot of decking. A weighty lid will also improve the cover's animal resistance, because heavy lids are hard for dogs and other determined critters to move. If you decide to go light with a piece of metal roofing or something similar, you can secure it with stones, bricks, or a utility tie-down (bungee cord) attached to stakes on either side of the pit.

Don't bother to line the walls of the pit with brick, concrete blocks, or wood, all of which will make digging around in the pit more difficult. (Bear in mind that even rot-resistant cedar or redwood, or chemically treated woods, will degrade when exposed to constant moisture and also may become termite terminals.) If you feel the need to line your pit with a material that will serve as a partition between the compost and surrounding soil, try lining the dug hole with pieces of scrap carpeting or two thicknesses of burlap; either will deter (but not eliminate) incursion from tree roots but will still allow water to drain out should the pit be flooded.

You can compost in a big plastic storage bin buried up to its rim (first drill drainage holes in the floor of the bin), but doing so requires precise digging, which may not be possible if you encounter rocks or roots as you dig the hole. Flexible liners made from carpeting or cloth are better, because they easily mold themselves to the quirky contours of a hole that has a big rock jutting in from one side, or a thick tree root that sticks up at the bottom. But lining your Pit-of-Plenty really is unnecessary. Earthen walls work beautifully for home-sized underground composts.

Working a Pampered Pit

Working a Pit-of-Plenty is similar to coaching compost along in an enclosed composting container, with a few unique differences. A Pit-of-Plenty's earthen sides and bottom moderate temperatures, keeping them cooler in summer and warmer in winter. The walls also affect moisture levels by bringing evaporative moisture loss to a near standstill, though they may wick away moisture should the surrounding soil become extremely dry. However, as in other enclosed composting situations, which utilize large amounts of kitchen waste, the material in a Pit-of-Plenty is more likely to get too wet than to suffer from dryness. Should the contents of your pit turn into sloppy compost stew from large deposits of kitchen waste, mixing in some shredded paper or cardboard or other brown material will usually fix the problem.

In summer, your pit will receive frequent visits from flies, wasps, and other insects, which are enticed by the aroma of rotting cantaloupe rinds and other sweet delicacies. If insects prove too bothersome, they can be partially controlled with a screened skylight that doubles as a ventilation pipe (see Versatile Vent Tubes on page 186). Better yet, simply accept them as part of your compost's ecosystem. Once you get over the aversion most of us have to seeing writhing mag-

gots (fly larvae) at work, they can be very interesting critters to watch! In late summer and early fall, give foraging yellow jackets a wide berth. They rarely sting when engaged in food-gathering work, but they can be irritating nonetheless.

THROW CRITTERS OFF THE SCENT

If raccoons, opossums, or other wild animals often visit your garden, defend your compost by using an enclosed composter (such as those discussed on page 142) or by composting underground. For those days when you have old applesauce, an abundance of egg shells, or other aromatic items to add to an open heap, deter invaders by covering your compost with a piece of fencing (plastic garden fencing is fine) held in place with heavy stones or bricks. You can also fight back with the deterrent scent of ammonia. Animals back off when they encounter ammonia's vapors, which can be released via small open saucers or by tying strips of cloth to a post or fence and soaking it with ammonia from a squeeze bottle (a great reuse for dishwashing liquid bottles). Ammonia will burn plants if it drips on their leaves, so be careful when handling it in your garden.

Top Off
a Plentiful Pit

After years of struggling to maintain some semblance of tidiness around the above-ground bin next to my deck, I replaced it with a Pit-of-Plenty topped with a plywood lid attached to a wood frame with a pair of hinges. A minor add-on — a piece of nylon cord tied between the handle and my deck railing — makes it possible to open the lid, dump out my countertop collection crock, and close it again in less than 20 seconds, without ever stepping off the deck. But here's the best part: Since switching to the pit, I have not seen a single errant banana peel or coffee filter strewn across the yard by my dog or by the moon-crazed 'possums that live in the woods.

TOOLS AND MATERIALS

- Spade or other digging tools
- Wheelbarrow or cart
- Carpenter's level
- Disposable paintbrush
- Measuring tape
- Hand or circular power saw
- Hammer
- Power drill
- Screwdriver
- Pencil
- One 2' × 4' (0.6 × 1.2 m) piece of ¾" (1.9 cm) untreated, exterior-grade plywood (a quarter sheet)

- Two 6' (1.8 m) long pieces of untreated 2×4 (38×89 mm) pine lumber
- Four 3" (7.6 cm) box nails
- 4 small metal corner brackets
- 16 or more 1" long (2.5 cm) wood screws
- 1 pint tinted water sealer, wood stain, or exterior-grade enamel paint
- 2 cabinet hinges
- 1 sturdy drawer or gate handle

1 Choose the location for your Pit-of-Plenty, and excavate a 14" (35.5 cm) deep hole no more than 42" (101.6 cm) long and 20" (50.8 cm) wide. As you dig, take care not to loosen the edges of the hole. Dump the excavated soil in an accessible place for future use in other composting projects. Don't worry if the bottom or sides of the hole are bumpy or uneven.

2 Using the level, adjust the edges of the hole as needed to make them level on all sides. Add soil to low spots first, and trim high portions of the edge only if necessary. Measure the perimeter of your prepared pit.

3 To make the frame, measure and precisely saw each of the 2x4s (38x89 m) into two pieces — one 46" (116.8 cm) long and the other 26" (66 cm) long. Many lumberyards will custom-cut lumber for a small fee.

4 Working on a level surface, such as a paved driveway or patio, butt one end of a long piece against the end of a short piece. Drive a nail through the long piece and into the shorter one to hold them together while you install a corner bracket.

5 Place the corner bracket on the inside of a corner and mark through the screw holes with a pencil onto the boards. Drill pilot holes for screws. Screw the bracket in place. (See the facing page.) ▶

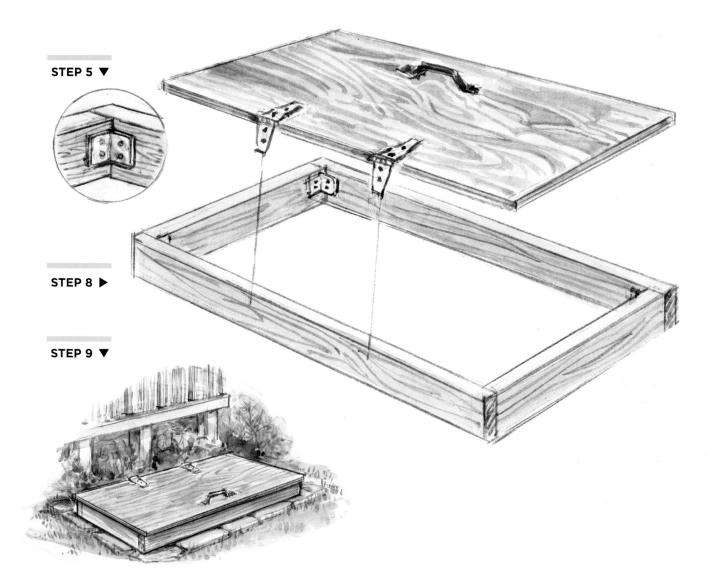

6 Repeat steps 4 and 5 with the remaining three corners of the frame.

7 Working outdoors when temperatures are above 60 degrees, place the finished frame and the plywood on a plastic drop cloth or tarp. Paint the exposed surfaces with tinted water seal or paint according to package directions. When dry, flip both pieces over and coat the other sides. Allow to dry for at least 12 hours.

8 Center the plywood on top of the frame with the back edges of both pieces flush. Attach the plywood top to the frame with two hinges, making sure that the screws are very tight. Install the handle near the front of the lid. ▲

9 Place the finished lid over your excavated hole, and start filling it with kitchen waste and other compostable materials. ▲

Managing Space

As with other types of composts, the materials in a Pit-of-Plenty will shrink in size as they decompose, and decomposition tends to be quite rapid once the pit is colonized by fungi and bacteria. But if the material does not shrink quickly enough to make room for the new material you are adding, you can face a space crunch. Like a landfill manager, you'll need to decide which waste really needs to go into the pit and find other accommodations for bulky stuff that's taking up limited space in the hole. We suggest using a Pit-of-Plenty as a disposal point for unsightly and stinky kitchen and garden waste, and using other methods to compost bulkier materials.

Another easy way to make more space is to remove some of the partially rotted material and move it to another composting project. If your pit holds a mixture of finished, intermediate, and fresh material, use a digging fork or a garden rake to push the fresh stuff to one side and mound up the rest in a separate pile. Stop adding material to the more advanced side for a week or so, and then scoop it out and place it in a wheelbarrow or cart or spread it over a tarp. Allow it to dry for a day or two if necessary, sift out the undecomposed pieces (there's more on sifting and screening on page 220), and return them to the pit. If you think the sifted compost is rife with unwanted seeds (be they tomato seeds or weeds), combine it with other materials in a high-heat Banner Batch (see page 136) or use one of the other de-weeding methods discussed on page 222.

Accommodating Earthworms

Don't be surprised if your pit morphs into a hub of activity as the materials attract the attention of crickets, beetles, and thousands of earthworms. These and many other small creatures find plenty of food and luxury lodgings in a Pit-of-Plenty that receives fre-

VERSATILE VENT TUBES

A Pit-of-Plenty has much in common with an actual latrine, including the production of methane gas and a tendency to attract flies. In outdoor pit toilets, these issues are resolved through the use of a wide ventilation pipe topped with a piece of window screening that rises from just above the composting material straight up through the roof. As long as people remember to close the toilet lid, flies and other insects trapped in the dark will fly up toward the light at the top of the pipe, and then die from exhaustion as they struggle to escape through the screening.

The same concept works in a Pit-of-Plenty. All you need to do is to install a short piece of pipe (18" [45.7 cm] long will do) at least 3" (7.6 cm) in diameter through an opening made in the lid. PVC pipe 3" (7.6 cm) in diameter works well, and is easy to install. Any type of vent tube can be camouflaged by paint-

ing it or slipping terra-cotta stovepipe tiles over it. You can even make a hand-crafted, Daniel Boone–style faux chimney from stones or sticks. Locate the vent tube where it won't interfere with opening and closing the lid, and be sure you can secure a piece of polyester screening over the top with a broad rubber band. In winter, remove, clean, and store the vent tube, and cover the hole in the door with a piece of scrap wood or roofing shingle, loosely screwed into place.

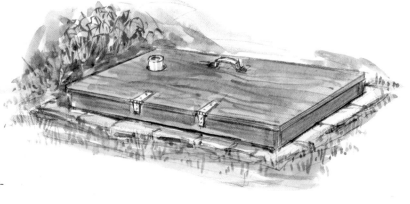

quent infusions of kitchen waste. As you poke around in your pit, keep a close watch for clusters of reddish earthworms, because these are precisely the kind of worms you will need should you decide to practice Catch-and-Release Vermicomposting (see chapter 7). These worms may be smaller than most of the ones you encounter in your garden, and you can guess at their species based on the descriptions on page 199. Don't get hung up on this, because any earthworm that proves itself as a processor of kitchen waste in a pit can perform the same services in a vermicompost bin kept indoors through the winter. If you want to release the captive worms in spring, put them back into a pit or add them to any compost project that includes plenty of rich kitchen trimmings.

Working with Treasure Troughs

Let's say, for the sake of argument, that compacted subsoil is a fact of life in your landscape, but you've managed to enrich your topsoil to the point where it does a good job of supporting plants. You're still bothered by your subsoil, so you'd like to open up the hardpan as you enlarge existing beds. Now let's add another factor: You have lucked into a supply of animal manure that's easy enough to get but is likely to be rife with weed seeds. Or maybe you have another potentially putrid material at your disposal, such as a big bucket of food waste you collected while volunteering to wash dishes at your church's covered-dish dinner. The solution is to turn to the composting technique we call Treasure Troughs — on-site excavated trenches in which compostable materials are buried deeply, where they stay forever.

A Treasure Trough can be of any size or shape, but an oblong trench dug along the edge of an existing garden bed is the most versatile plan. If you dig carefully, you can eventually extend the bed without injuring plants that are growing along its edge. A Treasure Trough is a great technique for adding a few square feet of growing space to an established perennial bed, or you can Treasure Trough your way to a bigger and better "color bed" planted with long-blooming annuals. In your food garden, a new Treasure Trough can be put to work immediately as a home to deeply rooted plants, such as sunflowers or amaranth, which love to tickle their toes in underground caches of rich organic matter.

Creating a new Treasure Trough is fast and easy work. Simply dig out the soil as deeply as you can, and pile it up next to the excavated hole. Place 4" to 5" (10.2 to 12.7 cm) of compostable materials you never want to see again in the bottom of the trench, and then backfill it with the set-aside soil. Allow for future shrinkage of the buried organic materials by using enough soil to raise the surface level of the refilled trough 2" to 4" (5.1 to 10.2 cm) higher than surrounding ground.

Discourage Determined Diggers

A Treasure Trough (or a Cathole Compost, described later in this chapter) filled with kitchen wastes may prove to be a magnet for the same curious critters that are drawn to food scraps in aboveground compost piles. Animal noses are much more adept than human olfactory organs at sniffing out subterranean goodies — even those that you think are buried too deeply to be discovered. If dogs, raccoons, or other scavengers start raiding your Treasure Trough, take steps to stop this behavior before it becomes a habit.

A trough at least 12" (30.5 cm) deep with 8" (20.3 cm) of soil over the compost ingredients is your best defense; shallowly buried or lightly covered materials are most likely to attract the unwanted attention of prowling varmints. Even if your Treasure Trough is well secured with soil, once an animal discovers it you'll need to add another layer of protection. A roll of 18" (45.7 cm) wide poultry netting, also called chicken wire, works well for guarding the buried treasure, and you can roll it out to cover your trough (or a series of catholes) if you're filling it little by little instead of all at once.

Secure the end of the wire netting a few inches beyond the edge of your Treasure Trough and roll it out until you've covered every bit of buried treasure. If you're covering a completed trough, use metal snips to cut off the wire and fasten down the other end. You may want to pin or stake down the netting at intervals along the trough, too, for extra security. For a fill-as-you-have-ingredients trough, leave the roll attached and roll out more netting as you fill and cover more of your trough.

A poultry netting barrier is a good way to keep animals out of a new Treasure Trough, but you should consider it to be a temporary measure. After three weeks or so, before weeds can grow into a tangle within the wire (or you forget it's there and it gets discovered by a lawn mower), take it up and replace it with a mulch of cardboard or newspaper covered with a more attractive mulch. If you like, leave spaces between the pieces of cardboard or newspaper and fill them with fast-growing sunflowers, zinnias, marigolds, or other annual flowers.

Roll out the poultry netting as a temporary barrier to keep animals from excavating your newly created Treasure Trough.

> ## TOPPING OFF A TROUGH
>
> A Treasure Trough is a lasting cure for drainage problems caused by compacted subsoil, and helps to supply foraging plant roots with the nutrients they seek, but it does little to enrich the entire root zone with organic matter. You can meet this need by mixing finished compost with the soil as you refill your trough, but it's much easier to work from the top down by adding other compost gardening methods. For example, a Treasure Trough tucked under a flattened mound of Comforter Compost, or a thick layer of biodegradable mulch, becomes a snug habitat for earthworms, which will distribute organic matter through the soil as they move about. After a few months, you can dig the decomposed organic matter from the surface into the soil below. You now have a dream space for plants that require great drainage and fertile soil, such as Asian and Oriental lilies, reblooming daylilies, or the finest tomatoes you've ever grown.

Hardworking Honey Holes

Before fertilizer became available for sale in bags, people came up with interesting ways to stash away nutrients in the soil. Some Native American tribes regarded the burying of a fish beneath each corn seed as a spiritual necessity, and early peach growers in Georgia are said to have buried an old leather boot at the bottom of planting holes. In both cases, these traditions created hidden caches of bioactive nutrients that were slowly released as the materials degraded, which is part of what happens when you make compost in a Honey Hole. We don't recommend planting right on top of a Honey Hole, mostly because it's filled with a more massive amount of active organic matter compared to a fish or a shoe. In addition, planting in a Honey Hole would compromise its secondary function as a reservoir for moisture when there is little water to be had.

Because of these dual talents, a Honey Hole is best used as the heart of a planting plan for four to six upright plants that encircle the hole. You can grow any plants you like around a Honey Hole, but the best candidates are those equipped to take advantage of all that Honey Holes have to offer:

▶ **Tomatoes** and other plants that send out strong lateral roots will take advantage of both the nutrients and moisture they find in the Honey Hole.

BUILD A BETTER BIOWALL

If you set things up right, the microorganisms that break down organic matter will neutralize many chemical and biological pollutants, forming a bio-active filter to help purify tainted water. When used this way, a compost-filled trench is sometimes called a "biowall" because of the way it walls off polluted water before it can cause problems.

Biowalls are used by farms and some industries, and the idea can be adapted to home landscapes as well. For example, if you have a dog run or another animal enclosure that drains in the direction of your vegetable or herb garden, a compost-filled trench can catch the contaminants that flow into it before they reach your garden.

Leaves, sawdust, wood chips, and other slow-rotting materials are good choices for filling a biowall trench because they serve as a strong substrate for decomposing fungi, which break down all sorts of unwanted compounds, including bacterial and chemical pollutants. Cover the trench with a grate or other cover (an old door or several boards work well).

To maintain its effectiveness, re-dig the biowall once a year and refill it with fresh organic matter, preferably in the fall when leaves and other tree-based materials are in good supply. Small populations of *E. coli* or other unwanted pathogens may be present, so play it safe by using the excavated compost only on nonedible ornamental plants.

Moisture and nutrients from a nearby Honey Hole help keep tomatoes healthy and productive even during dry spells.

Blueberries

Blueberries (*Vaccinium* spp.) deserve a place in more gardens. One of the few cultivated native fruits of North America, blueberries are relatively untroubled by pest problems, and they make attractive additions to the landscape, bearing glossy green leaves, white-to-pink flowers, and red fall foliage. Packed with vitamins and disease-fighting antioxidants, blueberries have even been found to increase stamina for runners and other athletes. Blueberry bushes bear their fruits at heights just right for easy picking, the plants have no thorns, and you can eat them right off the bush.

Unfortunately, their reputation for being persnickety about soil pH has discouraged many gardeners from even considering these delightful plants. It's true that blueberries prefer soil pH that ranges between 4.5 and 5.5, but it's also true that compost gardening methods can make pH much less of an issue. In soil that's been well-amended with compost, shallow-rooted blueberries find the combination of moist soil and good drainage they need. Organic matter also improves the soil's population of beneficial microorganisms, including ericoid mycorrhizal fungi, which colonize blueberry roots and enhance their ability to take up nutrients and fend off diseases. A 5″ to 6″ (12.7 to 15.2 cm) thick mulch composed of aged sawdust or leaf mold further enhances blueberry growth. For the ultimate blueberry patch, encircle a Honey Hole packed with shredded leaves, manure, and garden waste with blueberries appropriate for your climate — highbush varieties in the North (*V. corymbosum*), and rabbiteyes (*V. ashei*) in the South.

▶ **Roses** and other plants that need wide spacing to ensure good air circulation benefit from the open space created by a central Honey Hole, and earthworms moving in and out of the Honey Hole help to maintain good drainage.

▶ **Blueberries** and other shallow-rooted shrubs with limited drought tolerance are much less likely to be damaged by extremely dry weather if some of their roots are able to access a reliable supply of moisture from the Honey Hole.

No matter what compostables you put into a Honey Hole, or what you plant around it, after a year, it will change from a compost project into a remarkably fertile, well-drained spot in your garden. By then you will probably be so hooked on adjacent Honey Holes that you'll get yippee-happy when you see an opportunity to set up a new planting that revolves around a simple hole filled with stuff that rots.

Materials for Honey Holes

As in other compost compositions, a balance of nitrogen-rich greens and high-carbon browns will help a Honey Hole decompose quickly. But maybe you don't care how fast the process moves along, because you have no plans to do anything with the finished compost except to spread it around a bit. If you can be patient until the growing season ends, constant moisture (rather than an exact balance of greens and browns) will have turned the materials into finished, cured-in-the-hole compost.

Very absorbent materials — even if they are high in carbon — are always welcome in Honey Holes. Corncobs make fantastic Honey Hole filler, as does weathered sawdust or hand-sized pieces of cardboard. For greens, you can use early season grass clippings, foliage from alfalfa or another Compost Fodder Crop (see page 276), or newly pulled juvenile weeds. Rough layers or coarse mixtures are fine, because each material will support a slightly different community of microorganisms, which can go about their business in peace, without being set back by mixing and turning.

Do think things through before using a Honey Hole as a depository for a glut of high-nitrogen manure, and use restraint should you decide to activate the mix with a high-nitrogen meal. Plant roots that wander into a moist environment that's rich in nutrients may suffer damage from chemical overload, or frenzied microorganisms may mistake them for dead and eat them for lunch.

When Every Drop Counts

In the event that the drought you've been dreading has finally hit, you must choose which plants to irrigate while letting many others go. Allotting precious water to compost doesn't make good sense in this situation, unless that compost is a Honey Hole. As long as the Honey Hole is kept moist, the plants around

---

HOW TO MAKE A HONEY HOLE

1. Select a bed that is approximately 8' (2.44 m) square, or a similarly sized rectangle, circle, or oval. If you have a raised-bed garden, you may be able to use the space between adjoining beds for a Honey Hole.

2. In the middle of the space, dig out a hole 20" to 30" (50.8 to 76.2 cm) in diameter, and up to 24" (61 cm) deep (or as deep as you can go). Set aside the excavated soil for another use.

3. Fill the hole with compostable materials: mix, spread in layers, or allow them to accumulate over a period of several weeks. The hole should be completely filled by the time the companion plants are planted or emerge from dormancy.

4. As the season progresses, water the Honey Hole each time you water your garden, or use one of the super-efficient watering methods described under When Every Drop Counts at right. Mulch beneath plants after the soil warms to conserve water in their primary root zone. Pile garden trimmings and pulled weeds over the top of the Honey Hole to reduce moisture lost to evaporation.

it have a lifeline to enough water to keep them alive. There are several ways to water a Honey Hole without wasting a drop.

▶ **PVC "smokestack."** If summer drought is part of your climate's normal rainfall pattern, plan ahead by installing a piece of 2" to 3" (5.1 to 7.6 cm) diameter PVC pipe down the middle, like a smokestack. Before setting it in place, use the smallest drill bit you have to make few holes on all sides of the pipe, about 6" (15.2 cm) apart. Fill the pipe with water several times, or find a large plastic jug or bottle that fits inside the pipe when turned upside-down. Fill the container with water, and let it drip through the pipe into the compost.

▶ **Wicking.** Help the compost retain water by including a few "wicks" made by tying newspaper into tight, 1" (2.5 cm) diameter rolls secured on each end with biodegradable string. Place them throughout the hole in vertical or diagonal positions.

▶ **Slow leak.** Dig out a depression in the top of the Honey Hole large enough in diameter to nest a cracked or leaky bucket in. Fill the bucket with water in the evening. During the day, keep the Honey Hole covered with a tarp or cloth to reduce evaporation.

Digging into Compost Gardening Methods

All of the underground composting methods described in this chapter have one thing in common — they force you to get behind a spade and dig. Deep digging gives you an honest look at your soil in its raw, unimproved state, and the more you know about what's down there, the better you can customize composting methods to your soil's particular needs.

In the short run, soil improved using underground composting methods may seem chunky and littered with undecomposed materials compared to soil that is mixed with finished compost. Stop worrying about the short run. You're keeping a composter's garden now, where time is not measured in days or weeks, but in months and years.

CATHOLE COMPOST

When backpackers head to the woods, they take with them a small spade with which to dig single-use-size latrine holes, called catholes. You can compost the same way, by burying bits of compostable waste here and there in your garden. The cathole method is a casual but easy way to compost: As long as you are digging a bed or preparing a planting hole for a tomato, why not bury something luscious at the bottom? Corncobs, for example, can improve drainage when buried a foot or more below the ground, and they later serve as a nutrient source when plant roots find the buried treasure.

The cathole method does have limitations. It can accommodate only small amounts of waste, and the holes will tend to sink as the material degrades. One of the best uses of Cathole Composting is burying little treasures in several spots a few feet away from the base of a shrub or tree. As the material in the cathole rots, it will attract earthworms and provide nutrients for wandering lateral roots. This is a good use for weedy manures because the buried weed seeds will never see the light of day. Or, you can cathole your way through a sudden excess of gloppy kitchen waste from a session spent making applesauce or canning tomatoes.

7
Catch-and-Release Vermicompost

MANY COMPOST GARDENERS think of their entire gardens as earthworm estates, because they are! Earthworms are nature's mightiest workhorses when it comes to transforming half-rotted organic matter into compost. When used in seasonal sequence, the earthworm-based composting methods in this chapter comprise what we call Catch-and-Release Vermicomposting. Like catch-and-release fishing, Catch-and-Release Vermicomposting involves borrowing earthworms temporarily from outdoor heaps or beds and putting them to work in special compost projects or raising them indoors in bins through the winter months. In spring, when their services won't be needed for a while, they can be set free in the garden.

Catch-and-Release Vermicomposting is rewarding, but mostly it is just plain fun. Work really does feels like play when your goal is to host and nurture nature's most gentle form of livestock.

Vermicompost Basics

Compost that is processed primarily by earthworms is called vermicompost. To some extent, every compost pile is a vermicompost pile, because earthworms are usually major players in the latter stages of the composting process. Yet earthworms also can be used as primary decomposers provided the material they are given to work with meets their needs for food and habitat. Intensive vermicomposting is emerging as an important waste processing technology used by hog farmers, sewage processing plants, and even school cafeterias. Industrial-size vermicompost operations often are the composting approach of choice in situations where large amounts of food or manure must be dealt with quickly to neutralize its pollution potential. Like other commercial types of compost, large-scale vermicomposting operations must be closely managed and are typically done in an indoor environment where water and temperature can be controlled.

Commercial vermicomposting makes good sense, environmentally speaking, but compost gardeners can take a much more casual approach when working with earthworms. Enter Catch-and-Release Vermicomposting. Here are the four main phases of the catch-and-release method, which will be discussed in detail beginning on page 200:

▶ Avoid unwanted casualties by practicing earthworm conservation

▶ Enhance earthworm habitats by locating compost where you want earthworms to work

▶ Foster compost colonization by adding worms to heaps at opportune times

▶ Keep an indoor bin in winter using worms gathered from outdoor heaps

Sounds easy enough, and it is, though you will find the entire process much more interesting if you understand how earthworms live, eat, and reproduce.

All earthworms are similar creatures, but they are not all alike. Some make better behaved bin inhabitants than others, while larger species that burrow deep into the soil do a superior job of moving organic matter from the surface to the root zones of plants. So, before we move on to great ways to put earthworms to work, let's spend a little time getting to know them.

The Benefits of Earthworms

Historically, humans have been slow to recognize the good work done by earthworms (*Lumbricus* spp., *Eisenia* spp.). For centuries people feared earthworms, because of mistaking them for snakes. European gardeners poisoned them with salt or ashes to rid their soil of what they thought were nasty vermin. Fortunately, earthworms caught the interest of the famous 19th century British naturalist Charles Darwin, who studied them closely and even tested them to see if they could hear the difference between an oboe and a whistle. Darwin published his findings in a book, *The Formation of Vegetable Mould Through the Action of Worms* in 1881.

Were he alive today, Darwin would surely be impressed with what scientists have recently discovered about "vegetable mould," or worm castings. Carrots, cucumbers, tomatoes, peppers, corn, grapes, strawberries, and even marigolds have been found to produce better when grown in soil that includes worm castings. When handled properly, earthworms also can help clear contaminated soil of chemicals such as polychlorinated biphenyls (PCBs), which are cancer-causing compounds that were widely used in industrial adhesives and oils until they were banned in 1977. In a recent study of soil taken from a badly contaminated site in Gary, Indiana, redworms (*Eisenia* spp.) set up to work as composters removed 80 percent of the PCBs in the soil in 200 days. Of course, the researchers ended up with toxic earthworms, but dried, powdered earthworms are easier to dispose of than toxic sludge.

Earthworms can also help prevent pest problems in the garden by serving as food for pest predators. For example, earthworms are sometimes used as an alternate food source by carabid beetles and other slug predators when slugs become hard to find. Then, when a slug hatch occurs, the beetles stop eating earthworms and go back to gobbling their favorite prey. Earthworms also are an important food source for dozens of animals, from ants and moles to turtles and birds. Many of these predators consume other garden insects, too, so hosting plenty of earthworms is a simple way to encourage a robust population of generalized bug-eaters in your yard.

In the garden, earthworms improve the soil *physically* by making tunnels and burrows that help air, water, and plant roots move through the soil, and they improve it *chemically* by transforming decomposing organic matter into nutrient-rich morsels that provide food for plants. Those morsels also contain compounds that enhance plants' resistance to root-rot diseases, improve germination rates of some seeds, and promote fast, strong growth of lateral roots. Earthworm castings often are high in available nitrogen and phosphorous, as well as calcium and iron. Many plants that grow in acidic soil, for example azaleas and gardenias, often have trouble taking up sufficient iron, but worm castings somehow solve this problem by enabling iron uptake even when soil pH levels are low.

The Who's Who of Garden Earthworms

Ready to get to know the earthworms that call your yard home? In the next few pages you'll be introduced to a wide variety of them, so that you can then get ready to make use of the many services earthworms can perform for you and your garden. Whether you want to improve drainage by turning a low or compacted spot into a hangout for giant-size night crawlers, or produce concentrated worm

PERFECT MATCH

Carrots

Soil that's been worked by worms makes a dandy place to sow a carrot crop: Consider the empty spot left behind after a Walking Heap takes its first step as prime carrot territory. The carrots will make good use of the loose, moist soil where the worms have been dwelling beneath the compost, and they'll benefit from the improved biological activity and nutrition provided by the castings the worms have deposited there.

You can further enhance the site for your carrot crop by adding vermicompost to the soil prior to planting. Unlike more potent animal manures, vermicompost supplies a gentle nutrient boost without supplying too much nitrogen, which causes carrots to develop off-flavored, "hairy" roots. Compost-enhanced soil also helps protect carrots against infection by root-knot nematodes, microscopic wormlike organisms that cause lumpy, misshapen roots with numerous hairlike side roots.

As your carrots grow, mulch them with yard-waste compost or thin layers of grass clippings to keep sun exposure from turning their shoulders green, while retaining soil moisture and suppressing weeds.

WHERE DO BABY WORMS COME FROM?

Earthworms are hermaphroditic, meaning they possess both male and female reproductive organs. Still, it takes two to tango (for most worm species). Earthworms copulate by lying close together, often with their heads at opposite ends, so they can exchange fluids produced in their clitellums (the ringlike collars present in the midsection of any earthworm). After fertilization has taken place, the exchanged secretions slowly harden into a tube. As the tube hardens, the worm wriggles backward until the tube passes over its head and is released as a lemon-shaped cocoon. Although a cocoon may contain up to 20 fertilized ova, it is unusual for more than two or three to hatch into live earthworms. Cocoons produce hatchlings rapidly in summer, often within a few weeks. If produced in fall and winter, cocoons may not bear hatchlings until the following spring.

castings in a basement bin during the winter months, the methods in this chapter will make it simple to join forces with the hardworking creatures that Aristotle called "the intestines of the soil."

Earth is home to more than 2,500 species of earthworms. Depending on where you live, you may find only two or three species in your yard, or you may find a dozen. West-coast and coastal-south gardeners may encounter increasingly rare native species from time to time, but for most of us, the earthworms that inhabit our beds, heaps, and bins are among (or closely related to) the species described below. Basic characteristics are given here, but garden-dwelling earthworms do tend to look alike, and it is impossible to correctly identify earthworms without using a 20x microscope to examine the bottom section of the clitellum — the broad band or collar that divides the worm's short front half from its longer back half. You may have to guess at your resident worms' identities at first, but as you get to know them and watch what they do in your garden and compost projects, it will become easy to tell who's who.

Large Worms

Night crawler, dew worm
(*Lumbricus terrestris*)

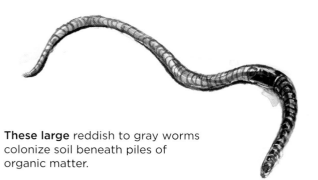

These large reddish to gray worms colonize soil beneath piles of organic matter.

▶ **Color.** Brick red to purplish red, becoming grayish with age, with a dark anterior (front end), paler posterior (tail end).

▶ **Size.** Adults can grow to 10" (25.4 cm) long, though most garden specimens are half that size. Bodies are comprised of 110 to 160 segments. Young worms closely resemble *L. rubellus* (at right).

▶ **Life span.** Individuals mature within 350 days, live 3 to 6 years, produce about 38 cocoons per year.

▶ **Habitat.** Make vertical tunnels into the soil to 6' (1.8 m) deep. At night, or under blankets of compost or mulch, night crawlers gather organic matter at the surface and pull it into their burrows. When disturbed, they quickly retreat and press their sides against the tunnel walls, making them difficult to pull up.

▶ **Value in gardens.** Transport organic matter from surface to deeper soil. Tunnels improve drainage. Produce nutrient-rich castings.

▶ **Look-alikes.** Several earthworms native to the West and South resemble night crawlers, as does the Asian jumping earthworm (*Amynthas* spp.), a recently imported species regarded as invasive. When disturbed or exposed to high light, jumping worms suddenly contract into a tight S shape, often jumping several inches (centimeters) into the air.

Medium Worms

Red worm, red marsh worm, red wriggler, dung worm
(*Lumbricus rubellus*)

These reddish worms with an iridescent sheen are common in rich compost.

▶ **Color.** Deep brownish red, iridescent on top, often with a hint of pale yellow on underside.

▶ **Size.** Adults 1" to 4" (25 to 105 mm) long, bodies comprised of 95 to 120 segments.

▶ **Life span.** Individuals mature in 170 days, may live for 2 to 3 years, and produce 70 to 100 cocoons per year.

▶ **Habitat.** Found in top few inches of soil, beneath leaf litter or mulch, and often in rich kitchen compost heaps or manure piles. In wet weather, these worms often gather beneath containers or other objects.

▶ **Value in gardens.** These versatile, adaptable worms enrich soil with their castings while aiding in the decomposition of compost and mulch. They are easy to manage in indoor bins.

▶ **Look-alikes.** Field or pasture worms (*Aporrectodea* and *Allalobophora* species) are reddish gray to pink, and better adapted to living in open soil than in rich compost or bins. However, they go where the food is and often show up in outdoor heaps.

Small Worms

Compost worm, manure worm, brandling worm, tiger worm (*Eisenia fetida;* formerly *E. foetida*)

These little worms reproduce quickly in enclosed composters or heaps that receive abundant kitchen waste.

▶ **Color.** Purple, red, maroon, or red with yellow stripes in alternating bands.

▶ **Size.** Adults 1" to 5" (35 to 130 mm) long, bodies comprised of 60 to120 segments

▶ **Life span.** Individuals mature in 6 weeks, may live for a few months to up to 4 years. Well-fed individuals can produce up to 400 cocoons per year.

▶ **Habitat.** Inhabits rich manure or compost piles. These worms do not burrow into soil, yet they do migrate toward compost piles, and often are found in barnyards or other places where manure is present.

▶ **Value in gardens.** Because they like a rich diet and reproduce quickly, these are the most popular types of worms to use in enclosed indoor bins. They may not persist as well in open gardens, where conditions are less to their liking.

▶ **Look-alikes.** The India blue worm or spike-tail (*Perionyx excavatus*) is similar, but has no bands. A fast-moving worm, this species is fine for outdoor bins but prone to staging escapes when kept indoors.

Getting Started in Catch-and-Release Vermicompost

As a compost gardener, you will never have to look far to find compost-loving worms. Even if you live in an area where few earthworms are present (see Exotic Earthworm Ecology on page 202), eventually earthworms will find the wonderful food sources available in your beds, heaps, or bins. You may unknowingly import a few as you collect various compostable materials that come your way, and some may even hitch rides to your garden in plant containers. Of course, you can always buy worms (see the resources on page 293) to get your population off to a booming start, but you will do better to find a composting neighbor who has an established heap and plenty of worms to spare. That way, you will get worms that are adapted to your climate *and* to the varied diet they will be served in your compost. Knowing the species name of an earthworm is not nearly as important as knowing that it has a successful track record as a compost colonizer in your climate.

Earthworms may lack brains, but they invariably manage to make themselves at home when they find a good habitat. Over time, you may find that the types of worms you see most often in your beds differ from those that rule in your compost projects, though there also will be quite a bit of crossover. For example, you may start out with hundreds (or thousands) of small redworms or red wigglers in a Comforter Compost made by layering half-rotted kitchen compost — or vermicompost made in an indoor bin — with grass clippings or other materials (see page 154). A few weeks later, the little guys may move on (or make it back to the mother heap), only to be replaced by a population of larger night crawlers.

We will walk through the phases of Catch-and-Release Vermicompost in the next few pages, but it's important to never lose sight of matters relating to *habitat* when you shift from one project to another. Do you need worms to chow down on material you just buried in a Layered Crater? Look beneath an old compost heap for worms that are accustomed to living a few inches below the soil's surface. Want worms to move organic matter that's been layered into a Comforter Compost built on top of a patch of grass? Night crawlers are the best worms for the job. On the other hand, when you need worms for a new indoor bin, naturally you want worms with a healthy appetite for kitchen scraps. They are ready and waiting for you in the composter or heap where you've been putting your apple cores and coffee grounds.

Ready to get started? The first step along the Catch-and-Release path is to know how to keep the earthworms you have.

MINIMIZING CASUALTIES

When using a tiller is the most practical way to plant or replant a row or bed, you can minimize earthworm losses by planning ahead and luring or moving worms out of the area, and by cultivating in midday, when many earthworms burrow down deep to escape heat and light at the soil's surface. Even if you cultivate by hand, the three strategies described below make it easy (and fun) to grow a good garden and protect the health of your earthworms.

Lay down a hay haven. A few days before you plan to till, lay down a spine of damp hay, pulled weeds, or fresh grass clippings parallel to the row you need to till. Make the spine 6" (15.2 cm) deep and at least 10" (25.4 cm) wide, and wet it down to make it irresistible to earthworms. If you work mostly in raised beds, place whole or half bales of hay between beds in need of renovation. Then thoroughly wet the hay. Earthworms will think they've found the greatest resort in the world beneath the bales.

Serve up box lunches. Collect several small cardboard boxes (shoebox size is ideal). A few days before you plan to till, cut 3" (7.6 cm) wide windows in the sides, bury the boxes in the rows, and fill them with fresh food scraps and rough compost. Close the lids or cover the Box Lunches with cloth to keep them dark and damp. Before tilling, lift the boxes and set them in the shade. Release the collected worms back into the soil when you finish cultivating.

Grow legume islands. Make intermittent small plantings of bush beans or other legumes in long, wide rows, and mulch them with straw or grass clippings. Skip over the Legume Islands as you till by raising the tines of your tiller. Earthworms often congregate around legume roots and move out into surrounding soil at night. When the legumes are ready to be pulled, loosen the soil with a digging fork and pull the plants by hand to protect the worms.

As you get to know the earthworms in your garden and the situations that please them, you will probably think of more ways to herd your earthworms out of the path of your tiller or spade. Or perhaps you will simply cultivate your soil gently and less often. This happens naturally when you become a compost gardener, because soil that is constantly enriched with compost becomes fluffier and more fertile with each season, so it requires less digging. Working in such soil is so pleasurable that you may find yourself looking forward to cultivating with gloved hands rather than hefting a digging fork.

Practicing Earthworm Conservation

As a compost gardener, it's important to understand the two biggest threats to earthworm health: pesticides and cultivation. Several common pesticides are lethal to earthworms, with carbaryl (Sevin) often causing nearly 100 percent mortality when allowed to drip into worm-inhabited soil. Even organic pesticides can be harmful, so you are wise to take safety precautions on behalf of your earthworms when using them in your garden. Before applying an organic pesticide to a plant, cover the ground below it with a plastic sheet to keep the pesticide from dripping or drifting into the earthworm's habitat. Be especially careful in spring, when earthworm activity is high as they mate and reproduce, and again in fall, when earthworm populations close to the surface are at their peak.

Tillage presents a dilemma, because seeds need a well-worked planting bed if they are to germinate and grow, and many soils (especially heavy clay soils), require cultivation to help them regain oxygen lost through rain or natural compaction. There is plenty of evidence that turning soil over with a plow or tiller can damage earthworm populations. Contrary to common belief, earthworms that are cut into pieces do not immediately regenerate replacement parts. Some species do grow new "tail" ends quickly, but others, including the common night crawler, are more likely to die than to develop replacement parts when they are chopped into pieces by a tiller or spade. Although earthworm populations vary greatly with climate (soils in dry climates always have far fewer earthworms than soils in moderate to high rainfall areas), there is a direct correlation between frequency of tillage and number and size of earthworms. Soil

EXOTIC EARTHWORM ECOLOGY

Some agricultural historians credit a teeming local earthworm population as an essential factor in the success of the planet's first farmers, who worked the fertile Nile River Valley. Indeed, it is quite possible that the redworms and night crawlers you find in your garden are descendants of species native to the Nile River basin, because most garden earthworms are not native to this continent. The last ice age (10,000 to 50,000 years ago) wiped out most of the earthworms in North America's northern half. As colonists arrived, they were often accompanied by Eurasian earthworms. These species have since become permanent members of many disturbed ecological communities.

Take note that the word "disturbed" is important here, because the introduction of non-native earthworms to northern forests, which evolved in a wormless state for 10,000 years, caused huge environmental changes. Thick natural mulches of leaf litter and fallen conifer needles persist when no earthworms are present, but a few bait worms, left behind by a fisherman, or perhaps several clusters of earthworm cocoons transported within the treads of a tire or hiking boot,

can quickly give rise to a teeming population of earthworms. As the worms harvest the forest's natural mulch, a shift in plant communities occurs that favors fast-growing annuals at the expense of ferns and many native woodland wildflowers. Once earthworms enter such an ecosystem they never leave, and the most common worm species spread at the rate of 15' to 30' (4.5 to 9.14 m) a year. In the interest of preserving northern woodlands and the unique native plants and animals they support, even fans of earthworms are helping to educate the public on the importance of preventing the accidental introduction of earthworms into the few remaining wild lands of the North.

The situation is far different in places where people live and grow food and flowers. Humans radically rework ecosystems everywhere we go, and the earthworms that follow us help to heal the damage we do with chainsaws, bulldozers, tractors, and spades. Although earthworms are rightly regarded as a damaging exotic pest in pristine northern forests, they are a mighty ally in efforts to restore balance to natural environments, which people alter.

that is not cultivated for several years typically has 3 to 10 times more earthworms than soil that is cultivated annually. Earthworms that enjoy the peace of untilled soil tend also to be larger.

What's a worm-minded gardener to do? Machine cultivation with a plow or tiller endangers many more earthworms than cultivating by hand, especially if you use a digging fork rather than a spade to work the soil. And, you will find that after several seasons of using Compost Garden methods, the tilth of your soil will improve to such a point that hand-cultivation is both practical and pleasurable. Until then, use the methods described in Minimizing Casualties on page 201 to reduce earthworm losses.

Enhancing Earthworm Habitats

Many of the things gardeners do every day benefit earthworms. When you water, you raise soil moisture levels, making earthworms more comfortable. When you mulch, you insulate the soil from temperature fluctuations, which also appeals to earthworms. Earthworms are more numerous in fertile soils, so the same organic fertilizers you use to nurture your plants help to energize earthworms. And adding lime to raise the pH of acidic soil, or sulfur to lower the pH of alkaline soil, often has dramatic effects on earthworm populations. Like plants, earthworms prefer a pH between 6.0 and 7.0.

This symmetry between plants and earthworms should come as no surprise, because plants and earthworms work together for the mutual benefit of both. Plants provide shelter when they are alive and food after they are dead. In exchange, earthworms help to supply the nitrogen plants need to grow along with other growth-enhancing substances. The bottom line is that fundamental organic gardening practices benefit earthworms.

Composting every chance you get will make you an even better earthworm host or hostess, as will maintaining uncultivated buffer areas that are mowed from time to time. Many earthworms are attracted to well-kept lawns because of the constant supply of food offered in the form of grass clippings, but a

PERFECT MATCH

Strawberries

Planting strawberries in a site where you've taken steps to encourage earthworm activity is an easy way to provide the loose, rich soil your berries need to thrive while preventing problems with common soil-borne diseases. Research conducted by scientists at Ohio State University found that improving soil with vermicompost suppressed the soil-borne fungal disease Verticillium wilt on strawberries and increased populations of beneficial fungi-eating nematodes while reducing the numbers of nematodes that injure plants. To give your strawberry patch these benefits, you can work a 1" (2.5 cm) layer of vermicompost into the soil prior to planting, or add 2 T (29.57 ml) of vermicompost to each hole when planting strawberry crowns.

If you're thinking ahead, plant your future strawberry patch with a worm-welcoming, cold-hardy cover crop, such as crimson clover (page 282) or hairy vetch in the fall (page 276). In addition to attracting worms to do some of the soil-prep work, a Compost Fodder Crop will help with weed control, a necessary element in strawberry success. Cut down the fodder crop in early spring, use the greens in a compost project, and plant your strawberries!

rougher area, such as a wildflower meadow that is mowed only once a year, also makes an outstanding earthworm habitat.

There are also many ways to attract earthworms to specific spots. A pile of manure waiting to be used in a composting project will work like an earthworm magnet, as will any large, wet chunk of organic matter. One gardener we know collects collapsed Halloween pumpkins in her neighborhood and piles them where she wants to attract earthworms. Another buries stale bread between perennial flowers as hidden treasures for wandering worms.

Do keep in mind that earthworm populations follow seasonal cycles. Activity near the surface is high in spring, when winter's surviving adults and hatchlings become active. When hot, dry weather arrives, most earthworms retreat to deeper soil. They become extremely active in the fall, as long as their moisture needs are met.

All of the low-temperature composting methods in this book — including Pits-of-Plenty and other underground methods, Comforter Composting, and even keeping Nursery Heaps — will do double-duty as earthworm habitats, and of course any bin or heap you keep will eventually be colonized by earthworms. The more you compost and the more you garden, the less you will want or need special tricks to attract earthworms to your beds.

Fostering Worm-Colonized Compost Heaps

Earthworms make willing, hardworking garden employees, but it is a mistake to think they can be enslaved to follow human whims. When temperatures get too hot or cold they will go deeper into the soil than you will ever care to dig, or they may simply die and leave their offspring behind to carry on when

Super-Size Your Night Crawlers

Coaxing night crawlers to stay where you want them, at least for a while, is surprisingly easy with the help of damp hay or straw — the best material to place at the soil's surface if you want to get night crawlers to colonize the soil.

1 Begin by digging out weeds, rocks and roots to a depth of 8″ to 10″ (20.3 to 25.4 cm), and mix in a 4″ (10.2 cm) thick blanket of partially decomposed compost, such as shredded leaves collected the previous fall and kept moist through winter. If you plan to use the bed to grow garden plants in its first season, mix in some organic fertilizer as well. If needed, correct the pH with lime or sulfur. ▼

2 Stuff in as much hay or straw as will fit into a plastic cart or wheelbarrow, and drown it with water. Leave the hay or straw to soak for at least an hour. ▼

3 Paw through your worm bin or an outdoor heap, and collect the largest worms, which are likely to be night crawlers. Place them on the cultivated, amended soil, and then plop the wet hay or straw on top. ▼

4 Cover the wet straw with an old blanket or Composter's Sling (see page 82), and forget about it. When you're ready to plant, use your hands to open up holes in the mulch and nestle plants or seeds into the soil. If you're skeptical about your night crawlers' ability to work unsupervised, you can rake back the straw and poke around in the soil a bit. Expect to see night crawlers that have grown to the size of small snakes! ▼

This scheme works because it gives night crawlers exactly what they need — nutrient-rich topsoil, firm subsoil that supports their burrowing, and an abundant stash of food at the soil's surface. Bearing these things in mind, you can probably think up many more ways to create enhanced night crawler habitats in your garden. A plain bale of hay placed over a grassy spot will work, or you can arrange a grid of sticks or other coarse material at the base of a cold compost heap.

better living conditions return. A hot compost pile will send them running, too, and sometimes a comfortably cool heap that seems worm-worthy will be mysteriously devoid of worms — or any other life forms, for that matter. Should you gather up some worms from another part of your garden, or borrow them from a bin when you think a heap needs a bit of worm working? This is always worth a try, and it is most likely to work if you include two things — a piece of their home in the form of a quart or so of the soil or compost from which the worms were taken, and a bribe. The bribe can be any of a number of well-known worm goodies, from a shovelful of manure to a few slices of dampened bread. Just be sure to place it inside the heap so your worm banquet will be cool and moist rather than hot (or cold) and dry.

The most common reason to put worms into a compost heap is that you finally got around to mixing and moistening materials that have been sitting around a while, so you suddenly have a suitable place for worms to live. Assuming you have an established heap or bin from which you can take a few worms, getting them to stay in the new heap is easy. Stop when you're half finished mixing and moistening, and make a well in the middle of the materials. Fill it with strips

of corrugated cardboard, which have been soaked in water for a few minutes and then torn into strips. Sprinkle on a dusting of corn meal or whole wheat flour, add the worms, and finish building the heap. The meal or flour will serve as high-energy food, and the worms will use the channels in corrugated cardboard as shelter. Eventually they will leave the little resort you made in the middle of the heap and carry on their good deeds in the rest of the compost pile.

Keeping Worms in Indoor Bins

Earthworms' natural home is the great outdoors, but they can easily be raised in bins that are kept indoors — a great way to continue composting through the winter in ruggedly cold climates. Any place where temperatures range between 55°F and 75°F (13°C and 24°C) is a good place for an indoor worm bin. When bins receive proper care, they are not smelly or messy, and the worms inside multiply like mad.

Step-by-step instructions for setting up an indoor worm farm are given on page 209, but before you get started, think about what you hope to accomplish by raising earthworms indoors. As a garbage disposal for kitchen waste, worm bins have definite limitations. Not all kitchen wastes are appropriate for enclosed bins, and the speed with which worms process the food they are given varies as well. True, keeping an indoor worm bin may reduce the trips you must make to your outdoor compost in winter, but it will not eliminate them altogether. Plan to keep outdoor compost going year round, and set aside a separate collection container in your kitchen for special foods that worms especially like.

Practicing source separation can also help limit unwanted seeds in the finished compost (earthworms seldom kill weed or tomato seeds). You are wise to go seed-free when deciding which kitchen scraps to

Worms can handle most types of kitchen waste (left). Multi-level worm bins (right) are an easy way to turn vegetable scraps into fertilizer.

feed to your worms and which ones should go into an outdoor compost heap or bin. Consider the container where you collect material for your worm bins to be a seed free zone; maintain a second container for material that will be composted outdoors and place seedy kitchen waste there. For example, if you cut up a cantaloupe, place the seeds in the "outdoor compost" container and tuck the rind into the "vermicompost" larder.

A second reason to keep a separate collection container for future earthworm entrees is that the pieces should be small. So, whereas you think nothing of throwing an intact banana peel into an outdoor compost pile, when you're catering to worms it's best to first snip it into thumbnail-size pieces (scissors work

better than knives). We have also found that earthworms won't touch anything that's not really and truly *dead*; they seem to have a supernatural sense for plant parts that might possibly come back to life, such as raw potato or peelings that contain eyes, or the tops of carrots, turnips, or beets. Then there are earthworm favorites, like crumbled moldy bread, leftover pasta, and used coffee grounds, which you won't want to waste on an outdoor heap when you have a herd of hungry worms to feed. Also consider sanitation issues, because materials that smell bad as they decompose (citrus rinds, Brussels sprouts, shrimp hulls) should go outside. The lists on page 208 suggest common items from a typical kitchen's waste stream to channel toward or away from your worm bin.

When Will the Vermicompost Be Done?

There is no fixed answer to this question, because life in the worm bin is complicated. In addition to the work done by the worms, fungi and bacteria are important parts of the worm community. New bins may seem to work slowly, showing little progress after six to eight weeks, but older bins that teem with an established community of life forms process waste much faster. In our experience, a new bin set up in October reaches full maturity the following April or May — though you can harvest chunks of vermicompost from the corners of the bin long before then. If you're willing to be patient and let your worms work at their own pace, you can easily harvest 5 gal. (19.93 L) of excellent vermicompost from a 15-gallon (56.78 L) plastic storage bin every four to five months.

FOOD FOR WORMS

DO include:

Coffee and tea, including filters

Most fruit pulp and peelings

Most seed-free vegetable trimmings

Eggshells (well rinsed)

Bread, pasta, rice, or cereals that are not heavily sweetened

Any cooked vegetable (without excessive salt or fat)

DON'T include:

Seeds from vegetables and fruits

Trimmings from cabbage-family crops

Garlic, onion or hot pepper trimmings

Citrus rinds

Salty foods

Set Up an
Indoor Worm Farm

Quiet and undemanding, earthworms are usually happy to snuggle into an indoor bin during the cold winter months — or year-round for that matter. When you get everything right, the bin should be odorless, pest free, and teeming with earthworms.

MATERIALS AND SUPPLIES

- Plastic storage bin with lid, 12 gal. (45.42 L) size or larger
- Drill
- ¼" (0.6 cm) bit, or hammer and sharp nail
- 6" (15.2 cm) tall stack of dry newspapers, including color inserts
- Bucket or sink filled with water
- Rubber gloves
- 4 cups (0.95 L) peat moss or finished, weed-free compost
- 2 cups (0.47 L) gritty garden soil
- 2 cups (0.47 L) plain corn meal
- Water in spray bottle
- Earthworms (at least 200; 500 is even better)
- 2 cups (0.47 L) vegetable or fruit scraps, cut into small pieces

1 Remove labels from bin, and decorate the top with acrylic paint if you like.

2 Use the drill, or a hammer and sharp nail, to make numerous holes in all sides of the bin. In the lower half of the bin, make holes about 6" (15.2 cm) apart. Reduce spacing between holes to 4" (10.2 cm) apart in the top half of the bin. ▼

3 Working with a few sheets at a time, dunk newspapers in a bucket or sink of water, tearing the paper into pieces no larger than 3" (7.6 cm) long and wide. Some pieces can be in thin strips, while others are ragged patches. ▼

4 Add newspaper bits to the bin until it is about half full of lightly moistened pieces. Move the bin to its permanent location before adding peat moss or compost, soil, and corn meal to the moist newspaper. Toss everything together thoroughly with your hands. Spritz on additional water until all of the materials are lightly moist. ▼

5 Place earthworms in the prepared bin. Divide vegetable and fruit scraps into four portions, and bury them in four sections of the bin beneath 1" of bedding. Put the top on the bin. ▼

6 After a few days, stir through the bin with a long spoon or a gloved hand, and spritz water on bits of newspaper that seem dry. You can now start feeding your worms kitchen waste up to 3 times a week.

Preventing Runaways

The most often heard problem with indoor worm bins is runaway worms that exit the bin at night. This often happens quite dramatically in new bins stocked with purchased worms that have been jostled around for days in delivery trucks. The trauma leaves them confused (perhaps they sense a prolonged earthquake), and it's not unusual for shipped worms to attempt a mass exodus from their new digs. To prevent this odd runaway behavior, leave the lid off the bin and turn on a light in the room for the first two days after releasing shipped worms. The light will discourage them from venturing out of the bedding, and they should settle in nicely within a few days. Similar runaway behavior can occur if you move a bin to a new location, so it's a good idea to leave a light on for a few days after a bin is moved.

There are many other reasons why worms may try to leave the bin, including high heat, excessive water, or overpopulation. Decomposing food often gives off biological heat, so the temperature inside a worm bin often is several degrees higher than the air temperature in the room. The situation can be aggravated if the bin is kept in an enclosed cabinet, where air circulation is limited. For this reason, a bin kept in a cool basement is less likely to give rise to runaway behavior than the same bin kept in a warm kitchen.

Too much water can send worms running for higher ground. If you accidentally overwater your bin, roll dry newspapers into 1" to 2" (2.5 to 5.1 cm) wide cylinders secured with rubber bands, and bury them in the bin for a few hours. They will wick out some of the moisture. Leaving the top off of the bin during the day also will help excess moisture to evaporate from the contents.

When a bin is teeming with worms, and you find more than a dozen clinging to the sides and top of the bin each time you open it, you are probably looking at an overpopulation problem. Especially in spring, worms in bins have lots of babies! Follow the steps for Adding New Bedding on page 212 to relieve population pressure in your bin. Or, you can return some to your garden or outdoor composter.

Caring for Captive Worms

Experience is great teacher when it comes to learning how to care for earthworms raised in bins. After a few months, you will develop an intuitive sense of how to satisfy your worms' appetites and maintain the right moisture level in the bin. Until you have shared company with captive worms for a while, the following discussion of food and water may be helpful.

Waiting on Worms

Earthworms in a bin won't wiggle up to the surface, grab a snack, and pull it down into the bedding, so you have to bury their food. Actually, it's a mistake to think of the worms as immediate consumers of most of the stuff you give them to eat, because they like for it to get a bit moldy first. Fungi work fast on food buried 1" or 2" (2.5 or 5.1 cm) deep, especially if you spray a bit of water on dry stuff (like pizza crust or uncooked oatmeal) before covering it with newspaper bedding.

As long as you're burying food you'll probably want to dig around in the bin to see what's happening, so it's a good idea to wear a glove. We like medical exam gloves, which can be reused several times, but any moisture-proof glove will do. If you find that the worms have not consumed the food you left for them a few days before, don't give them more to eat for another couple of days. There is also no need to worry about your worms if you leave town for a couple of weeks, or simply forget about your bin. When no fresh food is available, the worms will simply consume their bedding.

Should you want to step up the pace of life in your bin, the best high-energy food for earthworms is cornmeal. Sprinkle a generous dusting of plain cornmeal over the surface, gently rake it in with a fork or gloved fingers, and within a week you should see plenty of robust wiggling. Be sure to use plain cornmeal rather than cornbread mix; the high salt content of cornbread mix can cause worms to become uncomfortably dehydrated.

Maintaining Moisture

Earthworm castings have a claylike consistency, so once they become moist they tend to hold water very well. Keep a spray bottle handy for the first few weeks after starting a new bin, or when adding new bedding, because newspapers and cardboard often take a while to soak up water. When you run into a dry pocket of bedding while adding food to the bin, simply spritz on a little water.

Once the bedding is uniformly moist and the worms have begun producing castings, most bins kept indoors require little additional moisture. Indeed, giving them too much water is a bigger risk than giving them too little. Signs of excessive moisture include worms congregating on the sides or inner lid of the bin, the appearance of mold inside the bin, or a sudden population explosion of tiny white potworms

POTWORMS IN YOUR BIN?

As a bin evolves into a biological community, you may notice that your earthworms have company. Tiny, hair-thin white worms often appear in abundance, especially in the corners of the bin or clustered around chunks of decomposing paper. These are *Enchytraeid* species, often called potworms. White to pale pink and less than 1/2" (1.9 cm) long, pot worms thrive in the moist, acidic conditions of enclosed worm bins. Midget cousins to earthworms, potworms eat fungi and tiny bits of organic matter, and their castings are rich in nitrogen and many minor nutrients. They are present in gardens, too, where they help to move beneficial fungi about in the soil. Potworms are a prized food for tropical fish, and they are often used as biological indicators when soils are tested for heavy metal contamination because they avoid copper, lead, and other such contaminants. Potworm populations sometimes explode following the addition of new bedding and then level off as the vermicompost becomes mature.

(see Potworms in Your Bin? at left). To set things right, wipe out the mold with a paper towel, and then mix in a small amount of dry bedding (and the used paper towel, too). Leave the top off of the bin for a day or two and the moisture level should drop back within the normal range.

Keeping Worms Cool in Summer

Once summer gets under way, there is no need to keep worms indoors, so you can release them into your garden or to outdoor compost projects, move the worm bin to a cool place in the shade, or do a little of each. Retaining a small captive population eliminates the need to collect a starter colony of worms for a new bin. And you'll have a ready source when you want pure vermicompost to mix into bins of potting soil or sprinkle into the pots of container-grown plants.

Depending on your climate, it may be acceptable to simply stash your worm bin in a shady spot, but in most areas summer daytime temperatures are much too warm for earthworms. On an 85°F (29°C) day, for example, the temperature of the bedding and castings in a bin, even resting in a shady spot, will probably be nearly as hot as the air temperature. If they were free to roam, the worms would escape this level of heat by moving deeper into the soil until they reached a more comfortable (to them) 60°F (16°C) range. Or, they could cluster at the bottom of a compost pile to wait out the day, and do their food foraging at night. Stuck in a stuffy bin, they have neither of these options.

If hot weather is only an occasional event in your garden, you can keep your worms comfortably cool by making ice packs from zip-top sandwich bags, and burying them just below the surface of your outdoor bins, or by refrigerating or freezing food before you place it in the bin. Where daytime temperatures often top 85°F (29°C), the best way to keep your worms comfortable is to dig a snug hole into which a plastic vermicompost bin can be sunk at least halfway, so that the part of the bin that contains worms and bedding is surrounded by cool soil. The hole can be used as an underground composting project the following fall and winter, or you can make the summer "worm hole" a permanent part of your landscape by covering it with boards when you're not using it to provide climate control for a worm bin. Keeping your worms comfortably cool will improve their appetites, so you can continue to put small amounts of food into the semi-buried bin throughout summer. Moldy bread or bits of wet cardboard disappear fast when tucked beneath the surface of a sunken worm bin in summer.

Harvesting Finished Vermicompost

There are two challenges to gathering your goodies from a vermicompost bin — separating the worms from their castings, and drying the vermicompost to make it suitable for long-term storage. Both are surprisingly easy to do. You can use worms' natural inclination to avoid light and dryness to make them separate themselves from finished vermicompost. Then, simply allow the harvested vermicompost to air dry for a few days and it's ready to be stashed away in a bucket, bin, or plastic bag until you need it.

Depending on your needs, you can harvest your vermicompost bit by bit, in partial batches, or all at once. You will probably choose different options at different times, and sometimes you may want to collect and move worms to new bins or outdoor compost projects more than you want to harvest their castings. Here are four easy methods that can be adapted for a variety of situations.

Vermi-Volcanoes

When exposed to light and fresh air, earthworms naturally head downward in search of a cool, moist place to avoid drying out. Put this instinctive behavior to good use by piling vermicompost into volcano-shaped cones placed in a well lit place for an hour

Adding New Bedding

You can add more bedding to your worm bin at any time, but it's important to keep an eye on depth. A bin that's dense with worms, castings, bedding, and food can run short of oxygen if the material gets more than 10" to 12" (25.4 to 30.5 cm) deep. Should your worms reproduce so well that the bin seems to be wall-to-wall worms, you can start a second bin or release some of your current charges outdoors. Either way, you will need to add new bedding to the bin.

Follow step 3 on page 209 to prepare a fresh supply of newspaper bedding. Cardboard also is a great material to use for supplemental bedding, particularly corrugated cardboard. The ripples in corrugated cardboard help to aerate the bedding, and you will often find young worms using the channels as nurseries. You will need to tear the cardboard into small pieces first, which is easily done by soaking large pieces in water for a minute or two. Wetting cardboard before tearing it into pieces also limits airborne cardboard dust, which can irritate your lungs. To make the most of your effort, you may want to combine the addition of bedding with the harvesting of finished vermicompost, as we will suggest here.

1 Cut a piece of cardboard that fits snugly across the inside of your bin, so that it forms a straight or curved partition.

2 Tilt the bin, and hold the high side up by setting it on some food cans or other sturdy props. Use a hand trowel or gloved hand to scoop the material from the high side of the bin, removing up to one-third of the total volume in the bin. Place the vermicompost you remove in a pail, or pile it on the upturned top of the bin. ▼

3 Insert the cardboard partition between the cleared end of the bin and the working portion, leaving a 1" to 2" (2.5 to 12.7 cm) high open "gate" between the bottom edge of the cardboard partition and the bottom of the bin.

4 Fill the empty end of the bin with new bedding, some finished vermicompost taken from the mature end of the bin, and food in alternate layers: Place 2" (12.7 cm) of damp newspapers or cardboard in the bottom, cover with two to three handfuls of mature vermicompost, followed by a thin layer of coffee grounds or other kitchen waste. Repeat the layers, ending with a layer of damp newspaper or cardboard. ▼

5 By the time you're done, many of the worms in the vermicompost you set aside will have moved to the bottom of the bucket or pile. Gently remove the vermicompost from the top to another container; it should contain relatively few worms and be ready to harvest and store (see page 214). Return the worms that gathered at the bottom of the bucket or pile to your bin, or release them into an outdoor compost pile.

6 After a week or two, numerous worms will migrate into the fresh bedding, and the cardboard partition will soften and begin to degrade. Repeat the steps above from the opposite side of the bin, using the old partition as some of the bedding.

or two. If you are using a plastic storage bin as your vermicompost chamber, you can simply take off the lid, lay it on the ground or floor next to the bin, and pile on a cone-shaped mound of vermicompost. The width of the Vermi-Volcano is as important as height, because the worms will move inward from the edges just as they move downward from the top.

After the worms have bunched up in the center of the cone, lift handfuls of vermicompost from the top and sides and place them in a colander. Return the worms to the bin, or release them into a bed or compost pile outdoors.

Buckets and Bowls

Just as earthworms move to the bottom of a cone-shaped open pile, they will move to the bottom if you place worm-laden vermicompost into a bucket or large bowl. As long as you place the vessel in good light, the worms should promptly head downward, and you can gather the vermicompost from the top of the container after an hour or two. Then return the worms clustered at the bottom to your bin, or release them outdoors if conditions in the bin seem quite crowded.

Bottomless Buckets

If you want to move worms from your bin to an outdoor heap and retain the vermicompost for later use, you have the perfect job for an old plastic bucket that has a crack or hole in the bottom. Use a utility knife to enlarge the hole, but keep part of the bottom intact. Then fit the bottom of the bucket with some sort of grid that will hold in the vermicompost, but has open passages through which the worms can exit. For example, you can use an old piece of window screening with ½" (1.3 cm) diameter holes cut into it (taped into place with duct tape) or a number of sticks arranged in a criss-cross pattern over the open hole. Fill the bucket with worm-laden vermicompost, and place it on the bed or compost pile where you want the worms to work. In a day or two, the worms will exit through the bottom of the bucket. Sift and store the vermicompost left behind.

Drop-Through Screen

To harvest all of the vermicompost in a bin, place a 2" (5.1 cm) thick layer of damp compost in the bottom of a wheelbarrow or cart, and install a screen or sifter (see page 68 and 220) over the top. Dump the contents of your bin onto the screen, and park the cart in partial shade for a few days. Worms will migrate to the bottom of the pile and drop through the screen into the cart. Be sure to cover the vermicompost with a sheet of plastic, or move the cart or wheelbarrow into your garage, should rainy weather occur. Gather 1" or 2" (2.5 or 5.1 cm) of vermicompost from the top of the pile each day, and sift or store it. Use the worms that accumulate in the cart or wheelbarrow to start a new bin, or release them into your garden.

Sifting and Storing Vermicompost

Freshly harvested vermicompost is likely to have a moisture content of about 75 percent, so it must be allowed to dry for a few days before it can be stored. You can spread it out in an old baking pan lined with newspaper or simply place it in a large colander that fits inside the top rim of a bucket or pail. Use a hand trowel to fluff through the vermicompost whenever you think about it, and it should be dry enough to store within a few days.

You don't have to sift your vermicompost, but it's a satisfying process that produces a fantastic finished product — fluffy, chocolate brown compost, perhaps flecked with small bits of broken eggshells, which is ideal for topdressing plants in containers, or for mixing into potting soil. We like using a colander placed over a bucket to sift vermicompost, or you can simply work through it with a gloved hand, gently breaking up clods as you go. Should you encounter bits of intact bedding or food, simply return them to the bin.

KEEP A COMPOST COLANDER

Every compost gardener needs at least one inexpensive plastic colander that can be dedicated to garden use. A colander makes a perfect soil sieve when you want a very fine batch of compost or vermicompost to mix into potting soil. Look for a colander with very large holes or drainage slits that fits the top of your most often used buckets. Colanders with small openings clog quickly, and those made of metal may rust when left outdoors. In a pinch, you can use your compost colander as a temporary shade cover for newly transplanted seedlings. Lined with a piece of cloth, a colander makes a great flow-through filter for making a quick batch of instant compost tea for container-grown plants.

If you are trying to increase earthworm populations in any part of your garden, you can also pick out the cocoons, which look like BB-sized, yellowish beige pearls, and place them where you want more worms.

To preserve the biological vitality of vermicompost, it should still be lightly moist when it is placed in storage, and the storage containers should allow for limited circulation of fresh air. Clean buckets or pails with lids work well, or you can use small storage bins or big plastic containers like those used to package cat litter. Punch or drill a few holes in the sides of whatever storage container you use to permit modest circulation of fresh air.

Best Uses for Vermicompost

Vermicompost is a form of animal manure, and while it does contain soluble nitrogen and other nutrients, it is not rich enough to qualify as a true fertilizer. Instead, you might think of it as a soil tonic, or even call it "vita-verm," a high potency "vitamin" supplement for soil. Here are five ways to use it in your garden.

▶ **Add to potting soil.** As long as you mix in less than 20 percent by volume, vermicompost makes a wonderful addition to purchased or homemade potting soil. Like other forms of manure, vermicompost tends to be somewhat high in salts, so it should *always* be mixed with soil or potting soil to help dilute its salinity. Plants grown in 50 to 100 percent vermicompost seldom grow well; most studies suggest that the ideal balance is 15 to 20 percent vermicompost to 80 to 85 percent potting soil.

▶ **Topdress houseplants.** Houseplants respond beautifully to light topdressings with vermicompost. Apply a ¼" (0.6 cm) deep layer over the soil's surface in spring, just as new growth begins. Or, scratch it into the surface of houseplant containers that are too big and awkward to repot. Don't worry about smell, because vermicompost is nearly odor-free.

PERFECT MATCH

Petunias

When you've invested time and effort into making compost, it's easy to fall into the habit of playing favorites as you distribute the results of your labor. High-profile ornamentals, such as roses, and popular garden crops like tomatoes tend to get all the goodies, while unassuming annual flowers go begging. It's tempting to skip the annuals — they are going to die at the end of the growing season anyway. But by doing so, you may be missing the chance to see them really shine instead of merely limping along until frost finishes them off. Even easy-growing petunias appreciate a compost pick-me-up halfway through the growing season, and they'll repay your kindness with renewed vigor and abundant blooms well into the fall. When petunias start looking tired in the middle of the summer, cut them back by half their length and topdress them with a half inch of vermicompost, followed by a thorough drenching. Within a week, they will demonstrate their gratitude with a flush of fresh flowers that will make you glad you showed them a little tough yet tender compost love.

▶ **Rejuvenate containers.** The soil in containers of annuals kept on a deck or patio gets worn out by late summer, but the combination of vermicompost applied to the top and pruning back of leggy stems works wonders to stimulate fresh new growth. Be sure to follow up with a thorough drench of water to help move dissolved nutrients to the plants' roots.

▶ **Topdress beds.** Just as vermicompost can help revive containers, you can use it to keep tomatoes, peppers, and other vegetables going all summer long. Tuck handfuls under the mulch or simply scatter a thin layer over the soil's surface.

▶ **Prepare planting holes.** Some evidence suggests that substances in vermicompost stimulate rapid rooting, and because of its modest nitrogen content, vermicompost will not burn tender roots like some fertilizers can. Mix a handful or two of vermicompost into the soil as you prepare planting holes for perennials, shrubs, or trees.

Staying Focused on the Big Picture

Growing worms in bins is fun, so it's easy to become so involved with your captives that you lose sight of the basic purpose — to tie the compost garden year together by keeping decomposition moving along in winter. When practiced in rhythm with the seasons, Catch-and-Release Vermicomposting fits in beautifully with other compost gardening methods and ethics. It becomes the most active compost project of winter, yet it still relies primarily on resources found within your yard — including the worms! As you try other compost garden methods, you will invariably discover endless opportunities for enlisting earthworms to help make good compost even better.

8
Making the Most of Your Compost

ROM BANNER BATCHES and Honey Holes to Grow Heaps and Catch-and-Release Vermicomposting, we've covered more than a dozen methods and countless variations to help you on your way to full-throttle compost gardening. Next, you'll find many more ways to *use* all that wonderful finished compost. You can sift out irregular chunks (which may be used in another compost project) and have the finest, fluffiest compost imaginable. Learn how to rid your finished compost of weed seeds — without wiping out the microscopic good guys in it. You may want to experiment with making and using compost tea, and you will certainly want to try mixing compost-based potting soil. Last but not least, you will get to know a bit more about the wild things that share your interest in composting. Making the most of compost means understanding and using its dynamic powers to enhance the growth of your plants and the many other living beings with whom you share your landscape.

The Whys and Hows of Compost Screening

Sifting or screening compost removes undecomposed sticks or other materials, while reducing the particle size of your cured compost. Small, uniform particles hold more air than larger ones, so sifted compost has a unique velvety texture that makes it a joy to work with. Sifting compost does take time, but when it's done right, the process is almost as enjoyable as the result. Why bother to sift your compost through a screen? Here are six simple reasons:

▶ **Appearance.** Topdress houseplants, outdoor container-grown flowers, and established garden beds with screened compost for the loveliest, most soil-nourishing mulch ever. Screening removes the almost inevitable foreign matter that makes its way into your compost pile, so that the mulch you spread beneath your roses won't include flapping pieces of plastic tape or sticky fruit labels.

▶ **Seed security.** Garden seeds can get lost in the cracks and crevices of coarse compost, but this won't happen in finely textured, screened material. Screening also removes chunks of leaves and other undecomposed materials that can actually hinder plants' growth. After seeds are planted in beds, a light blanket of sifted compost will nurture them along while reducing the risk that a hardened crust will form over the germinating seeds.

▶ **Potting perfection.** Screened compost looks beautiful in containers, and its uniform consistency makes it easier to combine with other amendments in customized potting mixes.

▶ **Inoculate your next batch.** The material you screen out of your finished compost can help activate other composting projects. The stuff that won't fit through your sifter is still loaded with fungi and bacteria that will help a new pile get cooking.

Good looks are one of many reasons for sifting cured compost. Screening creates the perfect texture for potting mixes and seed beds.

▶ **Reduced storage space.** Screened compost is less bulky than unscreened and takes up less space in containers when stored for use another day.

▶ **Sifting compost is fun.** Sifting blends physical activity, sensual excitement (the texture, aroma, and hidden treasures), and the mysterious blending of past and present as the screen captures whole acorns, peanut shells, and occasional produce-department stickies. To better savor these moments, plan ahead for maximum enjoyment, which might include a chair in the sun, a clean pair of gloves, and no reason to hurry.

You need not sift all of your compost — we certainly don't! But we actually look forward to sifting our best Banner Batches as well as rich vermicompost. As for compost you plan to dig into your soil, the presence of large, slow-rotting woody pieces can be a good thing, because these holdouts will serve as reservoirs of microbial life long after the rest of the material has changed from active to stable organic matter (see page 8).

Sifting Made Simple

When it comes to sifting compost, necessity is truly the mother of invention. You can put together a sifting device using scrap materials, because all you need is some type of ½" (1.3 cm) metal or plastic mesh attached to a frame. A sturdy compost screen should

CART-MOUNTED SIFTERS

Brilliant minds think alike, but it's still a little spooky that both of us rely on similar cart-mounted sifters, which each of us made and thought were designs unique to us. My compost sifter consists of a piece of stiff ½" (1.3 cm) metal hardware cloth stapled onto a frame made of pieces of 1x3 (19x64 mm) scrap pine lumber. It's just wide enough to fit over the top of my garden cart. I pile on a few gallons of compost, stroke through it with a small spade, and harvest the fluffy stuff that falls into the cart. The rest goes back into a working heap.

Barbara's is a bit fancier. After she stapled flexible plastic hardware cloth with ½" (1.3 cm) mesh to a pair of 1x2s (19x38 mm), she screwed small cleats into each side piece. She hooks an elastic tie-down or piece of nylon cord over one cleat, then passes it under the cart and fastens it to the cleat on the other side of the screen to hold it in place. After she uses gloved hands or a hand trowel to fluff the compost over the screen to remove rocks, roots, and undecomposed chunks, the cords can be quickly removed to make the junk easy to dump (see page 68).

When we're not using our sifters to screen compost or soil, they come in handy for keeping neighborhood cats or other critters from digging in newly seeded beds.

add to your burden by working with a sifting device that is heavier than it needs to be.

To make sifting compost easier on your back and to cut out some of the lifting, buy or make a screen that fits over the top of your wheelbarrow or garden cart. If you like, you can line the inside of the cart with an old sheet or other cloth, which makes it easy to transfer the sifted compost into bags or pails for storage. If your sifted compost is destined for use in a special batch of potting soil, you can make a screen sized to fit over the top of a plastic storage bin, or simply use a colander that fits inside the top of a large, lidded, plastic pail.

Getting Rid of Unwanted Seeds

If your main composting operation is an "anything goes" affair, richly stocked with shriveled tomatoes, grass clippings, and random wilted plants from your garden, chances are good that it is also rich in weed seeds. The best way to approach this ever-present problem is to do a good job of separating materials that are likely to carry weed seeds from the materials that are comparatively clean, and then compost them separately. For example, you can meticulously avoid placing weedy materials in compost that is made primarily from leaves, and keep a separate Hospital Heap for the riskier materials (see page 123).

But even practicing good source separation will not completely eliminate this problem. Any compost project that includes soil will have its share of weed seeds, and kitchen waste may contain so many squash, tomato, and other vegetable seeds that the compost is unacceptably seedy. Weed seeds are nearly impossible to actually see in a crumbly handful of compost, but if you're wondering if a given batch of compost is weedy, you can have your answer within a week. Simply put some moist compost into a container, enclose it in a plastic bag, set it in a warm, sunny spot,

be able to handle both compost and soil, because you will also likely want to sift soil before mixing it with compost to make your own potting soils or planting mixes (see page 230).

Smaller sifters are usually better, because compost can be heavy stuff. A bushel of moist compost can weigh 50 pounds (22.7 kilograms), and soil is even heavier. Allowing very moist compost to dry for a few days makes it lighter and less likely to clog your screen. You will lift only a few shovelsful of compost onto your screen at a time, but there is still a lot of lifting and bending involved, and you don't want to

and see what comes to life. One cup of very rich, manure-based compost can contain thousands of seeds, compared to a scattered few in compost made from materials that seldom carry weed seeds.

If you know that a batch of compost is a weed festival waiting to happen, you have several choices. One easy option is to use the compost in projects that involve deep burial — for example a Treasure Trough or the lowest layers of a Layered Crater — or you can use it in the bottoms of large containers, such as a half barrel. Burial will suppress the emergence of most of the weed seeds, but because some types of weed seeds remain viable when buried for eight or more years, your sleeping enemy may awake with a vengeance when you cultivate the soil to plant a new crop. The best solution is to rid the compost of weed seeds using either high-temperature or low-temperature composting methods.

High-Temperature De-Weeding

If you're eager to use your compost, the fastest way to decommission weed seeds is to expose them to high temperatures accompanied by steam. This is not an altogether happy solution, because the high temperature of 140°F (60°C) needed to deactivate weed seeds can also kill beneficial microorganisms. Heat-treating compost therefore reduces its value as a source of dynamic soil life, but with a little help and time, the microbes can make a comeback. The weed seeds, however, will be dead forever. If you heat-treat your compost when it is not quite done, yet advanced enough so it has decreased in volume, you can then mix in a little cured, weed-free compost and a handful of wiggly worms. Enclose it in a plastic storage bin and set it aside to cure at room temperature for a few weeks; the microbes will multiply quickly and restore life and vitality to your heat-treated compost.

Forget trying to use your kitchen oven as a heat chamber, for two reasons. The lowest temperature setting on most ovens is 170°F (77°C), which is a little too hot. Soil chemistry can go haywire as temperatures approach 200°F (93°C), rendering compounds that are downright toxic to plants. And then there's

A light-colored garbage pail becomes a deadly germination chamber for weed seeds lurking in your finished compost.

the odor. Cooking compost or soil indoors releases odors that have a way of lodging in the human nose. Even after the cooking's done, you can pick up the scent for days.

A solar cooker set up in a sunny spot outdoors will not pose this problem. You can make one from a cardboard box in an evening and use it for months, provided that you remember to bring it indoors at night, so it won't get wet from rain or dew. People have devised dozens of designs for simple solar cookers, which intensify the sun's warmth by reflecting light to the center of the enclosure.

Make a Solar Soil Cooker

This cooker is based on the Barnard Box, a simple cardboard box covered with aluminum foil designed by contemporary French solar-cooking sage Roger Barnard. You can make one for under $10.

MATERIALS AND SUPPLIES

- 1 sturdy cardboard box, either square or slightly taller than it is wide (a 20" [50.8 cm] square box is a good size)
- Pen or marker
- Utility knife
- 1 roll of duct tape
- 1 small bottle of all-purpose glue
- One 75' (22.9 m) roll of aluminum foil
- Scissors
- Ruler

- 2 heavy stones, bricks, or other weights
- 2 metal food cans, filled with pebbles
- One 3 gal. (11 L) black plastic nursery pot
- Several clear plastic bags big enough to enclose the filled pot
- Twist ties
- One 3 gal. (11 L) plastic storage bin with lid
- 3 cups of active compost

1. Remove any tape or staples from the box so the top and bottom flaps fold out. Flatten the box. (See below left.) ▼

2. Working on a hard, scratch-proof surface, use the utility knife to remove all four top flaps from the box. Set them aside. Cut the front right edge of the box along the fold vertically, from top to bottom, and do the same with the front left edge.

3. Set the now three-sided box up vertically, with the bottom flap that is attached to the back of the box folded inward, and the two side flaps folded outward. Position the front piece of the box so it meets the edge of the infolded bottom flap, and tape the two pieces together with duct tape. Flip the assembly over, and reinforce the bottom by placing two of the reserved flap pieces across the base of the cooker. Tape them in place, and turn the cooker back over. (See below right.) ▼

4. Now you're ready to glue sheets of aluminum foil to all of the inner surfaces of the cooker. Working with one side of the cooker at a time, tear off a sheet of foil 2" (5 cm) longer than the size of the box pieces. Drizzle a thin thread of glue over the box, lay one edge of the foil in place so that it extends an inch or so beyond the cardboard's edge, and use the ruler to smooth the foil to the box. Wait until you're finished gluing on all the foil to trim the edges. Then use

STEP 2 ▼

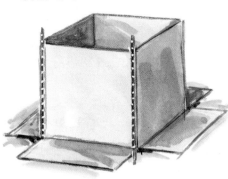

STEP 3 ▼

PROTECT YOUR EYES!

The intense light reflected inside your solar cooker can cause permanent damage to your retinas if you look into it, so it's crucial to avoid looking at the inside of the cooker in bright sunlight. Wear dark sunglasses as you get the hang of working with your cooker, keeping in mind that even sunglasses cannot exclude all of the potentially damaging rays. With practice, you will learn how to reposition the cooker from behind, with your eyes closed. Working from behind the box, it's easy to lift the weights from the side flaps and swivel the cooker until the shadow of the box lines up perfectly with your body as you stand behind it (you, the human sundial). Avert your eyes as you move to the front of the cooker to rearrange the cans, stones, or whatever you are using to raise the tongue to a 30-degree angle. Now you're done until the sun moves farther toward the western horizon.

duct tape to cover all the edges, which helps to keep the foil from tearing. (See below.) ▼

5 To use the cooker, place it in a sunny spot, oriented so that the shadow of the box centers on your legs as you stand behind it (See Protect Your Eyes! above). In the morning turn it to face east to southeast; in the afternoon face it south to southwest. Position the sides at 45-degree angles, and hold them in place by putting weights on the flaps. Use cans filled with pebbles to lift the front of the cooker slightly, to about a 30-degree angle.

6 Fill a 3 gal. (11 L) black plastic nursery liner with weedy compost, and moisten it well. Enclose the filled pot in a clear plastic bag, and place it in the middle of the cooker, about 3" (7.6 cm) away from the back. (See below right.) ▼

7 Every two hours, reorient your cooker for maximum solar gain. As you pivot the cooker westward, also rotate the pot to expose a different side to maximum heating. On a sunny, 70°F (21°C) day, the compost should heat up to 140°F (60°C) in two to three hours, and hold its temperature for most of the afternoon. Insert a soil thermometer midway into the pot of compost to check the temperature. Before emptying it from ther pot, wait until the compost cools to lukewarm, which often takes several hours.

8 Place the heat-treated compost in a plastic storage bin, and mix in several cups of finished, weed-free compost or vermicompost. After two weeks of curing, the compost should be revitalized and ready to use.

STEP 4 ▼

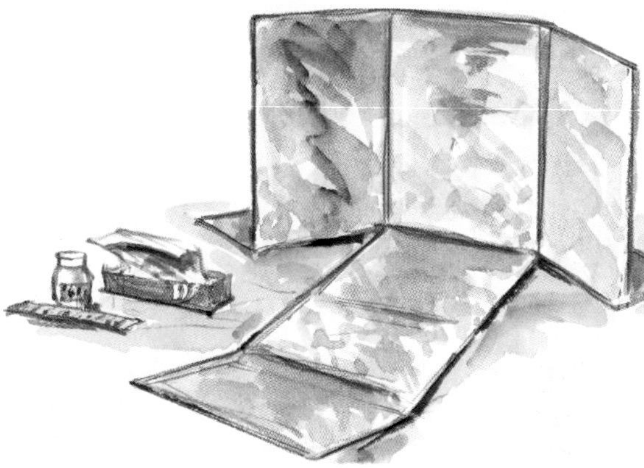

STEP 6 ▼

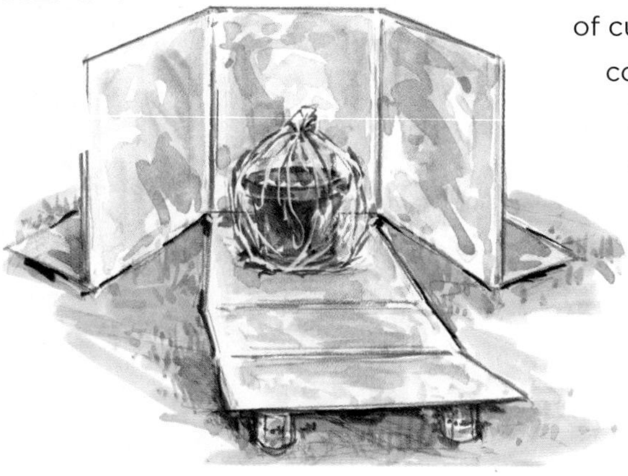

Low-Temperature De-Weeding

Killing weed seeds in compost without using heat takes more time, but two methods (and more you may dream up on your own) can be counted on to slash the number of weed seeds in a weedy batch by about 90 percent. The objectives of both methods described here — the Kicking Can and the Mummy Bag — are to create conditions that encourage the seeds to sprout. The fragile seedlings are then killed by roughing them up and depriving them of light.

▶ **The Kicking Can.** As long as temperatures are warm enough to promote germination (40°F/4°C nights and 65°F/18°C days), placing compost in a sealed plastic garbage pail and rolling it on its side every few days is a great way to exhaust the compost's supply of seeds. We suggest a white or other light-colored 12 qt (11.4 L) round, plastic garbage pail with a locking lid. Load the pail three-quarters full of moist compost (return earthworms to the mother heap). Fasten a strip of masking tape over the lid to secure it to the can. Place the can in a sunny spot and its interior will heat up during the day, triggering warm-natured weed seeds to sprout. At night, cooler temperatures will help activate germination of cool-natured weeds. Enough light will

get through the plastic to support the germination process.

Each time you roll the can, which can be done with a gentle kick, fragile sprouts get tossed about, and most suffer terminal injuries. Allow at least two weeks (three is even better) to deplete the viable seed supply within the can. Throughout this time, the composing process continues inside the can, so the resulting mixture is rich with microorganisms, enzymes, and castings from any earthworms that survive repeated tumbles. Strip off the masking tape and use your now excellent, nearly weedless compost any way you choose.

▶ **The Mummy Bag.** Like the Kicking Can, the Mummy Bag method reduces the number of viable weed seeds in compost by coaxing weed seeds to life and then killing them. The procedure is simple: Place a few quarts (liters) of moist, weed-bearing compost in a light-colored plastic bag, fold down the opening and secure it with clothespins, and lay the bag in a sunny spot. Every day or two, pick up the bag, give its contents a good shake, and then flatten it back on the ground. In two to three weeks, most of the weed seeds will sprout and then wilt to death. However, temperatures inside the bag will remain moderate,

Remove any earthworms from the compost as you put it in the pail (left).
Fasten on the lid and secure it with a few strips of masking tape to make sure it stays on (right).

preserving the lives of beneficial microorganisms that live in the compost.

Our experiments have shown that the best types of plastic bags to use are the thick bags often used by department stores. Bags that measure about 18" (45.7 cm) square are easy to handle, and you can even put the filled, flattened bags to work smothering weeds by placing them atop unwanted plants. Black plastic bags are prone to heating up so much that they actually begin to melt, and most clear plastic bags are too thin to work well. After the Mummy Bag has done its job, you can set the de-weeded compost aside to cure for a while without removing it from the bag, or go ahead and use the contents of the bag and refill it with a second batch of weedy compost.

▶ **Repurposed Mummy Bag.** Use your ingenuity to put the Mummy Bag method into action with whatever materials you have. Scraps of plastic sheeting can be fashioned into envelopes held together with clothespins, or you can make use of plastic bags used to package mulch, pebbles, or other landscaping supplies. If you have an unemployed opaque plastic storage bin, put it to work as a weed germination chamber. Fill two-thirds of it with moist, weedy compost, secure the lid with tape or elastic tie-downs,

Get your kicks. Every roll wipes out fragile seedlings of would-be weeds.

and place it in a sunny spot. Turn it over every few days to crush and mangle any weed seeds that have germinated.

Is Compost Your Cup of Tea?

Well-made compost is a superior soil amendment and excellent mulch. Its advantages over synthetic fertilizers and single-ingredient amendments are many. But the benefits of compost can take time to show up in your garden, so there may be times when you need a speedier "solution."

By making good-quality compost into a tea, you can spread its beneficial effects beyond the area of soil it might enrich in solid form. In solution with water, compost's micronutrients and beneficial microorganisms can be delivered directly to a plant's root zone, or even applied to the foliage. Compost tea can be useful when you have plants that are struggling in poor, unimproved soil, explains Dr. Paul Hepperly, director of research at the Rodale Institute in Maxatawny, Pennsylvania. "The best thing about compost tea is compost," says Hepperly, whose work includes studying the disease-suppressing effects of compost tea. "If you're going to do one thing, make compost and improve your soil," Hepperly recommends, noting that making and using compost tea is labor intensive. When applied to edible plant parts, compost tea also may present food safety issues because of its heavy load of bacteria.

Start with First-Rate Compost

Good compost tea starts with excellent quality, cured compost. Compost tea made from partially decomposed and/or bad-smelling compost may do your garden more harm than good because it may contain ammonia or dangerous bacteria. Making compost tea with poor quality or unfinished compost is a waste of time and compost.

PERFECT MATCH
Turf and Tea

A lawn consists of millions of individual grass plants (roughly 850 per square foot), each capable of forming complex relationships with soil microorganisms that help it take up moisture and nutrients and fend off disease organisms.

Much like other plants, lawn grasses grow better in soil that is improved with compost, but spreading compost over a lawn is a lot of work. First there's the quantity: A ½" (1.5 cm) thick layer of compost spread over a quarter-acre lawn equals nearly 17 cubic yards (15.5 cubic meters) of compost. Then there's the application: Most drop-type lawn spreaders are meant for distributing fine-textured grass seed or dry fertilizers. To pass through a spreader at its widest setting, compost must first be fully cured, drier than usual, and sifted through a ¼" to ½" (0.6 to 1.5 cm) screen.

Compost tea makes it easier to share the advantages of compost with your turf. You still need to start with Banner Batch–quality compost, but instead of tons, you need only a few pounds. You can apply compost tea to your lawn using a pump sprayer, hose-end sprayer, or even a watering can. Apply at a rate of 5 to 10 gal. (18.9 to 37.8 L) of compost tea per acre. For most lawns, one application in spring just as new growth is getting underway and another in fall when the trees start losing their leaves is sufficient.

Preferably, the compost you use to make compost tea will not contain animal manures. Although we recommend adding air to the mix when you "brew" your tea, aeration alone will not prevent bacterial pathogens, such as *Escherichia coli* (*E. coli*) from proliferating in compost tea. Rather than worry about whether or not your tea is supporting a population of pathogens that could make you sick, leave manure out of the equation and leave that worry behind.

Add Water and Air

Traditionally, gardeners and farmers have made compost (or manure) tea by simply steeping compost in water for a week or two. Without aeration, the resulting tea was smelly stuff that had modest nutrient content and not much in the way of desirable biological activity. Since spreading the biological wealth from

Make Compost Tea

An ever-growing array of compost tea-making kits is available for home gardeners, ranging from inexpensive bucket kits to elaborate systems with price tags to match. We suggest assembling your own compost tea brewer and trying a few batches to watch its effects in your garden. You may be inspired to move up to a bigger system that lets you make more tea, or you may decide that you'd rather spend your time gardening and pursuing less labor-intensive composting activities. As with all aspects of compost gardening, it's important to choose the methods that make sense for you and your particular garden's needs.

MATERIALS AND SUPPLIES

- One 5-gal. (18.9 L) plastic bucket
- 1 aquarium pump
- 1 aquarium air stone
- 4' (1.2 m) plastic tubing
- 1 shovelful (approximately 4–5 cups) cured compost or vermicompost
- Fine mesh bag for holding compost (a knee-high nylon stocking or the lower part of one leg from a pair of pantyhose will work well)
- De-chlorinated water

1 Set up your compost tea brewer in a spot out of direct sunlight where a little spillage won't hurt anything. You'll need access to an electrical outlet to run the pump. For safety's sake, use an outlet with a ground-fault circuit interrupter (GFCI) when making compost tea in places that get drenched by rain.

2 If your water supply is chlorinated, fill the bucket with water; connect the air stone to the pump with the plastic tubing, and "bubble" the water for a couple of hours to dissipate any chlorine in it.

3 Fill your mesh bag with compost and lower it into the bucket. This is optional — you can simply add the compost to the water. But if you plan to apply the compost tea with a pressure sprayer, you'll have to strain the finished tea before you can use it. Containing the compost will also help to keep it from clogging your air stone.

4 Aerate the tea for 24 to 48 hours. Foaming is normal, which is why you put your brewer where spills don't matter. Check at least once a day to make sure the pump is operating properly; stir the solution or swish the bag during each visit.

5 Pour the finished tea into a pump-type pressure sprayer or watering can for application. For best results, use your tea right away. If you can't apply it all at once, continue to aerate the remaining tea to keep anaerobic conditions from developing. The longer your tea sits, even with aeration, the less biologically active it becomes. Without other food sources, microorganisms will feed on one another and gradually die off.

6 As soon as you remove the tea from your brewing setup, clean the bucket, air stone, and plastic tubing. Undesirable bacteria are quick to occupy these surfaces and can negatively affect your future compost tea production. Plus, it's easier to clean everything while it's wet. Use a solution of 1 part chlorine bleach to 9 parts water or undiluted 3 percent hydrogen peroxide; rinse thoroughly with clear water after cleaning.

compost is the best reason for making and using compost tea, it makes sense to use a process that preserves that bio-activity.

Research into the uses and benefits of compost tea indicates that aerating the tea helps to loosen beneficial microorganisms from the compost so they enter into the tea solution. Thus, aerated compost tea is much more biologically active than nonaerated tea, and it has the same earthy fragrance as healthy compost. Aerating compost tea on a home scale is easy to do using an aquarium pump and an air stone purchased at a pet store.

Using Compost to Make Special Soils

Today's gardeners collectively spend over $500 million each year in the United States on special soils. At any large garden center, you will find a bewildering selection of these products, ranging from mixtures intended for use in containers to others labeled as "tree and shrub planting mix" or simply "garden soil." Most gardeners think they need these products; the numbers don't lie. In recent years, specialty soils have emerged as the fastest-growing category of lawn and garden products.

But do you really need to spend your money on designer dirt? As a compost gardener, you have the resources to reduce your bagged soil purchases to a precious few, or to phase yourself out of the store-bought soil loop altogether — a move that will not only save you money, but increase the overall sustainability of your gardening practices and add to the personal satisfaction you derive from working with your plants.

Declaring independence from purchased soils may feel a little scary, because bags that promise great results do provide a feeling of security. The more alluring the package, the more willing we are to believe that we are giving our plants their best possible shot at success. Question that belief, and open your mind! Give your plants a chance to show what they can do when grown in compost-enriched soils you make yourself, and expect to be delighted with what you see. Most plants will grow just as well, or even better, in homemade potting soils and planting mixes than they would if you grew them in soils purchased in bags.

We realize we are telling you to do something that may feel risky, because almost every gardening magazine, book, and extension publication you have ever read has instructed you to use a "soilless seed starting mix" to grow your seedlings and to buy a "good-quality potting soil" for your outdoor container plants and houseplants. As you watch your favorite gardening TV show, you will see planting holes for trees and shrubs prepared with the use of bagged planting mixes. Yes, these products will work, but so will thoughtful mixtures made with your own homemade compost. You may still buy bagged products from time to time in the interest of convenience, but as a compost gardener, you need not be totally dependent on them.

Turning Back the Clock

To help you warm up to the idea that you can, indeed, make perfectly good potting soil, let's go back a few decades. Gardening books published before the emergence of the boutique-dirt market provide wonderfully simple blueprints for making specialty soils from compost. Writing in 1973, Helen Van Pelt Wilson, author of a dozen gardening books including *The Fragrant Path* (still considered the bible of nose-minded gardeners), shared her thoughts on the best soil for geraniums (*Pelargonium* spp.), African violets, and other potted plants in her book *Houseplants Are for Pleasure* (Doubleday & Co., 1973):

> *You can be extremely fancy about the soil or "growing medium" for your plants or extremely plain. Mine is the plain policy. I grow practically everything in some variation of the Equal Thirds Mixture:*
> > *1 part soil from a well-worked garden bed*
> > *1 part compost or other humus*
> > *1 part sharp clean sand or Perlite*

In the same year, similar guidance was given by George Taloumis, garden editor for *The Boston Globe* newspaper and author of several gardening books, including *House Plants for Five Exposures* (Abelard-Schuman, 1973):

> *A simple soil combination for most house plants includes two parts garden soil, one part leaf mold, peat moss, or compost, and one part sand, Perlite, or vermiculite. On this sprinkle enough bone meal and a mixed fertilizer to whiten the surface. Mix all the constituents thoroughly with your hands or a trowel.*

We will come back to these simple formulas shortly, but first there is another story to tell: the dawning of the age of soilless mixes.

What About Soilless Mixes?

When you step into the greenhouse section of a modern garden center, much of what surrounds you can be traced to the work of Jim Boodley and Ray Sheldrake, Jr., two soil scientists at Cornell University. Starting in the 1960s, Boodley and Sheldrake foresaw the potential for a new horticultural industry that would mass-produce plants in climate-controlled greenhouses. Finding ways to prevent soil-borne diseases (which can spread like wildfire in warm, humid enclosed spaces) and to deliver nutrients to plants in irrigation water were fundamental challenges, which they overcame by creating what became known as the Cornell Peat-Lite soilless mixes (see basic formula below). By substituting chemically inert vermiculite or perlite for sand, and sphagnum peat moss for compost, they found that plants did not miss the soil component as long as they received adequate nutrition from chemical fertilizers.

For the next thirty years, most commercial plant growers used some version of the Cornell formula, and hundreds of extension pamphlets encouraged gardeners to fall in line with this trend. Among the benefits of soilless mixes are these three items:

▶ **Reduced risk of disease.** Peat moss is an extremely poor medium for the fungi that cause roots and stems to rot.

▶ **Excellent porosity.** Perlite and vermiculite readily absorb and release water, making it easy to keep soil moisture levels within an acceptable range.

▶ **Light weight.** Until it is moistened, any soilless mix is extremely light in weight, making it economical to ship and store.

The dependability of soilless mixes helped get the greenhouse industry off the ground, and many gardeners rely on this basic mix, widely sold as seed-starting mix, to grow their own seedlings.

THE CORNELL FORMULA

4 gal. (15.4 L) No. 2 grade vermiculite or perlite
4 gal. (15.4 L) shredded sphagnum peat
4 T (2 oz./57 g) powdered superphosphate
8 T (8 oz./227 g) ground limestone
1 c (8 oz./227 g) 5-10-5 formula fertilizer

WHAT'S WRONG WITH PEAT MOSS?

Over 10 million cubic yards (7,645,548.6 cubic meters) of peat moss are harvested each year from bogs in Canada, plus another million or so from bogs in the northern United States. Those are big numbers, but because less than 1 percent of North American peat lands are currently being harvested, peat bogs remain more plentiful here than in the British Isles, where harvesting has reduced peat acreage by nearly 80 percent. Peat comes from such very slow-growing, slow-rotting plants that it typically takes 1,000 years for a bog to add 1 yd (0.91 m) to its depth. Once harvested, peat bogs are changed forever. They can become forests or grasslands, but it will be centuries before we know the success or failure of efforts to restore them to peat.

Of equal concern are the environmental costs of the fuels required to dig drainage ditches, harrow and dry the peat, vacuum it up and bale it, and then ship it long distances. That's a lot of greenhouse gas emissions for stable organic matter, which is, of course, readily available in homemade compost.

Peat moss does have special characteristics that make it worth its costs when used as part of seed-starting mixtures. It absorbs and holds 10 to 20 times its dry weight in water, and it is a very poor medium for various soil-borne fungi, including those that cause the fatal seedling disease damping off. Beneficial bacteria *can* live in peat moss, so using small amounts of peat moss in seed-starting mixture is a sound practice. A three-way mixture of peat moss, sand, and heat-sterilized compost (see page 223) works well. Once seedlings grow big enough to transplant to larger pots or outdoors, you can drop the peat and start using homemade potting soil that includes your best Banner Batch of weed-free compost.

Compost Makes a Comeback

Technically, vermiculite, Perlite, peat moss, and lime are organic ingredients, so as long as an organic fertilizer is substituted for its chemical counterparts, you can grow plants in a soilless mix and claim that they have been organically grown. Yet there are several sustainability issues that have helped open the door to change. Peat moss is excavated from ancient cold-climate bogs, and it grows back so slowly that it is widely considered to be a nonrenewable resource (See What's Wrong with Peat Moss? on the facing page). In addition, more uses are needed for commercially produced compost made from forestry by-products, animal manures, yard wastes, and other biodegradable materials that are no longer allowed to take up valuable landfill space.

On the horticultural side of the situation, soilless mixes are too light and thin to serve as a long-term growing medium for plants, so plants that get their start in soilless mixes must eventually be transplanted to a richer medium. This is exactly what many gardeners do when they start seeds in a soilless mix and shift them to compost-enriched potting soil as soon as they are big enough to handle.

There are a few studies to backup this practice. In 2004, Melissa VanTine, a graduate student in horticulture at West Virginia University, wrote her master's thesis on the performance of tomato seedlings grown in soilless mix compared to various concentrations of composted horse and cow manure. Using composted manures produced on nearby farms, VanTine found that they made perfectly acceptable substitutes for peat moss — and for soilless mix. Interestingly, over the four-week period of VanTine's study, the pH of soilless mix dropped by a full point, becoming more acidic, while the composts remained above 6.0 on the pH scale.

Why wait for more science to validate what you already know? If you want proof that your compost is perfectly fine to use as a primary ingredient in potting soil, just do it.

Making Special Soils

You can make a nice batch of potting or planting soil using basic hand tools and a few simple ingredients, and then store your mixtures in moisture-proof containers until you need it. Use recipes in the chart on page 234 to make special soils to suit your purposes. You can mix up small batches in a wheelbarrow or large bucket, using a hand trowel or cultivator to blend the materials together. These basic recipes call for three categories of ingredients — soil, compost, and sand, perlite, or vermiculite.

▶ **Soil** provides the gritty texture that plant roots like, and serves as a reservoir of mineral nutrition. Use soil from your best beds when making potting soil. If you want to eliminate weed seeds in the soil, pasteurize it in a solar cooker (see page 224) before adding it to potting soil. You can also pasteurize moist soil by baking it in a tightly covered pan in a 200°F (75°C) oven for 90 minutes.

▶ **Compost** supports root function by supplying starter populations of mycorrhizal fungi and bacteria, and provides nutrition and growth-enhancing enzymes. Its high organic matter content helps the mixture absorb and retain water. It's best to use weed-free compost in potting soil (see page 222), or you can fill containers only two-thirds full of the weedy potting soil and top them off with purchased potting soil or heat-pasteurized compost.

▶ **Sand, perlite, or vermiculite** improve the drainage of the mixture, but add nothing in terms of nutrition. When garden soil with a sandy texture is used, you can cut back on these drainage-enhancing materials.

Finishing Touches

Once you've made a basic mixture, you may want to fine tune it to make it even better. Depending on the materials in the mix and what you plan to do with

Recipes for Special Soils

Mixture	Ingredients	Uses
All-purpose potting soil	2 parts soil; 1 part compost; 1 part sand, perlite, or vermiculite	Container-grown flowers, houseplants, vegetables and herbs
Rich mix	2 parts manure-based compost; 1 part soil; 1 part sand, perlite, or vermiculite	Fast-growing vegetable seedlings, perennials being held in containers
Light mix	1 part screened compost; 1 part sand, perlite, or vermiculite	Rooting stem cuttings or holding perennial divisions in a propagation bed
Planting mix	2 parts leaf-based compost, 1 part soil	Preparing planting space for new landscape plants

it, one or more of the following additions may be in order.

▶ **Vermicompost** is an excellent source of humic acids, which have been shown to enhance the growth of many plants. It is also high in salts, so it should never comprise more than about 20 percent of a potting soil's volume. Vermicompost-amended potting soil is ideal for flowers, herbs, or vegetables grown in containers outdoors.

▶ **Water-holding polymer crystals** (more properly known as potassium polyacrylamide copolymer crystals) help a potting mix retain water longer, so they are often added to potting soils intended for use in containers. Most large garden centers sell these crystals in small packages, which should be used at the rates suggested on the product's label.

▶ **Fertilizer** has quickly become a standard addition to potting soils, and you can add small amounts of plant food to your own batches. It's important to thoroughly blend organic fertilizers with other potting soil ingredients to avoid burning plant roots. Instead of taking a one-size-fits-all approach, wait until you are ready to use your homemade potting soil to add plant food. That way, you can tailor the type and amount of fertilizer to the preferences of the plants on the potting table.

▶ **Lime** is crushed limestone (calcium carbonate), which slowly raises the pH of very acidic mixes while providing calcium. Sprinkle on a light dusting when using compost made from leaves, sawdust, paper, or

other tree by-products as a major component of your potting soil.

▶ **Gypsum** (calcium sulfate) is another ground rock powder often added to potting soils to provide calcium, and it may help preserve fluffy texture in potting soils made with clay soil. A light sprinkling, or about 1 teaspoon per gallon (4.4 L) of potting soil mixed into the soil, is sufficient.

Rejuvenating Designer Dirt

If a purchased potting soil has earned your loyalty with consistent results, you can stretch your supply by using compost to reinvigorate it for a second tour of duty. This process can be as simple as mixing equal parts of worn-out potting soil and compost together, or you can follow the steps below to guarantee good results. Once the process is finished, you have excellent quality potting soil.

1. Dump used soil from containers into a large bucket with several small drainage holes punched in the bottom. Flood the soil with water, allow the excess to drain, and flood it again. This step washes away salts that often accumulate in containers. Spread the soil on a tarp in the sun and allow it to dry.

High-Energy Potting Soil

One of the credos often preached by my immigrant grandmother was to "learn something new every day." But sometimes learning that new thing requires setting aside an old belief, which, in this story, is the superiority of store-bought potting soil. After four experiments, good old chrysanthemums showed me that they prefer high-energy potting soil amended with compost rather than the store-bought version.

The lesson began when I decided to pot up some fine, late-blooming mums that had survived the winter. I dug the clump and selected six basal stems holding a few roots. I planted three of them in pots filled with a premium quality bagged potting soil and the other three in some homemade potting soil — a half-and-half mixture of slow leaf mold compost and a fast Banner Batch made from cow manure and straw.

Two weeks later, the mums in the commercial potting soil struggled to stay alive, while the ones in compost looked perky and green.

I thought it could have been a fluke, so I repeated the experiment with a different clump of mums. Once again, the compost clearly outperformed the potting soil. Thinking there could be something wrong with the potting soil; I bought small bags of two leading national brands and repeated the experiment. Once again, the mums liked the compost better.

Perhaps I should not have been surprised, but I was because I'd been so convinced, for years, that I really and truly needed the best potting soil money could buy. I was wrong. What I needed was the courage to trust what I suspected all along: Plants prefer soil that's every bit as alive as they are.

---

2. Mix the leached potting soil with an equal amount of rich, weed-free compost that has been sifted through a half-inch screen. It should include some undecomposed bits of leaf or straw, because its primary purpose is to restore structure with a fresh supply of organic matter.

3. Toss in a light sprinkling of lime and gypsum, and a small amount of a powdered or pelleted organic fertilizer. About 1 tablespoon of fertilizer per gallon (4.4 L) of potting soil is a good general rule of thumb.

4. Add enough water to make the mixture lightly moist, and then cure it in a converted container for two weeks. Microorganisms from the compost will recolonize the potting soil, the fertilizer will release some of its nutrients, and you may end up with the best batch of potting soil you've ever had.

Composting in Wild Company

Some of a gardener's finest moments are those shared with creatures that have wings instead of arms or that walk on all fours. Those that we like, including brilliant red cardinals and cute little chipmunks, we refer to as wildlife. Those we fear, such as snakes and rats, we regard as pests. But with few exceptions, the animals with which we share our gardens cannot be divided into good guys and bad guys, friends and enemies. Rather, they are all that remain of the once huge wild kingdom that we have replaced with our cities, towns, reservoirs, and highways. They are the

Thick mulches and the edges of compost piles catch the attention of brown thrashers, wood thrushes, and other birds that scratch up insects and seeds, and you may occasionally catch a glimpse of a salamander in a moist corner of your bin, should you turn a heap on a drizzly day.

So far, so good, and even though raccoons and opossums can cause problems if there are too many of them, most of us like to see them scuttling into the twilight from time to time. Some composters think nothing of throwing stale pizza and other items that these animals relish in the general vicinity of a compost pile, knowing it will disappear overnight. This can be irresistibly interesting, and while both of us are guilty of having fed ground-dwelling wild animals because we wanted to see more of them (Deb put out food for foxes; Barbara did it for a family of wild turkeys), it is not a good idea. Here is why we have mended our ways:

▶ **Overpopulation.** Supplementing the diets of wild animals increases birth rates (due to better nutrition), resulting in localized overpopulation. If the food supply is taken away, starving animals do desperate things to survive, or die.

▶ **Unwanted attractors.** Food that is not consumed by well-behaved animals will attract rodents, such as rats and mice, that invade human spaces and spread disease. And, pleased to find a good supply of insects, earthworms, and palate-pleasing rodents, snakes may make their homes in and around composting areas and make people scream.

Heard enough? Please limit feeding of wildlife to those that fly, and do what you must to keep wild animals from becoming regular guests at your compost buffet, especially rodents like rats, mice, and gophers. Sometimes the appearance of rodents has little to do with your or anyone else's compost, because you happen to be living in their territory. Instead of waging war with traps or weapons, first try your best to exclude unwanted animals with fine mesh fencing or screening, or switch to an enclosed above-ground composting system, such as a rotating barrel with a locking lid.

A pallet bin won't stop wildlife of all shapes and sizes from seeing your compost as a source of food and, in some cases, shelter.

survivors, and a lot of them have more than a passing interest in compost. For some, compost offers food. Others use a quiet heap as a home. When you introduce composting projects into the ecosystem known as your yard, you will probably see more wild things than you ever did before, because *compost supports life*.

In a composter's garden, the abundance of earthworms attracts animals that eat a lot of worms — robins, moles, toads, and turtles, to name a few. Toads think it's their lucky day when they happen upon a heap where slugs have set up shop, and lizards often patrol composting areas in summer in search of tasty insects.

Do Animals Make Compost?

Sure they do! Night crawlers stock their galleries with caches of compost, and abandoned rabbit dens are a natural form of underground composting. Ecologists have noted that decomposing salmon parts left behind by bears serve as an essential nitrogen source in forests of the Pacific Northwest. And then there are the Australian brush-turkeys, who build huge nests filled with precisely chosen, mixed, and moistened materials. Using their bills as compost thermometers, they peck, poke, and probe as needed to maintain the surface temperature at 92°F (32°C) — the perfect temperature for incubating their eggs. Instead of sitting on their eggs, brush-turkey parents keep them warm by depositing them in compost.

No animals native to North America are known to be such expert composters, though many have been reported to use a quiet compost pile as a nursery. In response to the question, "What's the strangest

PERFECT MATCH

Sunflowers

During times when birdfeeder filling becomes an almost daily task, it may seem as though the birds (and squirrels) are ultra-efficient diners who miss nary so much as a single sunflower seed. In truth, birds drop plenty of whole seeds here and there, which can give rise to a pretty patch of sunflowers with the help of a seed-friendly bed of compost.

Choose a spot for your feeder where you want sunflowers to grow the following year, and cover the ground with a Comforter Compost or a 2″ to 3″ (5.1 to 7.6 cm) layer of partially rotted materials (it need not be finished or cured). In spring, watch for the appearance of bird-sown broad-leafed sunflower seedlings, which often emerge before the last frost has passed. Pull out any weeds that appear, add mulch to keep the plants' root zones moist, and you're done. The plants will likely grow into different types of sunflowers, so you might want to tuck a few seeds of your favorite sunflower varieties into the compost among the bird-sown seedlings. Allow the plants to stand until the seeds are ripe, and the birds will harvest them for you. Stout sunflower stems make great materials to place at the bottom of a heavy heap to keep air channels open.

SCARED OF SNAKES?

Fear is a natural response to an unexpected snake encounter, but if you know what kind of snake you have, chances are good that you can eventually replace that fear with appreciation. Most snakes are harmless to humans, so the main thing to do is to identify a snake's species — or at least determine that it's not venomous. When you see a snake in or near a composting project, or anywhere in your garden, for that matter, take its picture. A digital camera is great because you can magnify details once you get the image on your computer, and from there you should be able to identify the species by consulting a good field guide. Nine times out of ten, you'll decide to watch the snake to learn more about its mysterious ways as opposed to chopping it up with a shovel and composting it.

Sammy the Skunk

Hungry wild things frequently visit compost in search of goodies, and the more you compost, the more likely you are to find yourself sharing with wildlife. At my house, the first serious trespass incident involved a knee-high stand of snow peas planted in Comforter Compost. During the night, the offender had pulled up most of the peas and dug through the compost beneath them. I saved the peas, and the creature left them alone for the rest of the season.

When my mystery guest returned the next year, it liked what it found — a half dozen composting projects, including thickly mulched Layered Craters where I'd been releasing captive night crawlers. Every few nights, the varmint would dig around in at least one of my masterpieces. When I shared my troubles with Tom Goforth, a native fern propagator who lives in a woodsy setting similar to mine, he had a ready answer. "Sounds like a skunk," Tom said. I didn't believe him and tried to blame the raids on wild things I had seen with my own eyes — raccoons, foxes, groundhogs, opossums, or the wild turkey that scuttled off into the woods when I went outside.

By process of elimination it became clear that my visitor was a striped skunk. The 4" (10.2 cm) deep conical holes, 3" (7.6 cm) wide at the top and tapering down to 1" (2.5 cm) wide, matched the size of a skunk's nose, a marvelous sensing device that helps it find earthworms hidden in the soil. In spring and summer, a large percentage of a skunk's diet is earthworms, supplemented by beetles, grasshoppers, and other insects.

Worried that my dog would soon dash through the door smelling of skunk, I looked into remedies. Urban wildlife specialists recommended motion-activated sprinklers or lights, but my checkbook balance nixed that plan. I did read about a man who relocated skunks that caused problems in his garden, and I'm still wondering how he managed to transport them in the trunk of his car. I decided to try a live-and-let live approach of barriers and deterrents coupled with giving the skunk access to a compost heap populated with worms.

Physical barriers included a cage made from plastic garden fencing erected around my Grow Heap of winter squash, and a cover of black fabric weed barrier secured over a big Banner Batch set aside to cure. To protect a Treasure Trough planted with flowers, I stuck bamboo stakes into the corners of the bed and connected them with horizontal strands of fishing line. All three skunk barriers proved 100 percent effective.

The scent deterrent I found easiest to manage consisted of strips of cloth drenched with ammonia, which I tied to the pen around my Comforter Compost beds. Ammonia can burn foliage, so it must be handled carefully. To minimize spillage, I filled an empty liquid soap bottle with ammonia, and pumped a few squirts onto the pieces of cloth every few days.

In the interest of peaceful coexistence, and to get some small benefits from the skunk's foraging, I removed the pen from around a slow-working heap, forked the material to fluff it up a bit, and added a few hundred earthworms from my indoor bin. Sure enough, the skunk began checking his special heap once or twice a week, mixing and turning it in the process. From then on, I made sure that at least one worm-bearing heap was available for his or her dining pleasure. It became a winning situation for both of us.

thing you've ever found in your compost?" readers of *Organic Gardening* magazine have told stories of baby rabbits, box turtles, kittens, skunks, mice, and even bumblebees (as well as lost watches, wedding rings, cell phones, and sunglasses). Wild things are most likely to make homes in heaps that are seldom disturbed, so approach a long-neglected heap carefully and be prepared for surprises.

Hosting Garden Allies

There is a big difference between feeding wild animals and providing habitat for homeless toads, lizards, and snakes, which are perfectly capable of feeding themselves. Give reptiles and amphibians a place to live, and they will devour more bugs, slugs, mice, and moles than you ever imagined lived your yard.

Eventually they may move on, but just in case a hungry toad or good-natured garter snake happens upon a composting project, here are a few ways to make these gardening allies feel at home:

▶ **Make a "hidey hole."** As you turn a finished heap that's ready to cure, outfit the base of the heap with a cardboard tube, a short length of 3" or 4" (7.6 or 12.7 cm) wide plastic pipe, or an A-frame shelter made from sticks that can serve as a moist, cool place for amphibians to hide from sun and predators.

▶ **Keep a stick pile.** A loosely stacked pile of sticks, stems, and other coarse material provides a comfortable habitat for amphibians, as well as ground-dwelling beetles that prey on other insects.

▶ **Add water.** Small water features like pocket ponds or ground-level fountains will attract numerous animals, so they are important elements in wildlife-friendly landscapes. Most visitors will be active at night, but broad, flat stones along the water's edge often become basking spots during the day.

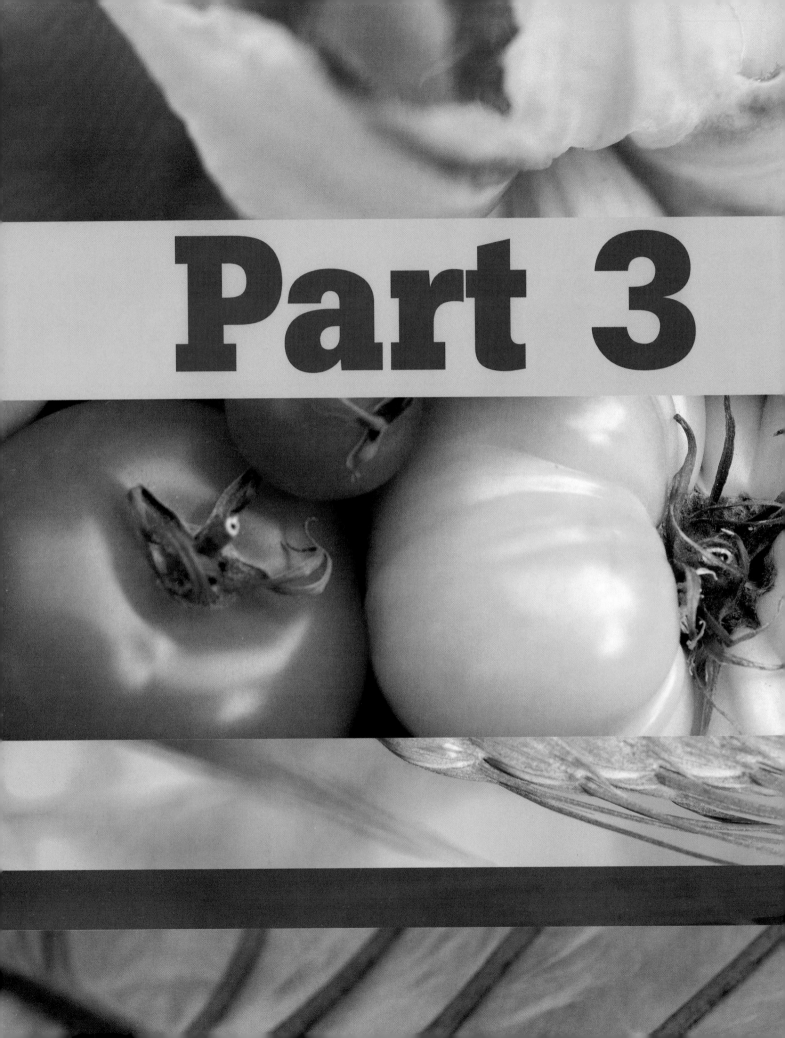

Part 3

Plants for the Composter's Garden

Mycorrhizo Walk of Fame

THE MODEST EFFORTS YOU MAKE to create more and better compost projects are returned to you in the form of healthy, productive plants. All gardeners have pet plants they can't get enough of, and most plants benefit from sinking their roots into compost in one way or another. Many scientists believe that eventually it will be proven that *all* plants benefit in some way from the activities of soil microorganisms. Compost gardeners find this easy to believe, because we see with our own eyes how dramatically some plants respond to compost-enriched growing sites.

The 25 plants profiled in this section are our nominees for the "Mycorrhizo Walk of Fame" based on their versatility and productivity in a composter's garden. Most are familiar; for example, green beans, watermelons, and tomatoes, but how about trying heat-tolerant yard-long beans with their red or purple pods, or tangy tomatillos? If you make a habit of trying some of the lesser-known members of the three plant families represented here (legumes, tomato relatives, and cucumber cousins), your garden will be more interesting, more productive, and a little closer to becoming sustainable.

How Plants Interact with Compost

We have also included a category called Compost Fodder Crops, which are plants you might want to grow to enrich the soil with organic matter and other nutrients, and to increase your supply of high-nitrogen greens for composting. The lists of hall of famers and Compost Fodder Crops could be much longer, so please do not assume that plants that are not included here are undeserving of compost. As you pay attention to how plants in your garden respond to different composts or different compost-garden methods, you will gain the best type of gardening wisdom you can have — wisdom gained through personal experience.

How Fodder Crops Enrich Soil

Like the fodder crops that farmers grow to use as food for livestock, Compost Fodder Crops are plants that compost gardeners grow to feed the soil, either directly, as a green manure, or indirectly via composting projects. Hundreds of different plants can be used as fodder crops, but the best ones are superior for building soil and making compost. Some, such as borage, stretch their taproots deep into the soil to retrieve nutrients that lie out of the reach of shallow-rooted garden crops. Others are noteworthy for profuse topgrowth that serves as a nitrogen source for carbon-heavy compost piles. Compost Fodder Crops with fine, dense, spreading root systems help to improve soil structure as they grow. When cut, nitrogen-fixing fodder crops, such as crimson clover, leave behind soil that contains more available nitrogen for the plants that follow, while the top growth may be incorporated into a Comforter Compost on the spot or added to any other compost-in-the-making. See page 276 to learn more about these super soil-building plants.

> ### PERFECT MATCHES FOR THE COMPOSTER'S GARDEN
> Throughout this book, we have suggested numerous great plants that pair up perfectly with certain composting methods. Check out these Perfect Matches:
>
> Asparagus, page 158
> Azaleas and rhododendrons, page 87
> Blueberries, page 190
> Carrots, page 197
> Garden cress, page 150
> Daylilies, page 159
> Forget-me-nots, page 167
> Hyacinths, page 84
> Johnny Jump-Ups, page 141
> Lawns, page 228
> Petunias, page 216
> Raspberries, page 155
> Roses, page 142
> Strawberries, page 203
> Sunflowers, page 237

Pondering New Plants?

Have you been thinking about a plant you want to grow, checked to make sure it's adapted to your hardiness zone, but still can't make up your mind? We can't do that for you, but we can offer these four points to ponder, which are especially relevant for selecting plants to grow in a composter's garden.

▶ **Will the plant thrive in biologically active soil?**
For most plants, the answer is a resounding "yes," but there are exceptions. Native plants that are accustomed to growing in very hot, dry, or cold climates may not be able to interact successfully with thousands of exotic (to them) soil-borne life forms. You can grow these plants as long as you give them soil that's not too rich for their "blood."

▶ **Are disease- or pest-resistant cultivars available?**
Pesticide use in a composter's garden should be reserved for emergencies, such as a nest of yellow

jackets that appears in your lawn. Fungicides are tricky to use successfully, and it makes little sense to let fungi-killing substances drip or leach into soil where an active microbial community is in place. On the practical end, there is no easier, or safer, way to prevent garden diseases than to grow resistant varieties. Resistance is usually noted on seed packets and in catalog plant descriptions.

▶ How good are the chances that a chosen plant will perpetuate itself with minimal assistance from you?

A composter's garden should be a low-input system, and your time is an "input." Among edibles, lettuces, chicories, arugula, and other gourmet greens will often reseed themselves if given the chance. Daffodils will naturalize easily if you dump piles of rich compost over the plants every spring; and foxgloves, forget-me-nots, and other biennial flowers can become permanent residents if their seed-producing cycles are allowed to reach completion, and the seed is then distributed to new beds in finished compost (see Grow Heaps Keep Bienniels Blooming, below).

▶ Is there a risk that a plant may become invasive?

Inclusion on federal or state lists of exotic invasives tells you what some plants can do when allowed to grow wild, so imagine the monsters they may become if given all the benefits available in a composter's garden. To learn about plants that have been identified as invasive or noxious in your area, check the Web site http://plants.usda.gov for listings by state or by plant species, or contact your local Cooperative Extension office. As a general rule, be especially careful when choosing berry-bearing shrubs or vines, because birds and other wildlife can spread the seeds far and wide.

GROW HEAPS KEEP BIENNIALS BLOOMING

When biennial flowers, such as hollyhocks, foxgloves, forget-me-nots, and others finish blooming, let compost help you spread your favorites to other places in your yard. Gather the mature, seed-bearing branches and tuck them into Grow Heaps (see Getting Started with Grow Heaps on page 163) created in spots where you'd like new flowers to blossom. Keep the heap lightly moist through the summer (cover it, if necessary). In autumn, chop up the compost and spread it in a layer about 2" (5.1 cm) deep over your future flower patch. The following spring will find the spot preplanted with seedlings preparing to put on their floral display.

Moving along. Let seed for biennials like these foxgloves germinate in compost, then plant the seedlings in the garden the following year.

The Legume Family
Leguminosae

In any garden, there is a delicious legume for every season. First come spring's early snow peas, then tender snap beans, followed by succulent edamame, heat-tolerant limas, or perhaps asparagus beans in climates where summer heat overwhelms regular pole beans. Dry beans such as pintos or kidneys sustain us with garden-fresh flavor and nutrition through the winter months when they serve as the base for hearty soups and baked beans. You can taste a dramatic home-grown difference in all of these legumes; peas and beans picked at their prime and eaten within hours of harvest carry hints of sugar laced with starch, which is as evident in a perfect pole bean as it is in a bowl of fresh edamame.

Legumes come in many different forms, from the familiar vines to shrubs and trees, and all have in common the ability to partner with soil-dwelling bacteria, which assist them as they convert airborne nitrogen into a soil-borne nutrient they not only can use right away, but also can store in nifty little root nodules until it is needed by the plant.

Legumes are often said to benefit the soil by manufacturing more nitrogen than they need, but this is

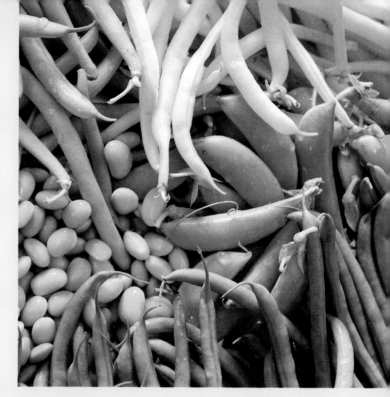

The roots of legumes form partnerships with soil-dwelling fungi that make it possible for them to manufacture their own nitrogen.

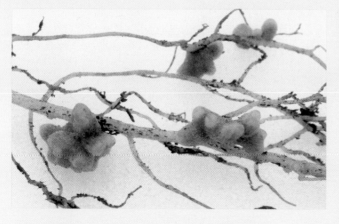

Legumes use nitrogen stored in root nodules to nourish a new crop of seeds.

SHOULD YOU INOCULATE?

Covering damp legume seeds with a thick dusting of ready-to-work, nitrogen-fixing bacteria seems like a good idea, and it is when legumes are grown in soil that is so lean that large amounts of fertilizer would otherwise be needed to keep them growing strongly, or when you're planting crimson clover or another Compost Fodder Crop (see page 276) that needs an unusual strain of rhizobia. On the other hand, if your soil is biologically active from constant composting, commercial inoculation may be a waste of time. Studies have shown that introduced nitrogen-fixing bacteria often fail to survive when added to soil where numerous other bacteria are present. Other things can go wrong, too. The bacteria inside packets of dry seed inoculant die after a year or so, or within days when exposed to poor storage conditions. And if dry weather hits before the inoculated seeds germinate, the bacteria can dehydrate or starve to death. Things work more efficiently in the secret wild kingdom of compost-activated soil, where the right rhizobia will team up with its preferred host plant when given a little bit of time.

probably stretching the truth for the legumes that grow as annuals. Plants are experts when it comes to allocating resources, and they never waver from their focus on what really counts — self preservation.

Not surprisingly, the bacteria that work with legumes do everything they can to keep their host plants happy, including conquering any competing bacteria that try to move into their territory. Different legumes utilize different bacterial strains, and we are constantly starting subterranean microbial wars when we plant asparagus beans after spring peas, or snap beans in a stand of alfalfa. You could try to give each new crop an edge by inoculating the seeds with an appropriate strain of bacteria, but most of the time it's best to let the beneficial bacteria duke it out among themselves (see Should You Inoculate? on page 245). It can't hurt to take a few spadesful of soil from the site where you grew a nice crop of bush beans last year and scatter it over this year's bean bed before planting, but the more important task is to provide great growing conditions for the plants.

Giving Legumes a Strong Start

When a legume seed sprouts and starts to grow, the roots exude substances that attract the right strain of nitrogen-fixing bacteria. More roots mean stronger signals, so it's important to provide enough nutrients to support vigorous early growth when growing legumes. For beans and other legumes that are planted after the soil warms in late spring, mixing an organic fertilizer into the soil, or starting a plantable composting project will do the trick, because organic fertilizers release their nutrients more quickly under warm conditions. Peas growing in cold soil are best fed with a water-soluble fertilizer at planting time, because soil-borne nutrients are less accessible when soil temperatures are below about 60°F (10°C).

Vining legumes, including peas, pole beans, and asparagus beans, require some sort of trellis, which should be installed just before the seeds are tucked into the soil. Thrifty pea vines are happy with a lightweight, 4' (1.2 m) tall trellis, but heavier vines need a sturdy 6' to 8' (1.8 to 2.4 m) tall trellis. A wire fence

or tomato cage will do, but the best pea and bean trellises follow a basic tripod or teepee design. As triangular trellises become heavy with vines, the weight of the plants actually increases their stability. You also can devise lean-to trellises to turn bean vines into a shade screen to cool down hot spots near your porch or deck, or to protect curing compost piles from the drying effects of summer sun.

Make sure that the trellis you provide for a vining legume is study enough to hold the plants aloft when they become heavy with pods.

Bush Beans
Phaseolus vulgaris

DAYS TO MATURITY: 50 to 60 days from direct seeding

SEASON: From late spring to early fall, while soil is warm (at least 60°F/16°C)

Bush beans are so easy to grow that they are the top crop suggested for new gardeners, but decades of experience does not diminish the pleasure of working with these generous plants. Green snap beans are the most popular types, and varieties offer plenty of variation in pod shape, size, and color. So-called Italian beans have flat pods, while most others have round, pencil-shaped pods. Most newer varieties are stringless, but you will need to remove the strings, or pod sutures, from older pods of most heirloom varieties.

Bush beans don't mind being a bit crowded, and they seem to grow best when planted in double rows. Thin plants to 6" (15 cm) apart, pull every weed, and then mulch with grass clippings or another material that will prevent mud from splashing on the plants, helping to keep the pods clean. Use two hands when picking beans to avoid injuring the plants (see illustration below). Bush snap beans often produce two or three flushes of pods, provided that the pods are kept picked, and plants are handled gently.

A purple-podded snap bean

When the plants decline, bush beans can be pulled up and composted. Keep a colander handy, because you will probably find quite a few beans you previously missed. Overripe snap bean pods become stringy and tough, but the beans inside taste great. Seeds harvested from pods that are allowed to dry to brown can be saved for replanting for up to five years.

Choosing Varieties

Bush snap beans can have green, yellow, or purple pods, and slender French filet beans can't be beat for in-garden snacking. All bush beans mature quickly and all at once, so unless you plan to can them, extend your harvest season by making several small sowings rather than one large one.

Bush Beans in the Composter's Garden

▶ Bush beans make excellent tenants for Comforter Compost (see page 154).

▶ Include a few bush beans at the base of large teepee trellises planted with pole beans or asparagus beans. The bush beans will grow faster and produce sooner while providing support for their taller neighbors.

▶ Plant a few bush bean seeds among cantaloupes, cucumbers, or watermelons, and let the beans serve as supports for floating row cover.

Careful two-handed picking helps to keep bush beans productive for a longer time.

Pole Bean
Phaseolus vulgaris

DAYS TO MATURITY: 60 to 70 days from direct seeding

SEASON: From spring to fall, while soil is warm (at least 60°F/16°C)

The most productive edible legume you can grow, pole beans become big, lush vines that bear beans for several weeks before they begin to decline. Their thick foliage shades out weeds, but you will need a sturdy trellis to support the twining vines. They are easy to grow, but pole beans are also popular with leaf-munching Mexican bean beetles, which can be hand picked and disposed of in all stages of growth, from clusters of orange eggs to spiny yellow larvae to mustard-yellow, black-spotted adults. Warm, muggy nights can cause pole beans to drop their blossoms, but the plants usually start producing again when the weather cools. In hot climates, use vining field peas or asparagus beans (see page 253) as summer alternatives to pole beans.

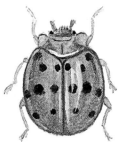

MEXICAN BEAN BEETLE ADULT

Pole beans often shed their oldest leaves while continuing to produce new vine growth and more good beans. Help feeble old plants to stay productive a little longer by collecting and composting failing leaves and mulching the plants' root zones with a fresh infusion of compost or vermicompost. When pod production declines, pull up plants and compost the vines, whole or chopped, in any type of composting project.

'Kentucky Wonder' pole beans

Choosing Varieties

Most pole beans are open pollinated, so you can choose from hundreds of varieties that vary in pod shape, size, and color, and save your own seeds. Try fast-cooking French filet types in salads, or grow flat-podded Romanos if you prefer the flavor of Italian beans. Numerous American heirlooms, including hairless, "greasy" beans and protein-rich "cut-shorts," offer incomparable flavor when allowed to grow until they begin to plump up with immature seeds. Be sure to remove the pod strings before cooking heirloom pole beans.

Pole Beans in the Composter's Garden

▶ Pole beans are a great pioneer crop for a new Comforter Compost bed.

▶ Plant pole beans after spring peas, using the same trellis, where summers are long enough to fit in both crops.

▶ Pole beans respond by producing bumper crops when grown in deeply dug Layered Crater (see page 179).

▶ Try growing pole beans on a large tripod erected around a Honey Hole (see page 189).

▶ Locate pole beans where they will form a visual screen to hide a messy compost heap.

Dry Beans
Phaseolus vulgaris

DAYS TO MATURITY: 80 to 100 days from direct seeding

SEASON: From late spring to early fall, while soil is warm (at least 60°F/16°C)

A rainbow of dry beans

Botanically speaking, dry beans are indistinguishable from familiar bush snap beans, but these legumes are harvested later, after the seeds are mature. The best dry beans (which can be eaten semi-dry, straight from the pod) have large, firm seeds that retain their flavor and texture when cooked. Growing your own dry beans gives you access to splashy colors and subtle flavors that you'll never find in a 1-pound bag on the supermarket shelf. You'll also discover that home-grown dry beans tend to have fewer gaseous side effects compared to dry beans from the store.

Plant the seeds in double rows after the danger of frost is past, thin plants to 6" (15 cm) spacing, and mulch with straw or grass clippings to keep the beans clean and to thwart weedy competitors.

Pull up entire bean plants in early fall when they begin to shed their leaves. If your crop is small, you can shell your beans by hand. Thresh large crops by beating whole plants against the inside of a clean trash can or by placing the pods inside an old pillow case and beating it against a paved surface or stepping on it. Separate the threshed beans from the pods and plant pieces, spread them out on clean window screens to air dry them for three days, and then store them in airtight containers. For optimum texture when cooked, use within a year.

Choosing Varieties

Dry bean varieties reflect their regional origins. 'Great Northern' is an heirloom "navy bean" ideal for soups and baked-bean dishes, while kidney-shaped cannellini beans are Italian favorites. Maroon-splashed, white Jacob's Cattle Bean is both beautiful and tasty, while brown-speckled pinto beans are essential for traditional Mexican dishes.

Dry Beans in the Composter's Garden

▶ Comforter Compost makes a perfect plot for dry beans (see page 154).

▶ Some dry bean varieties may be "half-runners" or semi-vining plants that you can grow on a teepee trellis erected over a Honey Hole (see page 189).

▶ The dried plants and shattered pods left after threshing dry beans make an excellent brown addition to any composting project.

▶ Use extra seeds to put dry beans to work as a summer Compost Fodder Crop. When used this way, pull up the plants as soon as they begin to bloom.

Lima Bean

Phaseolus lunatus

DAYS TO MATURITY: 72 to 88 days from direct seeding

SEASON: Summer, when weather is warm and humid, and soil temperatures are above 70°F/21°C

Protein-rich lima beans

Many people who think they don't like lima beans change their minds after their first taste of fresh-from-the-garden limas. Shaped like little three-quarter moons (hence the botanical name *lunatus*, for moon-like), garden-fresh limas are a rare delicacy well worth rediscovering. Beyond their beauty, flavor, and nutrition (limas are packed with protein, iron, and fiber), the fact that limas thrive in hot, humid weather wins the hearts of many summer-weary gardeners.

Plant limas in early to midsummer, and expect fast germination in warm soil. After that, the plants will take their time producing well-filled pods. Limas can tolerate heat, but they will produce more plump pods if they receive weekly doses of water during dry spells. Lima bean plants typically bloom prolifically for several weeks, but only a small percentage of flowers develop fertile pods. Limas do not ripen all at once, so a single sowing may yield five or more good pickings in late summer and fall. When a hard freeze ends the harvest season, pull up the plants and compost them with the last of autumn's falling leaves.

Choosing Varieties

Most limas are open-pollinated, and varieties may be compact bushes or vigorous vines that require sturdy support. Bush-type limas, such as 'Jackson Wonder' or 'Fordhook' are easy to grow in a range of climates, while long-vined 'Christmas Calico' or 'King of the Garden' perform best when summers are long and warm. All limas are at their best when harvested while still slightly immature, though they also can be allowed to mature into dry beans. The green color of the pods fades as the beans inside begin to dry, but varieties that feature splashes and speckles need to be close to full maturity to develop their best colors.

Lima Beans in the Composter's Garden

▶ Limas are a good choice for new Comforter Compost beds in warm climates.

▶ Where summers are hot, follow spring peas or lettuce with limas.

▶ Erect a tall, tripod-type trellis for pole limas, and compost garden waste beneath it.

▶ Grow bush-type limas around a Honey Hole (see page 189) in late summer.

Snow, Snap, and Shell Peas
Pisum sativum

DAYS TO MATURITY: 55 to 65 days from direct seeding

SEASON: Spring, when the soil temperatures range between 45°F/7°C and 60°F/15°C; also can be grown in fall in some climates

The snow, snap, and shell peas sold in your grocer's produce section must be picked quite early to assure good shipping quality, so enjoying the extraordinary flavors of perfectly ripened peas is a pleasure known only to gardeners. Be forewarned: Vegetable-hating kids will pick you clean if they get one taste of the treasures inside a garden-grown pea pod.

Snow, snap, and shell peas are all grown the same way. Two to three weeks before your last frost date, soak pea seeds in water overnight before planting them 2" (5 cm) apart on both sides of a 4' (1.2 m) high trellis. The seedlings are quite cold-hardy and benefit from a drench of water-soluble plant food such as fish emulsion when good weather encourages strong growth. Daily taste testing for ripeness is the only way to learn the pea picker's art.

To save seeds, allow pods to dry to a light tan color. Pea vines tend to break off at the soil line when you pull them, which can endow the soil with residual nitrogen from the decomposing root tissues. Pea vines make great greens for compost.

Choosing Varieties

Shell peas rapidly convert their sugars to starch, but long-holding varieties like 'Eclipse' give you a bigger harvest window. Variety in snow peas is all about pod size; tendrils gathered from thinned plants are a great addition to stir-fry dishes. Snap peas are the productivity kings of the pea patch. Team up an early, compact variety like 'Sugar Sprint' with later, long-

A young snow pea

vined 'Sugar Snap'. The early variety will start bearing a week or more ahead of the tall one and will provide physical support as well.

Garden Peas in the Composter's Garden

▶ Set up a circular Comforter Compost in spring, outfit it with a teepee trellis, and plant it with your favorite peas.

▶ Encircle a Honey Hole with a sturdy wire cage, and plant peas around the outside of the cage.

▶ Compact peas can be grown over a low wire arch like those used to support plastic grow tunnels. Pile up compostable materials beneath the arch in the cool shade provided by the peas.

Edamame
Glycine max

DAYS TO MATURITY: 65 to 90 days from direct seeding

SEASON: From late spring to late summer, while the soil is warm (at least 60°F/16°C)

Demand for soy-based, processed foods has increased by 15 percent each year for the last decade, but tender, immature soybeans, called edamame, are just being discovered by food- and soil-minded gardeners. Sometimes called vegetable soybeans, edamame (pronounced ed-a-MAH-may) must be picked soon after the hairy pods plump up with green seeds. Like spring shell peas or sweet corn, the sugars in the seeds convert to starch as they mature. To cook edamame, rinse the pods clean, dump them into a pot of lightly salted boiling water, reduce heat, and simmer for five minutes. The nutty flavored beans are great fun to eat straight from the pods, like peanuts. Any extras can be shelled and frozen.

Because of this bean's need for warmth, it makes a fine replacement for lettuce, spinach, and other spring greens. Sow seeds 1" (2.5 cm) deep and 3" (7.6 cm) apart. Thin tall varieties to 6" (15 cm) spacing when the seedlings are a few inches tall. Edamame thrives under hot, humid conditions, but the plants will produce better if they receive water during severe droughts.

Deer love to nibble edamame foliage, and Japanese beetles often stop in for a snack. Deer are impossible to deter once they have found this crop, but you can gather Japanese beetles first thing in the morning by jiggling them into a bowl of soapy water. Otherwise, edamame has few pest problems.

To save seed for replanting, allow one of your healthiest plants to stand until the plants begin to die back. Gather and dry the seeds, and store them in a cool, dry place. Layer or mix spent edamame plants into any type of composting project.

Succulent green soybeans

Choosing Varieties

If your garden is small or laid out in raised beds, try a dwarf variety, such as 12" (30.5 cm) tall 'Hakucho'. 'Sayamusume' grows to 2' (.61 meters) tall, and adapts well to cool climates. Highly regarded for its fine flavor, black-seeded 'Black Sugar' grows best where summers are hot.

Edamame in the Composter's Garden

▶ Grow edamame in Comforter Compost located in a sunny spot.

▶ To stockpile great dried greens for winter composting, dry edamame plants in the sun after you pull them up, and then tie them into bundles.

▶ Dress up your edamame patch with sowings of colorful sulfur cosmos, zinnias, or other heat-tolerant flowering annuals.

Asparagus Beans

Phaseolus unguiculata ssp. *sesquipedalis*

DAYS TO MATURITY: 80 to 85 days from direct seeding

SEASON: In summer, when soil temperatures are above 70°F/21°C; needs hot weather to produce well

More closely related to crowder peas and black-eyed peas than to regular snap beans, asparagus beans are also called yard-long beans and noodle beans. We like the noodle-bean name, and we love how this low maintenance, vining legume grows during the hottest part of summer. Once asparagus beans start producing, only frost will stop them.

The lanky twining vines can reach 12' (3.7 m) in length, but they will make do nicely with a 6' to 8' (1.8 to 2.4 m) tall trellis. A broad tepee with six diagonal posts and supplemental support from hemp string works great because it allows plenty of vertical hanging space for the long pods, and you can reach inside for two-handed harvesting.

Pods grow quickly in hot weather and should be picked when they are 12" to 14" (30.5 to 35.6 cm) long and still firm, because the pods become dry and hollow as the beans inside the pods mature. The flavor of asparagus beans varies with variety, season, and the age of the pods. Sometimes, mellow hints of mushroom become evident, especially when the pods are cut into 2" (5.1 cm) pieces and stir-fried in a small amount of sesame oil until they are soft and partially dehydrated. Tied in bundles of six pods, asparagus beans are also great when cooked on the grill.

All asparagus beans are open-pollinated, and you can easily gather enough seeds for replanting from only two or three fully ripened pods. Select pods for seed early in the season, but wait until the pods feel dry and brittle to gather the seeds.

Yard-long, or asparagus, beans

Choosing Varieties

Green-podded asparagus beans have been around for a while, but recently Asian varieties with more colorful pods have become available to gardeners. 'Red Noodle' and 'Mosaic' are pretty enough to qualify as edible ornamentals. 'Yard Long' bears pods more than 24" (24 cm) long, compared to 16" (40.6 cm) for most other varieties.

Asparagus Beans in the Composter's Garden

▶ Before planting asparagus beans around a teepee-type trellis, pile up garden debris and other compostables in the center of the teepee. The bean vines will keep the compost nicely shaded.

▶ Grow asparagus beans where a cowpea Compost Fodder Crop grew in previous years. They use the same type of nitrogen-fixing bacteria.

The Tomato Family
Solanaceae

Tomatoes and their close kin — eggplants, peppers, potatoes, and tomatillos — thrive when they enjoy a strong association with compost. Compost benefits tomato family crops in three major ways:

▶ **Nutrient availability.** Compost adds modest amounts of nutrients to the soil. More importantly, it improves the availability of nutrients that are already there. The biological activity that compost brings to your garden helps tomato-family crops to help themselves. Soil scientists and plant pathologists are just beginning to understand the many complex relationships that exist between plants and compost microorganisms. In the tomato family, plants whose roots are colonized by soil, or compost-borne endo-mycorrhizal fungi, are more successful at taking up nutrients from the soil. When they can tap into this subterranean energy source, tomatoes, eggplants, peppers, and tomatillos respond to the increased availability of nutrients by producing bigger crops of better quality fruits.

▶ **Disease suppression.** A number of soil-borne diseases can prove troublesome to crops in the tomato family, particularly the fungal organism *Phytophthora infestans*, which causes the leaf-, stem-, fruit-, and tuber-destroying disease called late blight of tomatoes and potatoes. In soil that's been improved with compost, disease organisms often fall prey to the larger population of beneficial microorganisms. The healthier, more vigorous growth of plants in compost-enriched soil makes them better able to resist the onset of diseases, too. Simply mulching the soil around tomato family crops with compost prevents some disease problems by keeping rain from splashing infested soil onto plants' leaves.

▶ **Better soil moisture retention.** Irregular soil moisture when fruits are developing causes fruit cracking, and promotes the calcium-deficiency disorder of tomatoes called blossom-end rot (it also may affect peppers and eggplants). In potatoes, fluctuating soil moisture contributes to cracked, misshapen tubers. By conserving soil moisture during dry periods, and by improving soil drainage during wet periods, compost helps to maintain the even water supply that allows plants to take up nutrients and moisture at a steady rate, avoiding growth spurts that contribute to split or deformed fruit.

Working with Tomato-Family Crops

The plants in this family are more than willing to take part in all kinds of composting projects, from Layered Craters and Honey Holes to Grow Heaps and Comforter Composts. They will not grow well, however, if their roots are exposed to fresh manure; potato tubers may be scabby and misshapen, and tomatoes and peppers may show growth spurts and delays when grown in compost that is rich enough to generate heat. Except for Honey Holes situated next to a planting of a tomato-family crop, stick with cold-composting methods when growing these vegetables directly in compost.

Potatoes grow best when planted during cool weather, but the other members of this family need an early start indoors. Plan to use some of your best, screened compost from your Banner Batches to get seedlings off to a strong start. See Making Special Soils on page 233 for information on using compost in potting soils for seedlings.

Rotate tomato-family crops with leafy greens, cabbage, or cucumber family crops, or various Compost Fodder Crops (see page 276), but not with each other. Growing tomato-family crops in the same place two years in a row sets the stage for several serious soil-borne diseases. Should you choose to adopt a volunteer seedling that pops up in your garden or compost, move it to a spot where tomato-family crops were not grown the previous season.

COMMON TOMATO-FAMILY PESTS

The sap of tomato-family cousins is laced with solanine, which is a bitter poison to many critters. However, it is exactly what some insects love to eat, so you can expect a few of the following unwanted visitors.

◄ **Flea beetles** often appear first on potatoes, where they chew tiny holes in leaves but don't cause serious damage. Eggplant often does not fare as well, so you may need to help these plants by using row covers or by catching the 1/10" long beetles with yellow sticky traps.

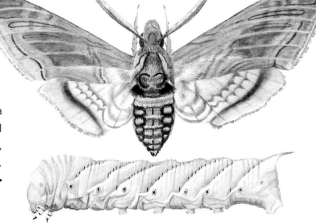

Tomato hornworms are the colorful larvae of a hummingbird moth. They are easiest to control by following their trail, picking them off by hand, and drowning in a jar of soapy water. They don't bite. ►

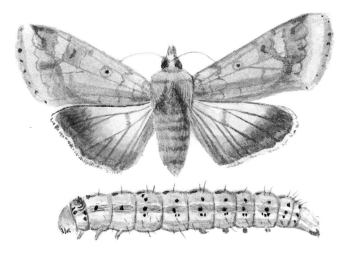

◄ **Tomato fruitworms** aren't a problem when there are only a few, but these little guys often appear in large numbers. Use a biological insecticide with *Bacillus thuringiensis* (Bt) as its active ingredient, applied while worms are young, to bring them under control.

Blister beetles travel in voracious packs, and they should only be hand picked with a gloved hand to prevent skin irritation and blisters. Use a biological insecticide that lists Spinosad as its active ingredient to control blister beetle outbreaks. ►

Tomato

Lycopersicon esculentum

DAYS TO MATURITY: 60 to 90 days from transplanting

SEASON: From spring to fall, while the soil is warm (at least 60°F /16°C)

Cherry tomatoes

To get a head start on tomato season, start seeds indoors about two months before the average last-frost date for your area. Use a seed-starting mix, such as equal parts of perlite or vermiculite, builder's sand, and screened compost, to get the seeds up and growing at room temperature, and then transplant the seedlings to containers filled with potting soil that includes your best compost or vermicompost. If you buy your seedlings, transplant them to roomier containers filled with compost-enriched potting soil as soon as you get them.

Speaking of seedlings, young tomato plants often pop up in finished compost or near places where tomatoes grew the year before. These volunteers stand a fair chance of bearing fruits that taste like cardboard, for example, when they are the offspring of hybrid tomatoes bred to be stalwart shippers. You can stock compost with desirable tomato seeds on purpose (see Saving Tomato Seeds on the facing page), but we recommend adopting random seedlings only in mid- to late summer when you may have no time for starting seeds and healthy seedlings are long gone from store shelves. In this situation, volunteer plants can mean the difference between plenty of September tomatoes and none at all.

In fall, when tomato plants are blackened by frost, gather up the ropy stems and layer them into a Walking Heap or one of your new leaf piles. Cut or chop the vines into pieces to make them easier to handle, but don't worry that the stems are too woody to decompose. In a matter of months, they will be finished compost.

If disease problems plagued your tomato crop, put the plant residue onto a weedy pile destined for hot processing. Also rake up the fallen leaves, which often harbor millions of fungal spores, and compost them in a hot pile.

Choosing Varieties

There's a tomato flavor, texture, size, shape, and color for every purpose and preference, and you can garden for a lifetime without having time to try them all. Begin this adventure by choosing varieties based on their growth habits.

▶ **Determinate** tomatoes are compact plants that produce a one-time, heavy set of fruit, and show little new growth after that. Choose determinate plants if space is tight, your season is short, or you want to can or freeze your crop.

▶ **Indeterminate** varieties, which include many heirloom varieties, grow and set flavorful fruit throughout the summer, usually on long, rangy vines that must be staked.

▶ **Vigorous determinates** typically produce a large crop of fruits, rest a few weeks, and then make a second crop later in the season. For long-season production, indeterminates or vigorous determinates are the best choices.

Compost garden techniques can help prevent some disease problems, but it's wise to grow resistant varieties if you know diseases are prevalent in your area. Resistant varieties are identified by letters that come after the variety name: V indicates resistance to verticillium wilt, F for fusarium wilt, N for nematodes, T (or TMV) for tobacco mosaic virus, and A for alternaria blight. Most disease-resistant tomato varieties are hybrids, so they are not good candidates for saving seeds.

Tomatoes in the Composter's Garden

▶ Make planting holes for tomatoes in a stand of hairy vetch, alfalfa, or another nitrogen-fixing Compost Fodder Crop.

▶ Tomato transplants will settle in when planted atop a Layered Crater or in Comforter Compost.

▶ Form a square with a tomato at each corner and a Honey Hole in the center.

▶ Grow tomatoes in earthworm-enriched soil left in the wake of a Walking Heap.

SAVING TOMATO SEEDS

If you want to save seeds from your tomatoes for next year's crop, it's best to save seeds from heirloom or open-pollinated varieties, which (unlike hybrids) will produce seedlings that will be similar to the parent plants. For your main-crop tomato, or perhaps an irrepressible cherry variety, the easiest way by far is to sow them in a Grow Heap (see page 163). Simply bury tomato pulp and rejected fruits in the heap, and cover it up over winter. As long as you don't pollute the heap with other seeds, the seedlings that pop up in spring can be left to grow or moved to other parts of your garden.

To store clean seeds indoors, you will need to ferment the pulp to remove germination inhibitors as described here:

▶ Scoop the seeds and surrounding gel out of a tomato, drop them into a clean jar, and add about ¼ cup of water. Put the lid on the jar, set it in a warm spot, and stir it twice a day for three days.

▶ When mold forms on top, add 1 cup of water, stir, pour off water and discard the floating seeds and mold (the viable seeds will sink to the bottom of the jar).

▶ Cover the remaining seeds with ¼ cup of water again, seal the jar, and let the mix ferment for another three days.

▶ Pour off the mold, rinse the viable seeds well, and spread them out on a piece of window screen to dry. When dried seeds are stored in an airtight container under cool conditions, they will remain viable for three to four years.

Potato

Solanum tuberosum

DAYS TO MATURITY: 90 to 120 days from planting sprouting tubers

SEASON: Plant in early to mid-spring; use blankets for late frost or freeze protection

Garden-fresh potatoes

If you are to be a happy compost gardener, you must like potatoes. Potatoes are never shy about replanting themselves wherever a little tuber happens to fall, including in most types of compost projects. Potatoes do need a well-drained, evenly moist growing medium in which to stretch their roots. Compost or compost-enriched soil satisfies this need. In addition, coarse compost mulch is like a mine field to Colorado potato beetles, a common potato-eating pest that must walk to find its preferred host plant.

As your potato plants grow, mound soil or mulch over their crowns to keep sunlight from turning the shallowest tubers green. Potato plants start to die back as their tubers mature. The tubers are ready in early summer in warm climates, but if you garden elsewhere, gather them in the late summer and fall (delicate, golf ball–size new potatoes can be gathered as soon as the plants make them). As you harvest mature spuds, set aside a few tubers to serve as seed potatoes for next year's crop. You can put them in a box and bury them beneath a mountain of chopped leaves, or keep them in a cool place indoors, such as a basement or garage. Gather up spent potato plants and layer them into a hot compost heap.

Choosing Varieties

Growing your own potatoes gives you the opportunity to try varieties that are rarely seen in stores. Don't miss the chance to try a rainbow of potatoes in shades of blue, purple, red, and yellow — we're talking flesh here, not just the skins. Start with seed potatoes that have been certified disease free to avoid common potato diseases.

Potatoes in the Composter's Garden

▶ Potatoes are happy to spread their roots in the loose contents of a Layered Crater.

▶ Plan a Treasure Trough (see page 187) next to a row of potatoes; use soil removed from the trough to mound up over the adjacent potatoes.

▶ Toss seed potato pieces over the top of a garden bed, then tuck them in beneath a Comforter Compost, adding layers as the plants grow and the compost settles.

WHEN GREEN IS NOT GOOD

Green potatoes are fine for planting, but they should not appear on your dinner table. The green tissue contains solanine, a toxic glycoalkaloid that is similar to the nicotine produced by the potato's cousin crop, tobacco. You'd have to eat a lot (2 pounds or more) of very green potato tubers to get seriously sick, which would be difficult, because green potatoes usually taste bitter. If a tuber has just a small, shallow green area, it's fine to cut it away and eat the rest of the tuber.

Pepper

Capsicum annuum var. *annuum*

DAYS TO MATURITY: 65 to 80 days from transplanting.

SEASON: From spring to fall, while soil is warm (at least 60°F/16°C); cannot tolerate frost

Piquant purple peppers

The three-way combination of warm soil, sun, and compost-enriched soil are the cornerstones of a great pepper crop. Like tomatoes, peppers may develop blossom-end rot on their fruits when fluctuating soil moisture affects the availability of calcium in the soil. By moderating soil moisture, compost helps keep this disfiguring disorder from doing a number on your peppers without overloading them with nitrogen. Peppers that are fertilized too well develop lush leaves, but few fruits.

Peppers benefit from compost mulch during the growing season, but wait until the soil is thoroughly warm before mulching. If you plan to save seeds, plant different open-pollinated pepper varieties in separate parts of your garden to prevent cross-pollination between sweet and hot varieties. To save seeds, choose a healthy, dead-ripe fruit, cut it open, and shake out the seeds. Let the seeds dry on a screen or a paper towel before storing them in an air-tight container in a cool place, such as a shed, garage, or refrigerator.

When cold weather brings pepper production to an end, pull up the plants and incorporate them into a composting project. If plants show thin, crinkled leaves, which is the most common symptom of viral infection, quarantine them in a Hospital Heap (see page 123).

Choosing Varieties

From candy sweet to fiery hot (with plenty of variations in between), there is a pepper for every palate. Small-fruited hot peppers are especially easy to grow and fast to fruit, while large-fruited sweet peppers bear their biggest crops in early fall. Viruses spread by leaf-sucking insects like thrips and aphids are common among peppers. If you've had trouble with viruses in the past, select resistant varieties with TMV (tobacco mosaic virus), PMV (pepper mosaic virus), and TEV (tobacco etch virus) after their variety name.

Peppers in the Composter's Garden

▶ Make planting holes for peppers in a thin stand of established alfalfa.

▶ Plant pepper seedlings atop a Layered Crater that includes several layers of soil.

▶ Make a Honey Hole in the middle of a square or circle of peppers.

▶ In late summer, sprinkle vermicompost over the root zones of your peppers to provide extra nutrients to support heavy fruiting.

Eggplant
Solanum melongena

DAYS TO MATURITY: 60 to 100 days from transplanting

SEASON: Summer, when the soil is warm (at least 60°F/16°C); tolerates high heat

Eggplants are easy to grow as long as you satisfy their need for warmth and rich, loose, evenly moist soil. Eggplants really like it hot, and they languish in chilly conditions. If you live in a cool climate, try growing the plants in 5 gal. (18.93 L) or larger, heat-absorbing black plastic pots.

Start seeds indoors 8 to 10 weeks before transplanting time, which should be 3 weeks or more after the last frost has passed. Meanwhile, enrich the planting site with cured compost and use black plastic or another dark mulch to prewarm the soil. After you set out the plants, consider covering them with floating row cover to prevent feeding by flea beetles, aphids, and Colorado potato beetles. Remove the row covers when the plants start blooming so that pollinators can reach the flowers.

Avoid growing eggplant where tomato-family crops have been grown the two previous seasons. This long rotation is needed to avoid eggplant's greatest weakness, verticillium wilt, a soil-dwelling fungal disease that is common in many climates. If limited space makes a long rotation plan problematic (or if you live in a cool climate), grow small-fruited eggplant in dark-colored containers that can absorb solar heat. In addition to keeping roots warmer, flea beetles are less likely to find eggplants grown in pots kept on a high table. In the fall, compost the frost-killed plants along with potting soil used to grow them.

Choosing Varieties

If you are a fan of sliced-eggplant recipes like eggplant Parmesan, you will want to grow traditional large-fruited varieties, such as 'Black Beauty'. Where short

A young purple-skinned eggplant

summers are the rule, or if you opt for container culture, choose small-fruited varieties or elongated Asian types, such as the hybrids 'Kermit' and 'Fairy Tale', which mature earlier than traditional large-fruited types. Regardless of size or shape, keep in mind that white-skinned varieties tend to be tough and bitter compared to those with black, purple, or green skins.

Eggplant in the Composter's Garden

▶ Mix a gallon of cured compost from a Banner Batch into each eggplant planting hole.

▶ Plant four eggplants in a square arrangement with a Honey Hole in the center.

▶ Transplant eggplants into a Layered Crater that includes several layers of soil.

▶ Grow eggplants in roomy containers filled with a heavy potting medium made of one part soil and one part cured compost.

Tomatillo
Physalis ixocarpa

DAYS TO MATURITY: 60 to 75 days from transplanting

SEASON: From spring to fall, while soil is warm (at least 60°F/16°C

A ripening cluster of tomatillos

Like super-charged versions of their tomato cousins, tomatillos grow into 4' (1.2 m) tall, lushly branched bushes. Sometimes called husk tomatoes, the sweet-tart tomatillo fruits resemble small, green or purple tomatoes, but with a papery wrapper surrounding each one. The robust plants are phenomenally productive, so most gardeners need only two or three. Tomatillo fruits are ripe when their husks begin turning brown.

Tomatillos tend to be more pest and disease resistant than other tomato-family crops, but the bushy plants may need staking to keep foliage and fruits off the ground, safe from soil-borne disease spores and foraging slugs and snails. Mulching with compost in early summer, after the soil is warm, also helps prevent disease problems and conserves soil moisture.

Like tomatoes, tomatillos are strong reseeders. Should they become weedy in your garden, dispose of tomatillo fruit trimmings and frost-killed plants in a Hospital Heap. If you don't mind volunteer tomatillos, you can knock down the plants where they stand and chop them with a sharp hoe or spade, or use them to give structure to loose piles of dried autumn leaves. The thin foliage will break down quickly, and the woody stems will disappear within a month or two.

Choosing Varieties

If you enjoy the flavors of Mexican food, particularly salsas, you should make tomatillos permanent residents in your garden. Most tomatillos are open-pollinated, so you can grow volunteer plants with a clear conscience. The varieties 'Toma Verde' and 'Green Husk' produce the familiar greenish-yellow fruits used in salsa verde; 'Purple' and 'De Milpa' yield deep purple or purple-and-green fruits. Tomatillos of both colors become sweeter and less tart as they ripen to gold or dark purple; harvest and use fruits while still green to take advantage of their tangy flavors.

Tomatillos in the Composter's Garden

▶ Transplant tomatillos into a bed vacated by spring peas or a hardy Compost Fodder Crop.

▶ Tomatillos flourish in a moist, rich Layered Crater.

▶ In late summer, grow a living mulch of lettuce or other leafy greens in the shade of tall tomatillo plants and enjoy two crops from the same space.

The Cucumber Family
Cucurbitacae

The cucumber family is a large and varied clan that includes juicy muskmelons, long-storing winter squash, and of course, cucumbers. Thanks to their big, flat leaves, members of this plant family are able to intercept and utilize plenty of solar energy. Below ground, they form partnerships with soil-dwelling microorganisms that help them to take up phosphorous and other nutrients. You can start seeds by planting them directly into warm soil a week or two after your average last-frost date, or start seedlings indoors and set them out when they are about three weeks old. Working with seedlings gives you a slight edge when it comes to pest control (keep reading), and also insures a uniform stand of plants.

All of the cucumber cousins are vining plants equipped with curling tendrils, though most varieties of summer squash grow into large, rounded bushes. As a space-saving measure, you can train cucumbers and other small-fruited cucurbits up a trellis made of wire, plastic garden fencing, or lattice. Cucumbers that develop long, slender fruits must be trellised to keep the fruits from kinking, but most other cucurbits are happiest when allowed to ramble over the ground. Weeds must be controlled early on, which is easiest to do by surrounding the plants with a five-sheet-thick layer of newspaper or a single layer of cardboard topped with an organic mulch, such as spoiled hay, compost, or straw. Once the vines have set fruit, avoid stepping on and mangling them as you tiptoe through the patch to check your crop. Vines that become twisted or bruised often fail to provide the nutrients needed by growing fruits, causing them to ripen unevenly, if at all.

Cucurbit Planting Plans

Traditionally, cucumber-family crops are planted in enriched hills spaced 6' (1.8 m) apart, with 3 plants in each hill. But because the plants are so productive, few gardeners want or need more than one or two hills of cucumbers or squash. With these crops, it is better to make two or three small successive plantings than to start all of your plants at once.

You can plant cucurbit crops in hills enriched with 2 to 3 gal. (7.5 to 11.4 L) of finished compost from a Banner Batch, or use other compost garden techniques to create cushy homes for your plants. Cucumber relatives thrive when grown in Comforter Compost that includes a few thin layers of soil, or you might opt for a Layered Crater, which is a great way to accommodate the plants' deep roots in sites with hard, compacted subsoil.

Melons and winter squash are not harvested until their seeds are mature, and the seeds will easily survive cold-composting methods. This makes these crops ideal candidates for Grow Heaps, which can be created in the fall and forgotten until spring, when they explode with robust seedlings. Growing a large crop of long-vined pumpkins, winter squash, or watermelon can leave little available space for other veggies, so look for areas near your garden's edge for these space-mongers. You can allow the vines to ramble over a patch of lawn if you're willing to forego mowing that area for the summer, or you can watch them wind their way into nearby plantings of upright corn or sunflowers. Because vine crops take up so much space, it's tempting to try to redirect them as they grow. Unfortunately, those long, juicy vines don't take kindly to being rearranged; even if you don't break the stems while moving them, unseen damage often results in misshapen, unevenly developed fruits.

Managing Cucurbit Pests

Several formidable insect pests feed on cucumber-family crops. You can prevent pest problems from the get-go by starting seedlings indoors, in roomy 4" (10 cm) pots, and setting the seedlings into the garden when they have two or three true leaves. As soon as you get the seedlings in the ground, cover them with lightweight, floating row cover with the edges securely tucked into the soil, and keep the covers on until the plants show a heavy set of flowers. Then remove it to allow insects to pollinate the plants.

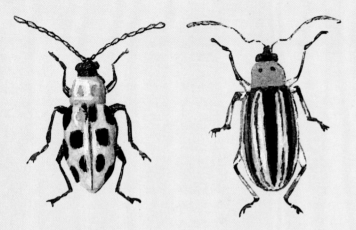

Spotted (left) **and striped** (right) **cucumber beetles** weaken plants and may transmit diseases.

Expect plenty of striped and spotted cucumber beetles to fly in when you remove the row covers to let bees and other pollinators work the open flowers. On the ground, squash bugs are on patrol for the host plants they require, and on warm evenings, the plants will likely be discovered by fast-flying moths whose larvae are the dreaded squash vine borers. These inch-long, super-maggots devour the spongy material on the inside of squash stems, girdling them from the inside out. Infested plants may struggle along, producing a small crop of undersized fruits and eventually succumbing to attack by some other pest or disease problem. Left unchecked, squash vine borer feeding usually kills the plant before its fruits reach maturity.

Squash vine borers weaken or kill many types of pumpkin and squash. The borers (top) are larvae of a large moth (bottom). ▶

Big, healthy plants can tolerate a bit of insect feeding, but because cucumber beetles can transmit bacterial wilt, a disease that causes melons and cucumbers to suddenly wilt and die, you may decide that the only good cucumber beetle is a dead cucumber beetle. You can put a big dent in your local cucumber beetle population by sucking them up with a vacuum cleaner. Practice on weeds until you learn how to handle the vacuum without mangling leaves, and work late in the day, when pollinators tend to be less active. Hand-pick squash bugs and their clusters of oval mahogany eggs. When you see sawdustlike frass (insect excrement) pushing out of a hole in the basal stem of a borer-infested squash, using sewing pins to pierce the stem sections where you think the borers are feeding can eliminate some of the offenders. You can also slit open affected stems with a sharp knife, cutting lengthwise along one side of the vine until you locate the pest(s). Remove and destroy the borer(s), then bury the slit stem under moist soil or compost. Vines treated this way often recover from their injuries, root in the soil, and go on to produce a healthy crop.

Cantaloupes and Muskmelons

Cucumis melo

DAYS TO MATURITY: 75 to 90 days from direct seeding or transplanting

SEASON: From late spring to early fall, while soil is warm (at least 60°F/16°C)

The delicious soft-fleshed melons we call cantaloupes are really muskmelons, but the two subspecies are easily confused. Most muskmelons have netted rinds and emit a sweet melon fragrance as they ripen, while cantaloupes have harder rinds without the familiar netting of a muskmelon. Honeydews and small specialty melons fall in between these two groups. If you've never grown melons before, start with a small-fruited muskmelon that matures quickly and "slips" from the vine when ripe; this is a great talent that eliminates guesswork as to when the melons have reached their peak of ripeness. For maximum nutritional value, grow muskmelons with deep orange flesh. They are delicious and an excellent source of vitamin A and other antioxidants.

Your patch will need to include at least four plants to ensure good pollination. Use floating row covers as described on page 264 to prevent problems with cucumber beetles and squash bugs. If raccoons visit your garden, they will keep their eyes on your melons and harvest them as soon as they think they are ready, so it's prudent to fence in your melon patch. At the end of the season, if the foliage shows white patches of powdery mildew, a fungal leaf disease, dispose of the vines in a Hospital Heap that will later be subjected to high-temperature processing methods.

To save seeds from open-pollinated varieties, simply rinse the seeds from ripened fruits and allow them to dry for a few days before storing them in a cool, dry place. Or, let a Grow Heap keep some of your cantaloupe seeds for you, as described on page 163.

Choosing Varieties

Try open-pollinated 'Minnesota Midget' or 'PMR Delicious' if you want to save seeds (the PMR stands for Powdery Mildew Resistant). Among hybrids, 'Ambrosia' is famous for its exceptional flavor, aroma, and disease resistance.

Cantaloupes in the Composter's Garden

▶ Cantaloupes are easy to grow in Grow Heaps or in Comforter Compost that includes several nutrient-rich layers.

▶ If you have hard, compacted subsoil, accommodate the plants' deep roots by growing muskmelons in a Layered Crater.

▶ To save space, small-fruited varieties can be grown up a trellis made of wire or plastic garden fencing supported by sturdy stakes. You'll need to provide support for each melon as it starts to mature.

PUT YOUR MELONS IN A SLING

You can conserve space in your garden by growing rambling melon vines up a sturdy trellis, but the heavy fruits need support to keep them from pulling down the vines. Cut off the legs from a pair of pantyhose and — presto! — you have two ready-made melon slings. While muskmelons are still the size of large eggs, carefully slip each developing fruit into the toe of a nylon stocking and pull the stocking up over the fruit. Without twisting the attached vine, tie the upper end of the stocking leg to the trellis. The stocking will stretch as the fruit grows, while protecting it from insect pests.

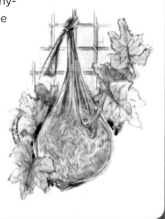

◀ Table-ready muskmelons

Cucumber

Cucumis sativus

DAYS TO MATURITY: 55 to 70 days from transplanting or direct seeding

SEASON: From spring to fall, while soil is warm (at least 60°F/16°C)

All cucumbers bear bountiful crops of fruits, which range from stubby, thumb-size gherkins, or picklers, to foot-long beauties, depending on variety. There is a loose correlation between leaf size, vine length, and fruit size, in that small-fruited varieties tend to be compact plants clothed with 3" (7.6 cm) wide leaves, while larger leaves and longer vines are typical of varieties that bear bigger cukes. Any cucumber can be trained to grow up a trellis, but trellising is most worthwhile with large-fruited Asian and Armenian varieties.

To insure good pollination, grow at least four plants together in a hill or broad row. You will enjoy a longer harvest season if you make two or three small plantings rather than one large one. As long as you use floating row covers to protect the plants from cucumber beetles and the bacterial disease they transmit (see page 264), cucumbers can be counted upon to grow quickly and produce a heavy set of fruit all at once. Pick ripe cucumbers daily, because the plants will stop producing if fruits with mature seeds are left on the plants.

With open-pollinated varieties, allow a selected fruit to grow until it turns hard and yellow, and save the seeds inside for future planting. Separate the hard-shelled seeds from the cucumber flesh, rinse the seeds clean and let them dry for a week at room temperature before storing them in an airtight container in cool, dark conditions. Gather cucumber vines when the plants begin to fail, and chop them into any type of compost.

Choosing Varieties

Slender-fruited hybrid gourmet cucumbers, descended from Middle Eastern types, are easy to grow and offer great texture and flavor. Among traditional American cucumbers, various open-pollinated 'Marketmore' varieties have good disease resistance. 'Lemon', 'Boothby's Blonde', and other heirlooms are especially suited to growing in late summer and fall.

Cucumbers in the Composter's Garden

▶ Cucumbers grown in hills piled on top of Layered Craters will produce like gangbusters; or you can use cucumbers to encircle a Honey Hole.

▶ Make a Comforter Compost in spring, install a simple tripod trellis, and you have an ideal site for a quick crop of cukes.

▶ In a traditional bed or row, enrich the planting site with 1 gal. (3.8 L) of compost per plant, worked into the soil.

CUCUMBERS WITH EXTRA APPEAL

In recent years, cucumber breeders have created special cucumbers to help meet needs of cucumber eaters and growers.

▶ Burpless cucumbers lack the "bitter" gene that causes compounds to form in cucumber peel that trigger the production of intestinal gas.

▶ Greenhouse cucumbers produce all female flowers that fertilize themselves, so these hybrids can be grown in greenhouses or under row covers that are never opened. They are easy to grow in a garden, too.

▶ Little-leaf pickling cucumbers carry genes from wild cucumber relatives that make them highly resistant to bacterial wilt and other diseases.

Pumpkins

Cucurbita pepo, C. moschata, C. maxima

DAYS TO MATURITY: 85 to 120 days from direct seeding

SEASON: Grow from spring to fall, while soil is warm (at least 60°F/16°C)

The deep orange winter squashes that most Americans recognize as pumpkins like nothing better than to sink their roots into compost-rich soil. Compost-gardening methods give these vigorous viners just what they need: a rich, evenly moist, well-drained site. Open-pollinated pumpkin varieties are excellent candidates for inclusion in Grow Heaps (see page 163).

Pumpkins are space hogs — a single plant may produce 20' (7 m) of rambling, leafy vine. Combined with their long growing season, this means that pumpkins will monopolize a lot of garden space; trellising is impractical for all but the most-small-fruited varieties. Still, few kids will forget the fun of watching a pumpkin develop from a barely perceptible bump at the base of a blossom into a robust Jack-o'-Lantern-to-be. And few pies are as tasty as one made with pumpkins plucked from your own patch!

Pumpkins can cross-pollinate with other squashes of the *C. pepo* species, so you may want to limit your crop to pumpkins or select less closely related squashes if you hope to save seeds. You'll get more complete pollination (and more pumpkins) if you have at least three plants; if space limits you to just one or two, you can use a soft brush to transfer pollen to the female flowers. Rinse and dry seeds before storing in cool, dry conditions. Pumpkin seeds remain viable for four to five years.

◀ Big, beautiful pumpkins

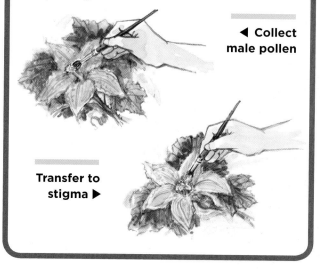
Choosing Varieties

Pick large-fruited types for Halloween displays; 'Howden' yields 10 to 20 lb (4.5 to 9 kg) carvers; 'New England Pie', also known as 'Small Sugar', produces classic 5 to 8 lb (2 to 3.5 kg) pie pumpkins. 'Jack Be Little' bears adorable 3" to 4" (7.5 to 10 cm) round fruits.

Pumpkins in the Composter's Garden

▶ Let pumpkin vines sprawl from a Treasure Trough at your garden's edge onto an area mulched with thick layers of newspaper where you plan to expand your planting space.

▶ Add the "guts" from your Jack-o'-Lanterns to a Grow Heap and stand ready to thin a healthy crop of seedlings when the weather warms up the following spring.

Summer Squash
Cucurbita pepo

DAYS TO MATURITY: 55 to 60 days from direct seeding or transplanting

SEASON: Grow from spring to fall, while soil is warm (at least 60°F/16°C)

A newborn yellow zucchini

Along with the squash we think of as summer squash — yellow squash, pattypans, and zucchinis — this species also includes acorn, delicata, and spaghetti squash, as well as some pumpkins. Because the latter four are normally picked after the seeds have matured, they can be sown in Grow Heaps, using the same techniques used for winter squash (see facing page). If you compost overripe summer squash or storage types of this species, seedlings are likely to appear in the following year's compost, which is a good reason to be meticulous about what seeds make their way into a properly managed Grow Heap. You can identify volunteer *C. pepo* seedlings by their broad, angular leaves. Most winter squash have lobed leaves.

When grown in any compost-enriched site, summer squash grows so exuberantly that you will probably need only two or three plants. The different types cross-pollinate one another, so you can grow a green zucchini, a yellow one, and a colorful pattypan in close company. Even compact bush varieties need plenty of elbow room, so space plants at least 2' (0.6 m) apart. Summer squash flowers are edible and delicious.

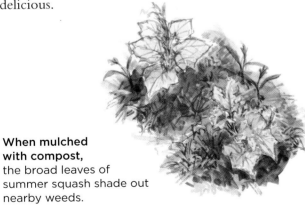

When mulched with compost, the broad leaves of summer squash shade out nearby weeds.

Squash vine borers often damage this species, although vigorous plants may continue to bear despite borer problems. Pull up plants when they stop producing and throw them onto a sheet of clear plastic that can be quickly tied into a bundle. Set the wrapped squash-plant skeletons in the sun for a few days to steam-kill insects before composting the wilted plants.

Choosing Varieties

Several hybrid varieties offer incredible vigor, which is paired with fruits featuring beautiful gold and green color patterns. Among open-pollinated varieties, old-fashioned 'Yellow Crookneck' is a true delicacy, while classic 'Black Beauty' and 'Golden Bush Zucchini' have stood the test of time.

Summer Squash in the Composter's Garden

▶ Summer squash adapt well to Grow Heaps and Comforter Compost provided soil is added to help anchor the plants' shallow roots.

▶ Plan ahead to provide water during dry spells. Use the Layered Crater composting method if you live in a hot, dry climate.

▶ When planting summer squash in hills or rows, generously line seed furrows or planting holes with cured compost.

Winter Squash

Cucurbita pepo, C. mixta, C. moschata, C. maxima

DAYS TO MATURITY: 80 to 100 days from direct seeding or transplanting

SEASON: Grow in summer, when the soil is warm (at least 60°F/16°C)

Among vegetables, winter squash are second only to potatoes in their ability to perpetuate themselves in a composter's garden. The fruits produce plenty of ripe, thumbnail-size seeds that easily survive cold composting methods, including vermicomposting. There are plenty of shapes and sizes of plants and fruit to choose from, though it's worth mentioning that 'Hubbard' types are the most attractive to squash bugs and squash vine borers. Butternut types have the fewest pest problems (they are rarely damaged by borers), and you can eat some of the immature fruits as summer squash if you like.

Buttercups and other varieties classified as *C. maxima* produce flavorful, nutritious fruits perfect for roasting or making into "pumpkin" pies, and sound fruits will store for months at normal room temperatures. These are big, robust plants capable of taking on pest challenges, and they pick up extra growing power from supplemental roots that develop where stems come into contact with moist ground. You can help them along by dumping a spadeful of compost over vine sections that have taken root. Even if the basal crown of a plant gets girdled by borers, the new roots often can keep the plant alive to ripen its fruit.

Winter squash are ripe when their rinds cannot be easily pierced with your fingernail. Leave a short piece of stem attached as you harvest each fruit to avoid making an entry point for decay and prolong storage.

Choosing Varieties

Work with good open-pollinated varieties, such as Cornell-bred 'PMR Bush Acorn' or 'PMR Bush

Single-serving delicatas

Delicata' (PMR is for Powdery Mildew Resistant). Among heirloom winter squash, 'Potimarron' is famous for its flavor and aroma. Many gardeners in warm climates get extraordinary yields from 'Tahitian' or other deep-rooted cushaw squash types (*C. mixta*), which bear long-storing fruits and edible seeds.

Winter Squash in the Composter's Garden

▶ Let Grow Heaps show you what they can do when planted with winter squash.

▶ When growing long-vined varieties, let them ramble over straw- or tarp-covered curing compost heaps or distant edges of your lawn.

▶ Dump seeds from hybrids into their own heap, and use the finished compost to grow a quick Compost Fodder Crop of cucurbit greens.

Watermelon
Citrullus lanatus

DAYS TO MATURITY: 85 to 95 days from direct seeding or transplanting

SEASON: Grow in summer, when the soil is quite warm (at least 70°F/21°C)

A sun-sweetened watermelon

Watermelons probably got their garden beginnings growing in compost piles near villages in North Africa many centuries ago, so this species has a long education in how to behave in a composter's garden. Research has shown that compost can increase watermelon yields and flavor while suppressing soil-borne diseases. If you give watermelons plenty of warmth and sun, the fast-growing vines studded with lobed leaves will quickly form a thick carpet of green. Pruning off the vines' tips when they are about 6' (2 m) long limits their spread and triggers the emergence of lateral branches, but you will still need a 15' (4.5 m) square of running space for the vines. You can let watermelons run over lawn, a curing compost pile covered with a tarp, or a mulched area of your garden.

Like pumpkins, watermelons take to Grow Heaps (see page 163) like ducks to water. For best results with this technique, work with a productive, open-pollinated variety that produces small fruits that weigh less than 10 pounds (4.5 kilograms). A 3' wide (1 m) flattened heap will support three nice watermelon plants; each should bear three or more juicy melons.

Watermelons accumulate sugars during the latter stages of ripening, so do don't pick them too soon (see How to Determine Ripeness on the facing page).

Choosing Varieties

Superior open-pollinated watermelon varieties to grow as perpetual Grow Heap crops include 'Black Tail Mountain', 'Sugar Baby', and orange-fleshed 'Orange Glo'. Pollen from these varieties can also fertilize the flowers of hybrid seedless watermelons grown nearby.

Watermelons in the Composter's Garden

▶ If you live in a warm climate, watermelon is a top plant for growing in a summer Grow Heap.

▶ Use watermelon rinds to help gather earthworms from your kitchen compost or vermicompost bin: Simply place large pieces of rind on the surface, juicy side down. Collect the worms that gather beneath the watermelon rinds.

▶ Plant watermelons in a mound of soil located atop a Layered Crater.

▶ Excavate an 18" (46 cm) wide Honey Hole, and use the soil to create a donut-shaped raised ring around the hole. Fill the Honey Hole with compostable materials, mix cured compost into the ring, and plant it with watermelons.

Compost Fodder Crops

In agricultural lingo, a fodder crop is one that is grown primarily to be consumed by animals. Many traditional fodder-producing plants have earned places in composter's gardens because they produce an abundance of fodder, or green material, that can be fed to compost, which is a big plus in landscapes that produce huge piles of leaves and other high-carbon brown materials. Compost Fodder Crops provide a supplemental supply of juicy green leaves and foliage that can easily be gathered and put to work in compost projects, or you can chop or mow down the plants and let the debris dry into weed-suppressing mulch. Meanwhile, the roots left behind in the soil rot into organic matter. In addition, nitrogen-fixing leguminous Compost Fodder Crops, such as alfalfa and hairy vetch, boost the soil's fertility so much that you often can cut back radically on how much organic fertilizer you use to meet the needs of nitrogen-hungry garden plants.

Plants that have strong talents for producing large amounts of leaf, stem, and root while taking up a lean supply of nutrients qualify as biomass plants. All plants accumulate biomass, but the big-time biomass plants are simply better at this task. Working green "biomass-ters" (see Ten Top Compost Fodder Crops on the facing page) into your garden often has additional benefits including hosting beneficial insects, protecting the soil from erosion, suppressing weeds, and breaking up compacted subsoil with their extensive

Cereal rye produces plenty of "fodder" for your compost projects, as well as dense, weed-suppressing roots.

roots. Compost gardeners like to use biomass plants as compost fodder or mulch, but farmers often turn them under and let them rot as "green manures" or use them as food for animals.

Whenever a bed or row is expected to be unemployed for more than a month, you have an opportunity to grow a Compost Fodder Crop. The best seasons for Compost Fodder Cropping (the term used by the 20th Century American Grow Biointensive gardening guru John Jeavons) depend on your climate and what you are trying to accomplish in your garden. There are Compost Fodder Crops for every season and need, including several that also produce delicious food. Compost-fodder crops are beautiful, too. Lush waves of buckwheat (in summer) or tangles of hairy vetch (in spring) serve as inspiring reminders of the determination with which soil and plants work together to create vigorous new life.

Choosing Compost Fodder Crops

In the following pages, we will profile 10 versatile Compost Fodder Crops that are easy to grow and can be planted during different seasons of the year. There are many more than we can cover in the space allotted, so we encourage you to study the possibilities of using other plants as compost fodder, including well-known

◀ **Bees love** borage's blue blossoms, while compost gardeners appreciate the herb's abundant foliage and deep, soil-penetrating roots.

vegetables, such as bush beans or vigorous grains like amaranth, canola, or quinoa. The plants we chose, whose characteristics are summarized briefly in the chart below, have a low risk of becoming invasive, which can be a garden problem with perennial clovers, vetches, and some grasses. Seed of most of these plants is available at farm supply stores or through seed catalogs, listed under cover crops.

DEALING WITH ROOTS, SHOOTS, AND SEEDS

Weediness is never a welcome trait, so you are wise to watch a fodder crop closely the first time you grow it. Pull up or chop down species that show a strong inclination to take over the world. Allow fodder crops to reseed only after they have shown a consistent pattern of good behavior in your garden.

Ten Top Compost Fodder Crops

Crop	Growing Seasons	Characteristics	Handling Tips
Alfalfa (*Medicago sativa*)	Year-round	Perennial, nitrogen-fixing legume.	Can be grown alone or as a companion plant with upright vegetables. Cut foliage in summer.
Austrian winter pea (*Pisum sativum* ssp. *arvense*)	Fall to spring	Hardy annual, nitrogen-fixing legume. Seeds are edible.	Combines well with rye or wheat. Cut down in late spring.
Borage (*Borago officinalis*)	Spring through summer	Vigorous taprooted herb; beautiful blue flowers.	Ornamental and edible. Good choice for small gardens. Cut in summer between flushes of blue flowers.
Buckwheat (*Fagopyrum esculentum*)	Summer	Fast-growing annual grain. Seeds edible but difficult to hull.	Very rapid growth. Can be cut for composting 3 to 4 weeks after sowing.
Crimson clover (*Trifolium incarnatum*)	Fall to spring in Zones 6–9; spring to summer in colder climates	Hardy annual, nitrogen-fixing legume.	Vivid flower spikes top lush foliage. Easily killed by mowing or hoeing. Cut down in spring or early summer.
Crowder peas (*Vigna unguiculata*)	Summer	Heat-tolerant, nitrogen-fixing legume. Seeds edible.	Top choice for hot weather. Fast, easy, and productive. Cut when plants begin to bloom.
Hairy vetch (*Vicia villosa*)	Fall to spring	Hardy annual, nitrogen-fixing legume.	Tremendous soil-enriching plant. Can naturalize with encouragement. Cut down in mid- to late spring.
Mustard (*Brassica rapa*)	Fall or spring	Fast-growing, leafy green. Tastes best after exposed to frost.	Best fast fodder crop for late summer to fall. Cut in early winter if plants are not killed by cold temperatures.
Rye (*Secale cereale*)	Fall to spring	Hardy grain with dense root system. Suppresses weeds.	Combines well with peas, vetch, and other hardy vining legumes. Cut in early summer.
Wheat (*Triticum aestivum*)	Fall to spring	Hardy grain with dense root system. Seeds ornamental and edible.	Combines well with peas, vetch, and other hardy vining legumes. Cut down in early summer.

Alfalfa
Medicago sativa

DAYS TO MATURITY: 70 to 90 days from direct seeding

SEASON: Grow as a perennial; sow seed in early spring (4 weeks before your last frost date) or in early fall (4 weeks before your first frost date)

Alfalfa is often called the queen of cover crops, and it makes a fabulous Compost Fodder Crop as well. A perennial, nitrogen-fixing legume hardy to Zone 4, alfalfa is a welcome permanent presence in a compost garden. You can give alfalfa its own space in a sunny bed or you can grow upright vegetables like broccoli or tomatoes in openings made in the stand by ripping out several fistfuls of stems or by cutting them off at the ground. New stems will sprout from the intact roots left behind.

Other Compost Fodder Crop legumes, including hairy vetch, winter peas, and crimson clover, are great for improving lean soil, but alfalfa needs fertile, well-drained soil with a nearly neutral pH (one also preferred by most garden plants) to prosper. In such a setting, alfalfa will recycle nutrients already present in the soil, while boosting the amount of soil-borne nitrogen available to other crops. Start new plantings of alfalfa in spring by sowing seeds where you want the plants to grow. Once an alfalfa planting is established, you can lift and move plants to other parts of your garden.

Just as alfalfa begins to bloom in early summer, harvest and dry foliage if you don't need it right away for your composting projects. Protected from rain, alfalfa hay retains its nutrients and makes a great addition to any type of compost. A large infusion of fresh or dry alfalfa will often lead to rapid heating in an intensively worked heap.

Vigorous, nitrogen-fixing alfalfa

Choosing Varieties

The 'Lucerne' variety is widely available, but there are many others developed for use in different climates. You can get inoculated seeds of regionally adapted varieties at local garden centers or farm stores.

Alfalfa in the Composter's Garden

▶ Use thin stands of alfalfa as companion crops for broccoli, tomatoes, or other upright crops that demand rich, fertile soil.

▶ Layer fresh or dried alfalfa hay into Comforter Compost to balance chopped, dry leaves or other materials that are high in carbon.

▶ Stud newly constructed Grow Heaps with a scattering of alfalfa seedlings. The plants' roots will add structure to the heap.

Austrian Winter Pea

Pisum sativum ssp. *arvense*

DAYS TO MATURITY: 6 to 7 months from direct seeding

SEASON: Grow from fall to spring. Cool weather required for good growth

A primitive form of garden pea, winter peas (sometimes called field peas) fix nitrogen and store it in root nodules. Well-rooted seedlings from August or September sowings stop growing when cold weather arrives and then take off in early spring. Plants grow to 26" (66 cm) tall by the time they produce purple-and-white, pocketbook-shaped flowers. For maximum benefits to soil and compost, cut the plants off at the soil line as soon as blossoms appear and layer the lush vines with overwintered leaves or other high-carbon materials. The roots left behind boost the soil's nitrogen content and ensure a ready-and-waiting population of nitrogen-fixing bacteria eager to team up with other types of peas.

Starchy winter pea seeds are as hard as rocks and benefit from soaking in water overnight before planting. If you allow a few plants to produce seeds, they can be saved for replanting for up to three years, or you can use them as soup peas, edible sprouts, or feed them to wild birds. The green pea vines also can be fed to animals, though in rare cases cattle have shown euphoric behavior when allowed to gorge on pea vines in spring.

Winter peas seldom have problems with diseases or pests when grown in well-drained sites, but they can suffer from root rot where winters are rainy. And although they are often hardy to Zone 4, winter peas grow best in Zones 5 to 7. If plants are allowed to stay in the garden until they produce mature seeds, they become susceptible to powdery mildew.

Winter peas with cereal rye

Choosing Varieties

'Austrian Winter' is the best-known variety; others include 'Early Dun' and 'Pennant'. Winter peas often are included in winter cover-crop seed mixtures.

Winter Peas in the Composter's Garden

▶ Many gardeners intermingle upright wheat with winter peas; the wheat serves as a low trellis for the peas' delicate vines.

▶ When gathering the vines for composting, use a sharp knife or hand scythe to cut them just above the soil line.

▶ Follow winter peas with heavy feeders, such as broccoli or spinach.

Borage
Borago officinalis

DAYS TO MATURITY: 70 days from direct seeding

SEASON: Sow in spring for foliage to compost; can be grown through winter in warm climates

A familiar plant to herb gardeners, borage deserves wider use as a Compost Fodder Crop. The plants produce a new flush of thick stems and broad, hairy leaves each time the older ones are cut back, and bumblebees can't resist repeat visits to the plants' star-shaped blue flowers. Many people eat young borage leaves in salads and freeze the edible blossoms in ice cubes for use in drinks. Both have a cucumber-like flavor and are perfectly fine to eat in small amounts. However, borage contains compounds that can be toxic to the liver if you eat too much, which is not likely, due to the thick coating of coarse hairs that help protect the plant from feeding by insect pests and people.

Plant jet-black borage seeds in spring and thin the plants to 2' (0.5 m) apart. Plants grow 3' tall (0.9 m) and 2' (0.5 m) wide and often flop over when they become heavy with flower clusters. This is your cue to harvest leaves and stems for composting, an operation that can be repeated every three to four weeks throughout the summer.

Young borage plants will stand through several frosts, but it's best to pull up and compost older ones as you clean up your garden in the fall. If you grow borage often, expect to see volunteer seedlings in your garden. To move the seedlings, gently lift them from beneath the roots to avoid injuring the vertical taproots and quickly transplant them where you want borage to grow.

Choosing Varieties

Species borage is known for the beauty of its sky-blue flowers, but there is also a white form 'Alba'.

Blue-flowered borage

Borage in the Composter's Garden

▶ Grow borage in places that can benefit from the probing powers of its deep taproot, which can penetrate compacted subsoil.

▶ Use pruning shears to cut leaf-bearing stems into pieces less than 1' long (0.3 m) before layering them into any type of compost project.

▶ Borage leaves contain abundant moisture, so they are a good addition to compost heaps that tend to dry out quickly.

Buckwheat

Fagopyrum esculentum

DAYS TO MATURITY: 30 to 50 days from direct seeding

SEASON: Grow in summer, when the soil is warm (at least 60°F/16°C)

Free-blooming buckwheat

If you have never grown a cover crop before, a few handfuls of buckwheat seed scattered over a plot of cultivated soil will show you how it's done. As long as the soil is moist and warm, the buckwheat seeds will sprout within a few days, forming a beautiful, weed-resistant sea of green. Although buckwheat is a grain, it is not a grass, so the plants are much easier to pull, mow, or cut down than wheat or rye. When the aboveground parts of buckwheat are removed, the roots promptly die and add to the soil's supply of organic matter.

About six weeks after sowing, buckwheat crowns itself with pollinator-friendly white flowers. If you like, you can allow a healthy cluster of plants to grow until they produce hard, black seeds for replanting. For eating purposes, the seeds must first be hulled, which is difficult and time consuming without special equipment. Buying buckwheat groats or flour is more practical than growing and processing your own.

Buckwheat is so quick and dependable that every compost gardener should keep a ready supply of seeds on hand. Buckwheat foliage and stems make a great substitute for grass clippings in summer composting projects, and a late sowing made in early fall is invaluable for combining with dry, chopped leaves. Just be sure to harvest the buckwheat plants before frost turns them to mush.

Choosing Varieties

Buckwheat seeds are generally sold by species rather than by variety. Seed companies usually list buckwheat under cover crops. You can buy seeds in bulk at any farm supply store.

Buckwheat in the Composter's Garden

▶ Sow freely from spring to late summer for use as compost fodder. Small plantings are great for filling gaps in rows or beds.

▶ In fall, you can use buckwheat as a "nurse" crop when planting hardy Compost Fodder Crops like winter peas, vetch, or crimson clover. The buckwheat will sprout faster than the legumes and then be killed by frost, making room for its neighbors.

▶ Open planting pockets in a stand of buckwheat by pulling up clusters of plants. Fill the holes with seedlings of vegetables or flowers.

Crimson Clover
Trifolium incarnatum

DAYS TO MATURITY: 80 to 180 days from direct seeding

SEASON: Grow from fall to spring in mild winter areas, or from spring to summer in cold climates

Well-behaved crimson clover

The same crimson clover used to create waves of color along roadsides makes a fine nitrogen-fixing Compost Fodder Crop. When sown in fall, seedlings stay small through winter, but below ground, they are busy developing heavy root systems. As days lengthen in spring, crimson clover explodes with green growth, and crowns itself with strawberry-red flower spikes by early summer.

Remarkably pretty for a cover crop, crimson clover is great for growing along fence rows or the outer boundaries of a garden. To harness crimson clover's nitrogen-fixing abilities, take the plants down before they expend their stored-up nitrogen producing seeds. This is easily done with a single pass of a mower or sharp hoe, because crimson clover cannot recover from close decapitation. Once its tops are gathered, the roots quickly die.

Before ordering mail-order seeds, check with local farm supply stores to see if they have pelleted seeds that have been coated with clay and inoculant for fool-proof planting. Be choosy about clover species. A few perennial clovers bloom red, but they carry a higher risk of becoming invasive compared to crimson clover. Crimson clover's imperfection is its limited cold hardiness. Well-rooted seedlings easily survive winter in Zones 6 to 9, but must be grown as summer annuals in colder regions.

Choosing Varieties

Crimson clover is rarely sold by variety name, though several have been developed by forage plant specialists. 'Dixie' and other "hard-seeded" varieties are best for sowing in fall. 'Cherokee', 'Frontier', and other "soft-seeded" varieties germinate faster and are better for summer-sown crops.

Crimson Clover in the Composter's Garden

▶ A small mass planting will produce plenty of high-nitrogen greens for spring compost projects.

▶ If you keep a wildflower meadow, sowing a few pinches of crimson clover seeds each fall will insure a colorful spring.

▶ Combines beautifully with hardy, self-seeding annual bachelor buttons (*Centaurea cyanus*) and corn poppies (*Papaver rhoeas*), easy-to-grow wildflowers that follow the same growth schedule as crimson clover.

▶ Can be mixed with other hardy annual Compost Fodder Crops, such as Austrian winter pea, hairy vetch, and cereal rye.

Crowder Peas
Vigna unguiculata

DAYS TO MATURITY: 65 to 80 days from direct seeding

SEASON: Use this heat-loving legume as a midsummer source of lush greens

Heat-tolerant crowder peas

If you live in the sultry South, July and August are good months to lay back a bit in the garden. While you take a break, you can put crowder peas to work improving your soil, shading out weeds, and serving as greens for your compost. Crowder peas are great to eat, too, and the reason you want to plant *crowders* (as opposed to black-eyed, pink-eyed, or lady peas) is that they are such enthusiastic nitrogen fixers. This talent shows in the seeds, which grow so large that they crowd the pods, squaring off shoulder to shoulder. Unfortunately, crowders tend to perform poorly in the long-day summer climates north of the 39th latitude, but in those cooler areas, gardening in midsummer is actually fun.

Sow crowders in very warm soil, usually as a follow-up to bygone spring or summer crops. Supplemental water may be needed to get the seeds up and growing, but once the plants have several leaves, they tolerate heat and drought beautifully. Pull up plants as you need them for composting projects, or mow them down and let them dry into weed-smothering mulch, which is a great way to prepare space for fall greens. If you want a crowder Compost Fodder Crop and some to eat, too, broadcast the seeds over a wide bed, and press them into the soil with your feet. When the plants are ankle high, pull up the ones that stand where you want pathways.

Choosing Varieties

Seed companies may list crowders as southern peas or cowpeas (long grown as fodder crops). Two old strains worth trying are 'Calico' and 'Polecat'. Local farm supply stores often sell several varieties.

Crowder Peas in the Composter's Garden

▶ Crowders are great plants to grow after spring Grow Heap plantings of summer squash or cucumbers.

▶ The glossy-leaved plants look great when grown as a green skirt around open piles of garden refuse. If you want more color, mix them with sulfur cosmos (*Cosmos sulphureus*).

▶ The plants' stiff stems add structure to heaps that handle kitchen waste, which is always plentiful during the watermelon days of late summer.

Hairy Vetch
Vicia villosa

DAYS TO MATURITY: 80 to 180 days from direct seeding

SEASON: Top nitrogen-fixing legume to grow from fall to spring

Vigorous hairy vetch

One of the best ways to use this hardy nitrogen-fixing legume is to sow seeds in late summer and then mow the plants down in spring, just as the purple and pink blossoms appear. Then simply allow the foliage to dry into a weed-suppressing mulch. Research has shown that when hairy vetch precedes tomatoes, the vetch increases the soil's supply of nitrogen and organic matter, and enhances the disease resistance of tomatoes. Many organic growers use hairy vetch as a winter cover crop and make their final decisions on where to grow sweet corn (a nitrogen glutton) based on where they find their strongest stand of vetch.

Seeds sown in late summer germinate within two weeks and make modest growth until cold weather lulls them into dormancy. Rapid growth occurs as the days lengthen in early spring. You can cut vetch down (or pull it up) anytime you would like to use the vining stems and foliage as compost fodder or mulch. If you live where summers are cool, you also can sow hairy vetch in spring and harvest armloads of greens during the summer months.

When growing hairy vetch in new garden soil, plant vigor is improved by inoculating the seeds with nitrogen-fixing bacteria before planting, or by amending the seedbed with cured compost. Vetch uses the same bacteria as do peas and beans, so scattering soil from a place where these legumes were recently grown over the seeded area can help pioneer plantings of hairy vetch.

Choosing Varieties

Most seed companies sell hairy vetch seeds by species, but you may find special regionally adapted varieties at local farm supply stores. Crownvetch (*Coronilla varia*) is a hardworking alternative choice, but it can become invasive and is on the noxious weed lists of some states.

Hairy Vetch in the Composter's Garden

▶ Sow in late summer in places where you plan to grow tomatoes, spinach, or sweet corn the following spring. Foliage not used as mulch makes great compost fodder.

▶ Combine hairy vetch with rye or wheat when growing it primarily as a Compost Fodder Crop. The upright grains help provide support for rangy vetch vines.

▶ Hairy vetch will naturalize as a useful weed if you allow it to reseed in parts of your garden.

Mustard
Brassica rapa

DAYS TO MATURITY: 40 to 50 days from direct seeding

SEASON: Best grown from late summer to fall; killed by temperatures below 20°F/7°C

The easiest leafy green to grow, mustard quickly produces lush green leaves for both compost and table — and suppresses the growth of several species of nematodes (microscopic "worms" that injure plant roots). In spring, a quick crop of mustard is worthwhile, but warm weather causes mustard's flavor to sharpen and lengthening days trigger premature flowering. If you use mustard mostly as a fast-growing fall Compost Fodder Crop, expect the plants to show bursts of exuberant growth after every rain or thorough watering. Light to moderate frost mellows the flavor of the leaves, which is further tamed by cooking. Cooked mustard greens can be substituted for spinach in casseroles, quiches, and many other dishes.

Sow seeds directly in the garden in late summer, just before rain is expected. When barely covered with moist soil, seeds sprout within a few days. Provide water if needed to support strong early growth. Mustard shades the surrounding soil with its broad leaves, which can be twisted off as they are needed. The plants are killed by hard freezes, but often survive winter from Zones 7 to 9. In spring, overwintered plants produce tasty, broccoli-like buds, which open into clusters of bright yellow flowers if left unpicked. Elongated seed pods quickly follow the flowers. Mustard seeds stay viable for 4 years or longer, when stored under cool, dry conditions.

Mustard is seldom bothered by pests other than aphids, which can be rinsed from leaves that are destined for dinner. Just before a cold blast kills the plants, pull them up and chop or layer them into any type of composting project. Follow mustard with spring peas, potatoes, or another unrelated vegetable.

Broad-leafed mustard

Choosing Varieties

Varieties vary in color and texture, and include red-tinged 'Red Giant' and beautifully frilly 'Southern Giant Curled'. Green, smooth-leaved varieties, such as 'Tyfon', are fast, vigorous growers.

Mustard in the Composter's Garden

▶ Combine fistfuls of mustard greens with shredded leaves in fall compost piles.

▶ Use mustard's broad leaves to help suppress unwanted vegetation in weedy sites.

▶ Chop plants down with a hoe, and use the debris as a base layer for Comforter Compost.

▶ In fall, grow mustard greens around the base of compost bins or pens.

Cereal Rye
Secale cereale

DAYS TO MATURITY: 180 to 220 days from direct seeding

SEASON: Sow in fall and harvest leaves and stems in late spring

Green seed head of cereal rye

An ancient grain, cereal rye has much to offer when grown as a Compost Fodder Crop. Rye leaves and roots produce chemicals that work as natural herbicides, so this is the best Compost Fodder Crop to grow in soil that's overrun with weeds like lambs quarters, pigweed, or ragweed. You also can combine cereal rye with hardy vining legumes including Austrian winter peas or hairy vetch. The legumes will cling to the upright rye foliage with curling tendrils, making it easy to harvest compostable greens by grabbing a bunch in one hand and using the other to lop them off near the soil line with a hand scythe or very sharp knife.

Handle rye seeds with care, and grow this Compost Fodder Crop only in sites where you can manage its seed production, if you allow it to go to seed at all. Cereal rye is considered invasive in many climates, though it is not nearly as invasive as annual ryegrass, which is a different plant.

Wheat (on facing page) is grown like cereal rye, but the more rugged rye grows better in poor soil, and it does a superior job of choking out weeds. The biggest challenge of working with rye is killing the plants, which are anchored by a huge, fibrous root system. The easiest method is to harvest the "hay" by cutting the foliage off close to the ground, followed by close mowing a week or two later. Once the tops stop regrowing, rye roots left in the ground decompose rather quickly.

Choosing Varieties
Many vigorous varieties have been developed for cover crop use, including 'Abruzzi' and 'Merced'.

Whole rye "berries," purchased at health food stores, can be used to grow small garden-sized plots.

Rye in the Composter's Garden
▶ Combine with hairy vetch or another vining legume for off-season soil improvement and erosion control from fall to spring.

▶ Use to raise the organic matter content of soil in need of extensive restoration.

▶ Add rye greens to composting projects that involve leaves. The rye will help retain moisture.

Wheat
Triticum aestivum

DAYS TO MATURITY: 80 to 180 days from direct seeding

SEASON: Grow hardy types from fall to spring, or sow in spring for cutting in summer

Ripe heads of wheat

Like rye (on facing page), wheat is an upright grain that combines well with hairy vetch and other hardy legumes, or you can grow a small plot in its own space. Wheat grows best in fertile, well-drained soil, and if you grow the right kinds, you can get edible seeds and high quality straw from the same plants. Growing a small crop of wheat "berries" can be fun, especially for kids, or you can try ornamental strains that feature showy awns that look great when used in dried flower arrangements and various crafts.

Plant hardy "winter" wheat in fall, and expect to see very little growth during the winter months. First thing in spring, however, the plants will start growing again. Spring wheat and most ornamental varieties can be sown two to three weeks before the date of your last spring frost.

When well pleased with its site and the season in which it is grown, wheat grows up to 4' (1.25 m) tall. You can harvest the foliage for composting at any time, and it's easy to cut, dry, and bind any surplus into small bundles for future use. Wheat foliage near the base of the plants begins to die back several weeks before the seeds are ripe, so if your main mission is to grow plenty of compost fodder, it's best to cut the plants back close to the ground as soon as green seed heads appear. This approach also prevents the accidental emergence of wheat seedlings in compost that you make using low-temperature methods.

Choosing Varieties

In addition to the dozens of modern varieties grown for high grain yield, there are several interesting ornamental varieties of wheat, including 'Black Emmer' (*Triticum dicoccon*), which has dramatic black awns, and blue-hulled 'Utrecht Blue'.

Wheat in the Composter's Garden

▶ Combine with hardy legumes in mixed winter plantings. In spring, harvest greens and mix them with overwintered leaves for composting.

▶ Save dried wheat straw, and use it to blanket the surface of various composting projects. It will look great while conserving moisture.

▶ Fresh or dried wheat foliage placed at the base of any aboveground compost project attracts earthworms, while ensuring good aeration.

Appendix

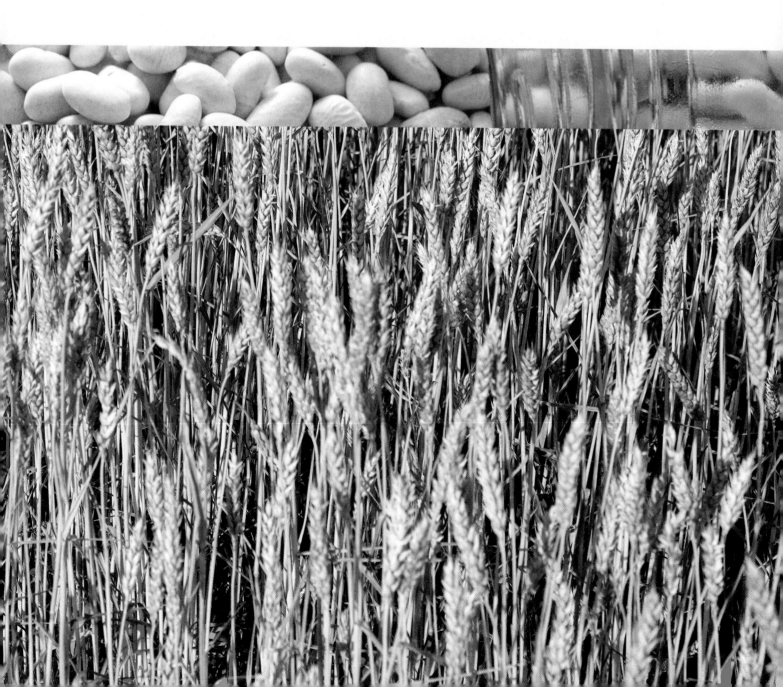

Glossary

Actinomycetes. Filament-shaped bacteria often involved in breaking down organic matter.

Aerobic. Organisms or processes that require oxygen.

Aeration. The process of creating openings within a compost heap to increase air. In closed composters, aeration is accomplished by rotating the container or stirring the contents. Slow, cold heaps aerate themselves as they shrink and settle.

Anaerobic. Organisms or processes that function without oxygen.

Banner Batch. Excellent-quality compost made with available materials and managed carefully in terms of air, moisture, C/N ratio, and temperature.

Biodynamic gardening. An advanced organic system that emphasizes food quality and soil health.

Biointensive gardening. An intensive approach to gardening that emphasizes sustainability and high food yields.

Biomass plants. Plants that produce unusually large amounts of leaf, stem, and root, while taking up a lean supply of nutrients. When used to support compost, they are referred to as "compost fodder crops."

Caliche. Light-colored layers of rock-hard subsoil in which soil particles are cemented together by carbonates of calcium or magnesium, predominantly present in the American Southwest.

Closed composting. Composting that takes place in barrels, plastic composters, or other enclosures.

Cold compost. Compost in which little or no heat is generated as the materials decompose.

Compost tea. A plant-nutrient solution made by swirling or aerating compost in water.

Cover crop. A crop grown to improve the soil, protect the soil from erosion, and block out weeds.

Compost. A soil-like mixture of decayed and decaying organic matter and minerals, which is the foundation of organic gardening.

Comforter Compost. Layers of compostable materials spread over the soil like a comforter; intensification of an older method called "sheet" compost.

Compost gardener. One who nurtures the soil through a variety of site-appropriate composting methods with the goal of producing healthy, productive plants. (See **www.compostgardening.com**.)

Compost miles. The cumulative distance that materials travel to reach your compost pile. The costs of compost miles are both financial and environmental.

C/N (carbon to nitrogen) ratio. The relationship between the carbon content and the nitrogen content of a compost material or a compost pile; 30 parts carbon to 1 part nitrogen is ideal for balancing a compost pile's C/N ratio.

Earthworms. Soil-dwelling worms of the family Lumbricidae that feed on decaying organic matter and enrich the soil with their castings

Edaphon. The collective community of plant and animal life present in soil.

Endomycorrhizal fungi. Beneficial fungi that colonize a plant's roots; these organisms can help a plant take up water and nutrients more efficiently and fend off soil-dwelling disease organisms.

Floating row cover. Spun-bonded (nonwoven) polyester fabric designed to protect plants from pests and/or frost damage. So light it "floats" over rows of plants, this translucent cover is air and water permeable but serves as a barrier against pests and provides a few degrees of frost protection.

Fodder Crop. Plants that compost gardeners grow to feed the soil, either directly by digging them into the soil as green manure or indirectly by including them in compost.

Green manure. A crop grown specifically to be dug into the soil while still fresh and green, thereby adding nutrients and organic matter, and stimulating the soil food web.

Grow Heap. A specially designed cold-compost heap that contains several layers of soil, making it suitable for growing many types of plants.

Hardpan. A compacted layer of soil, often with a high clay content that is nearly impossible for roots to penetrate. Hardpan may be the result of compaction by heavy machinery or of repeatedly tilling topsoil to the same depth.

High-protein meals. Processed grain (for example, corn) or legume (such as soy or alfalfa) products usually sold for use as animal feeds or organic fertilizers.

Honey Hole. An unlined pit, dug near garden or landscape plants, that is filled with compost ingredients; the pit is covered over with soil, and the contents are allowed to decompose.

Hospital Heap. A compost pile built to receive hard-to-handle ingredients, such as disease- or insect-ridden plants or seed-bearing weeds, which is later subjected to high temperatures to kill pathogens and neutralize these problems.

Hot compost. Compost in which carbon, nitrogen, moisture, and air are closely monitored to induce high temperatures within the heap.

Humus. Dark brown to black decomposed animal or plant matter resulting from the actions of bacteria and fungi; an essential part of the organic matter portion in the soil.

Induced systemic resistance. The enhanced ability of plants grown in compost-enriched soil to respond quickly and effectively when challenged by plant disease organisms.

Inoculant (as for legumes). Beneficial bacteria that may be applied to seeds or soil prior to planting of beans, peas, and other legumes to improve the crop's nitrogen-fixing abilities.

Layered Crater. A pit in which approximately half of the soil removed is replaced with layers of compost materials, with the goal of creating a deep, fertile planting bed.

Leaf mold. A dark, crumbly, earthy-smelling material resulting from the decomposition of tree and shrub leaves. The transition from whole leaves to leaf mold usually takes two years.

Muck soil. A soil type found at the bottom of bogs and shallow lakes or along the banks of slow-flowing rivers; it is made up of a large amount of active organic matter (up to 30 percent), combined with extremely tiny soil particles.

Mycorrhiza. The symbiotic relationship between fungal mycelium and plant roots; derived from "myco" (fungi) and "rhiza" (root).

Nursery Reserve. A slow, cold compost or leaf pile used to shelter dormant container plants over winter, or to provide a place for chilling potted, spring-flowering bulbs.

Open composting. Composting that takes place in an unrestrained pile or in an easily accessed pen or compost bin.

Organic matter, active. Material that is still actively decomposing.

Organic matter, stable. Plant or animal material that has decayed into humus.

pH. The measure of acidity or alkalinity in soil or compost materials, rated on a scale in which the neutral point is 7.0. Higher numbers indicate alkaline conditions, while soil with a pH below 6.0 is considered acidic.

Pioneer plants. Plants such as legume or squash family crops that grow well in soil that is in the early stages of improvement.

Pit-of-Plenty. A deep, covered pit intended for composting wet and/or odorous materials, such as kitchen scraps and trimmings, out of sight (and smell) of humans, pets, and foraging critters

Potting soil. A plant-growing medium made of a mixture of compost, soil, and various additions, such as sand, Perlite or vermiculite, that alters the texture of the mix according to needs of specific plants.

Rhizomorphic bacteria and fungi. Soil-dwelling microorganisms that enhance plants' ability to take up nutrients from the soil.

Root exudates. Compounds (often sugars) produced by roots, which serve to attract and retain populations of beneficial microorganisms in the surrounding soil.

Roguing out. Removing plants with undesirable characteristics, such as small or poorly flavored fruit, or removing undesirable conditions, such as disease or insect infestation.

Root zone. The zone in the soil where most plant roots reside; also called the rhizosphere.

Siderophores. Specialized large molecules produced by soil-dwelling microorganisms that help plants absorb iron and other nutrients present in the soil.

Soil community. The microorganisms (for example, bacteria and fungi) and macroorganisms (for example, earthworms and ants) that live in the soil.

Soil food web. The community of life forms that inhabits the soil, which includes thousands of microorganisms that process organic matter, as well as plants, earthworms, mites, and other tiny animals. "Web" reflects the complex relationships that exist between diverse life forms that live in the soil.

Thermophilic bacteria. "Heat-loving" decomposers that are most active when temperatures range from 113° to 158°F (45° to 70°C).

Transpirational pull. The pumplike movement of water from roots to stems, leaves, flowers, and fruits.

Treasure Trough. An excavated trench in which compostable materials are buried deeply to decompose and improve the soil on the spot.

Vermicompost. Compost made primarily through the activity of a concentrated population of earthworms.

Walking Heap. A compost pile that travels (is moved by increments) as it is turned and/or as new compost materials are added.

Further Reading from Compost Gardeners

Campbell, Stu. *Let It Rot!* North Adams, MA: Storey Publishing, 1990.

Gershuny, Grace. *Start with the Soil.* Emmaus, PA: Rodale, 1997.

Jeavons, John. *How to Grow More Vegetables,* 7th ed. Berkeley, CA: Ten Speed Press, 2006.

Lowenfels, Jeff, and Wayne Lewis. *Teaming with Microbes.* Portland, OR: Timber Press, 2006.

Martin, Deborah L., and Grace Gershuny, eds. *The Rodale Book of Composting.* Emmaus, PA: Rodale Press, 1992.

Authors' Web site

CompostGardening.com
www.compostgardening.com
A sharing space for compost gardeners, featuring photos, video clips, tips, and personal stories from creative home composters

Compost Gardening Resources

A. M. Leonard
800-543-8955
www.amleo.com
Compost bins, tools, bags, and aerators

BiodegradableStore.com
303-449-1876
www.biodegradablestore.com
Biodegradable compost collection bags and biodegradable dishes

Cathy's Crawly Composters
888-775-9495
www.cathyscomposters.com
Bins, books, worms, and other vermicomposting supplies

Charley's Greenhouse & Garden
800-322-4707
www.charleysgreenhouse.com
Compost bins, tools, and vermicomposting kits

Clean Air Gardening
214-819-9500
www.cleanairgardening.com
Compost bins, pens, biodegradable bags, and other composting tools

EarthWormDigest.org
216-531-5374
www.wormdigest.org
A nonprofit Web site that publishes articles, tracks research, and hosts lively forums on earthworms and vermicomposting

Gardener's Supply Company

888-833-1412

www.gardeners.com

Activators, aerating tools, bins, and tumblers

Gardens Alive!

513-354-1482

www.gardensalive.com

Activators, bins, compost tea kits, and worms

GREENCulture

877-204-7336

www.composters.com

Enclosed compost bins and tumblers and numerous composting tools

Harris Seeds

800-514-4441

www.harrisseeds.com

Compost bins, garden supplies, soil test kits and meters.

Home Harvest Garden Supply

517-332-3688

www.homeharvest.com

Soil test kits, gardening, and composting tools

Johnny's Select Seeds

877-564-6697

www.johnnyseeds.com

Activators, aerating tools, bins, and tumblers

Lee Valley Tools

800-871-8158 in the United States
800-267-8767 in Canada

www.leevalley.com

Composting pails, thermometers, and other composting tools

Mulch & Soil Council

703-257-0111

www.mulchandsoilcouncil.org

Certifies bagged mulch and soil products sold to consumers

Park Seed Company

800-213-0076

www.parkseed.com

Earthworm castings

Peaceful Valley Farm Supply

888-784-1722

www.groworganic.com

Compost tools, activators, compost tea kits, and cover crop seeds

Planet Natural

800-289-6656

www.planetnatural.com

Composting supplies, row covers, and natural pest control products

Salt Spring Global Worming

250-537-1111

www.saltspringworms.com

Vermicompost bins and kits, worms, and other vermicomposting supplies

Woods End Laboratories

207-293-2457

www.woodsend.org

Solvita compost test kit, research papers, and books

Authors' Acknowledgments

To all of the visionary compost-makers who came before us — notably Sir Albert Howard; J. I. Rodale; Robert Rodale; and more recently, Dr. Harry Hoitink, of Ohio State University, and William Brinton, president of Woods End Laboratories — we are deeply grateful. We also received valuable guidance from Dr. Paul Hepperly, research and training manager of the Rodale Institute in Kutztown, Pennsylvania, as well as Dr. Casey Sclar of Longwood Gardens in Kennett Square, Pennsylvania. Rodale Press has been knee deep in compost since its beginnings in the 1940s, and the company continued this legacy by supporting this project from beginning to end.

As months of work turned into more than a year, we noticed that the very thing that was slowing us down — discovering innovative home-composting methods that needed to be shared — was also making this book what it needed to be: a comprehensive sourcebook on home composting, based on methods that make good use of materials generated within a gardener's home grounds. We are especially grateful to Ellen Phillips and Nancy Ondra for generously opening their gardens to our inquiring eyes.

Magic happened when Gwen Steege, editor at Storey Publishing, assembled a creative dream team to turn our pile of manuscript pages into a beautiful, hard-working book. Delilah Smittle is listed as project editor on the copyright page, but we quickly changed her title to Compost Visionary. Delilah's artful imagination, combined with years of composting and gardening experience, enriches each page of this book. And, as Mavis Torke turned our scribbled drawings and skewed photos into crystal clear art, and Donna Chiarelli and Tom Wolf braved July heat waves to capture hundreds of impeccable images in their cameras, we knew with certainty that this book would be better than we had dared to dream. That dream became a reality as Cynthia McFarland, art director, and Dan Williams, designer, poured awesome amounts of time and creative energy into this project. Thanks and more thanks are due to one and all.

Photographer's Acknowledgments

With appreciation for their gracious willingness to allow photography, I would like to thank the following:

Harold and Bertha Weaver and James Weaver
   of Meadow View Farms, Kutztown, Pennsylvania
Longwood Gardens, Kennett Square, Pennsylvania
Global Libations Coffeeshop, Kutztown, Pennsylvania

First Frost

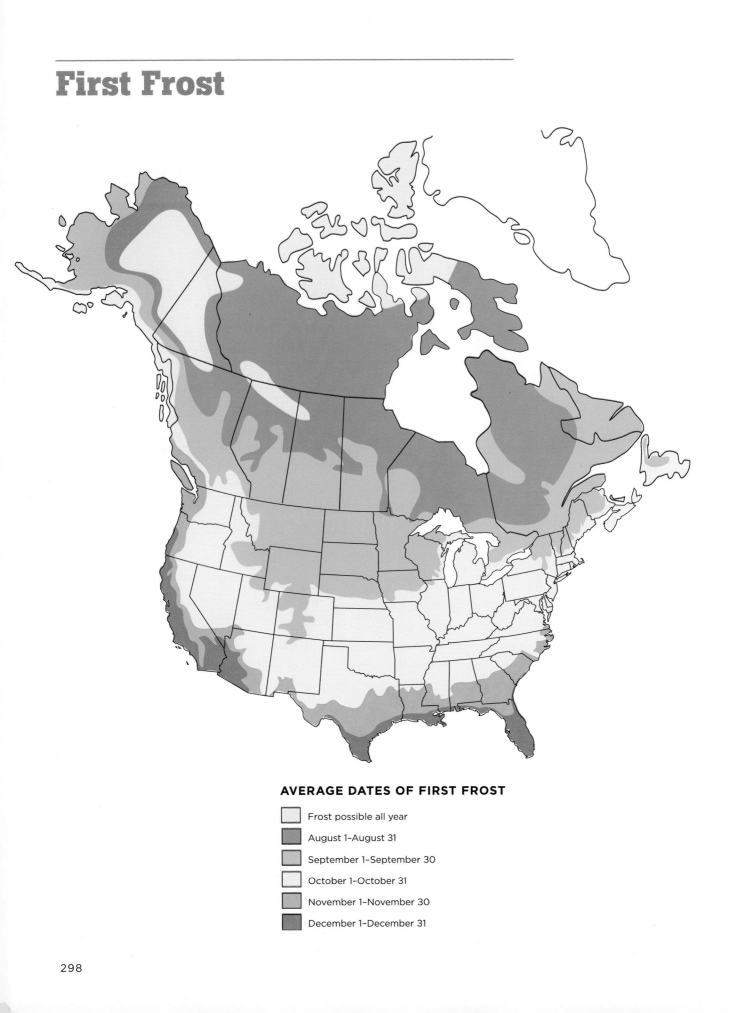

AVERAGE DATES OF FIRST FROST

- Frost possible all year
- August 1–August 31
- September 1–September 30
- October 1–October 31
- November 1–November 30
- December 1–December 31

Last Frost

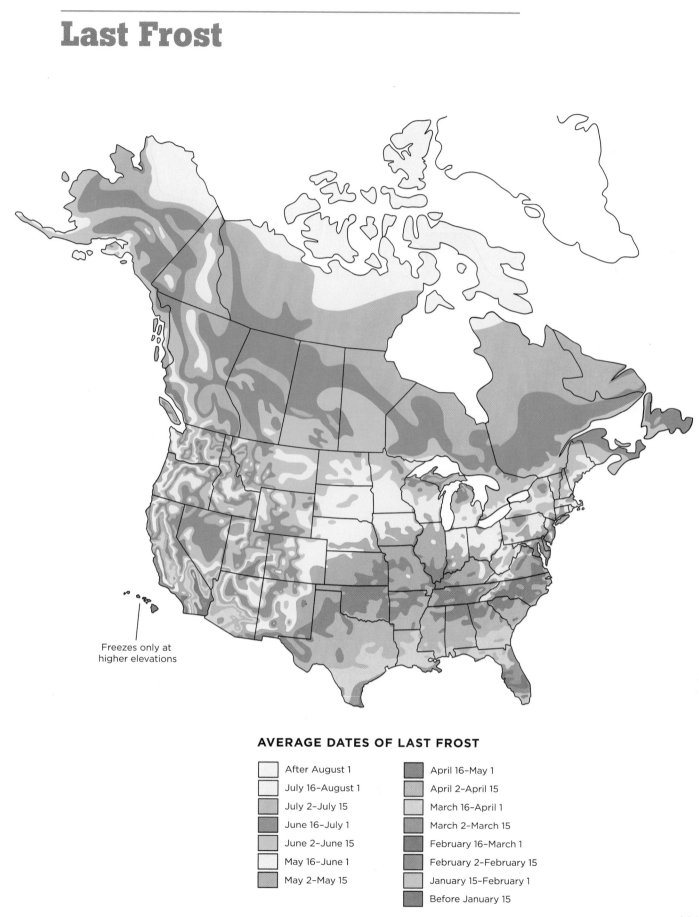

Freezes only at
higher elevations

AVERAGE DATES OF LAST FROST

After August 1

July 16–August 1

July 2–July 15

June 16–July 1

June 2–June 15

May 16–June 1

May 2–May 15

April 16–May 1

April 2–April 15

March 16–April 1

March 2–March 15

February 16–March 1

February 2–February 15

January 15–February 1

Before January 15

Zone Map

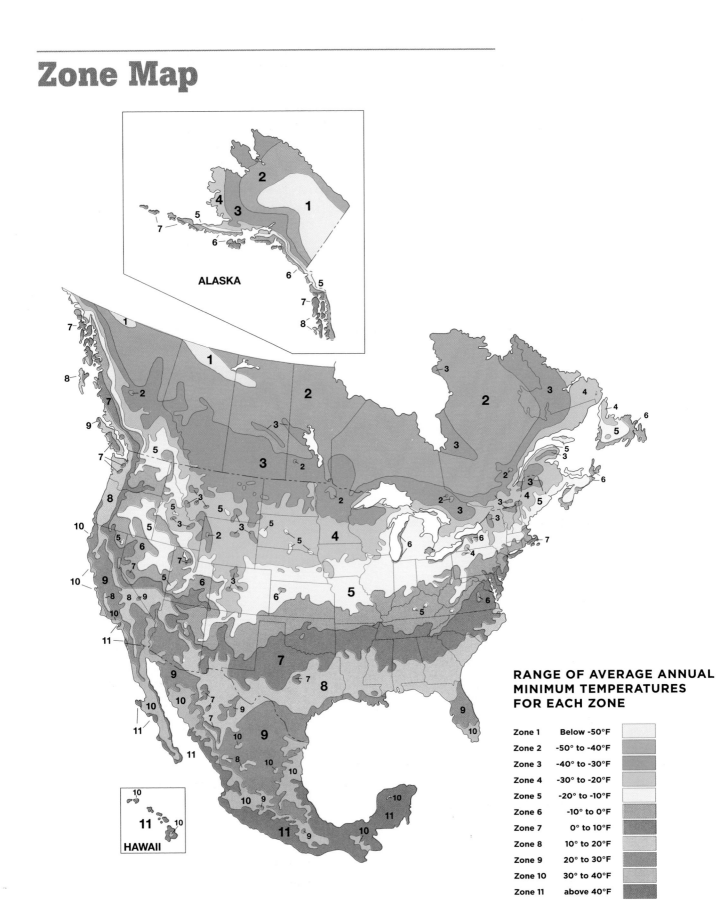

ALASKA

HAWAII

RANGE OF AVERAGE ANNUAL MINIMUM TEMPERATURES FOR EACH ZONE

Zone 1	Below -50°F	
Zone 2	-50° to -40°F	
Zone 3	-40° to -30°F	
Zone 4	-30° to -20°F	
Zone 5	-20° to -10°F	
Zone 6	-10° to 0°F	
Zone 7	0° to 10°F	
Zone 8	10° to 20°F	
Zone 9	20° to 30°F	
Zone 10	30° to 40°F	
Zone 11	above 40°F	

Index

Page numbers in *italics* indicate illustrations or photographs.
Page numbers in **bold** indicate tables or charts.

evaluation of, 48

finished, 19

historical reference to, 163

in place, 12

ready-made blend, 113–14

re-composting of, 117

volume, 19–20

See also composting

compostable materials

animal by-products, 99

common, 54, 55

garden refuse as, 70–72

getting to know, 52–53

"imported" ingredients, 53–54

items to avoid, 125–26

making a comeback, 133

odds and ends, 125, **128–29**

"try it" pile, 126

compost activators. *See* activators

compost bin, 62–63, 142–48

barrel-type, *62*, 63, *127*

bin-type, 142–43

bottomless plastic, *62*, 63

considerations, 142

cylindrical plastic trash can, 62, 138–139

enclosed, *55*

feature comparison, **144**

of stacked bales, 104

three-bin system, 143, *143*

wire-enclosed pile, *62*, 63

wooden, *16*, *134*, *143*, *236*, *236*

See also compost pen; pit-type composters

"compost central," 71–72

compost enclosures. *See* compost bin

composter's conduit, 180–81, *180–81*

Composter's Sling, 82, *82*

Compost Fodder Crops, 73, 276–87

choosing from, 276–77

grains and vegetables as, 277

scythe for cutting, 43

soil enrichment and, 243

top ten, **277**

weediness and, 277

compost gardening

long term of, 192

"perfect plant" matches, 243

six basic rules of, 14–15

and view of garden, 71

See also garden in compost

composting

adventures in, 127

benefits of, 17–19

projects, mixing of results, 68

three "M"s of, 65

compost maintenance tools, 44–48

aerating tools, *45*, 45–46, *46*

storage containers, 47–48

thermometers, 46, *47*

watering tools, 46–57

compost miles

bagged compost and, 115, *115*

cost of compost and, **53**

counting, 52–53

manure and, 92

See also "buy local" movement

compost pen, 71–72, 83, *83*, 143

enclosure materials, **146–47**

fasteners, **148**

post materials, **145**, 147, *147*

compost tea, 227–30

aeration and water for, 228, 230

brewing steps, 229

colander for, 214, *214*

compost to use, 227, 228

E. coli and, 228, 230

for lawn turf, 228

manure and, 100

"perfect match" plant, 228, *228*

uses for, 228

compost worms. *See* Eisenia fetida

conservation of space

sling for melons, 267

trellises, 246, *246*

vine crops in bales, 104, *104*

See also raised beds

construction projects

cart-mounted sifters, 220

composter's conduit, 180–81

D

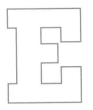

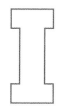

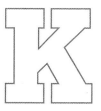

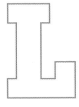

Nabhan, Gary, 53

Nancarrow, Loren, 206

Native Americans, 189

Native Seeds SEARCH, 53

need-nosed pliers, *42*

night crawler, 155, 201, 202, 237. *See* also
    Lumbricus terrestris

nitrogen
    animal manures and, 94
    content, finished compost, 149
    lost to air, 48, 98

nitrogen-fixing. *See Leguminosae*

nitrogen-fixing bacteria, 21, 22, 245

nitrogen sources. *See* "greens;" *Leguminosae;*
    manure

non-heap compost methods, 134

no-work composting. *See* Comforter Compost

noxious plants. *See under* hazard

N-P-K (nitrogen, phosphorus, potassium), 70
    of animal by-products, 99
    for grass clippings, 88
    in manure, 100

Nursery Reserve
    bales for framing, 104
    leaf pile as, 83, 84

nutritional activators, *120*, 120–21, 122

nut shells, composting of, 61

odd compostables, 125, **128–29**

Ondra, Nancy, 222

open-pollinated plants, 164

open vs. closed compost system, **143**

orange rinds, composting of, 61

organic farms, 117

Organic Gardening, 239

organic matter
    active, 18–19, 243
    gaining, 17–18
    hows and whys of, 18
    organic acids, 149
    percentage, healthy soil, 26
    stable, 18
    testing content of, 19–20

Pachysandra terminalis (Japanese spurge), 159

pails. *See* buckets

Papaver rhoeas (corn poppies), 282

paper-based compost, 109

paper for composting, 105–8
    adhesives and, 106
    inks, dyes, and coatings of, 106
    uncoated paper plates, *105*
    various applications, 107–8
    See also cardboard for composting

pasture worm. *See Allalobophora* spp.

pathogens. *See* health threats

peas. *See Leguminosae; Pisum sativum*

peat moss
    considerations for usage, 232
    potting soil and, 85

Pelargonium spp. (geraniums), 231

pen. *See* compost pen

pepper. *See Capsicum annuum* var. *annuum*

perennials
    chopped for compost, 71
    compost for, 161, 217
    as edging plants, 162

perennial vine propagation, 161, *161*

"perfect match" plants
    asparagus, 158, *158*

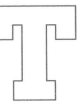

composting of, 72, 74, 90

controlling in compost, 102–3

deep burial and, 223

hot-composting to control, 104, 121, 124, 223

incoming, management of, 74

in manure, 93

origin of, 74–75

weed varieties

bindweed, 75

Canada thistle, 75, 154

chickweed, 74

crabgrass, 28, 74

ground ivy, 75

jimsonweed, 116

Johnson grass, 75, 93

quackgrass, 75, 93

smartweed, 125

West Virginia University, 233

wet compost ingredients, kitchen, 58

wheat. *See Triticum aestivum*

wheelbarrows and carts, 39–40, 220, *220*

white worms. *See Enchytraeid* spp.

wicking, 192

Wilde, Barbara, 142

wildlife, 235–36

allies, hosting in garden, 239

overpopulation of, 236

skunk deterrents, 238

snakes, 237

unwanted attractors, 236

See also animal pests; vermin

winter compost project. *See* Catch-and-Release Vermicomposting

winter pea. *See Pisum sativum* ssp. *arvense*

winter squash. *See Cucurbita mixta*

wire-enclosed pile. *See under* compost bin

wood chips and sawdust, 110–14

best uses for chips, 113

free sources of, 110–11

handling of sawdust, 113, *113*

handling wood chips, 111–12

ready-made compost blend, 113–14

using, 114

wood to avoid, 110

Woods End Research Laboratory, 49

worm, 66

multi-level worm bins, 207, *207*

by size, 199–200

See also Lumbricus spp.

Worm Book, The (Nancarrow and Taylor), 206

worm farm setup, 208–9

yard-long beans. *See Phaseolus unguiculata* ssp. *sesquipedalis*

Photography Credits

Other Storey Titles You Will Enjoy

The Flower Gardener's Bible, by Lewis and Nancy Hill
All the advice you need on flower gardening, from the basics of plant care
to inspiration for theme gardens.
384 PAGES | PAPER: ISBN 978-1-58017-462-6 | HARDCOVER: ISBN 978-1-58017-463-3

The Gardener's A–Z Guide to Growing Organic Food, by Tanya L. K. Denckla
An invaluable resource about growing, harvesting, and storing for 765 varieties of
vegetables, fruits, herbs, and nuts. **496 PAGES** | PAPER: ISBN 978-1-58017-370-4

Incredible Vegetables from Self-Watering Containers, by Edward C. Smith
A foolproof method to produce a bountiful harvest without the trouble
of a traditional earth garden.
256 PAGES | PAPER: ISBN 978-1-58017-556-2 | HARDCOVER: ISBN 978-1-58017-557-9

Mulch It!, by Stu Campbell
A practical guide to using mulch to protect soil, minimize weeds, cut down on labor, and
contribute to plant health. **128 PAGES** | PAPER: ISBN 978-1-58017-316-2

The Organic Lawn Care Manual, by Paul Tukey
A comprehensive volume of natural lawn-care information to answer the growing
demand for organic grass.
256 PAGES | PAPER: ISBN 978-1-58017-649-1 | HARDCOVER: ISBN 978-1-58017-655-2

The Vegetable Gardener's Bible, by Edward C. Smith
A reinvention of vegetable gardening that shows how to have your most
successful garden ever. **320 PAGES** | PAPER: ISBN 978-1-58017-212-7

The Veggie Gardener's Answer Book, by Barbara W. Ellis
Insider's tips and tricks, practical advice, and organic wisdom for vegetable
growers everywhere. **432 PAGES** | PAPER: ISBN 978-1-60342-024-2

These and other books from Storey Publishing are available
wherever quality books are sold or by calling 1–800–441–5700.
Visit us at *www.storey.com.*